a **LIVING** | **FREE** guide

The Home Preserving Bible

by Carole Cancler

ALPHA

A member of Penguin Group (USA) Inc.

To people everywhere who eat to live, and to the memory of my immigrant grandparents, who inspire me.

ALPHA BOOKS

Published by Penguin Group (USA) Inc.

Penguin Group (USA) Inc., 375 Hudson Street, New York, New York 10014, USA • Penguin Group (Canada), 90 Eglinton Avenue East, Suite 700, Toronto, Ontario M4P 2Y3, Canada (a division of Pearson Penguin Canada Inc.) • Penguin Books Ltd., 80 Strand, London WC2R 0RL, England • Penguin Ireland, 25 St. Stephen's Green, Dublin 2, Ireland (a division of Penguin Books Ltd.) • Penguin Group (Australia), 250 Camberwell Road, Camberwell, Victoria 3124, Australia (a division of Pearson Australia Group Pty. Ltd.) • Penguin Books India Pvt. Ltd., 11 Community Centre, Panchsheel Park, New Delhi—110 017, India • Penguin Group (NZ), 67 Apollo Drive, Rosedale, North Shore, Auckland 1311, New Zealand (a division of Pearson New Zealand Ltd.) • Penguin Books (South Africa) (Pty.) Ltd., 24 Sturdee Avenue, Rosebank, Johannesburg 2196, South Africa • Penguin Books Ltd., Registered Offices: 80 Strand, London WC2R 0RL, England

Copyright © 2012 by Carole Cancler

International Standard Book Number: 978-1-61564-192-5
Library of Congress Catalog Card Number: 2012935358

14   13   12   8   7   6   5   4   3   2   1

Interpretation of the printing code: The rightmost number of the first series of numbers is the year of the book's printing; the rightmost number of the second series of numbers is the number of the book's printing. For example, a printing code of 12-1 shows that the first printing occurred in 2012.

Printed in the United States of America

Note: This publication contains the opinions and ideas of its author. It is intended to provide helpful and informative material on the subject matter covered. It is sold with the understanding that the author and publisher are not engaged in rendering professional services in the book. If the reader requires personal assistance or advice, a competent professional should be consulted.

The author and publisher specifically disclaim any responsibility for any liability, loss, or risk, personal or otherwise, which is incurred as a consequence, directly or indirectly, of the use and application of any of the contents of this book.

Trademarks: All terms mentioned in this book that are known to be or are suspected of being trademarks or service marks have been appropriately capitalized. Alpha Books and Penguin Group (USA) Inc. cannot attest to the accuracy of this information. Use of a term in this book should not be regarded as affecting the validity of any trademark or service mark.

Most Alpha books are available at special quantity discounts for bulk purchases for sales promotions, premiums, fund-raising, or educational use. Special books, or book excerpts, can also be created to fit specific needs. For details, write: Special Markets, Alpha Books, 375 Hudson Street, New York, NY 10014.

Publisher: *Mike Sanders*

Executive Managing Editor: *Billy Fields*

Senior Acquisitions Editor: *Tom Stevens*

Development Editor: *Lynn Northrup*

Senior Production Editor: *Kayla Dugger*

Copy Editor: *Monica Stone*

Cover/Book Designer: *Rebecca Batchelor*

Indexer: *Celia McCoy*

Layout: *Ayanna Lacey*

Proofreader: *John Etchison*

Cover Images:
Pressure Cooker © Pixtal / SuperStock
Frozen Mackerel vacuum packed © Westend61 / SuperStock
Dried Tropical Fruits © Marka / SuperStock
Preserved Vegetables © donatas1205 / Shutterstock

Contents

Appendixes

Introduction

When I was presented with the opportunity to write a book about food preservation, I jumped at the chance for a whole bunch of reasons. This book really brings together my education in food science, a love of food history, a lifetime of meal preparation and home entertaining, experience in the food industry, and an interest in sustainability. Since studying Food Science and Nutrition at the University of Washington, I have enjoyed a varied career at several different companies, including restaurant management and product development.

The Home Preserving Bible is near and dear to my heart. I have been canning for about 50 years, starting when I was a young girl helping my mom. Today, I mostly can fruits to use on plain yogurt every morning, and an array of pickled vegetables, from corn to pepper relish and beets.

Over the years, I've enthusiastically used frozen food to make meal preparation easier. I've also dabbled with curing pastrami, smoking salmon, making cheese and wine, and fermenting vegetables. Several years ago, I started drying food; it's much easier than canning, and produces shelf-stable food. (If you have ever lost power with a freezer full of food, you know why this is important.)

Today, I'm very concerned about our centralized food system. Yes, we produce more food cheaply than we have ever done in the past. Nevertheless, there are negative impacts on our economy, environment, and nutrition. We're also raising second and third generations of individuals who are increasingly distant from the source of their food. Instead of coming from the ground or hoof, food comes from a can or box and needs a label to explain what it is and why it's good (or not so good) for you.

What's most disturbing about our current system is how narrow and unnatural it has become. Our preservation methods are limited to antibiotic-filled fresh food, and pasteurizing everything so that no microbial life exists. The same hamburger, french fries, and chicken are served the world over. Industrialized food systems produce a handful of crops that increasingly put a nitrogen load on the soil that it cannot sustain. One can't help but wonder if Mother Nature is going to stage a backlash very soon.

Unfortunately, standard U.S. government guidelines for food preservation recommend sterilization of all food by heating or pasteurizing. In other words: heat the food to kill all microbes, good or bad. Our industrialized methods promote—and even require—the use of antibiotics during the growing and processing of food to keep it "safe." While it may be safe from "bad" bacteria, our food supply is less nourishing than it was a generation ago. In other words, we're producing more food, but you have to eat more of it to get the same nutrition; still more of it is simply empty calories.

There is clearly something wrong with the system. Many Americans are overweight and unhealthy. New strains of antibiotic-resistant pathogens are causing new diseases for which there is no treatment. There is a lot of conflicting information about food preservation, and even the experts don't always agree. But if you learn and practice even one food preservation method, you can be rewarded with a sense of accomplishment and delicious, healthful foods to eat.

A comprehensive book about food preservation with a broad historical context seems timely. People around the world have been preserving food for centuries. They figured out what worked, even before they knew how or why it did. I think it's time we revisited some of their methods.

In the past, people preserved food because they had to; unlike today, they lacked a year-round supply of fresh food and mechanical refrigeration. In times of pestilence, war, famine, tsunamis, and earthquakes, people simply wanted to make sure they had some food "put by." They preserved food mostly by trial and error. Yet the diversity and cleverness of the methods they used is astonishing.

The Home Preserving Bible summarizes the ways in which people have been preserving food for thousands of years. They packed it in salt. They spiced it and dried it. In cold climates, they let it freeze. It hot climates, they buried it and let it ferment. They stored it in animal stomachs and hides. They used every bit of it, beasts from nose to tail and plants from fruit to vine. As you can see, preserving methods go well beyond freezing food in an electric appliance or canning it with special equipment.

A few of the techniques might surprise you. Cultures throughout western and central Asia dry eggplant routinely; it is easy to do and has many delicious uses. The French preserved meat as confit, but so did the Maori in New Zealand. Hawaiians buried and fermented food in their tropical climate, and Native American cultures were making a kind of meat jerky called *pemmican*—both long before Europeans came exploring. Fermenting and pickling have been used by everyone everywhere for eons, using vinegar or lemon juice as well as pomegranate juice, whey, salt with oil, miso, or soy sauce.

I hope you find this information interesting and useful. Above all, enjoy good health, food security, and freedom.

Acknowledgments

Small local and regional farmers are the people who most often inspire me. Their constant work, resilience in the face of weather and economic vagaries, and willingness to share stories add much joy to the everyday task of meal preparation.

Friends and family with whom I've shared many delicious meals generate the warmest memories. These include compatriots who often share in meal making, as well as the hearty and thankful eaters who are the *raison d'être* for any good cook.

My grandparents, who immigrated to America as teenagers and spent a lifetime working the land on their Midwest farm, transferred a love of good food to my mother, who passed it to me.

Julia Child, whose landmark work *Mastering the Art of French Cooking* opened the door to expanded horizons in food preparation techniques.

Students in my cooking classes, who are eager to tackle new techniques, motivate me to continue to meet their enthusiasm for learning. I thoroughly enjoy their company to share recipes with them and the food we have prepared together.

Food scientists and agriculturalists, who conduct painstaking research for which I am very grateful. I could not have written this book without the results of their hard work.

Everyday people in countries throughout the world whose homes, markets, and restaurants I've been privileged to enjoy. I dream of a day when we can replace war with the potluck garden party. Who can think of fighting when the weather is agreeable, the communal food abundant and delicious, and the company congenial?

Special Thanks to the Technical Reviewer

The Home Preserving Bible was reviewed by an expert who double-checked the accuracy of what you'll learn here, to help us ensure that this book gives you everything you need to know about preserving. Special thanks are extended to Trish Sebben-Krupka, a master food preserver.

Trademarks

All terms mentioned in this book that are known to be or are suspected of being trademarks or service marks have been appropriately capitalized. Alpha Books and Penguin Group (USA) Inc. cannot attest to the accuracy of this information. Use of a term in this book should not be regarded as affecting the validity of any trademark or service mark.

Essential Concepts

⌐∞⌐ **1**

The first thing you need to know about preserving food is that people have been doing it for thousands of years. Since a lot of it happened by accident, some of the methods are very easy. You can hang it up and dry it out. You can bury it in the ground to keep it cold. You can cover it with salt. Most of the old ways use simple equipment that you probably already own. For others, you can buy the latest gadget.

In Part 1, I explain the essential steps and available equipment for eight different methods of food preservation. You can use these methods to preserve all kinds of food. Some methods have more than one technique, so whether you like the do-it-yourself approach or are interested in the latest in modern technology, you can find one that will work for you.

Overview of Food Preservation  1

Throughout history, the primary reason people have preserved food is to provide during times of scarcity. In modern life when we run out of food, we simply go to the grocery store and buy more. It's a little hard to comprehend a time when there might not be any food to go get.

There are many reasons why people want to preserve food today. Maybe you want to keep food as pure as possible, are a mother with an allergic child, have a family with aging parents, or are a locavore (a person who eats foods grown within 100 miles of home) who wants more food security. Maybe you have a large garden or a small farm and want to preserve foods for use in the winter. Perhaps you are a survivalist who wants an emergency stash, or a chef who needs to stretch food dollars as far as you possibly can. Maybe you are a foodie who wants to do it all!

Deciding what and how much food to preserve is a critical step in a successful home preserving plan. The most important decision you can make about preserving food is to be practical. Preserve familiar foods that you and your family like. Whether your goal is preserving food for health, security, convenience, seasonal eating, or a long-term emergency supply, plan to store only as much food as you can reasonably consume.

For example, you may be blessed with a bounty of quince from your tree, but 50 pints of quince preserves may not be practical if you have a small family who prefers strawberry jam. However, unsweetened quince purée combined with applesauce makes a delicious and healthy natural sweetener for breakfast yogurt or freshly baked muffins. A few jars of quince marmalade make fine homemade gifts, and quince pickles are an exciting morsel for holiday relish trays. When used wisely, home preserving bestows the joy of making something with your own hands and provides a ready supply of useful and delicious foods for pleasurable eating every season of the year. With a well-stocked pantry, you can save money, save time during meal preparation, and keep an emergency supply of shelf-stable foods.

To preserve fruits and vegetables at their peak, it helps to understand the difference between maturity and ripeness. Maturity means the produce will ripen and become ready to eat after you pick it. Ripeness occurs when the color, flavor, and texture is fully developed. Once it is fully ripe, fresh produce begins the inevitable and declining spoilage process. Here's a guideline:

* Mature, slightly underripe produce is optimal for canning, pickling, and jamming.

* Ripe produce is best for fresh eating, drying, cellaring, and freezing.

* Overripe produce is suitable for fermenting. (And may have started without you!)

Before you learn food preservation methods, it helps to learn a little bit about why food spoils. Once you know how you can control spoilage, then the methods to preserve foods make more sense. You are unlikely to take unsafe shortcuts if you understand what's important.

Food Spoilage

Just as we enjoy eating fresh fruits, vegetables, and meats, so do all kinds of tiny living organisms. As soon as you pluck a strawberry from the field, bacteria consume the sugar and release enzymes. These enzymes begin to soften the fruit. If you don't eat the berries soon, yeasts ferment the juice and mold grows. We delay these natural processes by washing produce to remove bacteria, yeasts, and molds. We refrigerate fresh food to slow down microbial activity and delay spoilage. These microorganisms are everywhere, so washing and refrigerating are only temporary measures that preserve foods for a short while and give us a chance to eat those foods before the organisms!

WHAT ARE ENZYMES?

Enzymes are proteins that act as catalysts to cause chemical changes in living tissue, including our bodies and our food. There are thousands of types of enzymes, each one designed to do a specific thing. In fruits and vegetables, enzymes cause apples and potatoes to turn brown when you cut them open. Our body creates the enzymes it needs at any given moment. In order to digest milk, you need the enzyme lactase to break down the lactose. If you are lactose intolerant, you lack the ability to make the enzyme. Without the enzyme, you get an upset stomach when you consume dairy products. Lactose-free dairy already has the lactose broken down.

When there isn't enough water or air, microorganisms become inactive. Cold temperature slows down their growth, while heat stops enzyme activity and kills other microorganisms. Salt or acid in high concentration also stops microbial activity. However, at lower levels of salt, you might encourage "good" bacteria that produce acid for you.

Bacteria, yeasts, and molds are everywhere. To preserve food safely, you need to learn the rules and follow all procedures so that unintended microorganisms do not survive. Safety in food preservation cannot be overemphasized.

Food Poisoning

Food poisoning (also known as food-borne illness or food-borne disease) occurs when you drink water or eat foods contaminated with harmful microorganisms. Bacteria, yeasts, and molds are companions in our environment. Many of them are beneficial and necessary to life. A few are not. There are a number of different bacteria associated with food poisoning outbreaks. Those of most concern to the home preserver are shown in the following table, based on information from *HACCP User's Manual* by Donald A. Corlett Jr. (Springer, 1998).

Control Factors for Pathogenic Bacteria in Home Preserved Foods

Bacterium	Some Common Sources	Minimum Salt	Maximum Acid (pH)	Maximum Temperature
Clostridium botulinum	Meat, poultry, canned vegetables, vacuum-sealed foods	10%	4.7	38°F
Escherichia coli	Ground beef, raw milk, leafy greens	8%	3.5	33°F
Listeria monocytogenes	Cured meats, raw milk cheese, fresh produce	12%	4.7	32°F
Salmonella spp.	Meat, poultry, dairy, eggs	8%	3.9	41°F
Staphylococcus aureus	Meat, poultry, dairy, eggs	20%	4.4	41°F

The bacteria that cause most food poisoning cases change over time. A century ago, botulism poisoning was a problem due to improperly processed *C. botulinum* in foods canned at home. After research agencies determined the correct methods (time and temperature) to can vegetables and meats safely in the home, the problem disappeared. Today, rare cases of botulism occur when incorrect canning procedures are used.

In the latter part of the twentieth century, *E. coli* in ground beef caused many deaths. As a result, national policies dictating the handling and preparation of meat were updated and greatly reduced the risk of *E. coli* in our meat supply. Today, *Listeria* infection is a recurring problem and research is underway to identify and correct issues in our produce supply that lead to it, including handling and traceability.

SPOILER ALERT

There are comparatively few reported cases of food poisoning in home preserved foods. When they do occur, it is usually due to improper handling. Other outbreaks tend to occur when a new technology or fad emerges—such as vacuum packaging, steam-pressure canning, refrigerator pickles, or meat curing. When you learn a new method of preserving, be sure to practice safe food handling and strictly follow the guidelines for the method and the type of food.

Organizations Where You Can Learn More

If you want to know more about food poisoning, here are the principal organizations in the United States that monitor, report, research, and provide education for consumers on the issue:

⚜ **Food safety information provided by government agencies:** foodsafety.gov

- **Bad Bug Book from the FDA:** www.fda.gov/Food/FoodSafety/FoodborneIllness/ FoodborneIllnessFoodbornePathogensNaturalToxins/BadBugBook

- **FDA Food Safety:** www.fda.gov/Food/FoodSafety

- **Centers for Disease Control and Prevention, Food Safety:** cdc.gov/foodsafety

- **USDA Food Safety and Inspection Service:** www.fsis.usda.gov/Food_Safety_Education

Common Mistakes

Food poisoning from home preserved foods is almost always due to handling the food improperly or using incorrect procedures. Be sure to review this list of the most common mistakes that people make when preserving food:

- **Improper hand washing.** Wash your hands for 20 seconds with soap and running water before and after food preparation tasks. Wash them whenever switching tasks—for example, from washing raw produce, to cutting raw meat or setting up food preservation equipment.

- **Carelessly washing produce.** Follow the guidelines in the section "Washing Produce" later in this chapter. Especially make sure you clean and sanitize the washing area before and after you prepare raw produce for preserving.

- **Thawing food at room temperature.** Always thaw ingredients for food preservation in the refrigerator.

- **Mingling raw and cooked ingredients.** Follow the guidelines in the section "Safe Food-Handling Practices" later in this chapter.

- **Pickling and curing at temperatures above 40°F.** Always pickle and cure foods in the refrigerator. Fermenting is a special type of pickling that is done at warmer temperatures, under strict control, and with special limitations.

- **Tasting a food to see if it's still good.** The best policy is always "when in doubt, throw it out" (without tasting it).

Symptoms

Symptoms of food poisoning resemble many other illnesses, and can include upset stomach, abdominal cramps, nausea, vomiting, diarrhea, blurred vision, and fever. In many cases, the symptoms can be fairly mild and do not require hospitalization. One of the best things you can do if you suspect you have food poisoning is to drink plenty of water. If symptoms persist or worsen, see a physician. Most types of food poisoning have effective treatments.

People at Risk for Food Poisoning

When healthy adults and children ingest food-poisoning bacteria, they usually do not become seriously ill. However, the following groups are at increased risk for serious side effects and even death from low levels of bacteria:

⚜ Newborn babies

⚜ Persons with weakened immune systems, such as people who have HIV/AIDS, have organ transplants, or take certain medications

⚜ Persons with certain diseases including cancer, diabetes, alcoholism, and liver or kidney disease

⚜ Pregnant women and their unborn children

⚜ Older adults

Foods Most Often Linked with Food Poisoning

Certain foods are most often associated with food poisoning; be careful when using or handling and preserving these foods. Choose preserving methods that control pathogens according to the needs of your family, especially when you or members of your family are in a high-risk group. The following foods are most often associated with food poisoning:

⚜ Raw meat, poultry, shellfish, eggs, and unpasteurized milk naturally contain bacteria. Refrigerating and freezing control bacterial growth, but only heating kills the pathogens.

⚜ Bulk foods that mingle with the products of many individual animals—for example, ground beef, milk, and liquid eggs.

⚜ Fresh fruits and vegetables that you consume raw can become contaminated in many different ways: in the field by wild animals or improper use of fertilizers, exposure during harvest and transport, or during the manufacture of fresh products such as bean sprouts or unpasteurized fruit juice. Washing decreases but does not eliminate this contamination. Only heating kills pathogens.

Safe Food-Handling Practices

Food preservation methods take advantage of the natural order of living things. However, you must approach food preservation with some common sense. This includes using high-quality foods at the peak of freshness, keeping the work area clean and sanitary, following all recommended procedures, and storing fresh and preserved foods properly.

Sanitizing the Work Area and Equipment

Before you begin any preserving process, you need to sanitize the work area. Before you sanitize, you need to wash the area with soap and warm water, and rinse with clean water. Spray sanitizing solution on the clean surfaces and utensils; let the solution stand for the required amount of time.

These sanitizing solutions are effective against *Listeria, E. coli,* and *Salmonella* when used on hard surfaces:

- **Bleach:** In a spray bottle, combine 1 scant teaspoon plain (unscented) liquid chlorine bleach in 1 quart water (or 1 tablespoon in 1 gallon). Spray on surfaces and let stand for at least 1 minute.

- **Vinegar (5%):** Heat 5 percent strength white distilled vinegar to 150°F and carefully transfer to a clean spray bottle. While the solution is still warm (at least 130°F), spray on surfaces and let stand for 1 minute. (If the vinegar is at room temperature, let stand 10 minutes.)

- **Hydrogen peroxide (3%):** Heat 3 percent strength hydrogen peroxide to 150°F and carefully transfer to a clean spray bottle. While the solution is still warm (at least 130°F), spray on surfaces and let stand for 1 minute. (If the hydrogen peroxide is at room temperature, let stand 10 minutes.)

It's best if you can then let equipment and surfaces air-dry or, at the very least, wipe with a clean paper towel.

SPOILER ALERT

Never combine bleach, vinegar, or hydrogen peroxide. Mixing any of these products together can create poisonous gases.

Washing Produce

Here are the guidelines you can follow when preparing produce for any recipe:

1. Keep produce chilled and wash immediately prior to use.

2. Wash hands thoroughly before washing produce. After washing your hands, you may wish to use disposable gloves. I find that washing produce can irritate the skin, especially when you have a lot to do at one time.

3. Wash and sanitize all surfaces and utensils before and after washing produce. This is also a good time to use disposable gloves.

4. Cut away any damaged or bruised areas on the produce.

5. Scrub firm produce—like apples, carrots, or potatoes—under running water with a clean, stiff brush. Scrub the surface of produce such as citrus, melons, and winter squash before cutting them, too—even when the skin is peeled—because the knife can drag bacteria from the surface to the inside if you don't scrub it off first.

6. There are several recommended methods for washing produce:

    • Rinse produce well under plenty of plain, cold, running water. Don't use detergent, soap, bleach, or commercial produce washes.

    • Spray produce with a vinegar solution. Rinse produce with water to remove surface dirt and dust, and then spray until coated with a solution of 1 part vinegar and 3 parts water. Rinse again with clean water.

    • Soak soft produce for 2 minutes in a vinegar solution. This includes produce with soft or uneven surfaces, such as soft berries, leafy vegetables, and broccoli. Before using this method, be sure to clean and sanitize your sink or bowl so that you don't cross contaminate your produce. After sanitizing, fill the washing basin with a solution of ¼ cup vinegar for every 1 quart water. After soaking, rinse produce under plain, cold, running water.

7. After washing produce, let it air-dry if possible, in a clean and sanitized colander or rack. Otherwise, dry it with plain (not printed) paper towels, clean cloth towels, or in a salad spinner.

Methods of Preservation

The first food preservation methods, drying and fermenting, are believed to have been discovered by accident at various times and locations around the world. Dried foods were light and easy to carry, and sustained travelers over land and sea. Simple, natural fermentation processes turned grapes into wine, cabbage into *kimchi,* and milk into yogurt. Without food preservation, we would have none of these delicious foods.

Many cultures around the world used salt as a preservative, whether by covering food in dry salt or immersing it in liquid brine made of heavily salted water. Canning and freezing are the newest forms of preservation, becoming commonplace in the past 100 years.

You can preserve almost any food to some degree. Which preservation method you choose depends on several factors: the type of food, the intended use, your knowledge of a particular method, and the equipment you have or are willing to acquire.

In the following sections, you can read a short description of each preservation method. It briefly explains how each method works to preserve food, along with its advantages and disadvantages. The rest of Part 1 discusses each method in detail.

Drying

Drying is the simple process of dehydrating foods until there is not enough moisture to support microbial activity. In addition to being very easy and safe, you can make shelf-stable products (nonperishable foods that you can store at room temperature). You can use dried foods as is, rehydrate them with water, or grind them into a powder. The primary factor affecting the spoilage of dried foods is inappropriate packaging or storage that lets moisture back in, leading to mold growth.

> ⚜ *Advantages:* Applies to all food types, very easy, shelf stable, similar nutrition as fresh product, usually requires no special equipment

> ⚜ *Disadvantages:* Some drying methods require energy or require special equipment, dried product has limited uses

Fermenting

Most fermentation processes are anaerobic. That is, they occur without air, in closed containers. The process produces acids that inhibit spoilage microorganisms and other components that improve texture and flavor. Fermented foods are very safe; in fact, they are teeming with desirable and edible microorganisms called probiotics, which reduce the risk of food-poisoning pathogens such as *Salmonella* and *Clostridium*. In the nineteenth century, French scientist Louis Pasteur was the first to demonstrate that fermentation was the result of microbial activity and that many different types of organisms caused fermentation.

Some fermented foods—such as cheese, yogurt, and sauerkraut—require refrigeration or canning for long storage, while others—such as wine, vinegar, and bread—are shelf-stable foods that you can store at room temperature. Learning how to ferment foods is relatively easy, if you follow procedures carefully. The primary factor affecting spoilage of fermented foods is incorrect application of necessary controls, especially by using unclean utensils or allowing air into the process.

> ⚜ *Advantages:* Applies to all food types, easy, some fermented foods are shelf stable, enhanced nutrition due to probiotics, usually requires no special equipment

> ⚜ *Disadvantages:* Some products are an acquired taste, requires superior cleanliness and attention to controls

Pickling

Pickling is the process of replacing or "binding" the water in a food by soaking it in a solution containing salt, acid, or alcohol. Pickling a food changes its color, flavor, and texture. Pickled foods have a relatively short shelf life. The primary factor affecting spoilage of pickled foods is incorrect application of the necessary controls—for example, by using dirty utensils, too little (or too much) salt, or too warm temperatures.

✤ *Advantages:* Applies to all food types, very easy, most methods require no special equipment

✤ *Disadvantages:* Pickled foods are not shelf stable without a complementary method such as fermenting or refrigerating, unsafe for those at risk for food poisoning

Curing

Curing works the same way as pickling by coating or soaking a food with salt, which binds the free water. In this book, I define curing as the process of controlling microbial growth in meats and fish with or without nitrites (compounds that more easily control the growth of *C. botulinum*). Modern curing methods usually reduce the amount of salt and nitrites, which may mean that you have to refrigerate the final product. Some methods combine curing with a secondary process such as drying, smoking, fermenting, or sealing. Curing changes the color, flavor, and texture of the food. The primary factor affecting spoilage of cured foods is incorrect application of necessary controls—for example, poor sanitary conditions or inaccurate measurements.

✤ *Advantages:* Applies to meat and fish, similar nutrition as fresh product, some methods require no special equipment, some cured products are shelf stable

✤ *Disadvantages:* Moderate to difficult, requires solid understanding of techniques, most cured products are not shelf stable, shelf-stable products require use of nitrites and a complex aging process, consumption of nitrites is cited as a possible health concern

Sealing

Sealing is a process of covering food to keep out air, delaying the activity of spoilage organisms. Sealing is relatively easy, but has limitations as a preservation technique. It is used mostly as a complementary process to other methods such as drying, curing, cellaring, or freezing. The primary factor affecting spoilage of sealed foods is seal failure. However, trapped air and intrinsic microorganisms can also plague sealed foods.

✤ *Advantages:* Easy, vacuum sealing considerably extends the shelf life of dried and frozen foods

✤ *Disadvantages:* Limited uses, vacuum method requires special equipment, fat method requires large amount of salt and nitrates (compounds that cure slowly to control the growth of *C. botulinum* over a long period) to be shelf stable

Canning

Canning combines pasteurization (controlled heating) with vacuum sealing. Canning destroys microorganisms by heating the product at a specified temperature for a specific length of time, and then vacuum sealing the pasteurized food in special glass jars designed for this purpose. The primary factor affecting spoilage of canned foods is lack of cleanliness, untested recipes, faulty equipment, or failure to follow required procedures.

   ⚜ *Advantages:* Applies to most food types, shelf-stable product, is a safe process if recommended practices and tested recipes are strictly followed

   ⚜ *Disadvantages:* Practice needed to develop adequate skill, requires special jars and two-piece lids, nutritional value of product is slightly less than fresh or other preservation methods

Cellaring

Cellaring is the process of storing foods in a temperature-, humidity-, and light-controlled environment. No matter where you live, you can use the concept of cellaring to some degree. A food cellar does not have to be a stand-alone building or a root cellar in a dirt-floor basement; it can also mean a cool basement closet, a box buried in the ground, or an attic. The cellaring method depends on your resources as well as on the type of foods to be stored. The primary factor affecting spoilage of cellared foods is the wrong environment for the type of food.

   ⚜ *Advantages:* Many different methods to use, scalable (can be one box or a specially constructed room), many methods are very easy and safe, maintains food in fresh state, low energy use

   ⚜ *Disadvantages:* Requires regular monitoring and control, many methods subject to invasion by pests (rodents and insects)

Freezing

Freezing is the process of chilling foods to at least 0°F. True freezing is not possible in the freezer compartment of your refrigerator where the temperature is typically well above 0°F. To freeze foods, you need to acquire a dedicated freezer and ensure the temperature control is set to chill foods to between −10°F and 0°F. The primary factor affecting spoilage of frozen foods is inadequate food preparation or packaging.

   ⚜ *Advantages:* Applies to all food types, easy, very safe, quality is most like fresh food, nutrition about the same as fresh products

   ⚜ *Disadvantages:* Requires expensive appliance, uses energy

Drying Foods ❦ 2

Drying is one of the simplest and least expensive forms of food preservation, requiring only warm temperatures combined with good air circulation. Drying removes the water bacteria, yeasts, and molds need to grow. If adequately dried and properly stored, dehydrated foods are shelf stable (safe for storage at room temperature).

The length of drying time can fluctuate widely and depends on several factors. Drying time is affected by the type of food (meat, fruit, vegetables, etc.); size of the portions to be dried (whole pieces, thick or thin slices, ground or diced); drying method (sun, air, oven); and weather (especially relative humidity, abbreviated RH). Humid weather greatly increases drying time (even when drying indoors using an oven or dehydrator). Food dehydrators offer more control than conventional ovens or sun drying. To stop the drying process at any time, simply cover the food and refrigerate.

You can dry almost every type of food, including fruit, vegetables, meat, fish, nuts, and seeds. However, there are a few types of food not suitable for home drying:

> ❧ Fruits with high fat content, such as avocados and olives

> ❧ Vegetables that you normally serve raw, such as cucumbers, radishes, and lettuce

> ❧ Dairy products and eggs, such as milk and cheese

Even though some of these foods are available in dried form, commercial manufacturers of these products use industrial equipment and processes. You cannot safely make powdered milk, cheese, or eggs using home drying methods.

Drying Methods

You have a choice of several different methods to dry food, including warm shade (circulating air), direct sun, trapped solar heat, conventional oven, electric dehydrator appliance, fire pit oven, or smoking. Some methods are more effective than others. Foods dried unprotected outdoors in the shade or sun are lower in quality and nutritional value compared to other methods. Solar dryers protect the food with a cover, and pit ovens and smoking use heat and smoke to deter outdoor pests. Conventional ovens and electric dehydrators are used indoors in controlled conditions.

Foods dried outdoors in warm shade or direct sunlight become contaminated with insects and their invisible eggs and larvae. Therefore, be sure to treat these foods after drying by freezing or pasteurizing:

- ⚜ Freeze by placing a package of dried food in a deep freeze (0°F or less) for 48 hours.

- ⚜ Pasteurize by placing dried food on a rack over a baking sheet in a preheated 160°F oven for 30 minutes. After heating, you may want to condition the food, if you have not already done so.

If you neglect to treat foods dried unprotected outdoors by either freezing or pasteurizing, the food deteriorates faster during storage and may even cause food poisoning.

Each drying method requires the same basic steps to prepare, dry, and store the food properly. The following sections describe each method in more detail.

TRAYS FOR DRYING FOODS

Trays used for drying foods need to be of a food-safe material such as plastic, stainless steel, Teflon, or wood (avoid green wood, pine, cedar, oak, and redwood). Avoid metals other than stainless steel; they can transfer a metallic flavor to food. You may simply stretch cheesecloth over an oven or cake rack or a wood frame, and attach it with masking tape, paper clips, or clothespins. You can have (window) screens made at a hardware store to use for drying. For large quantities of food, use rimmed trays with slatted, perforated, or woven bottoms. Place trays on a raised surface (such as wood or cement blocks, or glass jars) to maximize air circulation. A clothes-drying rack can also be repurposed to hold drying trays.

Warm Shade or Air Drying

Shade drying places food out of direct sunlight, in a location with very warm air or very good circulation, or both. Suitable locations may be outdoors—such as an open shed or covered or screened porch—or indoors in a well-ventilated attic or room, as well as inside a car or camper.

The most common shade-dried foods include hanging bean britches, pepper ristras, or herb bunches and tray drying nuts in the shell. You may also use shade drying as a finishing method for sun-dried foods that need to be shielded from additional sun exposure.

Sun Drying

Sun drying is limited to desert climates. This method requires temperatures above 90°F, humidity of 20 percent or less, and low air pollution. To sun dry, simply place trays of food in direct sunlight where there is good air circulation. Use screens or netting to protect against birds and bugs. Place trays for sun drying over cement or hard surfaces, rather than soil or grass.

DRYING BEAN PODS ON THE VINE

While sun drying usually requires high temperatures and low humidity, one exception is vine-drying beans—such as navy, kidney, lentil, or soybeans. At the end of the growing season, leave the bean pods on the vine in the garden until the beans rattle inside the pods. When the vines and pods are dry and shriveled, pick the beans, shell them, and then condition (conditioning is described later in this chapter). If conditioning shows that the beans still contain too much moisture, they will grow mold unless stored in the freezer or dried more completely. Dry the shelled beans completely using any method (such as solar, shade, oven, or dehydrator).

Solar Drying

If you don't live in a desert climate and want to dry foods in the sun, you must use a solar dryer. Solar drying utilizes a collector, which traps heat and makes it possible to dry foods in any climate. The collector is a specially designed covered box that increases the drying temperature and maximizes air circulation. You can find do-it-yourself instructions online or in books to build a simple to elaborate solar dryer (see Appendix C).

A good solar dryer has the following qualities:

✦ Vented for control of temperature and airflow

✦ Covered to keep food dry in the event of rain

✦ Shielded to keep food from direct sunlight

✦ Easy-to-raise covers for loading and unloading

✦ Design of solar collector is based on climate

✦ Moderately increases interior temperature

✦ Allows for variable angles during operation (greater angle in autumn versus summer)

Solar dryers use background material based on climate needs; for example, black is used for high latitudes, while other colors are used for low latitudes, hot climates, and high altitudes.

Conventional Ovens

Oven drying uses a conventional gas or electric oven. It is a good choice if you want to do occasional drying or are drying for the first time. It tends to be slower than other methods, but there is little or no investment in equipment and you don't have to depend on the weather. Caution: the oven-drying method is not safe in a home with small children.

Foods that are well suited to oven drying are meats; seafood; fruit leather; low-moisture foods such as herbs, potatoes, bread cubes, berries, and meaty tomatoes (roma or paste-type); and excess produce you might otherwise throw out, such as onions, celery, and bananas. Dry foods on days when the humidity is not high, space the food about an inch apart, and fill only half of the oven racks with food.

Here are the general steps for oven drying any type of food:

1. Preheat oven to the lowest temperature setting.

2. Maintain an oven temperature between 125°F and 145°F. Check the oven temperature with an accurate thermometer. Decrease the temperature by propping open the oven door with a wooden spoon or folded towel.

3. Maximize air circulation to speed drying. Place a fan on a chair near the propped-open oven door so that it blows away the hot, escaping air. Open nearby doors and windows to promote more airflow.

After drying a few foods, if you want to continue to use the oven method, consider investing in an electric food dehydrator.

Food Dehydrators

A food-dehydrating appliance has few weather dependencies, can consistently produce a quality product, and is less prone to problems. This makes it easier than most other methods. A good food dehydrator provides variable temperature control and good air circulation. A temperature control with a range of 85°F to 180°F provides full flexibility for drying all types of foods, from delicate herbs and firm fruits to meat jerkies. A temperature control with a maximum of 160°F or less will limit your ability to dry meats and fish.

You can purchase a basic model for as little as $50, which is a good choice for first-time users or those who want to dry foods occasionally and in small amounts. Basic models have limited temperature ranges, vertical airflow, single-wall construction, and limited drying capacities. Deluxe models cost $250 or more, and offer more temperature range, efficient horizontal airflow, double-wall construction, and larger drying capacities.

Pit-Oven Drying

Pit-oven drying is useful when other methods are impractical. Create a pit oven by building a fire in an earthen pit and using rocks to store heat. The stored heat in the rocks is used to dry food after the wood fuel has burned down to embers.

When the fire has burned down to embers and the rocks are red hot, place a tray of food over the fire. Drape the tray with breathable material, such as green leaves or thatched mats, to reduce heat loss. Stir the food occasionally. As the rocks cool, lower the tray to use the heat more efficiently.

The advantages and disadvantages of the various drying methods are summarized in the following table.

Advantages and Disadvantages of Drying Methods

Method	Advantages	Disadvantages
Sun	Low cost	Limited to desert climates
Solar	Less weather dependent	Requires skill to build
Shade	Adaptable	Limited to a few foods
Oven	Accessible	Uses more energy
	Good for first-timers	May cook fruits and vegetables
Dehydrator	Less error prone	Initial cost
	Less weather dependent	
Pit oven	Use when practical	Uses lots of fuel
		Food may have smoky flavor

Even though you can dry almost any type of food, you need to prepare, package, and store different types of foods correctly. If you skip critical steps, your dried foods may become moldy or infested with bugs. The following sections talk about specific requirements for different types of foods.

Drying Fruits and Vegetables

When drying fruits and vegetables, you need to prevent browning in susceptible foods, inactivate spoilage enzymes, inhibit harmful bacteria, and take steps to ensure even drying.

Pretreat to Prevent Browning

Some fruits and vegetables are susceptible to browning as soon as they are peeled or cut. Browning occurs in light-colored fruits such as apples, pears, peaches, apricots, and bananas; and vegetables such as artichokes, eggplants, and potatoes. Browning can also occur around the stem area of light-colored cherries and grapes. There are several easy ways to prevent browning, including using acid, heat, sugar, salt, or sulfur. Which method you use is a matter of personal preference.

Ascorbic acid (also known as *vitamin C*) is safe and effective for treating fruits and vegetables to retard the enzyme oxidation that causes browning. An added benefit is the increased acidity, which helps prevent bacterial growth. Over time, some foods treated with ascorbic acid may turn brown; sulfiting offers the best protection for long-term storage. I'll discuss using sulfiting chemicals later in this section.

Vitamin C is economical and available year-round where vitamins are sold. Be sure to buy plain tablets, not time-released, and without bioflavonoids, flavoring, or other ingredients. To prepare a soaking solution, use 3,000 milligrams per gallon of water (for example, crush six 500-milligram tablets and stir until dissolved). Allow prepared produce to soak 5 minutes, drain well, and pat dry. Ascorbic acid may also be added directly to sugar syrups or honey dips.

WHY DO FRUITS AND VEGETABLE TURN BROWN?

Here's the scientific explanation: When you cut into fruit (or drop and bruise it), you break the cell walls within the fruit. When this happens, the enzyme polyphenol oxidase (PPO) combines with phenolic compounds. If fruits contain PPO and colorless polyphenols, they oxidize or turn brown. This oxidative process isn't always detrimental. The same reaction contributes beneficially to the production of black tea, aged red wine, and raisins. To prevent oxidation when it is not wanted (for example, when you want to preserve apples, peaches, or eggplants), you need to deactivate the PPO enzyme by heating (blanching), increasing the acidity (adding acid like vitamin C), or removing oxygen (sulfuring). Sugar and chilling foods in the refrigerator will also slow down enzymes.

Besides ascorbic acid, there are several other products and methods that you can use to help prevent browning.

Citric acid prevents browning, but is not as effective as ascorbic acid. More often, it is used to raise acidity. To prepare a citric-acid powder solution, stir 1 teaspoon (5 grams) of citric acid into 1 quart (1,000 milliliters) of cold water. Cut fruits or vegetables directly into the citric-acid solution. Allow to soak 5 minutes, drain well, and pat dry.

Commercial antioxidants, such as Fruit-Fresh, are easy to use and readily available where canning supplies are sold. However, these products tend to be more expensive than plain ascorbic acid, contain additives (such as sugars and anticaking agents), may contain altered forms of ascorbic acid with no vitamin benefit (such as erythorbic acid), and may have a shorter shelf life. Follow the dosage and usage directions on the product label.

Fruit juice that is high in ascorbic or citric acid will help retard browning. Fruit juices you can use are apple, cranberry, white grape, lemon, lime, orange, or pineapple. They may be freshly squeezed or commercially bottled juices without added sugar. Cut fruits or vegetables directly into the juice. Allow produce to soak 5 minutes, drain well, and pat dry.

PERFECT PRESERVING

Which method you use to prevent browning is a matter of personal preference. Some methods change the flavor or texture in ways that you may or may not prefer. Sugar and salt work by binding water and making it unavailable to enzymes, which delays browning until drying takes effect. Sugar plumps up fruits and adds calories; salt tends to shrivel foods. Salt can be used on fruit to make sweet and salty snacks. I suggest you try simple, inexpensive methods first. If you don't like the result, then read through the other options.

Besides acids, there are several other methods you can use to help prevent browning. You may add ascorbic acid to any of these methods, if desired.

Water blanching immerses food in boiling water. However, it may contribute an undesirable cooked flavor and adds water. Therefore, it is not a preferred pretreatment for browning when drying foods. However, it is useful for "checking" fruit skins. (Checking is described later in this chapter.)

Steam blanching is one of my favorite methods to prevent browning in fruits and vegetables. It is inexpensive and doesn't add anything to the food. I've had great success using steam to pretreat everything from dried apricots and yellow cherries to eggplant and zucchini slices. Bring water to a boil in a pot or wok fitted with a steamer rack, add the pieces of food in a single layer, cover, and steam for 1 to 5 minutes, depending on the size and thickness of the pieces. You need to develop the skill for judging when blanching is sufficient. You should stop short of cooking the piece all the way through. Do not cool blanched food in an ice water bath; this adds water, chills the food, and delays the drying process. Pat food dry with towels and transfer immediately to the drying trays. See Chapter 9 for more on blanching fruits and vegetables.

Syrup blanching can be used to poach fruits before drying. It also reduces browning because the sugar reduces the amount of water available for enzymes to be active. Poached fruit becomes plump, soft, and very sweet after drying. Poach fruit gently in medium to very heavy syrup for 5 to 10 minutes (depending on size). Remove from heat, let fruit remain in warm syrup for up to 30 minutes, and then drain well. If desired, you may rinse off syrup under running water, and pat dry.

Honey dips also produce plump, soft dried fruits and are easier than syrup blanching. Dip sliced or halved raw fruit in honey syrup and let soak for 5 minutes. Remove fruit, drain well, and pat dry. See Chapter 7 for more on sugar syrups with honey.

Salt solutions may be used for fruits or vegetables. Salt binds water and inhibits microbial growth. Salty dried fruits are a common Asian-style snack known as *crack seed*. To prepare a salt solution, use 2 to 4 tablespoons salt per gallon of water. Soak produce for 5 minutes, drain well, and pat dry.

Sulfuring is the traditional method used to protect color and prevent browning of dried fruit as well as discourage insects during drying. Sulfur reduces the amount of oxygen available to the enzymes that cause browning. This method places the fruit in an enclosed box, ignites food-grade sulfur (not garden sulfur), and allows the fumes to penetrate the fruit. Burning sulfur is irritating to mucous membranes, as well as to plants, and needs to be performed outside in an open area. Do not use aluminum or galvanized metals, which will discolor and corrode from sulfur fumes. Also, do not additionally dry sulfured fruit indoors in an oven or dehydrator due to the irritating fumes.

Sulfiting chemicals are the modern alternative to sulfuring. Sulfites are widely used as an antimicrobial agent and to help preserve color in many processed foods available today. Sulfites can cause respiratory and skin reactions in sensitive people. For this and other reasons, the U.S. Food and Drug Administration (FDA) banned some uses of sulfites, including in salad bars and meats. Sulfiting agents are available where wine-making supplies are sold; ask for sodium sulfite, sodium bisulfite, or sodium metabisulfite. Be sure that the product you buy is USP (food grade) or reagent grade (pure). Prepare a fresh sulfiting solution according to package directions for each batch, just before you are ready to dry the food. Soak slices for 5 to 10 minutes and halves for 15 to 30 minutes, drain well, and pat dry. Use a longer soaking period for food that is not ripe, will be dried in the sun, or stored for longer than 6 months.

SPOILER ALERT

If you use a sulfiting agent, do not store the dried food in metal; use plastic bags inside of metal storage containers, or glass jars. Sulfated foods may react with metal and cause disagreeable color and flavor changes.

Blanch to Inactivate Spoilage Enzymes

As soon as fruits and vegetables are picked, enzymes start to break down the cellular structure. You can use blanching to inactivate these spoilage enzymes.

Enzymes become inactive at 140°F, which is the temperature at which vegetables are dried. So in theory, blanching is unnecessary if you're going to be drying the food. However, blanching will result in better-quality dried vegetables with longer storage capabilities. Steam blanching is the preferred method over water blanching. Find instructions for steam blanching in the previous section.

Blanching fruit is not necessary because its sugar and acids slow down enzymes until adequate drying is achieved. However, you may blanch certain fruits to prevent browning, as described in the previous section.

Pretreat to Inhibit Harmful Bacteria

Most fruits have enough acid to prevent microbial growth during drying. Vegetables dried until crisp have a low water content that also inhibits bacteria. However, you may wish to further control micro-organisms during drying and storage.

Ascorbic and citric acids lower the pH of foods, which inhibits microbial growth. A salt solution of 10 to 15 percent also helps to control bacteria. Find instructions for using ascorbic acid, citric acid, and salt solution in the previous section.

Pretreat to "Check" Fruit Skins

Treat fruits with tough, waxy skins (such as plums) that will not be peeled before drying. These thick skins hold in moisture. Therefore, to ensure even drying, you need to crack or "check" the skins. There are two methods you can use: water blanching and physically piercing or slitting the skin.

Water blanching creates microscopic cracks in the skins that are not visible to the naked eye. If you notice cracks after blanching, you have likely overdone it and cooked the fruit. After washing the fruit, dip in boiling water for 1 to 2 minutes, drain well, and pat dry.

Piercing physically cuts or slits the fruit. You may pierce the skins with or without blanching. Use a paring knife or fork to prick cherries on opposite sides, or pierce larger fruits like plums in three or four spots evenly around the fruit.

Checking is especially helpful when drying firm berries and small, whole fruits. Fruits to consider for checking pretreatment include blueberries, cranberries, cherries, figs, grapes, and small plums or fresh Italian prunes.

SPOILER ALERT

Don't underestimate the power of blanching to check fruit skins before drying. The short blanching process cracks or opens the pores in the skin (the same as a nice facial does for *your* skin). These openings let moisture escape, which ensures complete and speedy drying. Checking is desirable, even if you plan to pierce or cut the fruit after blanching—pitting cherries or cutting plums in half, for example. I once ruined a 10-pound batch of beautiful Italian prune halves because I thought cutting would be adequate. Despite thorough drying, too much moisture was still trapped under the skin; the prunes molded within a month. I'll never skip blanching of prunes again!

Drying Meats

In this section, you will learn about drying thin pieces of meat and fish, such as beef jerky and smoked salmon. Curing and drying thicker, larger cuts of meat are discussed in Chapter 5.

There are several pretreatments for dried meats: acid, salt, nitrites, and precooking. Pretreatments protect meats from microbial growth during the drying process. Following these treatments, you may dry meats by any of several methods, including air, sun or solar, ovens, food dehydrator, or smoking.

The best meats for drying are beef, buffalo, and goat. Lamb and pork are less suitable; the fat in these meats turns rancid quickly. For game meat, deer and antelope are best. Use only lean meats in excellent condition, either fresh or frozen.

Follow these safe handling guidelines when preparing meat:

- Wash your hands thoroughly with soap and water before and after working with meat products.
- Wear gloves or handle meat with tongs whenever possible, especially if you have cuts or sores.
- Clean and sanitize equipment and utensils before every step.
- Defrost frozen meat in the refrigerator, never at room temperature.
- Refrigerate all raw meats at 36°F to 38°F before preparing and during marinating.
- Never reuse marinade.
- Test the temperature of ovens, smokers, and dehydrators with a thermometer on the drying tray *before drying.*
- Do not use a microwave oven to precook or dry meats.

As with all preservation methods, the goal is to control the growth of bacteria, yeasts, and molds. Adequate controls ensure safe food with a longer storage life.

SPOILER ALERT

Many cultures around the world dry meat using sun-, solar-, and air-drying methods at temperatures below the minimum safe level of 140°F. However, these dried meats are cooked before eating rather than consumed as snack food, as we do beef jerky. To control bacteria, these traditional methods use freshly killed meat that is immersed in a strong salt solution before drying. To cook dried meats, you may pound them into a powder or shred and use in soups and stews. If you want to make beef jerky, your drying method should include cooking to a safe internal temperature (160°F for meats and 165°F for poultry). If you wish to use traditional methods, use high salt concentrations, nitrites, pasteurization, or other treatments to ensure a safe product.

Precooked Dried Meats

All meat contains bacteria. Precooking kills any pathogens that may be present. This safety step results in a product with a different color and texture than traditionally dried meat. The good news is, precooking shortens the drying time and tenderizes the meat. However, precooked dried meat is not acceptable to some people. The following considerations can help you decide when to use a precooking step:

꙳ High-risk individuals susceptible to food poisoning are strongly advised to consume only dried meat that has been prepared using a precooking step.

꙳ Aged meats are preferred by connoisseurs for cooking and eating. However, aged meats naturally contain higher levels of bacteria.

꙳ Ground meat jerkies justify a precooking step due to the possibility of higher bacterial counts, which is inherent in any type of ground meat.

꙳ Wild game meat must be sound and carefully handled. An animal that has a wounded intestinal tract, is not chilled after slaughter, or received careless field dressing is not a good choice for making jerky. Caution: some game meats—particularly bear, boar, wild feline (such as a cougar), fox, dog, wolf, horse, seal, or walrus—contain a strain of trichinosis-causing parasite that is not killed by freezing. Do not dry meat from wild game unless you precook the meat thoroughly to a minimum temperature of 160°F. These meats are most suitable for dishes that are thoroughly cooked, such as stews or soups.

꙳ Drying temperatures below 160°F, especially if prepared for snacking without another safety step (such as high salt, nitrites, or pasteurization), require the food to be precooked.

Use moist heat when precooking meat to prevent case-hardening. Meat becomes case-hardened when the surface dries prematurely and traps moisture inside, making it difficult to dry the interior meat thoroughly.

Curing Agents, Marinades, and Dry Rubs

You cure meat before drying to control the growth of bacteria. You can apply a cure by marinating meat strips in a liquid or by applying a dry rub. Curing agents include salt, acids, and nitrite.

Salt is the most important control to delay microbial growth in dried meat and the preferred choice of traditionalists over precooking or the use of nitrite. You will find many different recommendations for the amount of salt to use. Dipping strips of meat in brine of 20 to 26 percent strength inhibits pathogenic bacteria, including *E. coli, Clostridium, Listeria,* and *Staphylococcus.* However, modern brine recipes tend to use salt concentrations of 10 percent or lower, which will inhibit only *E. coli.* For more information on brine strength, see Chapter 4.

Acids enhance pathogen destruction and include vinegars, lemon juice, wines, soy sauce, and Worcestershire sauce. Acids with a pH of less than 3.6 are most effective against common meat pathogens, including *Clostridium, E. coli, Listeria, Salmonella,* and *Staphylococcus.*

Sodium nitrite or a fast-cure product is suggested if you use a salt concentration below 15 percent without a precooking step. For more information on curing with nitrites, see Chapter 5.

You may add other ingredients to either a wet marinade or dry rub to flavor and tenderize the meat, such as sugar and spices, in addition to curing agents. Many people also like to smoke dried meats for additional flavor, to control insects when drying outdoors, and to supplement the effect of curing agents.

Basic Steps for Drying Meat

Drying meat and fish requires rigorous attention to safe handling steps; efficient drying using plenty of warm, circulated air or heat (or both); and sufficient humidity to prevent case-hardening.

Here are the basic steps for drying meat by any method:

1. Prepare lean cuts such as flank, round, or loin. Trim meat of all visible fat; fat becomes rancid quickly during storage. Freeze for 30 minutes to firm for easier slicing.

2. For tender dried meat, cut against the grain; for chewy dried meat, cut with the grain. For fast, safe drying, cut meat in strips 1 to 6 inches wide, and no more than ¼ inch thick.

3. Apply a cure or marinate meat in the refrigerator using a wet marinade or dry rub.

4. Precook meat using moist heat method (optional; see steps for precooking in the next section). Preheat an oven, dehydrator, or smoker.

5. Dry by any method (sun, air, oven, dehydrator, or smoking). Place strips close together on drying trays, but do not overlap. To prevent case-hardening, ensure sufficient humidity during drying. Test a cooled piece; meat should crack when bent, but not break. Pat dry any beads of oil with clean, absorbent towels.

Your goal when drying meat or fish is to achieve uniform dehydration, which is indicated by even color, smooth surface, and hard texture.

Oven drying and smoking are the methods recommended by extension agencies for dried meat because they can cook meats to a safe internal temperature of at least 160°F. Meat temperature tends to lag oven temperature by 25°F; so preheat the oven or smoker to 185°F. Arrange meat on drying trays so that it is at least 4 inches from the heat source.

The requirements for a dehydrator are the same as for oven drying. If your dehydrator operates at temperatures below 185°F, you need to treat it like sun or air drying and consider a precooking or curing step.

Steps for Precooking Meat Before Drying

Precooking is a recommended step for drying meat that is to be consumed by high-risk individuals; made with aged, ground, or game meats; consumed raw without a subsequent cooking step; or prepared without adequate cure.

Here are the basic steps for precooking meat before drying:

1. Prepare a cooking liquid, which can be plain water or a marinade. If using a marinade, complete the marinating step before precooking.

2. In a saucepan, bring the meat strips and cooking liquid to a boil, and boil 5 minutes.

3. Heat strips to an internal temperature of 160°F for meats and 165°F for poultry. Check the temperature of several pieces by wrapping a strip around a thermometer.

4. Remove strips from the cooking liquid and drain.

Immediately dry precooked meat as described in the preceding section, "Basic Steps for Drying Meat."

How to Kill Trichinae in Pork and Wild Game

You must freeze pork before making jerky with the meat because it may contain *Trichinella spiralis,* a parasitic roundworm. Eating meat infected with trichinae can cause trichinosis. Initial symptoms of an infection include nausea, diarrhea, vomiting, fever, and abdominal discomfort. If you eat raw or undercooked meat and develop these symptoms, see your health care provider immediately for tests and treatment. A blood test or muscle biopsy can determine if you have trichinosis. Several safe and effective prescription drugs are available for treatment of trichinosis.

To kill trichinae in pork before making jerky, cut the meat in pieces that are less than 1 inch thick. Wrap to prevent freezer burn, and place them in a deep freeze (0°F or below) for at least 1 month; freeze thicker pieces at least 2 months.

Although freezing kills the trichinae, it does not reduce the number of bacteria in meat. You may want to take additional precautions to reduce the possibility of bacterial contamination. Also, though freezing pork is effective, freezing game meat may not kill some of the different species of *Trichinella* and tapeworm that infect wild animals. Only thoroughly cooking game meat can destroy all parasites and other pathogens.

Cool, Package, and Store Dried Foods

There are quick and easy postdrying techniques you can use to protect the storage life of your dried foods. It is good practice—even for brittle dried foods—to test for dryness and to condition the product before you seal dried food in airtight packages.

Cool Foods Before Packaging

Most foods are easier to handle if you leave them on the drying trays until cool. After drying foods on trays, arrange the trays in a dry, airy location out of direct sunlight. This can be your dining room table or covered porch. Cool the food for 30 minutes, or until no longer warm to the touch.

Fruit leather is one product you want to remove from the drying tray while still warm. Peel from the liner and place on a clean plate or tray. Since fruit rolls can stick together in storage, you usually want to cut it into serving-size pieces and wrap individually for storage.

Dried foods hung on a string line or in bunches are usually left in place, but may also be unstrung and packaged and stored as described below.

Test for Dryness

Test all foods at the end of the drying process. The extent of dryness is somewhat a matter of preference. You may dry foods until pliable, especially if you want to use them as a snack food. Less-dry products have considerably shorter shelf life—from 2 weeks to 2 months. If you want to store dried food longer or use it to grind to a powder (such as tomatoes) to make sauce, then you want them to be crisp and brittle. The disadvantage is, very dry foods take longer to rehydrate.

PERFECT PRESERVING

Someone asked the other day whether you could really grind tomatoes to powder. The trick is to slice them thinly (1/8 inch) and dry until crisp and brittle. An avid canner, I now prefer drying over canning for most of my tomatoes. Drying is easier, uses less energy and equipment, and dried foods take up less space. Dried tomatoes can be used in all the same recipes (spaghetti sauce, chili, etc.). I dry thin slices as well as quarters and halves. Cut large dried pieces into bite-size pieces to toss into soups and stews. The only dish where the rich flavor of dried tomatoes doesn't work well is a fresh-style salsa; for this, I still prefer canned tomatoes.

Condition Dried Foods

Individual pieces of food dry at different rates; some pieces will have more moisture than others. If there is too much moisture left in a few pieces, they can grow mold and contaminate the entire batch. To guard against mold growth, you need to condition dried foods before you store them.

To condition dried foods, place them in a tightly closed container at room temperature. Stir or shake the contents every day for a week. If you open the container to stir the contents, be sure to close it again tightly. During conditioning, the moisture will equalize—that is, excess moisture will transfer to drier pieces, until it is evenly distributed throughout the batch. During conditioning, if moisture forms on the inside of the container, the food is not sufficiently dry and you need to return it to the dryer. Alternatively, you may store partially dried foods in the freezer.

Seal Foods in Airtight Containers

Seal dried food in airtight containers that hold only enough food to be used at one time. This reduces the number of times a package is reopened. You can also limit air by taping over jar enclosures or using a desiccant to absorb oxygen. Ideally, you want to store dried foods at a constant temperature between 40°F and 70°F. Be sure to store foods in a closed cupboard or dark room, away from light.

If you live in a dry climate, your dehydrated foods will tend to stay fresh longer. However, if you live in a humid area, moisture can get in and shorten storage life considerably. In high-humidity locations, put dried food in zipper-lock plastic bags that allow you to push out excess air.

You can store properly packaged, well-dried foods at room temperature for up to 1 year. Less dry, pliable products have a shelf life of a few weeks to several months. Storage life decreases with packaging that is not airtight, reopening packages, and fluctuating temperatures. You can vacuum-seal, refrigerate, or freeze any dried food for longer storage.

SPOILER ALERT

Remember that dried foods can spoil quickly if not properly stored. Be sure to package food in an airtight container. Even if you live in a dry climate, check it monthly for spoilage—usually mold. Use dried foods before other types of preserved foods, such as frozen or canned. Most importantly, enjoy eating your dried foods and be sure to experiment with different ways of using your stored treasures.

Using Dried Foods

Pliable fruits and meat jerkies may be eaten as is for snacks or trail foods for camping and hiking. Very dry fruits and vegetables may be ground into powder to make soups, sauces, or beverages. Dry foods may also be rehydrated before using. To rehydrate dried foods (including jerkies): Place them in a bowl and pour hot or boiling water over them. Soak 20 to 30 minutes, or until they have plumped up to their original size.

Cold water may be used to soak dried foods; however, it will take longer for the food to fully hydrate; refrigerate soaking foods if they have been at room temperature for 2 hours.

You can add dried vegetables to soups or stews and they will rehydrate as the dish cooks. You may need to add liquid that is at least equal in volume to the dried vegetables. For example, if you add 1 cup dried peas and carrots to your stew, increase the stock or water called for in the recipe by at least 1 cup.

Don't expect dehydrated foods to taste like fresh, frozen, or canned. Just as each of these preservation methods affects flavor and texture, dried foods also look and taste different. In general, dried foods have a strong odor, yet delicate flavor after rehydrating. Many people find dried vegetables more useful and tasty than canned ones.

If you are new to drying, start with a few of the easiest foods to dry such as berries, banana slices, herb bunches, tomato slices, chopped onions, oven jerky, and smoked salmon.

Troubleshooting Dried Foods

Problem: **Moisture develops in the container of dried food.**

Remedy: Return food to the dryer or freeze food that develops moisture.

Prevention: Test several pieces of food, not just 1 or 2, for adequate dryness. Package the food in airtight containers promptly after drying to prevent the food from reabsorbing moisture. Store dried foods in a cool, dry, dark place. Check for moisture daily during the first week in storage, and then monthly throughout the year.

Problem: **Moisture repeatedly develops in the container of dried food, despite redrying.**

Remedy: Return food to the dryer or freeze food that develops moisture.

Prevention: Cut foods into pieces of equal size so that foods dry evenly. Use a lower drying temperature (140°F or less) to prevent case-hardening (when the outside hardens or cooks and traps moisture inside). Use airtight containers; use tape over closure if necessary.

Problem: **Moisture develops after several weeks or months in storage.**

Remedy: Return food to the dryer or freeze food that develops moisture.

Prevention: Reseal container after each use. Store food is several small containers rather than one large container.

Problem: **Mold growth develops in stored food.**

Remedy: Moldy food is not safe to eat and should be discarded.

Prevention: Follow all of the preceding prevention steps to avoid moisture development in dried foods.

Problem: **Browning occurs in fruits such as apples or apricots.**

Remedy: Browned fruits are safe to eat. Prepare as stewed fruit or use in baked goods.

Prevention: Pretreat susceptible fruits to prevent browning (such as apples or other pomes, stone fruits, and bananas).

Problem: **Brown spots occur in vegetables.**

Remedy: Browned vegetables are safe to eat. Prepare as a creamed soup or grind for use in sauces and stews.

Prevention: Do not overdry vegetables or dry at temperatures above 140°F. Pretreat light-colored vegetables (such as eggplants and potatoes) to prevent browning. When using the blanching method to pretreat vegetables, use adequate blanching time.

Problem: **Black spots appear on dried tomatoes immediately after drying is complete, or later during storage.**

Remedy: If black spots appear immediately after drying, tomatoes are not spoiled and safe to eat, but may have an "off" flavor. However, if dried tomatoes develop black spots over time (during storage), it could be due to mold growth caused by excess moisture, which means the food is unsafe and must be discarded.

Prevention: In dried tomatoes, black spots can be caused by low acidity; choose tomatoes with high acid content for drying. For moldy food, follow all of the preceding prevention steps to avoid moisture development in dried foods.

Problem: **Insects are present in stored food.**

Remedy: Pasteurize food and transfer to a clean container.

Prevention: Pasteurize foods that are dried outside to kill invisible insect eggs and larvae, which may become active in storage. Store dried foods in airtight glass or metal containers.

Problem: **Holes develop in bags that contain dried foods (indicating insect or rodent infestation).**

Remedy: Pasteurize food and transfer to a clean container.

Prevention: Store dried foods in airtight glass or metal containers. Store dried foods that are in bags in the refrigerator, freezer, or another pest-free area.

Fermenting Foods 〜 3

Fresh foods are alive with microorganisms. However, fermented foods are a virtual block party, teeming with "good" bacteria and other microorganisms that are thought to have probiotic effects—living organisms that can help to maintain your health. These helpful microbes make vitamins, aid digestion, prevent disorders such as allergies and intestinal diseases, improve food safety, and keep pathogens from gaining a foothold.

Fermentation bacteria, yeasts, and molds produce enzymes that break down the food, causing many desirable changes. Fermented foods taste great, last longer, and are a cheap and energy-efficient form of preservation.

The line between fermented and spoiled foods is sometimes a matter of opinion. Some fermented foods—such as sourdough bread, yogurt, cheese, and soy sauce—are enjoyed by many people. Other fermented foods—such as blue cheese and fish sauce—have odors and flavors that can be an acquired taste. However, fermented foods do not contain harmful microbes. Truly spoiled foods make you sick and fermented foods do not. In fact, scientific studies provide evidence that fermentation inhibits pathogenic bacteria. This antimicrobial benefit may be one of their most interesting qualities.

How Fermentation Works

Like drying, fermenting is one of the oldest and simplest forms of food preservation. No one invented it. As sure as the sun sets every evening, fruit juice or milk, left unattended, will slowly ferment. Just as you use cooking to transform the flavor and texture of raw meat and vegetables, you can use fermentation to change almost any type of fresh food into something that is tasty and nutritious, and one that you can enjoy over an extended period.

You use fermentation to take advantage of the natural spoilage process of food, by encouraging certain "good" microorganisms over ones that can be harmful. Fermentation is one of the safest preservation methods, if you make and store fermented foods appropriately.

You may already know that bacteria, yeasts, and molds are everywhere. When the environment is conducive to a particular type of microbe, it grows. Most fermentation bacteria like to eat carbohydrates (especially sugar), which they convert into alcohol or acid. When they run out of food or the product is chilled or heated, microbial activity stops.

How to Control Fermentation

You control fermentation by encouraging some microorganisms over others using temperature, salt, acid, oxygen or air, and food (often sugar or soluble carbohydrates). The microorganisms produce enzymes, which are proteins that facilitate chemical reactions and cause the changes in color and texture. A by-product of these enzymatic reactions is acids that contribute much of the flavor.

Enzymes are very specific to a particular process. They can only function within in a narrow range of temperature and acidity (pH). Even slight changes in the environment can halt their activity. However, you can easily control them by maintaining favorable conditions.

SPOILER ALERT

While fermentation is a natural process, it can also be a tricky one. Altering the conditions of the fermentation even slightly can change a desirable result into an undesirable one. For example, acetic fermentation ruins alcoholic fermentation by producing vinegar instead of alcohol. Yeast fermentation, used successfully in wine making, ruins lactic fermentation when making pickles. Likewise, lactic fermentations, used for making cheese and yogurt, ruin a good batch of beer.

Starter Cultures

Starter cultures are a very useful way to begin fermentation. A starter is a known quantity of microorganisms that you introduce into your process.

Simply allowing a bottle of grape juice to stand open to the air is one method of producing vinegar. However, even if you establish the ideal temperature and oxygen level, you may not necessarily have the right wild yeasts present to turn the juice into wine, or the right bacteria to turn the wine to vinegar. This is where you want to add a starter culture. In some cases, you can purchase starter cultures, and in others, you can make your own.

Before introducing a starter, you usually want to kill all existing microorganisms—good and bad. This helps guarantee that the organisms you add are the only ones present. For this reason, fermentation procedures often call for treating (by chemicals or heat) the initial ingredient, such as grapes for wine, or milk for yogurt.

Some products turn out best when you use a specific starter—examples include beer, wine, cheese, hard salami, and tempeh. You can buy a range of starters from retailers who sell supplies for cheese making, brewing beer, or wine making; or from those who specialize in one type of starter, such as tempeh or natto.

Often, starters are sold in small envelopes that look similar to packets of bread yeast from the grocery store. However, bread yeast is not interchangeable with other specific yeasts and bacteria cultures for other types of fermented products.

For vinegar, you can find a starter in unpasteurized, organic vinegar. This starter, called the *mother,* is a floating, gelatinous blob—I've always thought it looked like a small jellyfish. It is composed mostly of cellulose, a type of soluble fiber, and of course favorable *Acetobacter.* Don't mistake the gray powdery sediment at the bottom of the bottle for the mother. The sediment is composed of tiny bits of source material (such as apples or grapes), along with enzymes, pectin, amino acids, vitamins, and minerals. Many people consider both the sediment and the mother to be very healthful. However, the sediment isn't important in helping you get an acetic fermentation started. If you can't find a mother, then the simplest solution is to use beer yeast and add it to fruit juice.

You can make yeast cultures by encouraging wild yeasts, using unwashed, wild, or organic fruits or grains. Remember that chlorinated tap water, iodized salt, and filtered air (including centralized heat, air conditioning, or HEPA filters) inhibit wild yeasts.

Another way to get a starter is from your last good batch of product. For example, you can use a few spoonfuls of yogurt to inoculate a quart of milk to make more yogurt. Likewise, a cup of sourdough yeast sponge will start another bread dough. If you strain plain, organic yogurt overnight, the clear, yellow liquid that emerges is whey. This acidic liquid makes a good starter for lacto-fermented pickles and fermented bread batters (such as Indian *dosa* or *idli* and Ethiopian *injera*).

However, using existing product as a starter isn't always better. The juice from a batch of fermented vegetables (such as sauerkraut) does not make a good starter for a new batch. When you make sauerkraut, you begin with salt. This environment encourages bacteria that produce lactic acid. When you begin with sauerkraut juice, the initial acidity is too high, and the most favorable bacteria for developing sauerkraut are inhibited. In this case, you skip an important step and the result is a poor quality product that lacks tangy flavor and crunchy texture. For this reason, you can enjoy sauerkraut and *kimchi* juice as a beverage or ingredient in soup (both traditional uses). However, neither makes a good starter for the next batch.

Now that you know a little bit more about how to start and control fermentation, let's look at the different types in more detail. There are many different ways to categorize fermented foods. Next we'll look at four types of fermentation (alcoholic, acetic, lactic, and alkaline) and then specific types of fermented foods.

"GOOD" VS. "BAD" BACTERIA

Many of the bacteria groups used in food fermentation include beneficial as well as harmful species. *Streptococcus* is a good example. *Streptococcus salivarius* subsp. *thermophilus* is important in the production of cheese and yogurt. However, *Streptococcus pyogenes* and *Streptococcus pneumoniae* cause strep throat and pneumonia, respectively. To complicate matters, strains of *Streptococcus* have been reclassified as *Enterococcus* or *Lactococcus.* Consequently, you may recognize names that you associate with pathogens.

Types of Fermentation

Alcoholic fermentation is the breakdown of sugar by yeasts. When you put grape juice inside a closed vessel without air, the wild yeasts on grape skins convert the juice (sugars) to wine (alcohol, mostly ethanol). Cider and beer are variations on this process using different ingredients. If you start with high-quality product and clean conditions, you get a better product rather than simply allowing over-ripe fruit to spoil. Here is a simplified chemical representation for alcoholic fermentation:

$$C_6H_{12}O_6 \text{ (sugar)} + \text{yeasts} = 2\ CH_3CH_2OH \text{ (ethanol)} + 2\ CO_2 \text{ (carbon dioxide)}$$

Acetic fermentation is the breakdown of alcohol by bacteria, which converts it into vinegar (acetic acid). When cider, wine, or beer is exposed to air, *Acetobacter* oxidize the alcohol (add oxygen or O_2). Different vinegars will contain flavor components from the source materials. Cider and wine vinegar are the most prevalent, but vinegar can be made from other fermented liquids such as sherry, malt liquor, or fermented pineapple juice. Here is a simplified chemical representation for acetic fermentation:

$$CH_3CH_2OH \text{ (ethanol)} + O_2 \text{ (oxygen)} + \textit{Acetobacter} = CH_3COOH \text{ (vinegar)} + H_2O \text{ (water)}$$

Lactic acid bacteria (LAB) fermentations are the most prevalent type used throughout the world. It's easy to see why. LAB are low in cost and can be applied to many types of foods, including milks, vegetables, grains, and legumes, as well as meat and fish. You probably enjoy many LAB-fermented products, such as yogurt, cheese, fermented pickles, sauerkraut, kimchi, bread, soy sauce, salami, and ham. LAB come from several different genera. The most prevalent ones are *Lactobacillus, Leuconostoc, Pediococcus,* and *Streptococcus.* Here is a simplified chemical representation for lactic fermentation:

$$C_6H_{12}O_6 \text{ (sugar)} + \text{lactic acid bacteria} = 2\ CH_3CHOHCOOH \text{ (lactic acid)}$$

Alkaline fermentations break down proteins into components that raise the pH. This is in contrast to the preceding acid fermentations (alcoholic, acetic, and LAB), which break down carbohydrates into acids that lower the pH. Alkaline fermentations produce strong odors and flavors from sulfuric and ammoniac compounds. Here is a simplified chemical representation for alkaline fermentation:

$$\text{Protein} + \textit{Bacillus} = R\text{-}NH_2COOH \text{ (amino acids)} + CO_2 \text{ (carbon dioxide)} + H_2O \text{ (water)} + NH_4 \text{ (ammonia)}$$

Many fermented foods combine several methods. As you have already seen, vinegar is produced first by alcoholic fermentation of fruit juice, and then by secondary acetic fermentation to make vinegar. Sourdough starter contains yeasts that ferment and raise the dough, while LAB contribute the characteristic sour flavor. The following table lists the principle microorganisms and types of fermentation used to make many common foods.

Common Foods by Type of Fermentation

Fermented Food	Fermentation Type	Principle Microorganisms (Genus)
Wine, beer (grapes, barley)	Alcoholic	Yeast (*Saccharomyces*)
Chocolate (cacao bean)	Alcoholic, acetic	Yeast (*Saccharomyces, Hansenula, Pichia*) and bacteria (*Acetobacter*)
Sourdough bread (grain)	Alcoholic, lactic	Yeast (*Saccharomyces*) and bacteria (*Lactobacillus*)
Yogurt	Lactic	Bacteria (*Lactobacillus, Streptococcus, Bifidobacterium*)
Cheese	Lactic	Bacteria: *Lactococcus, Streptococcus, Lactobacillus;* secondary fermentation bacteria: *Propionibacterium* (Swiss cheese); secondary fermentation mold: *Penicillium* (Brie, blue)
Sauerkraut, kimchi, pickles	Lactic	Bacteria (*Lactobacillus, Leuconostoc, Streptococcus, Pediococcus*)
Dry sausage	Lactic	Pepperoni: Bacteria (*Pediococcus*)
Olives	Lactic	Bacteria (*Leuconostoc, Lactobacillus, Pediococcus*) and yeasts (*Saccharomyces, Candida, Hansenula*)
Tempeh	Lactic	Mold (*Rhizopus*)
Soy sauce, miso	Lactic	Yeasts (*Hanensula, Saccharomyces*) and mold (*Aspergillus*)
Vanilla bean	Alkaline, lactic	Bacteria (*Bacillus, Aspergillus, Penicillium,* and others)
Natto (fermented soybeans)	Alkaline	Bacteria (*Bacillus*)

During fermentation, the color, flavor, and texture of the food can change considerably. Cucumbers change from white and dark green to uniform olive green when you soak them in brine. Yeast transforms sweet and cloying grape flavors into ones that are clean and dry. Milk thickens when cultured with bacteria to make yogurt.

Next, let's look at specific fermentation methods that you can use to preserve a wide variety of delicious foods.

Types of Fermented Foods

The key to making wholesome fermented foods is to start with quality ingredients, use clean and sanitary equipment, and understand the environmental controls (like temperature and salt) for the type of fermenting you want to do.

Cider, Beer, and Wine

You use alcoholic fermentation to make a number of foods, including beer, wine, and yeasted breads. In each of these products, yeast breaks down the sugar to produce alcohol and CO_2. Although alcoholic fermentation produces both wine and yeasted breads, the resulting products are very different.

You make alcoholic beverages by fermenting sugar with yeast. The basic process—whether for cider, beer, or wine—involves several steps:

1. Sanitize all equipment and bottles. Clean and sanitary equipment helps control the fermentation to achieve the desired result.

2. Use tap water, unless it contains excess minerals, iron, or water softener. However, chlorine inhibits yeast, so let water stand for 24 hours to dissipate the chlorine before using it. If in doubt, use distilled water.

3. Obtain fermentable material (for example, apples, grapes, or malted barley).

4. For predictable results, use Campden tablets to kill existing organisms in fresh, unpasteurized liquids before you introduce yeast.

5. Add yeast starter formulated specifically for the product you want to make (cider, wine, or beer).

6. Add yeast food if needed to ensure complete fermentation.

7. If there is a first fermentation, it takes place with air and reduces most of the sugar to alcohol. Beer and wine usually use two fermentation steps.

8. The second fermentation takes place without air, using an airlock to let CO_2 escape.

9. Siphon the liquid using a hose, no closer than 4 inches from bottom of the fermenting vessel. This is so you leave behind the sediment (or *lees*).

10. Bottle and store at 55°F (40°F to 60°F), and age 6 to 12 months before drinking.

PERFECT PRESERVING

Campden tablets contain a premeasured dose of sulfites that you may use to sanitize equipment and add to wine to protect it from spoilage. Buy them from retailers who sell beer or wine-making supplies. Historically, sulfites were added by burning pure sulfur in wooden wine casks.

Here is a list of basic equipment you need for making any of these fermented beverages. Kits are available from many suppliers and can be convenient and economical for first-time users. The initial cost of brewing supplies is in the range of $50 to $150, depending on the type of beverage and the quality of the materials chosen.

- ✤ A new, clean food-grade plastic or glass container is used for first fermentation. Reusing plastic containers or those made from non-food-grade materials may contribute "off" odors or leach dangerous chemicals into your beverage. They range in size from $6\frac{1}{2}$ to 25 gallons, and are priced from $15 to $60, depending on size and materials.

- ✤ A carboy is used for closed fermentation during cider or wine making. Carboys are large glass or plastic bottles or jugs. They range in size from 1 to 6 gallons, and are priced from $5 to $60, depending on size and materials.

- ✤ An airlock for closed fermentation keeps air out and lets CO_2 escape. You can purchase an inexpensive airlock with a rubber stopper for under $5. You can make an airlock by drilling a hole in a bottle cap, inserting a plastic tube that fits tightly, and then putting the other end of the tube in a container of water.

- ✤ An acid-titration kit or instrument (wine making only) for home use ranges from $10 to $50 and measures acidity.

- ✤ A hydrometer is an instrument that measures sugar content, called Brix degrees. They range in price from $15 to $30.

- ✤ Glass jugs, wine bottles, or beer bottles with lids, corks, or caps begin around $15 per dozen for bottles and $5 each for $\frac{1}{2}$-gallon jugs.

- ✤ A corking tool inserts corks into bottles or jugs, and a capping tool secures caps on beer bottles. These tools range in price from $20 to $45.

Finally, there are a few other inexpensive, but necessary supplies:

- ✤ A room thermometer and/or one for measuring the temperature of liquids.

- ✤ Clear, flexible $\frac{1}{4}$- to $\frac{1}{2}$-inch-diameter plastic tubing is used to siphon liquids from one fermentation container to another, or into bottles.

- ✤ Cheesecloth, muslin, or a jelly-straining bag is used for filtering the beverage before bottling.

- ✤ Other basic kitchen equipment, such as saucepans, funnels, strainers, and stirrers.

This list of basic equipment can get you through your first project. Of course, there are always additional tools that can make the process easier or more convenient, such as bottle fillers, bottle brushes, crushers, and fermenters with spigots. As you gain experience, you may want to explore the use of more specialized equipment by talking with suppliers or reading advanced books on home brewing and wine making.

After making hard cider (see recipe in Chapter 11), beer or wine kits are the easiest and least expensive way to get started making fermented beverages. The kits start at under $50. While these kits make unsophisticated beverages, it's a good introduction to alcohol fermentation at a nominal cost.

HARD CIDER VS. BEER

Hard cider was the beverage of choice in the United States before the Civil War, largely due to the traditions of the pilgrims and English settlers of the time. The influx of German and Irish immigrants, along with the advent of Prohibition from 1920 to 1933, eventually changed the status quo toward beer. There are some practical reasons why beer became preferred over cider. Apple trees need 7 years to mature for good cider. The grain and hops used to make beer can be grown every year with less effort and expense. In addition, cider doesn't store as long as beer or wine.

Vinegar

You can make vinegar from fruit or grain such as apples (cider vinegar), grapes (wine vinegars), barley (malt vinegar), and rice (rice vinegar). Each ingredient produces vinegar with a distinct flavor. Vinegar making is a useful technique for using fruit peels before you discard them in the composter. To produce good quality vinegar, your raw material needs to be clean and in good condition. If you want to use fallen fruit or peelings, the material needs to come from clean, mature fruit, not green, overripe, or rotting fruit.

You can try to make vinegar by leaving a bottle of wine or hard cider open and allowing fermentation to occur naturally. However, without any other controls, this spontaneous process can take months, and often results in a poor quality product.

The French method for making vinegar, known as the Orleans method, continually produces vinegar by adding one fourth its volume in wine at weekly intervals. After 4 weeks, you can begin to withdraw vinegar at the same rate (one fourth the volume) as you continue to add wine. You should stir or agitate vinegar during the first 4 weeks of fermentation. After that, you need to add the wine carefully to the bottom of the barrel, so as not to disturb the mother (the floating bacterial mass on the surface of the vinegar). By inserting a tube into the container all the way to the bottom, you can easily add wine to the bottom of the barrel, through the tube.

A simpler home method is to use beer yeast to inoculate some type of alcohol. You can buy yeast from retailers that sell home-brewing supplies. Add 1 package of yeast to 1 quart of wine or hard cider and stir or shake to combine thoroughly. Pour the yeast mixture into a fermentation container. Add 1 to 5 gallons wine or hard cider; the fermenting container should not be more than $\frac{3}{4}$ full. Cover the container with cheesecloth to let in air and keep bugs out. Place the container out of direct sunlight in a cool to warm location (60°F to 90°F; 80°F to 85°F is ideal). Stir the mixture daily. Your vinegar should be ready in 3 to 4 weeks.

Temperatures above 90°F interfere with the formation of the mother. At 60°F or less, bacteria activity slows down and produces inferior vinegar.

Check your vinegar simply by tasting. It should be pleasantly tart or sour and have good flavor, reminiscent of the wine or other liquid that you used to make it (apple, pineapple, orange, etc.). If you wish a more scientific approach, you can use a test kit. Buy a titration kit from a retailer that sells beer- or wine-making supplies. Use the kit to check the alcohol and sugar content of your vinegar. The results tell you more precisely whether the acetic fermentation is complete.

Once it is complete, you need to prevent further oxidation. If this happens, eventually your vinegar becomes nothing but carbonated water. There are two methods to "finish" your vinegar:

- ☩ Strain the vinegar through a coffee filter. Many people prefer this method, so that they retain many of the natural components in vinegar.

- ☩ Pasteurize the vinegar to prevent formation of a mother, and to stop oxidation completely. Pasteurizing allows you to store the vinegar indefinitely. To pasteurize, heat the vinegar to 140°F to 160°F. Cool before bottling.

Pour the vinegar into sterilized bottles and store it in a cool, dark place. Vinegar tastes best when it has aged for a minimum of 6 months before use. Homemade vinegar is excellent in salad dressings and other recipes; however, do not use homemade vinegar for preserving, such as when fermenting pickles or canning. You cannot guarantee standardized vinegar of at least 5 percent acidity, which is the minimum needed in order to preserve foods safely.

SPOILER ALERT

The biggest problem when making vinegar is the presence of flies and other insects that are attracted to the fermenting liquid. It is very important that they do not get into your vinegar because they carry pathogenic organisms. You can manage this problem by sanitizing the equipment and storage area, and cleaning up any spills promptly. If insects are persistent during acetic fermentation, you should strongly consider pasteurizing your vinegar.

Yeasted Breads

You can make bread using only flour and water. Any other ingredient you add speeds up the process, influences the texture of your bread, or adds flavor. The flour you use can come from any finely ground grain, as well as legumes or seeds.

Wheat is uniquely qualified to create big loaves of raised bread. It contains gluten, which is a protein that helps to form thin, elastic pockets when you work (or knead) a ball of dough. Other gluten-containing grains include all forms of wheat (emmer, farro, graham, kamut, and spelt) as well as barley, rye, and triticale (a rye-wheat hybrid).

Gluten-free grains and legumes also ferment to make bread dough, perhaps in less spectacular, but no less delicious fashion. Since ancient times, people routinely baked grains like teff and millet into flatbreads. Other nongluten grains include amaranth, buckwheat, corn, oat, quinoa, rice, and sorghum.

Besides yeast, another grain-fermentation method used in many parts of the world involves souring the bread using lactic acid fermentation. There are many variations for this type of bread, which may include the use of (wild or added) yeast or another leavening agent such as baking soda.

If rolled thin and baked until crisp and dry, flatbread can be stored indefinitely. Serve crisp flatbread as a cracker, or soften with water to use as a wrap.

Baking yeast comes in two forms: dehydrated yeast granules and fresh yeast cakes. Dehydrated or dried yeasts come in small packets that make one loaf, or bulk packages for any size recipe. There are several varieties of dried yeast, including regular, fast-rise, and breadmaker. Dried yeasts have a shelf life of about 1 year.

Fresh cake or compressed yeast is used by the commercial baking industry. It requires two rises, but serious bakers appreciate the complex flavors that this type of yeast contributes to baked goods. Once common in grocery store refrigerator cases, fresh yeast is not generally available to the home user. You can still purchase it in quantity from wholesale suppliers. Fresh yeast has not undergone the drying process, so it is very perishable, with a short shelf life of about 1 month. It may be frozen for 3 to 4 months; just be sure to defrost thoroughly (24 hours) in the refrigerator before using.

Most types of yeasted bread lose moisture and become stale at refrigerator temperatures. If you want to extend the shelf life of a loaf of bread, wrap it airtight and freeze up to several months.

Salt-Fermented Vegetables

Dry salting is fairly easy and reliable. You simply layer vegetables with salt, and the salt pulls water out of the vegetables, forming brine. While the salt does not preserve the food directly, it plays a very important role in LAB activity.

When you use relatively low salt concentration ($2\frac{1}{2}$ to 5 percent), combined with cool temperatures (64°F to 72°F), you promote the activity of several types of LAB. Fermentation is complete in about 1 to 4 weeks, depending on the cleanliness of the conditions, amount of salt, and temperature. The acid lowers the pH to around 2 to 3 percent. The increased acidity controls the growth of spoilage organisms and contributes pleasant, tangy flavors that many people enjoy in pickled products.

The optimum salt concentration and temperature range is quite narrow. At lower (less than 2 percent) or higher (6 percent to 7 percent) salt concentrations, or temperatures below 60°F or above 75°F, you may get spoiled vegetables, or at least bad-tasting pickled food.

At still higher salt concentrations (above 10 percent), the fermentation activity stops. Although food packed in a high amount of salt does not ferment, it is preserved because all microbial activity—good and bad—is inhibited. (See Chapter 4 for more about preserving foods by salting without fermentation.)

Fermenting vegetables with dry salt requires a few basic techniques that you must follow:

‑ Use a clean, sanitized container (thoroughly clean any soft materials such as plastic or wood, which trap oil or dirt more than hard materials like glass and glazed pottery).

‑ Use a scale that weighs vegetables to the nearest tenth of a pound and salt to the nearest tenth of an ounce.

‑ Use high-quality, fresh ingredients.

‑ Use pickling salt or kosher salt (additives in other salts may prevent fermentation or neutralize the acid that you are trying to create as a preservative).

The role of salt is to extract the water from vegetables, and create the right environment for desirable LAB. Salt is difficult to measure by teaspoon, because the volume measure varies greatly from one type and brand of salt to another. Some brands of kosher salt weigh half as much pickling salt. So don't measure salt, weigh it for best results. Generally, you may use $3\frac{1}{2}$ to 4 ounces salt for each 10 pounds of food and $2\frac{1}{2}$ to 3 ounces for 7 pounds. For each pound of food, you can use $\frac{1}{3}$ to $\frac{1}{2}$ ounce or 10 grams.

Complete fermentation takes between 1 and 4 weeks, depending on the temperature. The optimum temperature for fermentation of sauerkraut and other vegetables is 70°F, with a range of 64°F to 72°F. Temperatures outside this range affect the quality in several ways. Higher temperatures inhibit LAB activity, encourage yeasts, and create off flavors. At cooler temperatures, fermentation slows down and the food may spoil.

PERFECT PRESERVING

Be sure to enjoy your wonderful product. You may want to keep a notebook and jot down notes about how much you made, how you served it, and what adjustments (if any) you want to make the next season. Maybe the level of fermenting is too strong, so you want to stop the fermentation early. Maybe you found a sauerkraut soup recipe that is now a family favorite, and you plan to make more next year. Perhaps you found an old recipe that adds spices, so you want to split your batch next year and try a flavored version.

Here are the detailed instructions for preparing fermented vegetables by dry salting.

1. Clean, sanitize, and air-dry the fermentation container (see Chapter 1). This step eliminates unwanted microorganisms in your preservation process.

2. Choose and prepare only the best quality, mature (not ripe) vegetables. Prepare and pack while produce is still crisp and tender.

3. Calculate the amount of salt needed, based on the weight of the prepared food (not the weight as purchased). Here is how to calculate how much salt you need:

Pounds vegetables × 0.02 × 16 = ounces salt for 2 percent by weight

Pounds vegetables × 0.03 × 16 = ounces salt for 3 percent by weight

For example:

- 10 pounds of trimmed beans × 0.02 (0.03) × 16 = 3.2 (4.8) ounces for 2 percent (3 percent) by weight

- 7 pounds of shredded cabbage × 0.02 (0.03) × 16 = 2.2 (3.4) ounces for 2 percent (3 percent) by weight

4. Weigh salt for accuracy, if you want to achieve consistently good results. For just 1 pound of vegetables or trial runs, you may use 2 teaspoons pickling salt per pound.

5. Mix food and salt evenly. Work in batches no larger than 5 pounds. Toss food and salt together in a large bowl. Be sure to scrape all salt from the mixing bowl into the fermenting vessel.

6. Pack salted vegetables into the container 1 to 2 inches at a time. Press or gently pound each layer until you draw juice from the food. Press using your fist, or some tool such as a meat pounder, potato masher, or the bottom of a bottle.

7. Fill the container no more than three quarters full, to avoid overflow as food ferments.

8. Cover and weight vegetables to help brine form. Brine formation usually takes about 24 hours. See the sidebar for suitable covers and weights.

9. In 24 hours, if juices do not cover the food completely, prepare very weak brine using $1\frac{1}{2}$ tablespoons pickling salt per quart of water.

10. Fermentation starts when bubbles appear around the edge of the liquid. If you use a water-filled bag to seal the crock completely, do not disturb the vegetables until fermentation is complete. If you use another type of weight that allows air in and around the cover, you should check the vegetables for white scum at least every other day.

11. To check for scum, remove the weight and cover. Look for white scum on the surface of the brine. It is not harmful, but if not removed regularly, it will eventually use up the acid, and the food will spoil. Skim it off with a spoon and discard it. Be sure to use a clean cover and weight each time you do this process.

12. If necessary at any time during fermentation, add more brine to cover the food by at least 1 inch.

13. Fermentation is complete when no more bubbles appear. If you prefer lightly fermented vegetables, you may refrigerate the product before fermentation is complete.

14. Store vegetables in the fermenting vessel or other sanitized container, in the refrigerator up to 6 months. Vegetables should be completely submerged in brine at all times during storage. As during fermentation, remove any scum that forms. Do not allow mold to form at the top of the liquid.

15. For shelf-stable storage, pack raw fermented vegetables and their brine into clean pint (quart) canning jars, leaving $\frac{1}{2}$ inch headspace, and process in a boiling water bath for 20 (25) minutes.

If you follow the basic rules for preserving vegetables, by using clean equipment, accurate measurements, and attention to the process, you'll find success with your first batch. Then, the sky is the limit!

SUITABLE CROCKS, COVERS, AND WEIGHTS

A 5-gallon or larger glazed pottery crock is a traditional salting container. However, you may use any nonmetallic, nonreactive vessel, such as glass, food-grade plastic (no garbage or storage bins), or wood. Glass jars work well, from 1 quart to $\frac{1}{2}$ gallon or larger. Cover vegetables with plastic wrap, cheesecloth, Swiss chard, grape leaves, or a cabbage-stem end (a thick slice cut from the stem end). Be sure to press the cover onto the surface of the food without trapping air underneath. Add a weight on top of the cover to prevent vegetables from floating, exposing them to air. Suitable weights include a brine-filled plastic bag (best modern solution), or a plate with a water-filled jar or canned food.

Brine-Fermented Vegetables

In addition to layering foods with dry salt, you can soak foods in brine, which is simply a solution of salt and water. With the dry salting method, you layer the salt and vegetables, and they make the brine for you. When using the brining method, you make the brine and pour it over the vegetables. This method is most commonly used when making naturally fermented cucumber pickles.

Brine with a salt concentration below 10 percent allows fermentation bacteria to remain active. Brine above 20 percent prohibits fermentation of most microorganisms. Between these two values, it's something of a mixed bag.

Pickling salt or kosher salt is preferred for all brine solutions, but especially weak brine that will be used to ferment vegetables. Natural or chemical salt additives inhibit fermentation; this includes minerals in natural sea salts, as well as iodine or anticaking agents added to table salt.

Water used in fermentation brine should also be as pure as possible. Impurities in water inhibit fermentation, including minerals in hard water, water-softening chemicals, and chlorine or fluoride in municipal water. Use distilled or filtered water for best control and consistent results.

Adding vinegar to weak brine enables you to use it for lower-acid vegetables. Since higher salt concentrations would prevent fermentation, you use acidic brine for some vegetables to protect the food from spoilage organisms until fermentation can begin.

When brining vegetables, it is essential that you prevent the food from floating on the surface of the brine, and keep it completely submerged at all times.

When brining cucumbers to make pickles, the most important thing you can do to make crisp pickles is to choose young, fresh, just-picked cucumbers. Each day past maturity, you lose crispness and pickle quality. However, if you wish, you may use alum (potassium aluminum sulfate) to firm fermented pickles. Use no more than $\frac{1}{4}$ teaspoon per pint jar; using more will reverse the benefit and soften, instead of crisp, the pickles. Note that alum has no effect on unfermented, quick-process, or refrigerator pickles. Other firming techniques are discussed in Chapter 4.

The following table lists brines of different strengths, the approximate salt concentration in degrees (SAL°), how many ounces of salt you use per quart of water, and common uses for each type of brine. See Chapter 4 for more information about making brine of various strengths.

Brine Strengths and Their Uses

% Salt by Weight	Approx. SAL°*	oz. Salt/ qt. H$_2$0	Uses
3.9	15	1.3	Ferment "half-sour" pickles; approximate salinity of seawater
5.7	21	2.0	Cure meats with nitrites; ferment sour pickles
7.5	29	2.7	Long brine fish (10–12 hrs); cure poultry
10.0	38	3.7	"Enough salt to float an egg"
12.6	48	4.8	Brine fish (3–4 hrs); brine olives
15.3	58	6.0	Cure meats; brine fresh vegetables; inhibit some spoilage bacteria
20.1	76	8.4	Cure meats; brine fresh vegetables; short brine fish (1–2 hrs); inhibit salt-tolerant bacteria
25.1	95	11.1	Brine fresh vegetables; inhibit salt-tolerant bacteria
26.4	100	12.0	Saturated salt solution

*Water = 60°F

Cultured Milk

Anywhere in the world that there are people who raise livestock for milk, you will find a dizzying array of fermented dairy products. The milk can come from cows, goats, or sheep, as well as buffalo, camel, moose, and yak. Fermented dairy products, known as *cultured* dairy products, means they are made by encouraging or culturing fermentation bacteria.

There are many ways to describe cultured dairy products. It's difficult to classify them, because there are so many variations. The common denominators are proteins in milk and acid.

There are literally thousands of kinds of cheese throughout the world, from mild to pungent and soft to firm. The goal of many traditional hard cheeses is to preserve milk by transforming it into low-moisture, high-acid food that inhibits spoilage organisms. Some types of aged cheese may be stored for years at cool cellar temperatures.

In any case, here is a list of the broad categories of cultured milk products, with a few specific examples of each type:

 ⚜ Cultured or acidulated milk products include buttermilk, yogurt, mascarpone, cottage cheese, cream cheese, sour cream, crème fraîche, and fresh cheeses such as ricotta and some goat cheeses.

✧ Soft and semisoft cheeses made from milk or cream may be cultured with additional bacteria or mold. Some examples include Brie, blue cheeses, Camembert, mild cheddar, Gouda, Swiss, some goat cheeses, Havarti, and pepper Jack.

✧ Hard cheese is made from cheese curds pressed into blocks. It can be cultured with additional bacteria or mold, and aged. These include Parmesan, Asiago, sharp cheddar, Manchego, and Romano.

Cultured or acidulated milk products are simple to make at home using common household equipment. However, to make soft, semisoft, hard, or aged cheeses you need a press and aging chamber. Depending on the type of cheese, you may also need to buy other equipment or learn additional processes, such as molds and waxing. Beginning kits are priced in the $50 to $75 range.

However, once you understand the basic principles of how to make cultured milk products and fresh cheeses, then other types are incremental processes that you can advance to with confidence. Several factors are crucial for successful milk culturing:

✧ Clean and sanitized equipment

✧ Pasteurized milk to eliminate any pathogens that may be present

✧ Heating and cooling at the right temperature and sequence to activate milk proteins

The simplest cultured milk product you can make is acidulated fresh cheese. To do this, simply add an acid such as vinegar or lemon juice to milk, and heat it until curds form. The acid helps the milk proteins line up together, becoming semisolid. Then you drain the curds, separating the clear, yellow whey from the white, opaque fresh cheese. For detailed instructions on making fresh goat cheese, see the recipe in Chapter 11.

In fact, if you start with buttermilk, you don't need to add the vinegar or lemon juice. Just heat a quart of buttermilk, and its natural acidity will coagulate or thicken the milk proteins.

Yogurt requires an additional step and a starter instead of acid. The basic steps involve pasteurizing the milk, adding a small amount of starter, then holding or incubating the mixture at a warm temperature until it thickens. Proper incubation temperature encourages the growth of desirable *Lactobacilli* and *Streptococcus* while inhibiting pathogens.

It's a great first project if you want to see how the culturing process works. Acquiring the starter is easy; you just use any plain yogurt that contains live lactobacillus culture. The hardest part is finding a way to insulate or incubate the container of warm, cultured milk. There are several ways you can incubate yogurt:

✧ Wrap the container in several kitchen towels and place in a warm location, such as a sunny window or on a heating pad.

✧ Place container into 110°F to 122°F water, in a covered slow cooker or large pan over a very low burner or in a warm oven, never hotter than 130°F. The water should come at least halfway up the culturing container.

⚜ Heat water to 130°F and pour into a clean picnic cooler. Add the culturing container; the water should come at least halfway up the sides. Close the cooler and place in warm location.

⚜ Pour the warm (110°F to 122°F) yogurt in a clean and sanitized thermos jar.

⚜ Buy a small yogurt-making appliance for around $50.

If you want to try your hand at making yogurt, you need an accurate thermometer and one of these methods to incubate the warm milk.

In yogurt-type products, the proteins thicken, but remain semifluid and runny. Draining the whey from yogurt is another method to make fresh "yogurt cheese," also known as *labneh* and *quark*. Cream cheese, sour cream, cottage cheese, and many others are all variations on these two basic processes: heating milk with acid or LAB culture, and separating curds from whey.

You can use rennet in fresh, as well as soft, semisoft, and hard cheeses. Rennet is an enzyme that helps to firm the cheese curd. Originally, rennet came from the stomach of the animal that also gave the milk. Today, the home cheese maker can purchase rennet in tablet, liquid, and vegetarian forms in grocery stores or from retailers who sell cheese-making supplies. Dissolve the tablet in water about 1 hour before use; the liquid form is ready to use.

You'll find recipes for fresh goat cheese made with lemon juice, cultured yogurt, and cream cheese using rennet in Chapter 11.

Fermented Fruits

You may not realize that many common everyday products are the result of fermentation. Listed below are a few popular products that are nothing more than fermented fruits:

⚜ Black pepper is the unripe fruit of the *Piper nigrum* plant, which is fermented and then dried.

⚜ Tabasco is a brand-name pepper sauce from Louisiana. Created in 1868 by Edmund McIlhenny, the sauce ferments peppers with locally mined salt, and finishes it with vinegar.

⚜ Cacao pods are fruits that contain the beans that are fermented and ground to make chocolate. Inside the pod, the beans are enveloped in a white, sticky, sweet pulp. Fermentation occurs naturally when the beans and their pulp dry in the humid, tropical climate where they grow.

⚜ Vanilla bean pods are the fermented fruit from a couple varieties of orchid plant. While people in different parts of the world use various production methods, the basic process involves blanching, fermenting, and drying.

⚜ Green (unripe) olives are treated with lye (sodium hydroxide) to remove bitter components that inhibit LAB fermentation.

⚜ Black (ripe) olive production specifically inhibits LAB, using instead enterobacteria, yeasts, and high-salt (10 to 14 percent) brine. Some black olives with a high fat content are fermented in dry salt to capture the bitter flavors.

These are just a few everyday products that are examples of fermented foods. As you can see, some of them use basic ingredients like salt and acid, and complementary processes such as blanching and drying. Many of these fruits in their natural form have limited use or shelf life. Fermenting transforms their flavor and texture into useful and delicious foods.

Fermented Legumes and Eggs

Several important fermented beans and seeds prevail in Asian and African diets. In the United States, some well-known fermented-bean products include soy sauce, Indonesian tempeh, and Japanese natto.

Traditional soy sauce brewing methods date to the seventh century. The basic process involves the use of *Aspergillus oryzae* mold and *Lactobaccillus bacteria,* which encourage yeast enzymes that produce numerous flavor components.

Tempeh production uses dry conditions and high acid to encourage the fermentation agent, *Rhizopus* mold spores. The low pH is caused by natural lactic acid fermentation in the soaking water, or by the artificial addition of acids (lactic or acetic) after the soaking process.

Natto is a healthful Japanese soybean product that is fermented with bacteria (*Bacillus subtilis* var. *natto*). It is renowned for strong odor and sticky texture. It is a popular breakfast food that enthusiasts eat with rice and garnish with seaweed, egg, miso, soy sauce, green onions, and pickles.

Fermented eggs are an unusual product, known as *pidan* or "thousand-year eggs" in Chinese cuisine. To make it, fresh eggs are soaked in lye (sodium hydroxide). The yolk becomes semisolid and turns a deep blue-green. Pidan has a long shelf life and fragrant taste, very much enjoyed by its fans.

PIT-FERMENTED FOODS

Burying foods underground causes an acid fermentation without the need for salt. The pH decreases from around 7 to less than 4 in a few weeks. Buried food becomes soft and pastelike, with a strong odor, and is often mixed with other ingredients for palatability. Fermented paste can be removed from the pit as needed and may be replaced with a batch of fresh material. The high-acid paste is long-keeping and may also be dried. Because pit fermentation is cheap and reliable, it is used the world over for a variety of foods. Historically, the Japanese made natto by burying soybeans underground. Traditional Korean kimchi, a naturally fermented vegetable pickle, is packed into earthenware jars and buried. Ancient Hawaiians buried taro root to make poi.

How to Get Started

As we have seen, there are many ways to begin fermentation. Deciding which methods to use depends on the type of food and the desired result. Each of the recipes in Chapter 11 demonstrates some of the most basic fermentation processes that are easy to learn and use at home.

If you learn to make country wines, yeasted breads, fresh cheeses, and fermented vegetables, you will learn what people around the world have known for thousands upon thousands of years. Using grains, fruits, milks, and vegetables, you can create delicious and nutritious foods.

Troubleshooting Fermented Foods

Problem: **Alcohol fermentation seems to have stopped, but the alcohol content is low and the sugar is high.**

Remedy: If during first fermentation, stir the must. Warm up the room. Add yeast and/or yeast nutrients.

Prevention: Fermentation temperature is too high, too low, or fluctuating. Prepare yeast starter correctly.

Problem: **Cider is very tart or has an off flavor.**

Remedy: Stir in sugar or honey for drinking, or use in cooking.

Prevention: Cider did not finish fermenting; use specific gravity gauge to test. Add 1 pound sugar or honey per 5 gallons juice before fermentation. Don't leave on sediment after fermentation is complete; rack and bottle.

Problem: **Wine has yeasty odor and taste.**

Remedy: Use in cooking, or discard if flavor is too offensive.

Prevention: Wine left on the lees too long, or not racked properly (no longer than 8 days).

Problem: **Beer has stinky sulfur odor.**

Remedy: If the fermentation is still vigorous, the smell should dissipate when fermentation nears completion. Otherwise, discard it (unfortunately).

Prevention: Temperature is too low or too high; use a thermometer to monitor temperature. Not enough food (sugar) for the yeast; test before beginning fermentation and add sugar accordingly.

Problem: **Beer has too much or too little carbonation.**

Remedy: Use in cooking.

Prevention: Fermentation wasn't finished. If flavor is yeasty, wild yeast got in during bottling. After bottling, temperature is too low or fluctuating.

Problem: **Bread is tough and dense.**

Remedy: Use for croutons or grind into crumbs to coat fried chicken or fish.

Prevention: Too little yeast, yeast was not fresh, or hot water killed yeast. Too much salt inhibited yeast. Too much flour or not enough water (dough was firm and stiff). Not enough rising time.

Problem: **Yogurt fails to thicken.**

Remedy: Check temperature and add more starter.

Prevention: Too hot milk (+115°F) can kill starter bacteria; use a thermometer to monitor temperature. Use culture that contains live bacteria. Use a fresh, recently purchased culture each time you make yogurt.

Problem: **Yogurt has whey on the surface.**

Remedy: Drain the yogurt in a cheesecloth-lined sieve or colander to remove excess whey.

Prevention: Occasional separation is natural. Excessive separation can be caused by incubating too long or by agitating the yogurt during incubation.

Problem: **Yogurt tastes or smells off.**

Remedy: Provided there are no signs of spoilage, use in baking.

Prevention: Overheating or boiling the milk causes off flavors; use a thermometer to monitor temperature.

Problem: **Yogurt is very firm and jelled.**

Remedy: Use in dips or spreads.

Prevention: Refrigerate yogurt immediately after it thickens during incubation.

Problem: **Fermented vegetables have white film floating on surface of brine.**

Remedy: Check the vegetables for white scum at least every other day. Skim it off with a spoon and discard it.

Prevention: White scum is normal, especially when fermenting vegetables in less than 10 percent salt. Remove the scum whenever it appears. It is not harmful, but if not removed regularly, it will eventually use up the acid, and the food will spoil.

Problem: **Fermented vegetables are pink.**

Remedy: If the food smells sweet or yeasty like bread, LAB activity has stopped; yeast is growing because the temperature is too warm; discard the food. If the food smells sour, it may be a harmless chemical reaction that occurs in some light-colored foods.

Prevention: Sanitize fermentation vessel before use. During fermentation, store container at 64°F to 72°F. Too much salt used; weigh, rather than measure, salt and calculate amount based on weight of prepared vegetables. Be sure to layer salt and vegetables evenly.

Problem: **Fermented vegetables are dark colored.**

Remedy: Vegetables are spoiled and should be discarded.

Prevention: Too little or too much salt used, allowing undesirable bacteria to flourish; weigh, rather than measure, salt and calculate amount based on weight of prepared vegetables. Be sure to layer salt and vegetables evenly. Not enough brine to cover vegetables allowed undesirable aerobic bacteria and yeasts, causing off flavors and discoloration. Fermentation temperature is too high, maintain between 64°F to 72°F.

Problem: **Pickles are hollow.**

Remedy: Provided there are no signs of spoilage, pickles are safe to eat.

Prevention: Cucumbers were large or overripe. Cucumbers were not fermented within 48 hours of harvest. If cucumbers float when washed, cut into spears or chunk for pickling, or use in relish.

Problem: **Sauerkraut is soft.**

Remedy: Use in soups or cook with apples as a side dish for pork or ham.

Prevention: Cabbage was overripe. Too much salt used; weigh, rather than measure, salt and calculate amount based on weight of prepared vegetables. Be sure to layer salt and vegetables evenly. Fermenting temperature fluctuated too much.

Pickling Foods ⌘ 4

Cultures around the world favor pickled foods because they make bland, starchy meals more interesting and enjoyable. Consider preserved lemons from Morocco, Persian eggplant relish (*nazkhatun*), *tsukemono* in Japan, or Haitian sour cabbage relish known as *pikliz*. For many Americans, the word *pickle* means sweet or salty cucumber slices used in potato salad or to accompany hamburgers. However, before refrigeration, people throughout the country routinely pickled many types of foods such as carrots, onions, beets, and even eggs and pigs' feet.

There are three types of pickles. "Quick-process" pickles are vegetables immersed in acidified brine using tested canning recipes. You process quick pickles in a boiling water bath. They are shelf stable for 1 to 2 years. You will find recipes for canned pickled fruits in Chapter 15, canned pickled vegetables in Chapter 17, and relish (another form of pickled food) in Chapter 18.

Next, there are fermented pickles, which you make by soaking the vegetable for several weeks in brine at a narrowly defined salt and temperature range. You can refrigerate fermented pickles for 3 to 6 months. For shelf-stable products (safe for storage at room temperature), use a tested canning recipe and process in a boiling water bath. Fermented pickles require some skill and practice to get them right. You can find additional information about making fermented pickles in Chapter 3 and recipes in Chapter 11.

Finally, refrigerator or fresh pickles simply soak food in acid such as vinegar. These pickles are comparable to fresh food, with a short shelf life of a few days. Blanching the vegetables before pickling increases their shelf life to a few weeks. Fresh pickles may be the easiest of all preservation methods. Making them requires fewer steps and less of your attention than fermenting does. You don't need agreeable weather or an electric appliance as for drying. Likewise, you don't need special equipment as you do with canning and freezing.

As with all food preparation, you need to be mindful of the need to reduce the risk for foodborne illness by following good sanitary practices. Of course, the problem with making fresh pickles is there is no research available for the home user, except for canning them in a boiling water bath. However, here is a summary of the steps you can take to make refrigerator pickles safely:

✢ Clean and sanitize the work area.

✢ Sterilize the pickling container.

✢ Wash produce adequately.

✢ Add salt and acid.

✢ Refrigerate fresh pickles.

✢ Understand your risk level for food-borne illness.

For many years, refrigerator pickles have been regarded as very safe. However, recent studies have indicated that they pose some risk. If you or members of your family are at risk for food-borne illness, you should carefully consider your consumption of refrigerator pickles. See Chapter 1 for more information about food poisoning.

SPOILER ALERT

Recent studies have concluded that *Listeria monocytogenes* survive and multiply in low-acid, refrigerator pickles for several months. If you are in a high-risk group for food-borne illness, treat refrigerator pickles as fresh food and consume them within 3 days. Otherwise, you should consume only fermented or canned pickles.

In this chapter, we will explore pickling with high salt concentration (without fermentation), acid (such as vinegar), and alcohol.

Pickling Ingredients

The simplest way you can make pickles is to cover food with an acid, such as vinegar or lemon juice. Besides acidifying, you may use dry salt or brine in the same ways that fermenting methods do, but with a higher salt concentration that prevents fermentation. Alcohol pickling is used for fruit in a method called maceration (discussed later in this chapter). The following sections talk about acids, salts, and alcohols that you can use in fresh pickles.

Acids

The most common acids used to pickle foods are acetic (vinegar), citric (lemon juice), and lactic (whey).

Acetic acid is the sour ingredient in vinegar. The stronger the vinegar is, the higher its percentage of acidity. Do not confuse acidity with the pH value. The pH of different types of vinegar varies from 2.3 to 3.3. Commercial white distilled vinegar ranges from pH 2.3 to 2.6, and cider vinegar ranges from pH 3.0 to 3.3. But they both have 5 percent acidity. When canning, you must use commercial vinegar of at least 5 percent acidity. However, in fresh pickles, you can use any type of vinegar, including home-made vinegar and vinegar below 5 percent acidity.

Vinegar strength is the percentage of acetic acid. If you multiply the percent by 10, you get the grain content; conversely, you can calculate the percent when you divide the grain by 10.

✤ 5 percent vinegar × 10 = 50 grain

✤ 50 grain ÷ 10 = 5 percent vinegar

✤ 7 percent vinegar × 10 = 70 grain

✤ 40 grain ÷ 10 = 4 percent vinegar

Therefore, 7 percent vinegar is stronger than 50 grain, which is stronger than 4 percent.

VIN AIGRE: SOUR WINE

The word *vinegar* comes from the French phrase *vin aigre,* meaning "sour wine." If a partially filled wine barrel is exposed to air, the alcohol (ethanol) breaks down into acetic acid—the sour component. Most historians agree that the French were the first to begin commercial production of vinegar in the sixteenth century. However, people around the world have used vinegar for centuries for cleaning, disinfecting, treating ailments, and preserving food. People also enjoy vinegar as a condiment, beverage, and tangy culinary ingredient. Today's white distilled vinegar is made primarily from soybean, corn, and sorghum (milo). Cider vinegar is made from apples. Other types of vinegar come from wine (grapes), rice, malt, sugar cane, palm juice, bananas, and pineapple.

Lemon juice is a citric acid and has a pH of 2.0 to 2.6. Other citric acids include pineapple juice (pH 3.2 to 4.0), orange juice (pH 3.3 to 4.2), lime juice (pH 3.2 to 4.0), grapefruit juice (pH 3.0 to 3.7), and tamarind juice (pH 3.0). Pomegranate juice (pH 2.9 to 3.2) is common in west Asian cuisine. Verjuice or verjus, which means "green juice," is sour juice extracted from underripe grapes (either purple or green varieties) in midsummer. It has a pH of 2.5 to 3.0.

Whey is a thin, watery, yellowish liquid that separates from the curds when making cheese. You can also get whey simply by draining yogurt in a fine mesh sieve, lined with damp cheesecloth. It is slightly acidic with a pH of 4.2 to 4.9. Whey is alive with beneficial lactic acid bacteria (LAB). People around the world who consume milk have many inventive uses for this nutritional product, including pickles, beverages, and as an ingredient in baked goods.

You can use other liquids with a low pH (4.6 or less). Soy sauce (pH 4.4 to 5.4) is mildly acidic, but is used often in Japanese pickles that are made to be consumed within a few hours. Another soybean product, fermented *miso*, contains acid and salt. White miso is great for quick pickle preparations. You can combine it with soy sauce and *sake* to marinate something as simple as blanched asparagus for just 30 minutes before serving.

Salts

When you make pickles by processing or fermenting, you must always use canning or pickling salt. When you want to use brine to preserve foods, you should stick to canning, pickling, or kosher salts. But when you are making fresh pickles, you can use any salt, such as table salt, sea salt, iodized salt, or coarse grinds of salt. You can also experiment with different salts, such as kosher salt (regular, coarse, or flake) or reduced-sodium or "lite" salts (such as potassium chloride). However, be aware that kosher and lite salts can affect the flavor—which you may or may not prefer. Coarse or flake salts have larger crystals, usually requiring that you increase the amount of salt listed in the recipe. Reduced-sodium salts result in flavor changes that many people find unacceptable.

You can also make quick, fresh pickles without salt or with salt substitutes. When fermenting pickles you must use the pickling salt in the required salt concentration (2½ to 5 percent); the process simply doesn't happen without it. However, when you make refrigerator pickles using an acid such as vinegar or lemon juice, you may reduce or eliminate the salt. It's a much more forgiving process.

All About Brine

Brine is simply a solution of salt and water. You can use brine to help preserve foods in several different ways. You can ferment vegetables in weak salt solutions (see Chapter 3), cure meat (see Chapter 5), and pickle foods in strong brine without fermenting (which I'll talk about in this chapter).

You prepare brine simply by adding salt to water and stirring until it dissolves. For best results, make brine with hot water and stir slowly while pouring in the salt. Cool brine to room temperature before using.

Pickling or canning salt is your best choice for brine because it is fine-grained, pure, and dissolves easily. Fine kosher salt is acceptable; coarse kosher salt takes longer to dissolve. When you are preparing brine for fermenting food or curing meats with nitrites, you must use pickling salt or kosher salt. The additives in other salts, such as anticaking agents and minerals, interfere with the fermenting and curing processes.

In dry salting, you measure salt as a percentage of the weight of the vegetables. When you make brine, you measure the salt in relation to the amount of water. Brine strength is expressed as a percentage of salt in proportion to the weight of the water.

You can measure brine strength with an instrument called a salometer, which measures the salt concentration in degrees (SAL°). A salometer looks like a large, bloated glass thermometer. You simply float the tool in the brine and take a reading. To get an accurate reading, be sure that all of the salt is completely dissolved. Using a salometer, you can easily create brine of any strength, determine how much salt to add to any amount of water, and use any type of salt without weighing. If you routinely preserve foods in brine, an inexpensive model ($15 to $25) can save time. Buy it where sausage-making supplies are sold.

The following table lists how much salt to use to create brine of different strengths.

Brine Formulas: Weight or Volume of Salt per Quart of Water

Brine Strength (% Salt)	Any Salt	MTPC*	MCK**	DK***
3.9% (very weak)	1.3 oz.	2 TB.	2 TB. + 2 tsp.	¼ cup
5.7% (weak)	2.0 oz.	3 TB.	¼ cup	6 TB.
7.5%	2.7 oz.	¼ cup + 1 tsp.	⅓ cup + 1 tsp.	½ cup + 2 tsp.
10% ("enough salt to float an egg")	3.7 oz.	6 TB.	½ cup less 1 tsp.	¾ cup
12.6%	4.8 oz.	½ cup less 1 tsp.	½ cup + 2 TB.	1 cup less 2 tsp.
15.3% (strong)	6.0 oz.	½ cup + 1½ TB.	¾ cup + 1½ tsp.	1 cup + 3 TB.
20.1% (very strong)	8.4 oz.	¾ cup + 1½ TB.	1 cup + 1½ TB.	1½ cups + 2½ TB.
25.1%	11.1 oz.	1 cup + 1½ TB.	1½ cup less 1 TB.	2 cups + 3½ TB.
26.4% (saturated)	12.0 oz.	1 cup + 3 TB.	1½ cup + 1 TB.	2 cups + 6½ TB.

*Morton Table, Pickling, or Canning (MTPC) salt weighs 10 ounces per cup

**Morton Coarse Kosher (MCK) salt weighs 7.7 ounces per cup

***Diamond Kosher (DK) salt weighs 5 ounces per cup

You get more accurate results when you weigh the salt rather than use a tablespoon or other dry measure. Different types and brands of salt have very different volumes. A cup of one type weighs 5 ounces and a cup of another weighs 10 ounces. Using a dry measure, you might use twice (or half) as much as needed. See Chapter 3 for more information about fermenting vegetables in brine and uses for different brine strengths.

PERFECT PRESERVING

Good brine recipes will give you the formula using the weight of the salt. If dry measures are given, they can be inaccurate unless they specify the type and brand of salt. Using weight, 5 ounces of any type of salt is equivalent to any other kind.

Alcohols

Macerating fruits in alcohol is very common in cultures throughout Eastern Europe. It is an easy process that you can do at home with fresh fruit and vodka. You can use other types of liquor such as rum or brandy, as well as add spices to the mix. Make sure the liquor you use is at least 40 percent alcohol (80 proof). Lower alcohol, such as wine (10 to 20 percent), doesn't preserve the fruit and creates "off" flavors after a few days.

Pickling Methods

You can make pickles simply by washing, trimming, and soaking fresh vegetables in salt, brine, or acid in the refrigerator for a few days. However, you may want to consider heat treatments that may increase the safety and storage life of refrigerator pickles. There are also several ways you can maintain crispness in pickled vegetables. These treatments and firming techniques are described in the following sections.

Heat Treatments

To increase the safety of refrigerator pickles you can heat fresh pickle preparations in one of the following ways:

- Boil the pickling solution. Bring your pickling solution to a boil before pouring over washed and prepared vegetables. Boiling liquid may decrease, but not eliminate contamination, if present. This method does not improve the safety of raw pickled vegetables that you want to refrigerate for more than a few days.

- Blanch the vegetables to destroy enzymes that hasten spoilage. Cover blanched vegetables with cold pickling solution, or use boiling solution for compound effect. Blanching may decrease, but not eliminate, contamination.

- Cook the vegetables to kill bacteria. Instead of blanching, you can simply cook the vegetables until tender, followed by rapid cooling. When cold, immerse the vegetables in a cold or hot pickling solution.

- Heat refrigerator pickles just before consuming. Place vegetables in a covered saucepan, bring to a boil, and boil for 2 minutes. Serve warm or at room temperature. You should consume these pickles within 2 hours and discard any leftovers. Do not re-refrigerate or reheat pickles a second time.

Unless you are in a risk group for food-borne illness, these heat treatments can increase the storage life of refrigerator pickles up to 1 month.

Firming Techniques

The primary enjoyment of pickles comes from the balance of sweet, sour, salty, and hot flavors. However, crunchy vegetable pickles seem to be everyone's favorite. Some pickled vegetables, like radishes, are inherently crisp, but many others may not be, like cucumbers and carrots.

Crispness comes from natural vegetable pectin. There are several methods that you can use to influence and maintain crisp texture in pickled foods:

- Soak vegetables in ice water for 4 to 24 hours before pickling.

- Soak vegetables in brine before pickling. The length of time depends on the strength of the solution and your tolerance for salty flavors.

✦ Add fresh grape leaves when pickling vegetables. You can add 1 to 2 leaves per quart to the brine or ice water presoak, or to the pickling jar. The tannins in grape leaves contribute "puckering" qualities and inhibit pectinase (enzymes that break down pectin and soften pickles). This enzyme is located at the blossom end of cucumbers, which is why you usually trim and discard it; if you do this, grape leaves are unnecessary (though still a charming addition to the pickle jar). Other fresh leaves with high tannins include horseradish, black currant, sour cherry, red raspberry, white oak (sometimes very strong and unpleasant), and black tea. Any fresh leaf with high tannin content could theoretically work.

✦ Soak vegetables in slaked lime (calcium hydroxide or hydrated lime). If used, be sure you buy food-grade, not industrial lime. Dissolve it in water and soak fresh vegetables for 12 to 24 hours. Calcium hydroxide is poisonous if ingested directly. For this reason, you must remove excess lime by draining the lime-water solution, rinsing the vegetables in 3 to 4 changes of water, and then soaking in fresh water for 1 hour. Finally, drain and rinse in several changes of water again.

✦ Soak vegetables in pickling lime (calcium oxide or quicklime). Prepare cucumbers for pickling (wash and trim). Mix according to package directions (usually 1 cup per gallon of water), and soak cucumbers for 2 to 24 hours.

✦ Add Pickle Crisp granules (calcium chloride) to the jar. This product is a brand of firming agent made by the Ball Corporation. The calcium combines with the pectin in cucumbers. Follow the package directions.

If you love crunchy pickles, be sure to try the recipe for Half-Sour Pickles in Brine in Chapter 11. These partially brined pickles are extra crunchy, refreshing, and not too salty.

PERFECT PRESERVING

Pickling demands the best quality food. You must select young, firm, preferably organic produce, free from any signs of spoilage. Never use overripe, bruised, spoiled, or fallen foods. Vegetables and fruits used for pickles should be tender, at the peak of freshness, and mature (neither underripe or ripe). Keep them refrigerated until ready to pickle, and prepare within 24 hours. Handle carefully during preparation to avoid bruising.

Processes for Pickling Foods

To pickle foods by fermenting, you use 2 to 5 percent dry salt concentration or weak brines with relatively low salt levels. LAB thrive in this range. The net effect is an increase in acidity. Therefore, in fermented foods it is not the salt, but the acid that hinders pathogens and preserves the food. If the salt concentration is above 5 percent, there is no acid production by LAB and you can promote pathogenic bacteria, yeasts, and molds. However, at salt concentrations above 12 percent, you begin to inhibit these spoilage organisms. Following is a summary of salt concentrations and their effect on microbial growth.

✤ Less than 2 percent salt concentration promotes pathogenic *Campylobacter* at warm temperatures (up to 86°F).

✤ 2 to 5 percent salt concentrations promote desirable LAB and fermentation at room temperature.

✤ 6 to 12 percent salt promotes most spoilage bacteria (*E. coli, Salmonella, Clostridium, Vibrio, Listeria, Staphylococcus*) at room temperature, and some (including *E. coli* and *Listeria*) at refrigerator temperatures, too.

✤ At 12 to 20 percent salt concentrations *Staphylococcus* remains active, but other pathogens are inhibited.

✤ 20 to 25 percent salt prevents the growth of most bacteria.

You may preserve vegetables without fermenting by using salt concentrations of 20 to 25 percent. When you prepare vegetables this way, they can stay fresh for several months when stored at cool temperatures. While this method takes less effort than fermentation, it requires an excessive amount of salt and you must desalt the food before using.

Keep salted vegetables covered with brine at all times to prevent the top layer from spoiling and remove scum immediately whenever it appears. Protect the brine surface from insects. If the product develops a bad odor, color, or soft or slimy texture, discard the product without tasting.

Dry Salting Vegetables

Dry salting is a practical and inexpensive way to preserve vegetables. This old-fashioned method was popular in the early twentieth century as an alternative to canning. At that time, it was promoted especially to conserve glass, tin, and fuel in time of war.

PERFECT PRESERVING

The heavy salt used in dry salting is out of step with today's tastes. You might want to try preserving a small amount of vegetables before preserving an entire crop with this method. You may find that learning to use the salted product requires some experimentation.

For cruciferous vegetables that are usually shredded and fermented, you can use dry salt concentrations of 20 to 25 percent to prevent fermentation and preserve them in their fresh state. This includes shredded cabbages, turnips, rutabagas, and kohlrabies. You can pack these vegetables raw, without blanching, just as you would for sauerkraut.

There are other vegetables that you can preserve by this method. These include cauliflower florets, leafy greens (spinach, kale, chard), shelled peas, and string beans. For best results, steam blanch these vegetables before dry salting.

Dry salting is nearly identical to the instructions for fermenting found in Chapter 3, except the latter uses only 2 to 3 percent salt:

1. Clean, sanitize, and air-dry the salting container (see Chapter 1).

2. Choose and prepare only the best quality vegetables. Wash, trim, cut, or shred as needed. After preparing, weigh the food to the nearest tenth of a pound. In contrast to fermenting, you should then steam blanch most vegetables before dry salting. After blanching, chill them on shallow trays in the refrigerator, and pat dry before packing with salt.

3. Calculate the amount of pickling salt needed, from 20 to 25 percent as desired:

   • pounds vegetables × 0.20 × 16 = ounces salt for 20 percent by weight

   • pounds vegetables × 0.25 × 16 = ounces salt for 25 percent by weight

   When dry salting, use either canning, pickling, or kosher salt; either fine- or coarse-grained salt works just fine.

4. Layer the food and salt evenly in the container, leaving 1 to 2 inches headspace. Cover and weight the vegetables to help brine formation. Brine formation usually takes about 24 hours. In 24 hours, if the juices do not cover the food completely, prepare brine of the same strength (20 percent or 25 percent), using the Brine Formulas table earlier in this chapter.

5. Cure the vegetables 2 to 4 weeks, preferably at refrigerator temperatures (36°F to 40°F), or in a cool area no higher than 50°F. Curing means that the vegetables absorb salt from the surrounding liquid until fully saturated.

6. Store vegetables at refrigerator temperatures (36°F to 40°F), or in a cellar at no higher than 50°F. You should check the container one or two times a week for scum or mold. Remove it immediately, if it appears. Keep the vegetables completely submerged in brine at all times during storage. Excessive mold, soft vegetables, or rotten odors indicate spoilage; discard these vegetables without tasting. Under ideal conditions, dry salted vegetables may be stored up to 6 months.

HOW TO USE SALTED VEGETABLES

When removed from the brine, salted vegetables will be firm and slightly darkened in color. You can prepare and serve them in the same ways you would if they were fresh, including eating raw or adding to salads. To use raw, rinse well in cold water. To remove excess salt, soak vegetables in three or four times their measure of cold water for 2 to 8 hours, or to taste. Change the water several times to speed up the process. Add vegetables to recipes without soaking when there is enough unsalted food and liquid to counteract the excessive salt. This method works best in dishes such as soups and stews, where there is lots of liquid and cooking time to redistribute the salt evenly throughout the dish.

Brining Vegetables

To pickle vegetables, use a strong acidulated brine (brine with added vinegar) to preserve whole beets, large cauliflower heads or branches, ears of corn, lima beans (in pods), whole okra or green beans, peas in the pod, stemmed and seeded peppers, pickling onions (silverskin type), and ripe tomatoes.

As the vegetables cure, water drawn from the vegetables dilutes the brine. To compensate, you need to add additional salt throughout the curing time to maintain brine strength.

The following instructions list the steps for pickling vegetables in brine. You may also want to refer to the similar instructions for fermenting vegetables in Chapter 3:

1. Clean, sanitize, and air-dry the brining container (see Chapter 1).

2. Choose and prepare only the best quality vegetables. Wash and trim as needed. Weigh vegetables and measure 3.2 ounces salt per pound of vegetables. For example, for 2 pounds of vegetables, weigh 6.4 ounces salt; for 5 pounds, use 16 ounces or 1 pound. Set this salt aside to add to the curing vessel in step 5.

3. Prepare strong acidulated brine by adding ¼ cup distilled vinegar for each quart of water in a 15.3 percent brine (see the table of Brine Formulas earlier in this chapter). Estimate the amount of brine at half the volume of the vegetables. For example, if you plan to fill a 1-gallon jar you will need 2 quarts of brine, or 2 quarts water, 12 ounces salt, and ½ cup vinegar. If you are filling a 5-gallon crock, you will need 2½ gallons brine, or 10 quarts water, 30 ounces salt, and 2½ cups vinegar.

4. Pack the food tightly into the container. Pour in brine to cover the food by 2 to 3 inches. Cover and weight the vegetables with a plate to keep them completely submerged at all times. The plate will be used for additional salt, and needs to be slightly submerged in the brine.

5. Carefully pour the salt from step 2 into a pile on the plate, under the surface of the brine. As the pickles cure and water is pulled from the vegetables, this salt will slowly dissolve and maintain brine strength. Cure the vegetables 2 to 4 weeks at refrigerator temperatures (36°F to 40°F). Check the container one or two times a week for scum or mold. Remove it immediately, if it appears.

6. Store vegetables at refrigerator temperatures (36°F to 40°F) or in a cellar at no higher than 50°F. Check the container one or two times a week for scum or mold. The vegetables should be completely submerged in brine at all times during storage. If necessary, prepare more 15 percent acidulated brine as needed. Excessive mold, soft vegetables, or rotten odors indicate spoilage; discard these vegetables without tasting. Under ideal conditions, pickled vegetables may be stored up to 6 months.

Acidifying Foods

Acidification means simply to soak a food in acid. When you add an acid, you extend the shelf life of fresh food from a few days to several weeks or more. The storage life depends on the strength of the acid and the use of heat treatments.

You can find recipes for several types of vegetables pickled with acid such as fruit juice and soy sauce in Chapter 12.

Macerating Fruits

Macerate means to soften or soak. The technique is commonly used to dress up fresh fruit with a sprinkle of sugar or splash of vinegar. You can also use this method to preserve fresh fruit in alcohol. Fruits that work best for macerating include firm berries, tropical fruits, melon, and dark stone fruits like cherries and plums. Avoid fruits that brown easily like apples or peaches, soft berries that break down and become excessively mushy, and the membrane and pith or rind from citrus, unless you want their bitter accent. For citrus, supreme the segments, or use only the zest and juice for sweetest results.

To preserve fruit in alcohol, wash and prepare it as you would for serving. Place it in a sanitized container. Add spices and sugar, if desired. Use liquor that is at least 40 percent alcohol (80 proof) and pour it over the fruit to cover completely. That's it!

You can begin using the fruit at any time; it's usually best after 3 to 5 days or more. The flavor will continue to develop up to 30 days. Store macerated fruit in the refrigerator up to 6 months.

Serve macerated fruit for dessert over ice cream, pound cake, or cheesecake. You get a bonus with this method, because as the fruit soaks up the liquor, it leaches juicy goodness into the alcohol. Sip the fruit liquor after dinner, top with club soda for a refreshing tall drink, or use in cocktails.

Troubleshooting Pickled Foods

Problem: **During curing or storage, salted vegetables have white substance floating on top of brine.**

Remedy: Remove the scum whenever it appears. If you see black or green mold, discard the food.

Prevention: Use a sanitized container. Earthenware is particularly susceptible to the development of white scum. Use adequate salt. Weigh the vegetables and measure salt accurately. Keep the vegetables completely submerged in brine. Store salted vegetables in the refrigerator or root cellar at 34°F to 40°F.

Problem: **Pickles seem soft or slippery.**

Remedy: If vegetables are excessively soft and slippery, they are probably spoiled and should be discarded.

Prevention: Use mature—not ripe, small, freshly harvested vegetables. Use stronger brine or add 5 percent vinegar. Keep the vegetables completely submerged in brine. Remove scum whenever it appears. Trim and discard the blossom end of cucumbers, which contain an enzyme that softens pickles. Use a firming agent. Store fresh pickles in the refrigerator or fermented pickles in a root cellar at 34°F to 40°F.

Problem: Pickles seem to have darkened or discolored.

Remedy: Pickles are safe to eat if there are no signs of spoilage.

Prevention: Use distilled water; hard water can cause discolored pickles. Use pans made of stainless steel or enamel, and utensils made of stainless, wood, plastic, or silicone. Avoid aluminum, brass, cast iron, copper, zinc, worn tinplate, or chipped enamel. Sea salts contain minerals that may darken pickles. Dark vinegar will darken pickles; use white vinegar if you prefer a brighter color.

Problem: Pickle flavor is too tart or too spicy.

Remedy: Make more pickling solution as called for in your recipe. Add sugar to taste. Pour off old brine and add new brine to pickles. Store at least 1 day and taste again.

Prevention: You may adjust sugar and spices (including pepper) to taste in pickle recipes.

Curing Meat
and Fish

5

The process of curing is equivalent to pickling. That is, curing "binds" the water in meat by saturating the tissue with salt. Like pickling, curing occurs when the salt transfers through osmosis from the curing medium, and is absorbed into the meat tissue. Curing works by decreasing water and increasing salt, both of which create conditions that inhibit the growth of harmful microorganisms.

Although some publications distinguish "curing" as the use of nitrites, I have found in my research of preserving methods for meat and fish that the use of nitrites is not universal. Therefore, I will explain meat and fish curing in the broadest sense—with and without nitrites.

Curing traditions include the use of salt with acid, salt to promote lactic acid fermentation, and salt with drying as well as with nitrites. Used correctly, salt and acid can serve a similar function as nitrites, one of which is to delay microbial growth until a secondary process fully preserves the meat. These secondary processes include drying, aging (controlled drying), and smoking. Nitrites, aging, and smoking contribute tangy, sweet, and smoky flavors, and reddish-pink colors that characterize cured meats.

Native Americans were salt curing and smoking venison and fish long before European settlers arrived. The taste of their smoked meats was different from the sun-dried methods that Jamestown settlers knew from their native England. Soon, they adopted the new process to use on the hogs they had brought with them. They evaporated seawater for salting the pork and then smoked the meat using hickory and oak woods.

There are commercial products still made today that do not use nitrites. For example, Italy produces *Prosciutto di Parma* and in the United States, we have Virginia ham (also referred to as *country ham*). While the specific process varies, each of these products uses carefully selected meats, generous amounts of salt, low temperatures, and a long aging or drying process. Virginia ham is smoked while Prosciutto di Parma is not. The red color results not from the action of nitrites, but the long and controlled aging process. This also results in the growth of beneficial bacteria that increase the acidity and protect the meat from harmful bacteria, including *C. botulinum*.

Industrial meat processing methods use a fast-curing process by injecting brine, nitrites, and other additives into the muscle. These modern products have a relatively short shelf life of 30 days and require refrigeration. They are but a shadow of cured meats prepared by traditional methods.

Although curing without nitrites can be safe, the process requires rigorous control. For all practical purposes, dry-aging meat without nitrites is not a realistic process for the home preserver. You can strike a balance between old and new methods, using nitrites when safety requires their use.

Curing Ingredients

Before the widespread adoption of mechanical refrigeration just 100 years ago, curing was a key method used to preserve meat and fish. The most important curing medium for many people around the world then—and now—is salt.

When you handle meat, you can introduce microorganisms from the air, your hands, and knives, to cutting boards and other equipment. At every step, you need to use safe food-handling practices. Botulism poisoning from eating improperly preserved meats is a real and present danger.

Nitrites can more easily control botulism. The conditions leading to botulin formation are lack of oxygen, slightly acidic environment, moisture, and warmth (between 40°F and 120°F, although 78°F to 95°F is optimal). In cured meats, you create these precise conditions in the interior of link sausage or rolled meat (such as *pancetta*), or when you age or smoke cured meat.

Saltpeter or Sodium Nitrate

Saltpeter (potassium nitrate, or KNO_3, and sodium nitrate, or $NaNO_3$) is a naturally occurring mineral that has been used to cure meat for at least 1,000 years. Nitrate prohibits the growth of spoilage bacteria, including deadly *C. botulinum*. The problem for you, the home user, is that the amount of saltpeter needed is very, very small; it is nearly impossible to measure and distribute it evenly throughout the meat. For this reason, you should avoid using saltpeter in pure form and use modern curing mixes instead.

As it turns out, nitrate isn't the active agent in meat curing, rather its derivative, nitrite (NO_2). Nitrites are the cause of the appetizing reddish-pink color, pleasing flavor, and preservative effects that we associate with cured meat. Sodium nitrite forms when naturally present lactic acid bacteria (LAB) on the surface of meat break down sodium nitrate:

$$2NaNO_3 \text{ (nitrate)} + \text{lactic acid bacteria} = 2NaNO_2 \text{ (nitrite)} + O_2$$

Actually, the same reaction occurs when you eat spinach; bacteria in your saliva convert the nitrate in spinach to nitrite.

Despite ongoing research, there is no better curing agent known today. Nitrites are generally recognized as safe (GRAS), because the benefits outweigh the risks. If you object to the use of nitrites, you should consider another method of preservation for meat, such as canning, drying, or freezing.

Many knowledgeable people in the food industry support the use of nitrates and nitrites in cured mixes for the following reasons:

- Nitrates exist naturally and you likely consume most of yours from foods such as celery, cabbage, root vegetables, and leafy greens.

✧ The risk of botulism poisoning is much greater than the estimated cancer risk from nitrites.

✧ Cancer risk is alleviated by eating a well-balanced diet, which can safely include modest amounts of nitrites.

✧ People around the world have used nitrites safely for centuries.

✧ Properly used, nitrites kill some really bad bacteria, as well as contribute wonderful flavor and appetizing color in cured meats.

People continued to use sodium nitrate only until sodium nitrite became available. Sodium nitrate is still used when a slow-cure method is needed for dry-aged raw meats. Fortunately, modern curing mixes make this easy.

Modern Curing Mixes

You can readily buy curing mixes for home use that make using nitrates and nitrites easy and safe. The following information explains the commonly available prepared mixes for curing all types of meats.

(American) cure #1 or **pink salt** is a "fast" cure that contains sodium nitrite. It is known by various brand names, including Insta Cure No. 1 (formerly Prague Powder #1), Heller's Modern Cure, DQ Curing Salt (or DC Curing Salt), or tinted curing mix (TCM). By law in the United States, these pink-tinted dry mixes contain 93.75 percent salt and 6.25 percent sodium nitrite. Because of the relatively high level of nitrite, the pink color ensures that users will not confuse it with any other type of salt. Use cure #1 in cured products that you will smoke, can, or cook before eating. This includes products such as smoked sausage, bacon, corned beef, fresh sausage, and jerky. Use cure #1 according to package directions, usually 1 level teaspoon (5 grams) for 5 pounds of meat, or a scant 1 ounce (25 grams) for 25 pounds of meat. You can buy 8 ounces of cure #1 for less than $10, and that will cure over 400 pounds of meat. Use cure #1 in dry or wet cure applications. Never substitute pink curing salt for any other type of salt.

(American) cure #2 is a "slow" cure because it contains sodium nitrate in addition to sodium nitrite. Brand names include Insta Cure No. 2, Prague Powder #2, and DQ Curing Salt #2. The nitrate acts like a time-release capsule that breaks down slowly into sodium nitrite. Depending on the brand and level of nitrite, this curing salt may be dyed pink; some brands are cream colored. Cure #2 is specifically formulated only for use when making raw-cured products that are dry aged for long periods (at least 4 weeks), and will *not* be smoked, canned, cooked, or refrigerated. Example products include dried pepperoni, dry salami, *sopressata,* dry *coppa,* and Spanish (not Mexican) *chorizo.* In 1978, the United States Department of Agriculture (USDA) prohibited the use of nitrate in cured products that will be cooked (such as bacon) to reduce the possibility of nitrosamine formation, which is a known carcinogen in test animals. Use according to package directions, usually 1 level teaspoon (5 grams) for 5 pounds of meat, or a scant 1 ounce (25 grams) for 25 pounds of meat. Add cure #2 to dry salt only; do not use cure #2 in brine. Never substitute curing salt for any cooking salt.

Morton Salt produces several types of cure mixes, including Tender Quick and many others, formulated for ease of use in home preserving. Follow the package directions for each type of mix. They are not interchangeable with curing salt #1 or curing salt #2.

Manufacturers of all these cures produce other mixtures. Depending on the intended use, they may contain varying amounts of salt, nitrates, and nitrites, in addition to sugar, spices, flavor enhancers, and curing accelerators. Examples of these products include Morton Sugar Cure, bacon cure, ham cure, and corned beef cure. Be sure that you follow the package instructions for each specific product, or contact the manufacturer about their appropriate use. They are not interchangeable with either cure #1 or cure #2.

European curing mixes are different from American cures, and vary from country to country. Follow the package directions for each type of mix. They are not interchangeable with curing salt #1 or curing salt #2.

Follow these guidelines when using curing mixes:

- Do not confuse cure #1 with cure #2; they are *not* interchangeable. Both mixes contain sodium nitrites, but only cure #2 contains the original, slow-cure sodium nitrate (saltpeter). If in doubt, check the ingredient list.

- Do not confuse pink curing salt with natural pink salts or flavored salts. Examples of natural pink and flavored salts include pink Himalaya, Australian, or Bolivian rose salt and specialty blends such as chili salt and orange Margarita salt.

- Do not exceed the amount of cure specified for the product you are using. Feel free to experiment with spices to suit your taste.

- Keep curing agents away from children and pets; label them as poisonous and store them in airtight containers out of reach.

SPOILER ALERT

Sodium nitrite is toxic if the powder is swallowed or dust from it is inhaled. Substituting sodium nitrite for table salt is known to cause toxic reactions. Slightly less than 1 gram is toxic for the average adult (14 mg/kg body weight) and can cause stupor, convulsions, blue lips or nails, and brownish blood. Higher doses of 5 grams can lead to cardiac arrest, coma, and death. Sodium or potassium nitrate (saltpeter), while relatively harmless, converts to nitrite once ingested. Nitrate is found naturally in many vegetables and water sources. Nitrate poisoning can occur in infants fed contaminated well water or large amounts of some vegetables, or through accidental ingestion from laboratory or garden chemicals.

You might find recipes for curing mixes that combine salt, sugar, and saltpeter (sodium nitrate). These recipes typically call for 7 to 8 pounds salt, 2 to 4 pounds sugar, and 1 to 4 ounces saltpeter. You apply this cure at a rate of $1/2$ to 1 ounce per pound of meat. However, the use of saltpeter has steadily declined because it presents a few problems:

- Nitrates work best at slightly elevated temperatures (46°F to 50°F) to encourage the acid-loving bacteria that break down nitrate into nitrite. Until this conversion occurs, there is no protection from the growth of harmful bacteria. By using nitrite, you can cure meats at safe temperatures (36°F to 40°F) and eliminate the need for developing sufficient acidity.

> ✢ The conversion of nitrate to nitrite depends on several other factors, including moisture content of the meat, salt concentration (especially in brine), and time. Therefore, there is not one correct formula for nitrate use. It is much more art than science.

> ✢ The amount of nitrate compared to the amount of salt and sugar is very small. The ability to measure sodium nitrate accurately in small volumes for home use is difficult, if not impossible. Preparing large volumes of potentially unsafe mix is more expensive than buying available curing mixes.

Most commercial food manufacturing operations have replaced nitrates with nitrites because they are much more reliable. Nitrites are preferred for most curing processes, unless nitrates are needed specifically for a slow cure. For home use, prepared mixes are easy to measure, curing begins immediately, and curing can occur at safe temperatures (less than 40°F).

If you wish to pursue the use of saltpeter, I recommend that you gain expert knowledge and practice with curing equipment, methods, and the available curing mixes for home use. After you successfully (and unsuccessfully) produce a variety of cured and aged meats, you will be better equipped to explore the use of sodium or potassium nitrate in pure form. Sodium nitrate and its chemical equivalent potassium nitrate are interchangeable.

To learn more about the use of sodium nitrate and sodium nitrite, begin by reading the *Processing Inspectors' Calculations Handbook* from the USDA. This publication is available online at the Food Safety Inspection Service website (www.fsis.usda.gov/) and details the complex formulas for the safe development of nitrate and nitrite cures.

Curing agents can be harmful; however, so is ingesting a large amount of pepper. Curing mixes are safe when you use them as intended and handle them with extreme care.

Salt Curing Without Nitrites

Curing without nitrites is used for jerky and other methods for dried meat strips. An acid may be included, whether added to brine or spread over the meat before dry salting. Meat cured only with salt has good flavor, but also a dark gray color, unless it is smoked.

When salt and acid are used without nitrites, meats must undergo a secondary process to be safe for consumption. Salted meats are often dried, smoked, or cooked to improve flavor as well as to control harmful bacteria. Examples include several air-dried meat products in Africa (such as *biltong, droewors,* and *kilishi*), *carne seca* in Mexico (beef cured with lime and salt and then dried), and *neua dad deo* in Thailand (brined, dried, and fried beef).

Keep in mind that after an animal (including fish) is killed, bacteria immediately start to multiply, even under refrigeration. When using a salt solution only, you can prepare the safest product when you begin with a large piece of freshly killed, well-chilled meat or fish, cut it into strips or flats, brine under refrigeration, and then dry it or smoke it promptly.

Strips or flat pieces of meat can be dipped in brine with a strength of 20 percent or stronger to inhibit pathogenic bacteria, including *E. coli, Clostridium, Listeria,* and *Staphylococcus.* However, modern tastes dictate salt concentration of 10 percent or lower, which will not inhibit *C. botulinum, Listeria,* and *Staphylococcus.*

The Role of Cure Ingredients

Following is a comprehensive list of the ingredients used in all types of curing, including some additives used in commercial curing operations. As indicated, some of these are appropriate for home use and some are not:

- Salt enhances flavor and acts as a vehicle for other cure ingredients (like sugar and spices) to spread throughout the food. Only in high concentration (20 percent) does salt inhibit the growth of microorganisms by decreasing the water activity (a_w).

- Nitrite prohibits the growth of spoilage bacteria, including deadly *C. botulinum,* turns meat a reddish-pink color, contributes unique flavor, and prevents fats from going rancid.

- Water is an important ingredient in brine. Using distilled or filtered water is recommended. If you use tap water, let it stand for 24 hours to dissipate the chlorine, which can interfere with curing processes. Hard water, water softeners, and fluoride also inhibit various preservation methods.

- Sugar contributes sweetness, counteracts the strong flavor of the salt, and provides food for beneficial organisms that convert nitrate to nitrite in slow cures. Recipes exist that use salt-to-sugar ratios of 4:1, 1:1, and 1:4; there is no correct formula. Cures with increased sugar tend to create products that readily develop mold. You can use any type of sugar, including granulated, brown, or dextrose.

- Dextrose is a refined corn sugar that you can use in wet or dry cures. Some users prefer it because it is less sweet and dissolves readily.

- Spices add flavor. Some have been shown to contribute minor preservative effects.

- Starter cultures come in many types. Brand names include Bactoferm, BactoFlavor, SafePro, Texel, and Lyocarni. You use these products when making dry, semidry, and fermented sausages to develop color and flavor, or to encourage the growth of "good" bacteria or (white powdery) mold. Use them to ensure consistency from one batch to the next, and during the aging process when your humidity isn't perfect.

- Citric acid speeds up curing reactions and stabilizes the red color in meat. It also increases acidity, which can help control fermentation in dry cured meat.

- Erythorbate or ascorbate (sodium erythorbate or sodium ascorbate) speeds up curing reactions, stabilizes the red color, and guards against rancidity. Manufacturers use these products to decrease curing time, and increase production. They are not recommended for home use.

⚜ Phosphates are used in wet cures to guard against rancidity, and increase the water-holding capacities of cured products. They are not recommended for home use.

⚜ Potassium sorbate prevents the growth of yeasts, molds, and select bacteria. It is not recommended for home use.

You can buy mixes for home use that contain the necessary ingredients for a variety of curing needs. They are easy to use and safe when used as directed.

NATURAL SOURCES OF NITRATES

Celery powder and more recently Swiss chard are being developed as sources of nitrate and nitrite for use in natural and organic cured products. However, according to research done in 2012 by Joseph Sebranek, PhD, these ingredients have demonstrated an increased likelihood of the growth of *Listeria* and *Clostridium*. Therefore, manufacturers using these natural curing products have implemented additional controls to avoid a food-poisoning outbreak. Research is ongoing, and the development of ingredients and changes to regulations remains active.

Beef, Pork, and Game

The meat you use for any type of curing should be the best quality that you can find. You definitely don't want to use curing to "rescue" spoiled or freezer-burned meat.

Your cured meat products will taste best when you use meat that evokes its *terroir*. This includes the animal's breed, its diet, the land where it grazed, and how it was slaughtered. Even heavily spiced sausages should reflect excellent meat flavor.

Commercially available meat in the United States tends to be younger (6 to 8 months) than traditional animal husbandry methods that slaughter animals at 12 to 14 months. Aged animals are more muscular and fattier. Their meat has more texture, flavor, and character; pork is "porkier" and beef is "beefier." Note that you want meat from aged animals; however, you don't want to cure aged meat. Aged meat has higher bacteria count by design. It is intended for optimal fresh eating, not preserving.

PERFECT PRESERVING

For dry curing, try to locate a farm that is raising old-style breeds by traditional methods. This meat produces the most flavorful dry-aged and fermented cured meat products.

You can coax better flavor out of young meat raised by modern methods if you use a wet cure, followed by a hot smoke. You can't produce shelf-stable meat by this method, but you will produce tasty products.

Composition of the fat in meat greatly influences the flavor of cured products. Modern U.S. meat tends to come from young animals bred for lean meat, clean flavors, and quick meal preparation. The meat contains more polyunsaturated fats, and less omega-3s and monounsaturated fats. In contrast, older breeds and husbandry methods produce meat that contains higher levels of monounsaturated fats, omega-3s, and dark, well-marbled meats. When cured, these fats don't go rancid as quickly, and the meat has better flavor.

It's the same reason that fatty porks (like bacon and ham) produce more intense flavor than loins (think of Canadian bacon), and cured duck is more succulent than chicken. In each case, the former contains more monounsaturated fat. Well-marbled, fatty meat is best for raw-cured products and lean meat is best suited to cooked and smoked cured products. Trimmings are ideal for sausage.

If possible, cure fresh meat that has never been frozen. There are some exceptions, such as treating pork and game for parasites (see Chapter 2). If you use frozen meat, be sure it is thawed completely (3 days) at 36°F to 40°F. Cures cannot penetrate frozen muscle. Commercially processed meat may have additives such as antibiotics that interfere with curing processes, especially dry aging and fermenting.

Pork is by far the best type of meat for curing. Cured pork products offer great color and flavor. The most common cuts used for curing are the rump (ham), shoulder (picnic ham), belly (bacon), and loin (Canadian bacon).

The most commonly cured beef cuts are briskets and strips of round. By contrast, lamb and veal do not show good color and flavor development, so are not prized for curing. Many game meats are also excellent when cured in the same ways as pork or beef, such as smoked leg (ham), corned or pickled meat, cured and dried for jerky, and sausages.

The following types of cured meat products are listed in order from easiest to the most advanced techniques:

- Salt-cured whole muscle meats and whole or filleted fish may be produced to be eaten raw (duck prosciutto, gravlax, salted salmon), while others are cooked (bacon, corned beef, pickled meat or fish, salted salmon).

- Smoked meats and fish are salt cured and finished with smoke. Examples include pastrami and smoked salmon.

- Dry-cured and fermented meat products use a carefully controlled aging process that dries the meat after curing, to make it safe for storage at room temperature. Examples include Virginia ham, Italian prosciutto, and *bresaola*.

- Cured sausages require thorough knowledge of fresh sausage-making techniques. They may be ready-to-eat (bologna, cotto salami), smoked (Polish kielbasa, mettwurst), or dry cured (summer sausage, Thuringer, Spanish-style chorizo, pepperoni, dry salami). Some are also fermented.

If you are new to curing meat, you might want to start with examples from the first two categories. As you gain experience and skill, you can confidently and safely move on to more advanced techniques. Likewise, you can work with whole muscle meats before you move into sausage making.

Poultry and Seafood

Both poultry and fish are good candidates for curing, especially fattier, darker meats such as duck and salmon. Fattier cuts such as duck or turkey legs and thighs take well to brining and smoking. Whole chicken takes well to brining, followed by smoking. Breasts of duck, goose, or wild birds can be cured in a manner similar to prosciutto, by dry salting followed by drying.

For lean seafood, brining firms the texture, helps delay spoilage, and retains moisture during cooking for all types of lean seafood such as cod and lingcod, shad, shrimp, scallops, sturgeon, striped bass, and whiting.

Fish with high oil content is best for smoking after curing. Species to consider are anchovies, black cod (sablefish), bluefin tuna, bluefish, candlefish or smelt, herring, mackerel, salmon, sardines, and wild trout.

To prepare whole fish for pickling, clean and scale the fish, and remove the head. Fillet large fish to remove the backbone; this step is unnecessary for small fish such as herring. Before curing fish, you must be sure to salt cure or freeze for several days to ensure no parasites are present. To treat for parasites using salt, bury it in dry salt or immerse in very strong (25 percent) brine for 5 to 8 days. Rinse well after curing to remove excess salt and soak up to 1 hour in fresh water, if desired. Salting or freezing is particularly important if using a brine-cure recipe that calls for very little salt.

Fish that will be raw cured should be frozen first at −10°F for at least 7 days to kill parasites. Any fish must be gutted before curing or preserving by any method.

Curing Methods

Meat curing requires cleanliness and attention to detail. Follow these tips when evaluating recipes or completing curing projects:

- ⚜ Review the recipe, your knowledge of meat spoilage, and techniques to control harmful microorganisms.

- ⚜ Clean and sanitize all equipment and the work area. If you have a curing chamber, clean and sanitize it after every load is completed, or a minimum of once per year.

- ⚜ Use nonmetallic containers for curing, such as plastic bags, or lidded containers made of plastic, glass, stoneware, or wood. Do not use metal containers.

- ⚜ Assemble all ingredients. Preferably, use scales for weighing ingredients, rather than using dry measure.

- ⚜ Use meat of exceptional quality. Chill the meat thoroughly (30°F to 38°F), without freezing.

- ⚜ Use salt to inhibit bacterial growth, in the range of 2.5 to 4 percent for cures with nitrites and a minimum of 10 percent (preferably 20 percent) if nitrites are not used.

- ⚜ Use nitrites to control *C. botulinum,* to develop color and flavor, and always when dry curing.

✢ Measure curing salt according to the weight of the trimmed meat you plan to cure. Too little cure creates dull color and flavor; too much cure leaves excess nitrites in the food.

✢ Clear enough space in your refrigerator. For safety, always cure meat in the refrigerator (36°F to 40°F). At colder temperatures, meat will not cure properly. At warmer temperatures, spoilage microorganisms may grow.

✢ To eliminate guesswork, after you estimate the curing time, determine the end date, when the product needs to be removed from the cure. Write the date on the package or container.

✢ After curing, if the meat is too salty, soak in cold water to remove excess salt.

✢ Cured meat turns pink or reddish when cooked. If the cure has fully penetrated the meat, it will be pink throughout the cut. When cooking poultry, use a meat thermometer to determine doneness, as meat will appear light pink, even when fully cooked.

Curing methods use either dry or wet application. Dry rubs and wet brines are equivalent in their ability to preserve food:

✢ Dry salting coats the meat generously with salt. As the meat absorbs the salt, liquid leaches from the muscle tissue. This method is best if you live in a hot climate, have no refrigeration, or any time you want to air-dry or smoke meat. Dry curing results in greater loss of meat weight, produces intense flavor and saltiness, and ensures longer storage life.

✢ Wet curing, also known as brining or sweet pickling, immerses the meat in a solution of salt and water. The method is the best choice for lean meat. This is a good curing method for beginners. It is less error prone and produces less salty product than dry salting.

✢ Injecting brine is used solely to speed up the curing process. The meat begins to cure from the inside at the same time as the outside. The method is used in the commercial industry to reduce costs by decreasing production time and increasing product weight. Injecting serves no practical purpose in home food preservation. However, it is commonly used as a flavoring technique before smoking, grilling, or roasting (like your Thanksgiving turkey).

How to Apply Dry Cures

When you rub salt into the surface of the meat, it begins to migrate into the interior, and water inside the meat starts to travel outward. This process is fast at first, and then slows down until the amount of salt inside the meat is equal throughout. The loss of moisture inhibits spoilage organisms; quite simply, they die of thirst.

In this method, salt penetrates the meat faster than wet cures and preserves the food longer. The products are saltier, and have more pronounced flavors and greater loss of meat weight (up to 30 percent). This method works best for meats and sausages that will be air-dried, with or without smoking. It is the best curing method if you live in a hot climate or have no refrigeration. With dry salting, there is less possibility that the meat will go sour at warmer temperatures.

Here are some guidelines for applying dry cures effectively:

- Evenly apply and thoroughly rub curing agent (salt or curing mix) into all sides of the meat. Meats with bones (such as hams) should have some of the curing mix applied around the bone to guard against souring.

- Divide the curing agent into 2 to 3 portions for thicker cuts. Meats that are 1 inch thick or less may have the entire curing agent applied at one time. Thicker meats should have the cure divided into 2 or 3 portions and rubbed in at intervals, 3 to 5 days apart. For example, loins up to 3 inches thick should have 2 rubbings, and larger cuts like ham (12 pounds or more) should have 3 rubbings.

- Refrigerate meats for curing between 34°F to 40°F. Avoid lower temperatures, which freeze the meat and stop the curing process. Higher temperatures speed up the curing process, but can lead to spoiled meat, or meat with a shorter storage life.

- When dry curing, overhaul the pieces of meat daily, or a minimum of every other day, until the curing time has elapsed. *Overhaul* means to massage the meats and turn them over. It is very important during the overhauling process to avoid touching the meat. For this reason, many people like to place curing meats inside zipper-lock plastic bags or airtight containers that they can simply rotate. Otherwise, use disposable gloves, tongs, or other methods to avoid handling meats directly, so you do not transfer bacteria from your hands to the meat.

Some traditional methods cure meats at temperatures between 40°F to 50°F. This is because they used nitrates, which work best at (46°F to 50°F). Therefore, use elevated temperatures only if you are curing with saltpeter (sodium nitrate or potassium nitrate). If you do not have access to refrigerated curing, or wish to cure products in a cold root cellar, under no circumstances should curing take place at temperatures above 50°F or the meat will spoil before curing can be completed. When curing at 40°F to 50°F, you must use nitrates to control *C. botulinum*. In this case, sugar should not be added to avoid fermentation and spoilage.

Salt barrels were commonly used to pack meat for winter storage or sea voyages. It sounds easy, but the practice requires some skill to master. In this method, you pack meat as tightly as possible with enough salt in between to keep any two pieces from touching. As the meat dries out, water leaches out. Some containers have holes that drain away the liquid or hold the meat on a rack above it. You need to unpack the meat every few days, rotate pieces from bottom to top, and repack with fresh salt. Repeat the process until curing is complete. When no more liquid escapes, you rinse the meat with water to remove any traces of blood, and pack again in dry salt for long keeping. Strong brine may also be added to the salt barrel.

The meat for a salt barrel needs to be cut into uniform pieces. For fish, you clean the fish and remove the heads before packing. Salt barrels use about 1 to 1½ pounds of salt for every 10 pounds of meat.

Dry Curing Times

Curing is more art than science. There is no one formula to determine how long it will take the cure to penetrate your meat completely. The curing time also depends on your tolerance for salt and the desired length of storage. If you are using meat with a different weight or size than specified in a recipe, you will have make adjustments. Here are two ways you can estimate curing time:

+ Cure for 7 days per inch. For example, if the thickest part of the meat is 1 inch, cure for 1 week. If the thickest part is 2.5 inches, cure for 17.5 days.

+ Cure 2 days per pound for small cuts like bacon and loin. Cure 3 days per pound for large cuts like ham and shoulder. For example, a 6-pound pork belly for bacon would take 12 days, and a 12-pound ham needs 36 days.

Curing time depends on several factors such as temperature, the size or thickness of the meat, and ratio of meat to fat. For example, when curing a ham, the cure will penetrate on the lean meat side and very little on the fatty skin side. While it might seem logical to trim the fat and speed up curing, the fat is effective at controlling the rate of cure and loss of moisture, and overall helps result in a more uniform product.

Guidelines for Brining

The wet-curing method soaks meat in a solution of salt and water. Brines may include additives such as nitrites, sugar, and spices. Sugar helps to counteract excessive salt flavor.

As in dry salting, salt in the brine migrates toward the center of the meat, and water inside the meat transfers to the brine. Diffusion stops when the amount of salt in the meat and brine is equal. Also during this phase, any additives in the brine travel into the meat tissue. Initially, there is a slight drop (1 percent) in the weight of the meat due to the loss of water. However, soon the salt causes meat tissue to swell, which allows it to hold more water than was initially present. The meat absorbs some of the brine and gains weight. Under normal conditions, this gain is about 3 to 4 percent of the original weight and occurs after 30 days of curing. Also during this time, brine additives will fully develop the flavor, color, and texture in the cured product.

Here are some guidelines for brining:

+ Prepare enough brine to cover the meat completely. Use noncorrosive containers, such as plastic, glass, stainless-steel, stoneware, earthenware, or pickling crocks. Use a plate or other weight to keep the meat fully submerged at all times.

+ Don't skimp on salt; brine strength is critical to the development of the flavor of cured meat. You are better off using stronger brine for shorter periods than weak brines for longer periods. Brines of 20 percent salt concentration give the best results.

+ There may not be enough natural bacteria in brine to convert nitrate into nitrite. If so, curing would be inadequate. For this reason, the use of nitrate (cure #2) is discouraged in wet cures.

✦ When preparing brines, always heat half of the quantity of water and dissolve the salt and the sugar completely before adding the remaining liquid. If the brine is not used immediately, store it in the refrigerator.

✦ Turn the meat over daily, especially at the beginning of the curing time. Rotation is necessary because curing solutions are not uniform. Salt has a tendency to sink to the bottom while nitrites float near the top. Therefore, rotating helps meat to cure evenly. Whenever foam appears on the surface of the brine, remove it immediately.

✦ After curing is complete, rinse the meat under cold running water to remove any additives or salt crystals. Drain the meat on a rack.

Wet curing is a slower process than dry salting; brined food has a shorter shelf life, and a net weight gain of up to 4 percent. However, wet curing is easier to do, less error prone, and makes foods less salty than meat cured in dry salt. The mild flavor tends to appeal to more people. After wet curing, meats are often smoked or cooked.

WHERE'S THE CORN IN CORNING?

Corning is an old English term that refers to pellets of salt, once called *corns*. Therefore, meat preserved by corning is salt cured, by either using a dry rub or pickling brine. Corned beef is synonymous with pickled beef, meaning beef preserved in a salt solution. Canned corned beef was an important Irish export in the late seventeenth century.

Start with short brining periods to avoid making food that is too salty to eat. Keep notes and increase brining time to increase storage life, while maintaining edible and tasty products.

To calculate the amount of brine you need, estimate between 0.3 to 0.5 pound of water per pound of food. One quart of water weighs about 2 pounds (33.4 ounces), which translates to about 1 cup of water per pound. Here are some example estimations, using 10 pounds of food:

✦ 0.30 × 10 pounds food = 3 pounds water ÷ 2 = $1\frac{1}{2}$ quarts

✦ 0.40 × 10 pounds food = 4 pounds water ÷ 2 = 2 quarts

✦ 0.50 × 10 pounds food = 5 pounds water ÷ 2 = $2\frac{1}{2}$ quarts

✦ 10 pounds food × 1 cup = 10 cups ÷ 4 cups per quart = $2\frac{1}{2}$ quarts

So if you have 10 pounds of beef brisket to brine for making corned beef, you can expect to need $1\frac{1}{2}$ to $2\frac{1}{2}$ quarts of brine. Use these formulas as a guide only. When brining, use a container that holds the food comfortably. Always make sure that the brine covers the food by at least 1 to 2 inches.

Using more brine than needed to cover the food won't cause any problems. However, soaking a 25-pound turkey in 20 gallons of brine won't speed up the process. Excess brine simply wastes salt and water.

Brine Curing Times

Soaking time varies based on the size and texture of the meat. Note that brining your Thanksgiving turkey for a few hours merely adds flavor or moisture to the meat for roasting. For preserving, brining time needs to be much longer.

To determine brining time, the general rule is $3^{1}/_{2}$ to 4 days per pound, or 11 days per inch. For example, a 2-inch-thick piece of pork belly (bacon) will take 22 days, and a 15-pound ham will take $52^{1}/_{2}$ to 60 days. However, you don't want to cure bone-in meats longer than 45 days or the bone may sour.

If the curing time is too short, you will see uneven color, especially at the center of the meat or under heavy layers of fat. If curing time is too long by a few days, you should not notice any difference.

After curing, rinse meats under cold, running water, or soak in 30-minute intervals with fresh changes of water. The reason you want to soak cured meats is to remove excess salt from the surface and encourage uniform distribution of salt inside the meat. The recommended times are 30 minutes for small meats of a few pounds, up to 2 hours for large cuts, or at a rate of 3 minutes for each day of curing. Drain and dry the meat after rinsing.

If a product is too salty, place it in cold water and refrigerate overnight. Soaking can be performed on any cured product, even after cooking or smoking. Cold water soaking removes curing ingredients that were introduced into the meat, and may shorten the storage life.

Wet vs. Dry Cures

There are no hard-and-fast rules about which method of curing to use and when. Your choice depends on the character of the meat, strength of the brine, length of curing time, sugar or other additives to affect flavor and texture, post treatments like smoking, and personal preference. Take bacon: some swear by dry salting and others like the sweet, mild flavor brining produces. When smoking salmon, I do not prefer one method over the other. Small pieces of fillet fit handily into a brining container. A large fillet is easier to place on a rack in the refrigerator with a dry rub. Dry rubbing is a satisfying activity, like kneading bread, but quickly becomes an annoyance when you are pressed for time. So which method you choose depends on a number of factors.

If you are experienced with curing and smoking, you may have well-defined preferences for rubs versus brines. If you don't, or this is all new to you, here are some guidelines that give you a place to start:

> ✣ Use wet cure for lean meats (loin, brisket, poultry).

> ✣ Use wet cure for meats that will be cooked, but not smoked (corned beef brisket).

> ✣ Use dry rubs for fatty cuts of meat (pork butt, duck breast, salmon).

> ✣ Use dry rubs for meats that will be smoked (pastrami brisket).

Keep in mind that there are exceptions to these rules. Canadian bacon is made from pork loin and usually wet cured, while Italian bresaola is made from lean beef and is dry salted. Even if you try bacon two ways and decide you like the dry rub better, you may reverse your opinion on the very next project.

Aging and Smoking

Following a wet or dry cure, you may use aging (controlled drying) and smoking to develop color and flavor in your product, and to further extend the shelf life.

Aging and Fermenting

Aging is a post-treatment process that dries cured meats. If the aging process includes the development of lactic acid in the product, then it is also a fermented meat. Aging results in shelf-stable meat, develops rich flavor and fine texture, and inhibits bacterial growth. If used, follow strict temperature and humidity requirements, and treat for mold growth.

Dry aging requires cool temperatures in the range of 50°F to 65°F and high humidity between 60 to 70 percent relative humidity (RH). A couple of things you should notice about these requirements are, first, that 50°F falls inside the food danger zone of 40°F to 140°F. Second, it is unlikely that you have these conditions in your home. Refrigerators are too cold (32°F to 40°F) and have low relative humidity. Modern homes with central heating and air conditioning average 50 percent RH or less. Moist areas such as basements and cellars tend not to make effective locations for aging.

If you use incorrect temperature or humidity, the meat may age too slowly (or too quickly). Either way, the result may be inedible meat that harbors *C. botulinum,* grows mold, or becomes rancid quickly. These factors make dry aging meat at home challenging, but not impossible with adequate preparation.

Fermented sausages are held at slightly higher temperatures (70°F to 90°F) for 1 to 3 days, during which time LAB ferment the sugar that was used in the cure. You can use a starter culture to facilitate the process and guarantee a good result. At this point, it is a semidry sausage and requires refrigeration for storage. With additional aging at cooler temperatures, you can make a dry fermented sausage that is shelf stable at room temperature.

Optimally, semidry and dry sausages grow a white mold on the exterior that contributes to the keeping quality. Dry sausages have had a good food safety record. The key to producing them successfully is to achieve rapid production of the beneficial acid and mold that act as complementary preservatives.

When using starter cultures, you need to be mindful of several issues that can cause spoilage. These issues include fresh rather than aged meat that can have higher levels of bacteria, meat raised without antibiotics that would interfere with fermentation, ideal meat-to-fat ratio, ideal moisture and salt to develop lactic acid, ideal temperature and time to develop lactic acid, and adequate humidity to prevent case-hardening.

WHAT IS CASE-HARDENING?

If you squeeze aged meat and it feels squishy, like raw meat, but has a hard exterior, then you have case-hardening. If possible, vacuum package the meat and place it in the refrigerator. After a few days, the moisture should distribute evenly through the meat. Continue aging the meat. Case-hardening is caused by low humidity, excessive airflow, or both.

Dry-aged and fermented cured meats are the most advanced food preservation method. If you want to learn how to age and ferment meats, first you need to learn thoroughly the sanitation methods required for food preservation. Next, familiarize yourself with pickling and fermenting. Successfully prepare several types of pickles, fermented vegetables, and pickled meats. Finally, prepare several types of cured products that are fresh and smoked.

Now that you have a deep understanding of food preservation by salting and fermenting, you need to acquire the necessary equipment for dry aging.

Additionally, if you want to prepare dry or fermented sausages, you first need to become adept at making fresh sausage. Grinding and stuffing links requires additional skills in order to get good results. Fortunately, you can have delicious fun while learning the techniques.

The method for making cured sausage is different from whole pieces of meat. Instead of a dry rub or immersion in brine, you combine the curing mix with the ground meat before stuffing into sausage casing. Curing takes place in the refrigerator. The sausage may be smoked, cooked, or aged after curing.

Equipment for Aging

One reason Italy is renowned for the production of dry-cured salami is their climate; it is ideally suited for aging. Most people live where the temperature and humidity are less than ideal for extended periods. Therefore, you have to create the right conditions. The three factors you need to control are temperature, humidity, and airflow:

- ⚜ **Temperature:** The recommended curing temperature range is 50°F to 60°F. Below 50°F, the curing process slows down, which means that it takes too long to achieve safe water content. Above 60°F increases the potential for harmful microorganisms to grow.

- ⚜ **Humidity:** The recommended curing relative humidity range is 70 to 75 percent. Below 70 percent, you run the risk of case-hardening, where the outside of your cured meat dries out too fast, traps moisture inside, and leads to spoilage. Above 75 percent, you run the risk of encouraging the wrong kind of mold growth. When you initially place meat into an aging chamber or room, you want the humidity higher—around 85 percent, which is only slightly less than the water content of the meat. Therefore, drying begins slowly. Over the course of the first week, you drop to within the recommended range.

- ⚜ **Airflow:** As moisture in the meat transfers to the surface, good air circulation helps pull the moisture away, and keeps bad (fuzzy white, green, or black) mold from developing.

While there are no readily available appliances sold for aging meats in the home, you have several options from DIY to increasingly expensive.

Locate an ideal area in your house, which might be a garage (that isn't used for cars, or storage for cleaning supplies or garden chemicals), attic, unfinished basement, pantry, or root cellar. Buy an inexpensive thermometer (to measure temperature) and hygrometer (to measure humidity) and test the temperature and humidity in various locations to see if you are lucky enough to have a location that could work. Most people aren't this lucky.

Another solution is to buy a wine refrigerator or used refrigerator and modify it for use as a curing chamber. Either of these options cost less than $300.

You can also buy a commercial bakery proofing cabinet for ideal temperature and humidity control. The catch? Proofing cabinets cost more than $1,000.

The following table provides a brief list and cost comparison for different meat-aging cabinet solutions.

Cured Meat–Aging Equipment with Cost Comparison

Equipment	Function	Used Frost-Free Refrigerator	New Wine Refrigerator	New Commercial (Bakery) Proofer
Refrigerator	Cool temperatures	$0–$150	$100–$200+	$1,400+
Temperature controller	Maintains 50°F–60°F	$50	Built-in	Built-in
Thermometer-hydrometer	Measures temperature and humidity	$10–$15	$10–$15	Built-in
Pan of water (free) or humidifier	Adds moisture	$50	$50	Built-in
Hygrostat	Controls humidity (70%)	$60	$60	Built-in
Circulating fan	Increases airflow	$15–$25	$15–$25	Built-in
Total Estimated Cost		**$185–$305**	**$235–$350+**	**$1,400+**

Mold is inevitable in aged meats. One type is desirable, several types are not good, and one type is definitely bad. Once you establish a good curing environment, the atmosphere tends to promote good mold in newly introduced pieces.

Only powdery white mold is good, a form of penicillin that has a strong ammonia smell. You can eat this mold, or trim it off when serving or eating. Fuzzy white, green, or blue mold should be wiped off with vinegar. To treat mold, use a clean towel soaked in vinegar and rub the surface thoroughly. Black mold indicates spoilage and means you must discard the meat.

You need to monitor aging meat daily to check the temperature and humidity, and to look for signs of fuzzy mold. Aged meats should lose at least 18 percent of the original weight. Strive for 25 to 30 percent loss within the recommended curing time of 7 days per inch.

SPOILER ALERT

Spoilage is a regular aspect of aging meat. Even commercial producers experience failure. Learn the signs of spoilage, and always discard spoiled meat without tasting it.

Smoking

Smoking after curing is a complementary process that helps preserve the meat, improves flavor, and greatly enhances appearance. Smoke acts both as a drying agent and as a complementary preservative. Smoked meats are less likely to turn rancid or grow mold, when compared to unsmoked meats.

Wood smoke deposits a coating that protects the surface from pathogens. Recommended woods are fruit or hardwood species such as hickory, apple, plum, oak, maple, or ash. Pine or other resinous woods create acrid smoke that is not good for food.

To use smoking as a preservation method requires the right type of wood and smoke with a high level of creosote that builds up slowly over time to penetrate the meat fully. Smoking in the home environment contributes more flavor and appearance benefits than food preservation.

Before smoking, you need to rinse the cured meat in fresh water. Especially when using dry salt rubs, you need to remove salt crystals on the surface of the meat that would prevent smoke penetration. However, if you smoke meat that is still damp, it will not attain a rich color and flavor. Therefore, you must dry the surface of the meat after rinsing, and before smoking. Place cured, rinsed, unwrapped meat in the refrigerator on a rack set over a rimmed baking sheet. Dry meat for several hours or until the surface is dry or tacky.

Hot smoking occurs at 180°F to 220°F, in a smokehouse or using a wood or electric smoker. Smoke until the meat is cooked to an internal temperature of 140°F. Sometimes I like to do a light smoke for flavor, and then finish the product in a moderate oven (350°F) until a safe internal temperature is reached. Salmon may smoke for as little as 30 minutes, and brisket or other large cuts of meat for 2 hours or more. Mastering the low-and-slow smoking technique of true barbecue is an acquired skill that can take years to perfect.

Cold smoking occurs at less than 90°F, over a smoldering fire or in a modified refrigerator. Since this process holds food in the temperature danger zone (40°F to 140°F), rapid microbial growth is a risk. Products that have been salt cured or fermented offer an additional degree of safety. Most food scientists cannot recommend cold-smoking methods because of the inherent risks. Those at risk for food-borne illness are advised to avoid cold-smoked products.

Liquid smoke is an easy way to add smoke flavors in cured food; however, it does not provide any preservative effect. Add liquid smoke to brine, or during a postcuring cooking process.

Storing Cured Products

If you plan to vacuum package the finished product, you must pay special attention to requirements for refrigerating vacuum-sealed meats or fish, especially if you cured them without the use of nitrites. Because vacuum packaging removes air, it creates the ideal conditions for the production of *C. botulinum*. Therefore, you must keep vacuum-sealed meats at less than 38°F. In the home refrigerator, this means storing them on a lower shelf, toward the back. If stored at slightly warmer temperatures, the safest approach is to break the vacuum seal by puncturing the package, or rewrapping with plastic wrap or foil.

If you freeze vacuum-sealed packages, be sure you also thaw them at less than 38°F. However, freezing tends to reduce the quality of cured meats and is not recommended.

Store well-cured and smoked fish in the refrigerator for up to 2 weeks, or wrap well and freeze for up to 3 months.

SPOILER ALERT

Many types of cured products are raw. Avoid cross contamination and store them so that they do not come into direct contact with other fresh or cooked foods.

Troubleshooting Cured Foods

Problem: **Incomplete color change in interior of meat.**

Remedy: Meat may not be fully protected; treat as fresh and consume or freeze within a few days.

Prevention: Increase curing time, or decrease amount of nitrate in long-cured products (too much nitrate inhibits color development).

Problem: **Color of cured meat fades over time.**

Remedy: Meat is safe to eat provided there are no signs of spoilage.

Prevention: Light and air will fade color; wrap meat to protect from light and air.

Problem: **Meat tastes salty.**

Remedy: Soak the meat in cold water in the refrigerator until saltiness is reduced.

Prevention: Use a shorter curing time. Add sugar to cure to counteract salt.

Problem: **Meat tastes bitter.**

Remedy: Soak meat in cold water in the refrigerator until bitterness is reduced.

Prevention: Decrease amount of nitrite or nitrate (too much cure turns meat bitter).

Problem: **Rancid flavor in cured pork.**

Remedy: Rancidity is the result of oxygen breaking down fat. It is not spoiled in the sense that it is due to microbial growth, and it won't make you sick. A rancid or ripe flavor in pork is subjective and actually preferred by some people. Meat is safe to eat provided there are no signs of spoilage, but if in doubt, throw it out. Use the meat in soups with lots of liquid or stir-fries with lots of spices to mask the flavor.

Prevention: To decrease this trait, decrease the strength of the brine and aging or curing time. Do not freeze cured meat or add ascorbic acid. Keep product well wrapped. Smoking decreases the development of rancidity. Buy and cure pork raised by traditional methods, rather than industrially raised meat.

Problem: **Sour or rotten odors in cured meat.**

Remedy: A sour odor indicates increased bacterial count, while a rotten odor indicates pathogenic bacterial growth. Depending on your tolerance and susceptibility to food-borne illness, the product should be discarded. If it is slightly sour, you might be able to use the meat if cooked thoroughly in soup or stew.

Prevention: Use freshly killed meat. Keep chilled. Prepare promptly.

Problem: **Mold growth on cured meat.**

Remedy: White powdery mold is normal and desirable. Black mold indicates spoiled product; discard without tasting. If fuzzy white, green, or blue mold is present, scrape off and rinse meat clean with a solution of $3\frac{1}{2}$ tablespoons vinegar in 1 quart water.

Prevention: Mold growth is a natural result of aging cured meat. Use a purchased culture to promote "good" white powdery mold when curing meat. Store cured meat in dry conditions, without touching other meats.

Problem: **Meat is infested with insects.**

Remedy: Trim deeply and discard the infested portion. Consume remaining portion promptly.

Prevention: Store in tightly closed paper bags in a cool, dry location. Clean the curing and storage area regularly. Cure and consume meats during cooler months, when insects are less active.

Problem: **Meat has case-hardening.**

Remedy: Try vacuum packing it and refrigerating for 2 to 3 days; the moisture may redistribute evenly, and you can continue the aging process. If not, chop or grate it, freeze it, and use it in soups or other cooked dishes.

Prevention: Age meats at correct temperature and humidity.

Sealing Foods 6

You and I need air to breathe, and so do bacteria, yeasts, and molds. By eliminating air, we can slow down (but not completely stop) the activity of spoilage organisms. Sealing provides no protection against harmful organisms. Therefore, you must usually combine sealing with another food preservation method, such as curing or chilling.

In the past, fat and paraffin sealing were common. People added large amounts of curing agents, such as salt and saltpeter (potassium nitrate), before sealing and storing food. The cures allowed the food to be stored at cool temperatures in a root cellar or through the winter months. Today, most people prefer to reduce the use of cures, because refrigerated and frozen storage is available year-round.

The two most frequent sealing methods used today include fat sealing and the newest method, vacuum packaging in specially designed plastic bags. Fat sealing is relatively inexpensive, while vacuum sealing requires a modest expenditure.

Throughout history, people have used many other sealing methods, including layering food with oil or fat, covering it with paraffin or wax, burying food in the ground, and wrapping it in thick pastry.

You can use vacuum sealing to extend shelf life indefinitely in frozen and dried foods. Of course, you must ensure the integrity of the vacuum package and maintain proper frozen storage temperatures.

Fat-Sealing Foods

To eliminate air, people around the world have used fats and waxes, both effective at keeping air out and food safe for consumption for an extended period. Before the widespread use of mechanical refrigeration, these methods were simple, effective ways to preserve meats from one season to the next.

Fat-Sealing Methods

The basic method for fat sealing involves cooking salted or dried meat in fat, and then storing the meat in its cooled, congealed fat. The storage vessel may be a stoneware jar, gourd, animal stomach, or hide. Many cultures throughout the world use this practice, especially to prepare meat for storage through the winter or dormant season.

In France, they favor *confit d'oie* (goose) and *confit de canard* (duck). The French prepare confit, which means *conserve,* by salting the meat, mixing it with saltpeter, and cooking it in its own fat. They pack the meat in an earthenware jar, carefully surrounded by fat. Originally, the French made it with large amounts of salt and saltpeter to allow for room-temperature storage.

Pioneers on the American frontier fried ground meat patties and packed them into crocks with rendered lard (pork fat). These meats would feed large groups of men gathered for projects such as threshing or barn raising.

Plains tribes in North America, particularly those in the northern latitudes, made a fat- and air-sealed meat product known as *pemmican.* To make pemmican, thinly sliced meat (bison, moose, elk, deer, caribou, buffalo, beef, or reindeer) was dried and sometimes smoked. They pounded the brittle meat into powder. During this process, they might add dried wild berries such as saskatoon or chokecherry. They combined the powdered food with melted fat, and poured it into skin bags. Finally, they folded and sewed or sealed the hide with fat to seal off air. Kept dry or buried in the ground, packaged pemmican could stay edible for 4 to 5 years or longer. Northwest tribes made fish pemmican by pounding dried fish with sturgeon oil. These products were an extremely valuable commodity for both Native Americans and Europeans who insinuated themselves with the local tribes. Pemmican was—and still is—compact, portable, and highly nutritious.

You can enjoy fat-preserved meats cold or hot. Use cold, shredded fat-preserved meat (called *rillettes* in French) as a spread for bread. Traditional hot preparations include frying the meat with eggs for breakfast (*khlea*), making pemmican into soup (*rubbaboo*) with added vegetables, or frying the meat briefly in its own fat (duck-leg confit) and serving with potatoes. You chew a piece of cold pemmican by gnawing since it is very hard. (See Chapter 14 for recipes using sealed foods.)

Whichever method you use, the best result (longest keeping quality) is obtained if you render and strain the fat twice to remove impurities, add salt and/or nitrate, store the product at cool temperatures (preferably 40°F or less), and protect the congealed fat from air by sealing in an airtight container. Fat-sealed meats may also be canned or frozen.

Preparation Steps

Sealing food from air creates an environment that might allow *C. botulinum* bacteria to produce toxin, causing serious food poisoning (in this case, botulism). Therefore, foods stored in the absence of air require that you control the sealed environment further.

In a sealed container, you control *C. botulinum* by sterilizing the container, cooking the food, removing moisture (with salt or dehydration), and adding ingredients such as acids or nitrates that inhibit microbial activity.

Here is a summary of the guidelines you need to follow. Completing these steps helps to prevent the development of botulinum toxin and extend the storage life as long as possible:

1. Fully cook meat to kill existing bacteria, yeasts, and molds. Use appropriate amounts of salt, acid, or nitrate to control *C. botulinum.* Do not include meat juices, which spoil rapidly.

2. Render fat to improve keeping quality (see instructions later in the following section). Surround the meat with fat (top, bottom, and sides).

3. To seal containers, use a thin (1/8-inch) fat layer for short storage (up to 1 month) or thick (1/2-inch) layer for long storage (up to 6 months). Protect the fat layer from air. Press foil or greaseproof paper on the top layer, or otherwise protect the fat from air.

4. Store fat-sealed products in a cool location (32°F to 40°F) for longest storage.

SPOILER ALERT

If you find an old (or new) recipe for fat-sealed food that does not call for heavy amounts of salt, acid, or nitrate, or a secondary method such as drying or canning, then treat the fat-sealed food as fresh, not preserved. Refrigerate this food and consume within 3 days, or freeze for longer storage.

Rendering Fat

Before using animal fat for sealing, you must first render or purify the fat, by melting and straining it. Melting eliminates moisture that would cause the fat to spoil quickly. Straining eliminates connective tissue and bits of protein. Pure, rendered fat keeps almost indefinitely.

Beef or lamb suet renders to make tallow. Pork back fat or leaf fat (surrounding the kidneys) makes lard. Rendered duck, chicken, or goose fats (*schmaltz*) are also excellent fat-sealing mediums.

To render fat, simply chop it into small pieces, melt it slowly, and then strain, cool, and store. Here are the steps in more detail. Render 1 to 2 pounds of fat on your first effort:

1. Trim any visible meat, reserving it for another use (such as making stock). Freeze fat for 30 minutes to make it easier to cut. Cut into 1-inch pieces. To speed up rendering, you may freeze cubes for 2 hours, and then pulse them in a food processor until pea size.

2. Place the pieces of fat in a saucepan or slow cooker. Optionally, add up to 1/4 cup water for every pound of fat, again to speed up the rendering process. This small amount of water will cook off as the fat melts.

3. Render fat in a slow oven (200°F to 250°F), or over low heat on the stove or in a slow cooker. Check and stir every 15 to 20 minutes. There should be no bubbling, smoking, or other activity—just slow melting. During rendering, the water evaporates and the fat melts. You will see browned bits floating to the surface.

4. After about 2 hours or when rendering is complete, remove your pot from the heat. Rendering is complete when the browned solids (known as cracklings) sink to the bottom of the pot, and the fat is completely liquefied and clear.

5. Line a fine-mesh strainer with cheesecloth. Carefully strain hot, liquid fat to remove cracklings. (Use cracklings as a topping for soups or salads, or add them to sautéed greens.) Pour hot, strained fat into lidded jars; pouring while still hot helps to eliminate air in the jar, which can promote mold growth. For easy cleanup, wash the pot and utensils with hot soapy water before fat hardens.

As fat cools, it turns from clear yellow to creamy white. Cover and refrigerate up to 6 months, or freeze for longer storage.

SPOILER ALERT

Be very careful when handling hot fat; it burns skin worse than boiling water.

Vacuum Packaging

Vacuum packaging has become popular due to the availability of low-cost machines suitable for home use. It is important to note that vacuum sealing does not prevent food spoilage. Like all sealing methods, vacuum packaging simply excludes air. Without a secondary process, it provides no protection against harmful organisms. Vacuum packing does not pasteurize food like canning does, nor does it remove moisture from food, like drying does. After vacuum sealing, you must store the food as you would without it. Therefore, store fresh foods in the refrigerator, frozen foods in the freezer, and dried foods at room temperature.

Uses for Vacuum Sealing

Many people use vacuum sealing to take advantage of lower-priced bulk foods, which they repackage into smaller portions for home use. Besides removing air, vacuum sealing reduces volume, resulting in efficient use of storage space.

One of the best uses for vacuum packaging is for dried foods, where it helps to prevent mold growth and extends storage time. It is also effective at delaying rancidity, preserving color, deterring insects in dried foods, and preventing freezer burn.

Vacuum sealing liquid foods requires the most attention. Liquids can seep into the seal area and prevent a vacuum from forming. As noted above, you must adequately refrigerate or freeze perishables to prevent any pathogenic bacteria that may be present from becoming active.

Effect on Storage Life

Vacuum sealing helps to extend the quality of stored foods—from 3 to 5 times longer than without vacuum sealing.

Note that there is a difference between quality and safety. For example, vacuum-sealed, frozen meat roast has an indefinite shelf life when stored at 0°F or less. Bacteria simply don't multiply at freezer temperatures. However, the quality of the roast may start to deteriorate after 1 year, the meat can become dried out, and the fat can start to become rancid.

Choosing a Vacuum Sealer

You can buy a small, hand-held, home vacuum sealer for around $20. Countertop models range from $50 to $300. The price you pay determines the features of your machine. Before you buy, check the price and availability of the vacuum bags, and consider whether you need the ability to vacuum containers, as well as bags. If you plan on light use and relatively short storage times, then a model on the lower end ($20 to $50) should prove satisfactory.

Other features you may want to consider are one-touch operation, noise level during operation, cool down or cycle time (number of seals per minute), ability to successfully vacuum liquids, metal versus plastic parts, sleeker design, and life of the appliance (or total number of packages it will vacuum before it stops working and needs to be repaired or replaced).

Machines that are more expensive, of course, have the most features. The best machines have some replaceable parts, such as the heat-sealing strip and rubber gasket. Commercial models range from $300 to $10,000. These vacuum packers use an internal chamber, rather than external bagging. They are also faster, repairable, use less-expensive bags, and offer additional features such as bag cutting and inert gas options for delicate foods.

All vacuum machines (home or commercial models) require specially designed, one-time-use bags (about $1 each), or reusable storage containers (about $5 each). Bags can be more economical if purchased in rolls that you cut to size.

Other Sealing Methods

To eliminate air, people around the world have used many clever methods to keep air out and food safe for consumption. Before the widespread use of mechanical refrigeration, these methods were simple, effective ways to preserve food from one season to the next.

Preserving in Oil

Vegetables covered by a layer of oil have a relatively short shelf life, making it more of a seasoning technique, rather than a preservation method. If you want to preserve vegetables in oil, you must add salt or acid (such as vinegar) or both. Alternatively, you can dry vegetables until crisp, before storing in oil. In either case, refrigeration is recommended for these products.

Oil excludes air and helps prevent spoilage. However, sealing foods against air is ideal for *C. botulinum,* which becomes active in low-acid (vegetables) and warm-temperature (more than 38°F) environments without air. Oil has no other preservative properties, nor do ingredients such as peppers, herbs, and garlic offer safeguards against food poisoning. Therefore, salt, acid, or dehydration to remove moisture, combined with cold temperature storage, is advised.

For dried vegetables, it is difficult in the home environment to ensure that the moisture content after drying is low enough to prevent botulinum toxin. *C. botulinum* can survive in just a drop of water.

Furthermore, the addition of acid to garlic may turn the garlic blue-green, which is not harmful, but unappetizing. To prevent discoloration, cure garlic for 4 weeks at room temperature (more than 73°F) before storing in oil.

For these reasons, preserving vegetables in oil is not recommended. You may add garlic and herbs to oil if you wash them well, dry them thoroughly, store them in the refrigerator, and use the product within 2 to 3 days. There are no other safe preservation methods.

Find recipes for preserving acidified vegetables with some oil in Chapters 12 and 17.

Paraffin Sealing

The paraffin-sealing process can have two problems: the product being sealed is not sufficiently sterile, or microscopic holes or incomplete seals allow air in or liquid to seep out. In either case, mold may grow under or on the surface of the paraffin. Molds may produce mycotoxins that can spread undetected, like the roots of a tree. Many people report that they have eaten plenty of jam after removing mold, and suffered no ill effects.

However, people with asthma, allergies, or immune suppression (such as people with HIV, chemotherapy patients, and organ-transplant recipients) are especially sensitive to mold mycotoxins. Reactions can be immediate or delayed and include stuffy nose, irritated eyes or skin, wheezing, or lung infections.

If you have the equipment, boiling-water canning is safer, less error prone, and less expensive than using paraffin.

HOW TO APPLY PARAFFIN SEALS TO JAM JARS

Paraffin takes extra care to apply correctly. First, melt paraffin in a double boiler until completely liquefied. To apply to jam, ladle cooked jam while very hot into sterile glass jars. Clean the inside rim of the jar to remove any jam. Pour a thin layer of melted paraffin over the jam and rotate the jar to ensure even distribution of the liquid wax completely around the inside edge. After cooling, pour a second layer of paraffin over the first, to ensure a complete seal. Don't store wax seals where it is too cold or the temperature fluctuates—these conditions cause paraffin to expand and contract, allowing air in and mold to grow.

Wax Sealing

Some people have erroneously assumed that you may wax any hard cheese (such as Parmesan or cheddar) as a method of food preservation. In fact, waxing modern cheese for the purpose of long-term storage promotes harmful bacterial growth.

Traditional cheese-making methods formulate cheese to have low moisture and pH (high acid). After pressing fresh curds, each wheel of cheese is coated with wax to promote fermentation. As the cheese ages, fermentation bacteria increase acidity and prevent growth of harmful bacteria. These cheeses store for several weeks at cool temperatures and controlled humidity.

Modern cheese is formulated for storage in the refrigerator and contains high moisture and pH (low acidity). Waxing modern cheese may minimize mold growth on the exterior of the cheese, but can promote the growth of harmful bacteria such as *C. botulinum* if stored above 38°F.

Burying

Buried food usually receives no other preservation treatment. When buried, food will remain cold, or will dry out (dehydrate) in arid climates and ferment in humid locales. As long as you protect buried food from insects such as beetles and worms, it can remain safe to eat for one or several seasons. See Chapter 8, which discusses garden mulching, trenches, pits, and other techniques for burying or cellaring foods.

Pastry Sealing

Sealing meat in pastry is really a fat-sealing method used primarily in medieval England. Old recipes (often spelled "receipts") from the time called for meat baked inside a thick, inedible pastry. After baking, melted fat (such as lard, butter, or suet) was poured through a hole in the top crust. Once the fat congealed, the pie could be stored at cool temperatures for a few weeks. When served, the pastry was discarded and only the meat and fat were eaten.

Troubleshooting Sealed Foods

Problem: Rillettes or pemmican is bland.

Remedy: Bring the product to room temperature, add salt or other seasonings to taste, and mix thoroughly.

Prevention: When seasoning warm foods, the mixture will taste saltier. If you serve the dish cold, oversalt the warm mixture slightly. Write the amount of salt you prefer on the recipe.

Problem: Potted meats or fish spoil or become rancid quickly.

Remedy: Unfortunately, the only remedy is to discard the food.

Prevention: When rendering or using fat for sealing, be sure to remove all solids and leave behind any meat juices, which spoil quickly. Cover meat completely with fat. The thicker the top layer, the longer the storage life. Enclose each piece of meat in fat—top, sides, and bottom. Meat pieces should not touch the container, or each other. Sterilize the jars. Refrigerate the potted meats and fish or use adequate amounts of nitrites for room temperature storage.

Problem: Mold grows on the surface of potted meat.

Remedy: If the amount of mold is small, you can remove it, plus ½ inch of surrounding fat. Otherwise, discard the food.

Prevention: Cover with foil or greaseproof paper pressed onto the surface of the fat; plastic tends to trap moisture and encourages mold growth.

Problem: Duck confit remains pink and does not appear completely cooked after 3 hours.

Remedy: Test with an instant thermometer; poultry is done if the internal temperature is 165°F. Prick meat all the way to the bone; if the juice runs clear or yellow (not pink or red), the meat is done.

Prevention: When using curing salts with added nitrites, fully cooked meat will remain pink. Omit curing salt if you don't want pink meat; however, without curing salt the product has a refrigerated shelf life of just 3 days.

Problem: Air is not being removed from vacuum bag.

Remedy: Clean the machine's sealing strip. Make sure the bag is lying completely flat against the sealing strip.

Prevention: Keep the bag and sealing areas clean and dry. Take extra care when sealing sharp objects, such as meat with bones, which can puncture bags and prevent sealing. Take extra care with liquids, which can be pulled into the sealing area and prevent sealing.

Problem: Several bags were successfully sealed, and now the vacuum machine won't work.

Remedy: Let the machine cool down.

Prevention: Check the sealing strip and gasket; wipe clean and dry thoroughly. Check the cycle time (seals per minute) for your machine and do not exceed the recommendation.

Problem: Air was removed, but has come back into the bag.

Remedy: Cut the bag open, and vacuum it again, or transfer food to another bag and seal.

Prevention: Check for a wrinkle, solids, or liquid along the seal area, which cause leakage and allow air in. Do not vacuum foods with sharp edges that can puncture the bag. Use a thicker bag, if possible.

Problem: Air was removed, but bag appears inflated after storing.

Remedy: Produce may be ripe or overripe; prepare and use soon.

Prevention: Some fresh produce—including tomatoes, (peeled or unpeeled) garlic, and cruciferous vegetables (broccoli, cauliflower, cabbage, and brussels sprouts)—give off gases, even under a vacuum. It is best to blanch, freeze, or dry fresh produce before sealing in vacuum bags.

Canning Foods   7

Canning is a relatively new form of food preservation, available for just over 200 years. Canning requires a modest investment in equipment and skills that are easy to learn and practice. Once you learn how, canning is a great way to turn fresh food into shelf-stable products.

You can store canned foods for at least 1 year. After 1 year, the quality of the food tends to deteriorate. However, experiments have shown that properly canned and stored food may remain safe for consumption, even after 100 years.

You might be surprised to learn that a Frenchman invented the canning process in the early 1800s. Nicolas Appert experimented with foods sealed in corked glass bottles. After heating and cooling, the bottled foods stayed fresh for an extended period. Napoleon sustained his army with these foods and Appert received a hefty prize from the Emperor for his invention. In Great Britain, Peter Durand used Appert's idea to seal foods in metal cans instead of glass bottles and canning was born.

About 50 years later, American John L. Mason patented useful improvements to Appert's bottle. This improved screw-neck jar had a threaded zinc cap that helped make the canning process easy and reliable.

Glass companies such as Ball, Atlas, and Kerr began to manufacture the new Mason canning jar. Over the next several years, various inventors tinkered with the design, including different styles of metal caps and glass lids with wire bails (known as *lightning jars*). Alexander Kerr developed the two-piece metal closure we use today. Kerr's invention consists of a flat metal lid with a sealing ring and a metal screw band. To use the two-piece closure, you place the flat lid on a jar of food and use the screw band to hold the lid in place during the heating and cooling process.

While the jar's design and closure has evolved, the fundamentals of canning have not changed since Appert put the process into practice over 200 years ago.

Canning Fundamentals

Like Appert, you still use a glass canning jar with a secure closure, and then heat and cool the jar to seal the food safely inside. The basic process involves just two steps:

1. You put food and liquid in special jars with lids.

2. You heat the jars.

The heat pasteurizes the food. When it cools, a vacuum forms, which greatly decreases the amount of air inside the jar and seals the food inside. This makes the food shelf stable—that is, safe for storage at room temperature.

There are four basic reasons why canning safely preserves food:

- Immerses the food in enough liquid to allow sufficient heating to take place
- Heats the food adequately to deactivate enzymes that spoil food
- Pasteurizes the food to kill harmful microbes that spoil food
- Forms a vacuum to maintain food safety during storage

The primary purpose of home canning is to preserve basic foods when they are in season. Preserved fruits and vegetables are a welcome respite through winter, when fresh, locally grown produce is usually not available. Home canned meats and other preparations give new meaning to convenience foods, made without additives.

There are a few essential concepts you need to learn to can foods successfully. People have the most trouble with canning when they don't understand why a step is necessary and, sometimes inadvertently, they take shortcuts. The fundamental tasks include choosing the right canning method, taking precautions to prevent botulism poisoning, and preparing and processing canned foods correctly. We'll look at all of these topics in this chapter.

Acidity and Canning Method

There are two canning methods: boiling water–bath (BWB) canning and steam-pressure canning. Each of these methods is described in detail later in this chapter. However, which method you use depends on whether the food you plan to can is high acid or low acid.

You can easily destroy most harmful microbes that spoil food by using the BWB canning method. If any "bad" bacteria remain, foods high in acid prevent the harmful growth of these heat-resistant microorganisms.

Remember, bacteria are everywhere. Foods that are high acid can deal with the bad guys and keep them in check. High-acid foods include most fruits, and products made from fruits such as applesauce and jam.

Pretty much everything else besides fruit is a low-acid food, including meat, poultry, seafood, milk, beans, and vegetables. Because low-acid foods offer no additional protection against heat-resistant organisms, you need to destroy more of the bad guys in these foods. Boiling water won't do the job. Therefore, you need to process low-acid foods at temperatures higher than boiling water.

It doesn't matter how long you boil a pot of water, it will never get hotter than 212°F. Only a pressure canner can achieve higher temperatures.

THE SCIENCE BEHIND PH

When ingredients dissolve in water (H_2O), they produce ions. If there are more hydrogen (H+) ions, the solution is acidic; if there are more hydroxyl (OH–) ions, it is alkaline or basic. Therefore, acidity is determined by measuring the potential hydrogen or pH. The pH can range from 0 to 14. A pH of 0 to 6 is acid, 7 is neutral, and 8 to 14 is alkaline. Lemon juice has a pH of 2 to 3. Tap water has a pH near 7 (neutral), while rainwater is around 6 (slightly acidic) and seawater is around 8 (slightly alkaline). Baking soda solutions have a pH around 9, and household ammonia has a pH of 11 to 12. High-acid foods have a pH of 4.6 or less.

So you choose a canning method based on the acidity of foods (summarized in the following table):

✣ For high-acid foods (pH 4.6 or less), use BWB canning at 212°F.

✣ For low-acid foods (pH greater than 4.6), use steam-pressure canning at 240°F.

pH of Common Foods and Canning Method

Type of Food	Acidity (pH)	Canning Method
Meat, poultry, seafood Grains and legumes Milk and cheese Most vegetables Combined foods (stews, soups, tomato sauces with meat, mixed vegetables) Melons Dates Papayas Persimmons	Low-acid foods (pH 5.2 or higher)	Steam-pressure canning (240°F–250°F)
Figs Tomatoes Mangos Bananas Pineapples	Medium-acid foods (pH 4.5–5.2)	Steam-pressure canning (240–250°F) Boiling water–bath canning (212°F) if acidified with tested recipe
Berries Most fruits Fruit and berry juices Jams and jellies Sauerkraut and kimchi Rhubarb Vinegars	High-acid foods (pH 4.6 or below)	Boiling water–bath canning (212°F)

continues

continued

Type of Food	Acidity (pH)	Canning Method
Pickled vegetables Vegetable relishes Cucumber pickles	Acidified foods (acid added to lower pH to 4.6 or below)	Boiling water–bath canning (212°F)

You may notice from this chart that a few fruits are low to medium acid, such as melons and bananas. In addition, pickles and relish are safe for water-bath canning, even though they contain vegetables. Pickles and relish have added acid in the form of vinegar.

When you add acid to lower the pH in fruits and vegetables, you must use commercially bottled lemon juice, commercially bottled vinegar of at least 5 percent acidity, or food-grade citric acid powder. You cannot use fresh lemon juice or homemade vinegar because the strength of these products is unknown. The following products effectively lower pH in canned foods, where called for in tested recipes:

- **Bottled lemon juice.** May contribute an undesirable flavor. Add 1 tablespoon to pint jars and 2 tablespoons to quart jars. Many traditional canners find the flavor of bottled lemon juice to be more objectionable than vinegar in canned tomatoes; can a few jars with each, if you're not sure. Add 1 tablespoon sugar to offset acid taste or use citric acid.

- **Commercial vinegar (5 percent or higher acidity).** May contribute undesirable flavor. Cider vinegar is milder than white vinegar, but adds color that may not be desirable. Add 2 tablespoons to pint jars and 4 tablespoons to quart jars. Add 1 tablespoon sugar to offset acid taste or use citric acid.

- **Citric acid powder (food grade).** Lemon juice or vinegar may be more readily available. Citric acid is available from suppliers selling nutritional supplements or candy-making supplies. Add $\frac{1}{4}$ teaspoon to each pint jar and $\frac{1}{2}$ teaspoon to each quart jar.

Besides fruits and some vegetable products, you cannot safely acidify other foods for BWB canning, including meats, fish, nuts, dairy, and products made from them, such as pickled pig's feet or pickled salmon.

You cannot determine from the pH how to safely acidify a food or choose a canning method; you must use a tested recipe. For one thing, the pH of a food fluctuates from one variety to the next (plum tomatoes versus beefsteak tomatoes, for example) and within a specific type (green, mature, ripe, or overripe tomatoes).

In addition to pH, something called *water activity* (a_w) influences the canning process. *Water activity is not the same as water content.* Water activity is a measurement of the free water on a molecular level—water that is available for microbial activity. Water activity indicates water that is available for food-borne microorganisms to grow. Ingredients in the water, specifically sugar and salt, influence water activity.

Pure water has an a_w of 1.0; acidified foods need a_w of 0.85 or below to prohibit bacterial growth. When you add salt or sugar, it binds the water and decreases a_w. It's no longer free water available for microbial activity. In actuality, the U.S. Department of Agriculture (USDA) defines low-acid foods as those with a pH 4.6 or below *and* an a_w 0.85 or below.

Tested canning recipes have determined the safe pH *and* water activity necessary to can food safely. Optimal water activity improves the color, flavor, and texture of canned foods, and maximizes their safety and shelf life.

If any of this information is confusing or overwhelming, don't worry. You don't need to remember it. All you need to know in order to choose the right canning method is to use recipes based on laboratory testing. The canning information in this book uses only recommendations and tested recipes based on the guidelines published in the USDA's *Complete Guide to Home Canning* and from county extension offices and university research.

Botulism Poisoning

Any discussion about home canned foods must include some facts about food-borne botulism poisoning. This rare but serious illness is caused by eating foods that contain botulinum neurotoxin.

Clostridium botulinum is a common, everyday bacteria found in soil and on food. Only under certain conditions does it become harmful. In the absence of air, such as in canned foods, *C. botulinum* may produce botulin, a toxin that causes food poisoning.

It is easy to make sure that *Clostridium* bacteria remain harmless. One way to prevent *C. botulinum* in canned foods is to process only foods that are high in acid. *C. botulinum* remains inactive in high-acid environments. For low- or medium-acid foods, you need to add acid if possible, or destroy these heat-resistant bacteria by heating the food to 240°F, which requires a pressure canner.

Inadequate processing of home canned vegetables is one of the primary sources of food-borne botulism poisoning. When you are doing home canning, be sure to use tested recipes. Tested recipes give the necessary information to can foods safely and guard against botulism. Of course, you need to practice other normal safety measures. Make sure that you sanitize the work area, wash produce thoroughly, adjust the processing time if you live and can above an elevation of 1,000 feet, follow all procedures accurately, and never take shortcuts.

In addition, before opening and consuming canned food, critically examine canned products for spoilage. As an added precaution, you can boil all home canned vegetables and meats without tasting for 10 minutes plus 1 minute per 1,000 feet above sea level (15 minutes at 5,000 feet). Boil home canned spinach and corn 20 minutes before tasting. If the toxin is present, it is readily destroyed by boiling.

SPOILER ALERT

Over the past couple decades, an average of 22 cases of food-borne botulism have been reported each year to the Centers for Disease Control and Prevention (CDC). In 2010, the number of cases reported was only nine, with no deaths. Most cases involving home preserved foods have been due to improperly home canned vegetables and fish; improperly cured meats; and canned tomato sauces using untested recipes. If untreated, the disease can lead to paralysis, respiratory failure, and death. Symptoms of botulism poisoning typically begin 18 to 36 hours after eating the contaminated food, but can occur as early as 6 hours or as late as 10 days later. Symptoms of botulism include double or blurred vision, drooping eyelids, slurred speech, difficulty swallowing, dry mouth, and muscle weakness.

Raw Pack vs. Hot Pack

In addition to the two types of canning methods (BWB and steam-pressure canning), there are two ways to pack food into canning jars:

- ⚜ Raw pack (also called cold pack) puts raw food into hot jars with hot liquid.

- ⚜ Hot pack puts hot food into hot jars with hot liquid.

Note that with either method, both the jars and liquids are hot. Which method you use depends on the type of food and desired result.

Use raw pack especially for delicate fruits such as soft berries (blackberries, raspberries, strawberries, etc.) and foods that are easier to pack when raw, such as whole green beans, strips of meat, and brined fish. You can also consider it for soft stone fruits (apricots, peaches, and plums) and pears, which can become mushy if heated before packing.

After packing the raw food into the hot jar, pour boiling liquid over it. For best results with raw-packed fruits, use a sweetened canning liquid, such as light- to medium-sugar syrup. If packed in water or unsweetened juice, raw-packed fruits may float above the canning liquid and turn brown or gray after a few weeks in storage. The color change is harmless and the food is safe to eat, but can be unappetizing.

Hot pack produces better products in most cases, so it is the method preferred by most who can foods. It works best for foods that are firm and maintain their shape even when boiled, such as peach halves or whole tomatoes. For hot pack, cook the food for the time specified by a tested recipe, and then pack while still hot into hot jars.

Both the raw-pack and hot-pack methods are used for BWB canning and steam-pressure canning. Processing times for raw-packed foods are usually longer than hot-packed foods. The advantages and disadvantages of both methods are summarized in the following table.

Advantages and Disadvantages of Raw- vs. Hot-Packed Foods

	Raw Pack	Hot Pack
Advantages	Retains better shape and texture in some foods such as berries and soft fruits	Destroys more bacteria during the cooking process prior to packing
	Easier to pack some foods when raw and firm, such as asparagus spears and sliced meats	Increases storage life by removing more air
		Increases jar capacity by shrinking food before packing
		More successful vacuum seals and fewer seal failures
		Retains better color and quality during storage
Disadvantages	Breakage increased due to cold product and hot jars	Soft foods may turn mushy during processing
	Shelf life decreased because food retains more air	More difficult to handle and pack some foods while hot, such as whole green beans
	Discolored foods and/or solids floating above liquid	

Methods to Prevent Browning

Fruits and vegetables that oxidize or turn brown when peeled or cut need to be treated for browning—for example, apple slices, pear halves, eggplant slices, or potato cubes. This section lists the various methods you can use to treat produce before canning. Note that you might use these methods in different stages of preparation and types of products. For example, you might use salt-vinegar holding water while preparing potatoes; then discard the water and use fresh hot liquid for canning. You might add lemon juice to sugar syrup to hold pear halves while peeling, and use the same syrup as the canning liquid. You may prefer the consistency of using ascorbic acid, and use it to treat holding water, as well as canning syrup.

During the planning phase, it's a good idea to think through these issues and prepare accordingly. See Chapter 2 for more information on where to buy and how to use these products, and methods to pretreat produce to prevent browning.

The best methods to prevent browning include using ascorbic acid powder, vitamin C tablets, or commercial products such as Fruit-Fresh. All are very effective at preventing browning and do not add flavors to the product.

Other good methods include the following:

✢ Lemon juice is less effective than ascorbic acid. You may brush fresh or bottled lemon juice directly on cut produce, or soak a large batch in lemon water; use $\frac{1}{4}$ cup lemon juice in 1 quart of water or 1 cup per gallon. Limit soaking time to 15 minutes or the acid starts to break down the produce and turn it limp or mushy. Bottled lemon juice is less expensive than fresh lemon juice, but adds an uncharacteristic flavor. Fresh-cut lemons may be rubbed on cut surfaces of produce, but is time-consuming for treating more than 1 to 2 pounds of produce.

✢ Apple juice is effective for holding prepared apples, has enough acidity to prevent browning, and contributes desirable flavor.

✢ A salt-vinegar solution can be used to hold fruit or vegetables for 15 minutes. Use 2 tablespoons canning, kosher, or table salt and 2 tablespoons white vinegar to 1 gallon water. Rinse well with fresh water after soaking to remove salt and vinegar flavors.

✢ Steam blanch produce by placing cut produce in a shallow layer over steaming water for 3 to 5 minutes, or until half-cooked.

The least effective methods include the following:

✢ Cold water is effective only for holding whole, peeled potatoes. Slices or cubes are best treated by some other method, such as ascorbic acid, salt-vinegar, or steam blanching.

✢ Citric acid powder is less effective than ascorbic acid or lemon juice in preventing browning.

Processing Time

How long to process or heat home canned food by either canning method has been determined by laboratory testing. The length of processing time depends on several factors:

✢ Ratio of solids to liquid

✢ Size of jar (half-pint, pint, quart, or half-gallon)

✢ Method (boiling water or pressure canning)

✢ Altitude (above 1,000 feet increases time and/or pressure)

Processing times stated in recipes assume that you are canning foods at sea level where water boils at 212°F. If you live or can at altitudes above 1,000 feet, you must adjust the processing time or pressure.

Altitude Adjustments

As altitude increases above sea level, water boils or steams at lower temperatures. Here's how to make altitude adjustments:

✢ BWB method: increase the processing time to compensate for the lower boiling point.

⚜ Steam-pressure canning method: increase the pressure to ensure the temperature inside the canner reaches 240°F.

The following table lists the adjustments you need to make at various altitudes for both canning methods and for both types of pressure gauges.

Altitude Adjustment Chart

Altitude (in feet)	Add Minutes to BWB Processing Time	Increase Pressure (weighted gauge)	Increase Pressure (dial gauge)
0–1,000	0	0	0
1,001–2,000	5	5	0
2,001–3,000	5	10	1
3,001–4,000	10	10	1
4,001–5,000	10	10	2
5,001–6,000	10	10	2
6,001–7,000	15	10	3
7,001–8,000	15	10	3
8,001–9,000	20	10	4
9,001–10,000	20	10	4

The following online tools can help you find the altitude for your location:

⚜ Download the free Google Earth app from google.com/earth. When you enter an address, the tool returns the latitude, longitude, and elevation.

⚜ Use the online U.S. Geological Survey Search Tool at viewer.nationalmap.gov/viewer/. When you enter an address, click the pull-down menu labeled "More," then select "Get Elevation."

Another way you can find the altitude where you live is to contact your local planning commission, zoning office, or Cooperative Extension office.

Misconceptions and Techniques to Avoid

Canning research is ongoing. In 2010, the U.S. government updated canning guidelines. In publications prior to 2010 and other sources such as online canning forums, you may find old techniques and misconceptions that are no longer recommended (or never were). Here are some common techniques to avoid:

⚜ **Do not use old recipes.** If you have a favorite old canning book or family recipe, consider using an alternate preservation method such as freezing.

✣ **Do not change tested recipes.** The only recommended changes you should make to tested recipes are to increase or decrease (but not eliminate) the sugar or the type of spices used. In canned pickle and relish recipes, never adjust the ratios of food, vinegar, water, and salt. You can always choose to ignore this advice, but do so at some risk.

✣ **Do not make up recipes.** How to formulate canning recipes depends on several factors, including acidity and ratio of solids to liquids. Instead of canning untested recipes, preserve some of the basic elements. For example, preserve tomato sauce, and make Grandma's special spaghetti sauce recipe using the tomato sauce, rather than canning her sauce.

✣ **Do not use litmus papers and pH meters.** The U.S. Food and Drug Administration (FDA) does not recommend testing pH in home canning to ensure adequate acidity. The pH is very recipe dependent, not stable during processing, and rises during storage. Tested recipes establish an initial acidity well below pH 4 and are also tested for a_w. Canning recipes may be verified safely only in a laboratory.

✣ **Do not use old-style jars.** Old canning-jar designs used wire bails with rubber gaskets and glass lids, or one-piece zinc with porcelain-lined caps. These old-style jars too often fail to seal properly. You can use old jars as containers for dried foods.

Older canning jar designs. Left: one-piece zinc with porcelain-lined caps; right: wire bails with rubber gaskets and glass lids. These old-style jars are no longer recommended.

✣ **Do not use open-kettle canning.** This old canning method boiled high-acid foods in an open kettle, and then sealed the hot product in hot jars without further processing. This method has been determined by testing to be unreliable.

✣ **Do not use steam canners.** Steam canners are a new type of boiling water canner that uses steam rather than boiling water to process jars. The processing times for steam canners have not been tested.

SPOILER ALERT

Don't confuse steam canners with steam-pressure canners. While both steam canners and pressure canners use steam heat, steam canners are not pressurized and operate well below 240°F. Furthermore, steam canners have not been tested for safe use; use a BWB canner instead. Only steam-pressure canners are safe for use for low-acid foods.

- **Do not use a microwave oven or a conventional oven as a processing method.** There are no safe methods for processing canned foods in either a microwave oven or conventional oven.

- **Do not use dishwashers as a processing method.** There are no safe methods for processing canned foods in a dishwasher.

It is important that you understand the difference between cooking and canning. These are two very different activities. Cooking is an art; canning is a science. The goal of canning is to preserve basic foods. I want you to enjoy canning and to stay safe and healthy. Keep your creative cooking activities *outside* the canning jar. Always use up-to-date guidelines and tested recipes, and follow procedures carefully.

Canning Equipment

Home canning requires special equipment, some of which you may already own. Canning kits, which include a BWB canner and enough tools to get you started, are an economical way to begin; kits start around $50. Steam-pressure canners are more expensive, and can double this initial cost. New glass jars with lids and screw bands cost between $8 and $12 per dozen, depending on jar size. New lids average just $3 per dozen.

Most of the equipment, except for the canning lids, is reusable from year to year. While there can be some initial investment, you will realize savings if you continue to can for several years.

The following sections describe the necessary canning equipment, as well as some equipment that makes food preparation tasks easier. Depending on the type of food or amount of canning that you want to do, there are many ways to make the tasks fast and fun.

Canners, Jars, and Lids

The following list is the canning equipment you must acquire in order to begin home canning.

Boiling water–bath (BWB) canner. If you can high-acid foods, use a BWB canner. The most common and least expensive type is made from enamel-covered steel and includes a jar rack and cover. If you have a flattop stove, be sure the canner you purchase is rated for your stove. However, you do not need a BWB. Any large, deep, covered stockpot that is at least 3 inches taller than your jars and allows at least 1 inch of water to circulate freely around the jars will work. You also need to add a rack to hold jars off the bottom. A pressure canner may also double as a BWB.

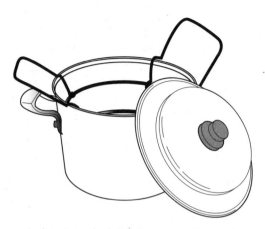

Boiling water–bath (BWB) canner with jar rack.

Steam-pressure canner. If you plan to can low-acid foods, you must use a pressure canner. There are two types: dial and weighted gauge. Today, the weighted gauge is more popular and slightly less expensive. The dial gauge is somewhat easier to use, but must be checked annually before each use by a qualified expert. You may have your dial gauge checked at a county Cooperative Extension office, or contact the manufacturer of your pressure canner. If you use a pressure cooker as a pressure canner, the cooker must be large enough to hold at least four 1-quart jars.

Pressure canners. From top left to right: dial gauge and pressure cooker;
bottom: weighted gauge.

Left: weighted gauge; right: dial gauge.

Jar rack. A jar rack ensures adequate heat penetration. It holds canning jars off the bottom of the pot, preventing breakage, and allows boiling water or steam heat to circulate under jars. A jar rack is included when you purchase either a BWB or pressure canner. A jar rack may also be fashioned from screw bands, foil, cake racks, or strips of wood.

Canning jars. Glass canning jars made from tempered glass have threaded tops that accept the two-piece closures. If you acquire used canning jars, be sure to check them for nicks around the rim or cracks along the sides and bottom, which can lead to canning failures. Canning jars may or may not be embossed with "Mason" or a manufacturer's name such as Ball, Atlas, or Kerr. However, all canning jars accept the two-piece closure. Do not use jars from commercially prepared products such as peanut butter, mayonnaise, or old designs.

Two-piece closures. The jar closure consists of a flat metal lid with a rubberlike sealing ring on one side and a metal screw band. You can reuse screw bands year after year, provided they are not bent or rusted and still screw easily onto the canning jar. You may remove screw bands after jars have cooled. Therefore, most people need only 1 or 2 dozen screw bands. However, you must purchase new, flat lids for each use.

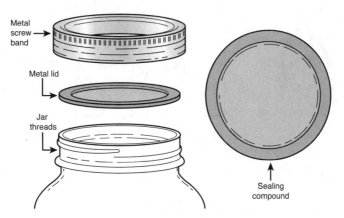

Metal screw band

Metal lid

Jar threads

Sealing compound

Two-piece canning lid, jar threads, and sealing ring.

Processing Equipment

Besides a canner, canning jars, and two-piece closures, there are a few essential tools you need to fill, process, and store canning jars correctly. The following list of equipment helps to ensure a smooth, accurate process and results in jars that form tight seals and are properly labeled. Most of these items are common in today's household kitchens.

Air-removal tool. After filling jars, you need to remove excess air trapped between food particles. You may already own a suitable implement, such as a narrow rubber spatula, a disposable plastic knife, or a plastic or wood chopstick. *Do not use metal utensils such as table knives because they can scratch and damage the glass.* You may purchase a specially designed air-removal tool at stores selling canning supplies. This tool often features markings to easily measure headspace.

Ruler. Check headspace using a common ruler, or an air-removal tool that includes this feature.

Sturdy tongs. Provide a safe way to lift empty jars and lids out of hot holding water.

Jar lifter. Used to transfer filled jars in and out of the canner safely. Regular tongs are not adequate for this task. A lifter is required if your rack does not suspend above the water, allowing you to transfer hot jars using potholders. Racks can be difficult to lift when fully loaded; many experienced canners consider a lifting tool a requirement.

Correct use of the jar lifting tool.

Wide-mouth funnel. The canning funnel fits snugly in the jar and makes it safe, quick, and clean to fill the jar with hot product.

Large ladle. Fills jars quickly and easily; an 8-ounce ladle is ideal for most sizes.

Magnetic wand. Easily retrieves flat metal lids from the hot holding water. My way is to put the flat lids inside the screw bands and immerse the two pieces together (bands facing up). Using regular tongs, you can easily grasp the edge of the screw band and bring the lid with it.

Slow cooker or saucepan. Holds canning lids in hot water; a slow cooker frees up burner space. As experienced canners know, the stovetop gets crowded during canning season!

Teakettle. Holds extra boiling water, which you may need to top off the canner or canning jars.

Potholders. Handle hot items safely using potholders.

Cloth towels or wood surfaces. Safe place to put hot jars after processing; protects jars from breakage and cools them slowly to form tight seals.

Paper towels. Dampened towels clean jar rims effectively; change frequently to keep the last jar as clean as the first.

Timer. Tracks processing times accurately.

Permanent marker. Use to label cooled jar lids with the contents and date before storage, or use other identification methods, such as jar labels.

In addition to the special canning and processing equipment, there are other helpful tools you may want to acquire. Which ones you need depends on the type and amount of product you wish to can and your skill in the kitchen.

General preparation equipment includes: a scale to weigh food, a vegetable peeler and scrub brush, colanders and strainers, cheesecloth for fine straining, nonreactive stirring tools (stainless steel or wood), nonreactive saucepans and stockpots (stainless steel or enamel), a steamer or wok for blanching, large bowls, sharp knives and cutting boards, measuring cups and spoons, and disposable gloves to protect hands when handling produce such as hot peppers.

In addition, there are many other tools that are by no means essential, but are handy to have for large batches requiring lots of chopping or slicing, or certain types of products such as applesauce or jelly.

Examples of these task-specific tools include: a fermenting crock, cider or wine press, bottle brush, jelly-straining bag, poultry shears, mandoline or vegetable slicer, meat or vegetable grinder, food mill or chinois, stand blender or hand (stick) blender, and food processor. In addition, there are many other task-specific tools such as a corn-kernel stripper, cherry or olive pitter, bean slicer, pea sheller, grapefruit spoon, and an apple peeler/corer.

In some cases, several forms of these tools are available, from hand-held tools to countertop models, as well as electric appliances.

Ingredients

You can preserve most foods by canning, including fruits, vegetables, meats, and fish. Besides whole foods like peaches, tomatoes, and green beans, you may choose from a delicious array of sauces, pickles, relish, jam, and soups to fill your larder and keep your family well nourished and happy.

To begin, select the best possible ingredients. We all like to save money, but while there are ways to cut costs, there are definitely mistakes you don't want to make when buying key ingredients. The following sections include expert tips that provide you with the best ways to save money and avoid pitfalls.

Foods That You Should Not Can

Some commercially canned foods may use processes that you cannot duplicate at home. Therefore, even if you find a jar or can of food in a store, you can't necessarily make it at home. One clue to whether it is safe to can a food is to look for a tested recipe from the USDA, an extension site, or a book published after 2010 that adheres to standards from these research groups.

Here is a general list of foods that you should not can:

- Untested recipes
- Untested fruits with unknown pH
- Thick products like mashed bananas and pumpkin or squash butter
- Infused oils (such as garlic oil, or oil with herbs)
- Breads or cakes
- Chocolate sauce

Many of these foods can be preserved some other way. For example, bananas, pumpkin butter, breads, and cakes may be frozen. Fruits with unknown pH may be dried or frozen. Untested recipes may be frozen, or might be freshly made from safe canned foods; for example, your family's special salsa or spaghetti sauce recipe can be freshly prepared from safely canned tomatoes and refrigerated for immediate use or frozen for longer storage.

Fruits and Vegetables

Choose quality fruits and vegetables if you want great canned products. Poor quality foods may spoil during storage, wasting the time you spent canning, as well as money. Consider these guidelines when you shop for or grow your own produce.

Choose locally grown produce in season. You will create the best canned foods from freshly harvested, locally grown, organic produce. If you don't grow your own fruits and vegetables, buy them from a farmers' market or farm stand, a community-supported agriculture program, or visit a "u-pick" farm. Supermarket produce is often several weeks out of the field, not always locally grown, and often chosen because it can stand up to mechanical harvest, long transport, and extended storage. It's great for eating fresh, but not ideal for preserving.

Choose suitable varieties. Some varieties of produce are better suited for canning or specific purposes. For example, roma or plum tomatoes make the best tomato sauce; these paste-type tomatoes have fewer seeds, less water, higher pectin, and more acidity and take less time to reduce for tomato sauces with good body. Juicy beefsteak and other salad tomatoes are best when enjoyed fresh. If you preserve peach halves, you probably want a freestone variety, with easy to remove stones or pits. Ask for recommendations from the farmers who grow the produce you are buying, or carefully read seed catalogs when planning your garden. These expert sources have the best information on varieties well suited to preserving.

Choose ripe or slightly underripe produce. You will make the best canned products when you buy produce that is firm and ripe or slightly underripe. Soft or overripe produce is best for eating fresh (quickly!) or freezing, but not for canning.

Choose good-quality produce. Choose produce free from insect damage or bruises. Be sure to trim thoroughly the occasional bruised or damaged area, which harbors microorganisms. You should not use badly damaged, moldy, or decaying produce for canning. Likewise, do not preserve produce from frost-killed plants, which may have low acidity. Instead, try freezing or fermenting.

Choose misshapen produce. You can save money by buying "seconds" that are misshapen. Just make sure the produce is firm, ripe, and otherwise of good quality.

PERFECT PRESERVING

If the available produce is not optimally suited for canning, consider other uses or methods of preservation. Commercially grown produce is intended for eating fresh any time of year, not preserving. Juicy tomatoes might be suitable for juice, but not tomato sauce. Bruised fruits might be suitable for fresh eating, if you trim and serve them promptly, or preserve by some other method, such as frozen jam or sauce. Overripe or badly bruised produce (trimmed of any decay) might be suitable for baked goods, such as zucchini or banana bread. Badly damaged, moldy, or decaying produce is suited only for the compost or worm bin.

Meat and Seafood

As with fruits and vegetables, the best quality canned meats and seafood come from fresh products that are handled properly and kept thoroughly chilled before processing. You cannot rescue poor quality products by canning. Consider these guidelines when you choose meat and seafood.

Choose fresh, not aged meat. Aged meat inherently has higher bacterial counts from the aging process. Aged meats are suitable for freezing, but not canning. Use fresh, commercially available meats or properly handled game.

Choose quality game. Game should always come from healthy animals, freshly killed, and carefully dressed. An animal that has a wounded intestinal tract, is not chilled after slaughter, or received careless field dressing is not a good choice for canning. This meat is more suitable for freezing.

Handle seafood properly. Clean your catch promptly. Avoid bruising and exposure to sun or heat. After the catch, bleed immediately to increase storage life. Within 2 hours, gut and rinse, and then ice, refrigerate, or freeze.

SPOILER ALERT

Dark tuna flesh has a strong flavor that overwhelms lighter meat; many prefer not to can dark tuna meat. Crabmeat takes on unacceptable flavors in canning, so it is recommended for freezing, not canning.

Chill before canning. Keep all meat and seafood well chilled until ready to can.

Keep ground meat very cold. Ground meat has a greater surface area, resulting in inherently higher bacteria counts. Take extra care to keep ground meat extremely cold during handling.

Thaw frozen foods completely. Meat or seafood that has been frozen needs to be completely thawed before canning. Cover meat and thaw only in the refrigerator, until no ice crystals remain.

Remove excess fat. Trim excess fat from meats and poultry. Excess fat may develop strong flavor or lead to seal failure. Poultry skin and bones may be included in the jar, if desired. Fatty fish and its skin may be included in the jar, if desired.

Soak game meat briefly in salted water. Wild game has strong flavors that may intensify in canned products. Soak game meat for 1 hour in cold water containing 1 tablespoon canning, table, or kosher salt per quart. Rinse meat under clean, running water before proceeding with canning. Otherwise, do not allow meat to stand in water.

Smoked seafood requires special processing. Smoked seafood is processed differently than other foods, so take extra care and use a tested recipe.

Sugar Syrups

Since acid is the key factor that prevents spoilage, you can adjust sugar to taste when canning fruits. Sugar helps retain shape, color, and flavor, but is not a safety factor in canned fruit. In fact, you may also pack fruit without sugar, using plain water or unsweetened juices.

Sugar syrups range from very light (10 percent sugar), to very heavy (50 percent sugar). The following table lists the amount of water and sugar to make 1 cup of any style syrup, from very light to very heavy. Honey or corn syrup may replace up to half of the sugar.

Sugar Syrup Formulas to Make 1 Cup

Syrup Type	Cups Water	Cups Sugar*
Very light (10%)	$1\frac{1}{8}$ cups	2 TB. ($\frac{1}{8}$ cup)
Light (20%)	1 cup	$\frac{1}{4}$ cup
Medium (30%)	$\frac{3}{4}$ cup	$\frac{1}{3}$ cup
Heavy (40%)	$\frac{3}{4}$ cup	$\frac{1}{2}$ cup
Very heavy (50%)	$\frac{2}{3}$ cup	$\frac{2}{3}$ cup

You may replace half of the sugar in any formula with an equal measure of honey or corn syrup. For example, for 10 percent syrup, use $1\frac{1}{8}$ cups water, 1 tablespoon sugar, and 1 tablespoon honey or corn syrup. For a 50 percent syrup, use $\frac{2}{3}$ cup water, $\frac{1}{3}$ cup sugar, and $\frac{1}{3}$ cup honey or corn syrup.

An average of $\frac{3}{4}$ cup syrup is needed per pint jar and $1\frac{1}{2}$ cups per quart jar. For a 7-pint canner load, you need about 5 cups syrup; for 7 quarts, about $10\frac{1}{2}$ cups.

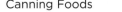

PERFECT PRESERVING

It is not necessary to can fruit in sugar syrup, but sugar does help it retain color, flavor, and shape. Therefore, fruit canned in water or unsweetened juice may turn brown, bland, or mushy. To overcome these issues, be sure to: can fully ripe fruit, use the hot-pack method, pretreat fruit for browning, add spices to canning liquids, and add a sugar substitute after canned fruit is opened for use.

Fruit-Pickling Syrups

In addition to sugar syrup, you may pack canned fruits in sweet-tart syrup to make fruit pickles. These pickling solutions use vinegar in addition to water and sugar. Fruit pickles can range from tart and tangy, to delicate and sweet.

Fruit-Pickling Syrups to Make About 1 Cup

Syrup Type	Sugar	Vinegar	Water	Fruits to Pickle
Tart	¼ cup	1 cup	None	Berries, stone fruits, figs
Tangy	⅔ cup	⅔ cup	¼ cup	Berries, stone fruits, figs
Mellow	½ cup	⅓ cup	¼ cup	Stone fruits, figs
Delicate	½ cup	¼ cup	¼ cup	Stone fruits, figs, apples, pears, tropical fruits
Sweet	¾ cup	¼ cup	¼ cup	Stone fruits, pome fruits, grapes
Very sweet	½ cup	1 TB.	¼ cup	Pome fruits, tart fruits: cranberries, sour cherries, lemons, quinces, rhubarb

Add spices to flavor the syrup, if desired. Start with ¼ teaspoon ground spices, ¾ teaspoon whole spices, or ½ stick cinnamon per cup of syrup. Use spices alone (such as cinnamon or cloves), or combined in a commercially prepared blend (such as ground pumpkin pie spices or whole pickling spices), or your own custom blend. Try combining 1 teaspoon ground cinnamon, ½ teaspoon ground ginger, and ¼ teaspoon each ground clove and nutmeg or allspice.

POME FRUITS

Pome fruits include apples, crabapples, pears, quinces, Asian pears (*nashi*), and loquats. What these fruits have in common is a tough core encasing a group of small seeds. The core is surrounded by a fleshy edible layer. Pomes can be preserved in many ways, such as dried leathers, canned fruits, jams, and sauces.

Sugar-Free Liquids and Sugar Substitutes

When you plan to pack fruit in water or unsweetened juice, be sure to choose fully ripe fruit and use the hot-pack method. Underripe fruit tends to float above the liquid during storage. Hot packing removes more air and prevents floating.

Many types of 100 percent juice are available to pack fruits; commercially bottled unsweetened apple, pineapple, or white grape juices work well for most fruits. You may also squeeze juice from fresh fruit.

Sugar substitutes, especially saccharin and aspartame, are usually not successful for use in canning. The general recommendation is to pack fruits in water or unsweetened juice, and add your choice of artificial sweetener at serving time. Various sugar substitutes exhibit different problems, including loss of sweetening power, bitterness, and aftertaste.

Sucralose, such as the brand Splenda, has fewer negative effects than other artificial sweeteners and offers the most hope for palatable canned fruit. You can substitute sucralose for sugar when making sugar syrup. A suggested approach is to begin with very light syrup and can only 1 or 2 quarts. If you prefer sweeter fruit, then test increasingly sweeter syrups until you find the concentration that satisfies your sweet tooth.

Fruit Pectins

Pectin, the substance that makes jams and jellies thick, occurs naturally in most fruits. To make pectin gel, you need to cook it with sugar and acid. The amount of pectin and acid varies with the type of fruit and its degree of ripeness. As fruit ripens, pectin levels decrease.

When making old-fashioned cooked jams and jellies without added pectin, combine $\frac{1}{4}$ underripe with $\frac{3}{4}$ fully ripe fruit. This will help to ensure sufficient pectin for a thick gel, as well as best flavor.

The ability of a fruit to gel depends on not only the pectin, but also the acid. Different varieties of the same fruit can exhibit very different pectin and acid levels. The following table summarizes pectin and acid levels in common fruits.

Pectin and Acid Contents of Fruits for Jam Making

	High Acid	Low Acid
High pectin	Apple peels and underripe apples	Ripe apples
	Underripe blackberries	Ripe blackberries
	Crabapples	Sour cherries
	Cranberries	Chokecherries
	Currants	Ripe loganberries
	Gooseberries	Ripe guava
	Grapes (wine, eastern Concord)	Bottled grape juice
	Grapefruit	Table grapes
	Underripe guava	Loquats
	Lemons	Melons
	Underripe loganberries	Quince
	Sour oranges	Ripe plums
	Underripe plums	
	Pomegranates	
Low pectin	Combine with high-pectin fruits: apricots, sweet cherries, figs, kiwis, pineapples, rhubarb, strawberries	Combine with high-pectin fruits and acid: peaches, pears, raspberries, elderberries, blueberries

You can use the information in this table as a guide when choosing fruits to make jam or jelly without commercial pectin. Ideally, you want to combine fruits to achieve both high pectin and high acid. If the fruit contains pectin but is low in acid, combine it with high-acid fruit or an acid such as lemon juice. For example, combine ripe guava with chopped pineapple, oranges, or lemon juice.

For fruits low in pectin, you need to combine them with a high-pectin fruit or add pectin (either commercial or homemade). For example, combine apricots with orange juice or add commercial pectin. Likewise, combine blueberries with blackberries or combine pears with quince and lemon juice.

To test fruit for natural pectin, place $\frac{1}{2}$ cup chopped fruit in a small saucepan. Add 2 tablespoons water, cover pan, and heat over medium heat for 5 to 8 minutes, or until fruit is soft. Mash the fruit with a fork or spoon. Strain the liquid to perform one of the following tests:

> ⚜ **Cooking test:** In a small saucepan, add $\frac{1}{3}$ cup fruit juice and $\frac{1}{4}$ cup sugar. Place over medium heat, and stir constantly until sugar is dissolved. Raise heat to high, bring mixture to a boil, and boil rapidly until it passes the spoon or sheet test. Pour jelly into a clean glass or ceramic bowl and allow to cool. If the mixture gels, the fruit juice contains enough natural pectin to make jelly. If not, use a recipe calling for added pectin.

⁂ **Alcohol test:** In a jar with a lid, add 1 tablespoon juice and 1 tablespoon of 70 percent rubbing alcohol, close and shake gently to mix thoroughly. Let stand for 1 minute. Fruit with high-pectin content will form one jellylike mass. If juice forms into several small lumps, it has medium pectin. If it shows lots of little lumps, there is not enough pectin for jelly. Caution: do not taste solution and be sure to discard after testing.

⁂ **Jelmeter test:** A jelmeter is a graduated glass tube with an opening at each end. The rate of flow of fruit juice through the tube gives a rough estimate of its jellying power. It can help you decide how much sugar to use to make a thick jam or jelly. You can buy a jelmeter where canning supplies are sold.

The easy, modern method for making jam and jelly simply adds commercially manufactured pectin. These products reliably produce thick jams and jellies and eliminate guesswork. They are available in powdered and liquid forms. When using commercial pectin, be sure to follow the instructions included in the package; they are not interchangeable.

To take some of the guesswork out of old-fashioned jam making, you can also add homemade pectin to any fruit when you want to make jam. Working with natural pectin to make jams and jellies takes practice but can be fun and rewarding. For more information on making and using homemade pectin, see Chapter 19.

Pickling Solutions

There are two types of canned pickles: Quick-process pickles are vegetables that are immersed in acidified brine (salt dissolved in water with vinegar added). The other type is fermented pickles, which are cured in brine to raise the acidity to a safe level by the activity of lactic acid bacteria (LAB). For more information about fermenting, see Chapter 3. Either quick-process or fermented pickles, when made from a tested recipe, may be processed in a BWB.

Alternatively, quick pickles that have unknown acidity and are not heat processed may be stored in the refrigerator. Not surprisingly, we call these *refrigerator pickles.* This method is useful if you have a favorite family recipe for pickles from an untested recipe. Simply make a small batch and enjoy them from the fridge. For more information about making refrigerator pickles, see Chapter 4.

As when canning fruits, the sugar and spices in pickle recipes may be increased or decreased. For a low-salt or salt-free pickle, be sure to use canning recipes especially formulated for this purpose, or make a small batch of refrigerator pickles.

Salts

You must always use canning (also called pickling) salt in pickling solutions for quick-process pickles or when brining naturally fermented pickles. Canning salt is pure and does not contain ingredients found in other salts that cloud pickling solutions or inhibit fermentation. You can buy canning salt at most supermarkets or locations that sell canning supplies.

Salts that contain anticaking ingredients or minerals are not recommended for any kind of processed pickle. This includes table salt, sea salt (regular, coarse, or flake), and iodized salt. These salts can cloud pickling solutions, darken pickles, or adversely affect the flavor.

Preparing to Can

In the previous sections, you learned about the science behind the canning process, necessary equipment, and ingredients. In the next few sections, I explain the process in detail and help you to discover that you *can* can!

If you are new to canning, you will want to refer to this chapter frequently. Don't worry, it takes a few projects to get familiar with the steps; even I need to be reminded of some of the details. If you are an experienced canner, you will appreciate the ability to get a refresher on any procedure, particularly at the beginning of a new canning season.

PERFECT PRESERVING

In Part 2, you will find many tested recipes, and many others are available at your local library or by download from extension agencies and research universities through the National Center for Home Food Preservation website. Check out Appendix C for a list of resources.

Probably the biggest mistake people make when canning for the first time is buying too much produce. A bushel of produce (40 to 50 pounds) makes for a very long day in the kitchen. Even the most seasoned canner may cringe at that much washing, cutting, jarring, and boiling. Fifty pounds of cucumbers is a lot of pickles to store and eat!

In fact, you can buy as little as 2 pounds of fruits or vegetables and have your first canned product finished in a couple of hours. Two to three pounds of produce will fill 1 quart or 2 pint jars. For some items—such as pickles, relish, or jam—that's all you and your family may want or need for an entire year. Think about it. How much jam does your family eat in a year, or in a month?

Today's devoted canners report that they preserve no more than 20 quarts of any one food, such as peaches or green beans. For prepared products such as jam, pickles, and relish, 20 *pints* is the maximum. Furthermore, for more than half of us, we preserve *less than half of these amounts*—10 quarts or 10 pints.

One canner load can hold a maximum of 7 quarts and requires 15 to 20 pounds of produce (about 1 box or *lug,* or less than half a bushel). Unless you are canning a food that you know your family eats with great frequency, then somewhere between 5 to 10 quarts of any food is a more realistic goal. This translates to somewhere between 10 and 30 pounds of produce. Ten pounds of pickles sounds a lot more doable than 50, doesn't it?

Now that we've whittled down the size of the average canning job, let's review the process in more detail.

Make a Plan

Canning is more fun and successful when you take the time to make a plan. The first tasks at the beginning of any canning project are to check equipment and supplies, choose a recipe, and assess what ingredients you need.

Check equipment. Check that you have all of the required canning equipment, and that it is in working condition. There is nothing worse than getting halfway through a project and finding out that you are missing something essential. For dial-gauge pressure canners, have the gauge tested every year before the start of a new canning season. For all pressure canners, inspect the gasket and any other movable parts and replace anything not in top condition. If your BWB canner has become rusted or bent, get a new one.

Check jars and screw bands. Check the condition of jars and screw bands (also called *rings*). Discard cracked or chipped jars and rusted or bent rings. Purchase new jars or screw bands as needed.

SPOILER ALERT

Use only tempered-glass canning jars that accept two-piece canning lids and screw bands. Jars that are not tempered break easily during processing and cooling. Do not recycle jars from commercially prepared foods such as mayonnaise, peanut butter, jam, or any other store-bought product. These jars aren't designed to accept the two-piece canning closure, which is required to form the vacuum seal necessary for safe canned foods.

Buy new lids. *Always use new lids when canning.* It is also best practice to buy only enough lids for one season. I try to end the year with less than one box. Although you may store new canning lids for 2 to 3 years, the longer they are stored the greater the chance of seal failure when you finally use them.

Check the harvest calendar. Find out when locally grown fruits and vegetables are available in your area. Create a rough schedule for the produce you want to preserve.

Choose tested recipes. Use tested recipes that are safe for canning. Read the recipe carefully and make sure you have the necessary equipment and supplies.

Purchase the ingredients. Before you buy produce or meat, purchase any other ingredients (like sugar, pickling salt, or ascorbic acid) and any other necessary equipment (jars, lids, and supplies). There is nothing worse than buying fresh food and finding out the store just ran out of jars or lids, and spending the day hunting down supplies while your produce wilts.

Select suitable foods. Carefully read the canning recipe to find out what foods you need to buy. Select a variety that is suitable for your canning task and at its peak of freshness.

Prepare Jars, Screw Bands, and Lids

Before any canning project, inspect and clean the canning jars and screw bands. Always heat jars before filling to reduce the chance of breakage. Here are some tips:

- **Select sound jars.** Select tempered-glass canning jars of the size specified in a tested recipe. Examine jars for cracks and run your finger around the rim to check for nicks. Discard any jars with cracks or nicks.

- **Select usable screw bands.** Inspect the bands before every use. Discard ones that are rusted, bent, or don't screw easily onto jar threads.

- **Wash jars and screw bands.** Use detergent to wash jars and screw bands by hand in hot water, rinse well, and drain; or wash them in an automatic dishwasher.

- **Keep jars hot.** Use the rinse and hold cycle in an automatic dishwasher; or plan to heat the jars in the canner when you set it up. Hot jars prevent breakage when you fill them with hot product (hot pack) or hot liquid (raw pack or hot pack).

- **Keep screw bands clean.** Set clean screw bands aside in a bowl or container to keep them clean. Using a container makes it easy to transport the screw bands to the workspace or get them out of the way quickly.

- **Keep canning lids hot.** Place new, unused lids in a pan and cover with water. Bring to a simmer (180°F to 190°F) over high heat. Cover pan and adjust heat to keep lids in simmering water until ready to use. Do not boil lids, it may damage the rubber sealing ring and cause seal failure. Note: A slow cooker set on high heat typically maintains a temperature of 180°F to 190°F and can be a convenient way to keep lids hot, as well as free up space on the stove.

I always heat a big teakettle of water at this time; when it boils, turn the heat down to low and keep it available in case you need to add water to the jars, lids, canner, or for any other purpose.

Now that the jars, screw bands, and lids are ready to go, it's time for you to prepare the canner.

PERFECT PRESERVING

One easy way to retrieve canning lids from a hot holding bath is to nestle each lid inside a screw band and place both in the hot water, band facing up. When retrieving a lid, grasp the edge of the screw band with tongs and bring the lid up with the band. Drain the excess water into the holding bath, and flip the screw band and lid onto a clean towel. Fill the jar and clean the rim. Put the lid in place. The screw band has usually cooled sufficiently to be safely secured over the lid by screwing down firmly. Alternatively, purchase and use a magnetic wand to retrieve flat lids from the hot holding bath. Keep screw bands clean and dry in a separate container.

Prepare a BWB Canner

It takes 30 to 60 minutes after setup for a BWB canner to heat up and be ready for filled jars. Review the recipe to decide when to set up the canner. If your recipe requires several hours of peeling, chopping, or soaking, you don't want the canner heating, if you are still several hours away from using it. However, the canner should wait for the jars; the jars should never wait for the canner.

Here are the steps to prepare a BWB canner:

1. The canner must be clean and in good condition or it may contribute to canning failures. If it is bent or rusted, replace it. If it's dirty or dusty, wash it with soap and water, rinse it well, and dry the outside. Place a jar rack inside the canner.

2. I usually put the clean, empty canning jars in the canner at this time. Whether you are using raw pack or hot pack, jars are always hot. So fill each clean jar with fresh, hot tap water, and place it in the canner. The alternative is to put the jars in the dishwasher. If they are clean, run a heated rinse/hold cycle. If they are dirty, put them through a wash cycle, and then hold on a heated cycle.

3. With or without water-filled jars in it, fill the canner about half-full with clean, hot tap water. This may be too much for quart jars, but I find it easier to put in too much, rather than too little, water. With experience, you will learn to adjust as needed.

4. Take care when hoisting the canner full of jars and water; get help if you need it. Place the canner over a large burner, put the lid on, and turn the heat on high.

5. Heat the water to 140°F if you are using raw pack and 180°F if you are using hot pack. When the water reaches temperature, turn the heat down to maintain it.

Now that you have the BWB canner, jars, screw bands, and lids ready, it's time to prepare the food for processing, using the recipe you have chosen. Visit these hot items occasionally, and check that everything is still at the proper temperature.

WHY AND WHEN TO STERILIZE JARS

Recent testing has determined that canning process times of 10 minutes or longer adequately sterilize the jars. Therefore, recipes in this book are standardized to a minimum of 10 minutes. If you have recipes for jams, jellies, and pickled products listing less than 10 minutes process time, you need to sterilize the jars before you fill them with product. To sterilize empty jars, put them right side up on the rack in a BWB canner. Fill the canner and jars with hot tap water to 1 inch above the tops of the jars. Boil 10 minutes (at 0 to 1,000 feet elevation). Hold sterilized jars in a hot water bath until ready for filling. If you put them back in a cupboard, they are no longer sterilized.

Prepare a Steam-Pressure Canner

Check the vent pipe before every use and make sure that it is not blocked. It takes about 30 minutes for a steam-pressure canner to heat up and be ready for filled jars. Review the recipe to decide the best time to set up the canner. The canner should wait for the jars; the jars should never wait for the canner.

Here are the steps to prepare a pressure canner:

1. Make sure the pressure canner is clean and in good working condition. Annually inspect and replace working parts as needed; have the dial gauge verified if you use one. If it's dirty or dusty, wash it with soap and water, rinse it well, and dry the outside.

2. Fill the canner with hot tap water as specified by the manufacturer. Usually the water is 2 to 3 inches deep, unless the manufacturer or the specific recipe you are using calls for a different amount. Longer processes require more water. Place the jar rack in the canner. Place the pressure canner on a large burner.

3. I usually put the clean, empty canning jars in the canner at this time. Whether you are using raw pack or hot pack, jars are always hot. Put enough clean, hot tap water in each jar to keep it from floating on the water, and place it on the rack inside the canner. You can also use your dishwasher to keep jars hot in the dishwasher. If they are clean, run a heated rinse/hold cycle. If they are dirty, put them through a wash cycle and hold on a heated cycle.

4. Be sure to inspect and clear the vent, if you have not already done so. Put the lid on loosely during the preheating phase so you don't build up pressure in the canner at this time. Turn the heat on high.

5. Heat the water to 140°F if you are using raw pack and 180°F if you are using hot pack. When the water reaches temperature, turn the heat down to maintain it. Be careful not to boil the water or heat it long enough without a cover to cause evaporation that decreases the water depth in the pressure canner.

Now that you have the pressure canner, jars, screw bands, and lids ready, it's time to prepare the food for processing, using the recipe you have chosen. Visit these hot items occasionally, and check that everything is still at the proper temperature.

Filling Jars

All jars need to be hot before filling with product. For hot-pack food, all ingredients are hot, including solids and liquids. For raw-packed foods, the jar and canning liquid are hot, even though the product is raw and cold.

Be sure to fill, close, and replace jars in the canner one at a time, before you begin another jar. This keeps the jars and product hot, and keeps your timing accurate. Following this rule helps to reduce jar breakage and ensures good vacuum seals and safely canned foods.

Add Product to Jars

After you fill the jar, adjust the headspace, clean the rim, secure the canning lid, and replace it in the canner, before you fill another jar. Here are the steps:

1. Using tongs or a jar lifter, carefully lift one jar from the canner and tilt to drain the hot water back into the canner. Place the hot, drained, empty jar on a folded towel.

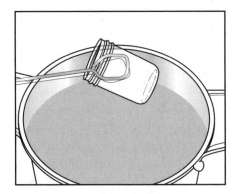 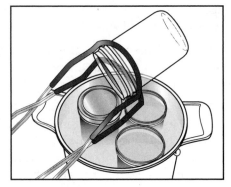

Retrieving hot jars from the boiling water bath with tongs (left) and a jar lifter (right).

2. Use a wide-mouthed funnel and ladle to fill jars to the approximate headspace (listed in the recipe). Too little is easier than too much; you will adjust the headspace next. The filling technique is slightly different for thick, uniform foods than solid/liquid foods.

    • For raw-packed products such as peach halves, asparagus spears, or brined fish, first add the solids to the jar by hand until they are filled to just below the threaded neck. Use a wide funnel to add liquid to the approximate headspace.

    • For hot-pack products in large pieces—such as peach halves or whole tomatoes—use a large spoon, which tends to work better than a ladle. Add solids until they are just below the threaded neck. Use a wide funnel to add liquid to the approximate headspace.

    • For hot-pack, combination solid/liquid products that can be ladled easily—such as cut, chopped, or sliced fruits and vegetables—use a wide funnel and ladle solids with some liquid until the solids are just below the threaded neck. Then add liquid only to the approximate headspace.

    • For hot, uniform products such as jam, relish, sauce, or juice, ladle product using a wide funnel. Fill to the approximate headspace and remove the funnel.

After the product has been added, you remove the funnel and adjust the headspace to the exact amount specified in the recipe.

Adjust Headspace

After you fill the jar with product, you need to remove trapped air. Removing air tends to lower the level of product in the jar. This means you have to add a little more product, until level is at the exact headspace specified in the recipe.

1. If you have not already done so, remove the wide funnel. Place a thin, nonmetallic tool on the inside of the jar rim. *Note: Do not use metal utensils such as knives because they can scratch the glass, resulting in jar breakage.*

2. Slide the tool down the inside of the jar all the way to the bottom. Tilt it toward the center of the jar, compressing the food gently to release trapped air. Air bubbles may not be visible; however, air that is trapped between pieces of food is removed by this process.

Remove trapped air from jar.

3. Pull the tool back out of the jar. Repeat the process in three to four different places around the inside of the jar.

4. Use a ruler or markings on an air-removal tool to check the headspace as required by the recipe. Add or remove liquid or product with a small, clean spoon as needed.

Correct headspace is more important than it seems. Headspace allows for product expansion during processing and ensures a good vacuum seal as the product cools. Eliminating this step can result in poor quality, discolored foods—or worse, seal failures, and unsafe or spoiled food.

After you have corrected the headspace, you need to clean the rim before closing the jar.

Clean the Rim

After filling jars and checking headspace, it is common to have gotten some food or liquid on the jar rim. You must clean the rim before putting the lid on the jar:

1. Use a clean, dampened paper towel and wipe the jar rim to remove any trace of product or liquid.

2. Refold or change the towel frequently so the last jar is as clean as the first. Water, pickling liquid, sugar syrup, or any other deposits on the jar rim will prevent a good vacuum seal from forming.

Take care not to introduce water by using a wet, rather than damp, towel. I usually use a half-damp, half-dry towel, wiping first with the damp side and then with the dry side. I use one towel, rather than two, so I don't have to pick up and put down multiple towels (and keep track of them). This may seem obsessive, but using just one towel can save quite a bit of time. It's a good trick to know when you have a lot of canning to do.

After cleaning the rim, immediately close the jar with a two-piece lid.

Secure the Lid

Be sure to fill, close, and replace jars in the canner one at a time before you begin another jar. Here are the steps:

1. Immediately after cleaning the rim, retrieve a flat lid from the hot holding water.

2. Place the flat lid, sealing ring facing down, briefly on a clean folded towel to remove excess water. Then place the lid on the jar with the sealing ring facing down on the rim.

3. Place a metal screw band over the flat lid and screw it down until you feel resistance and the band is firm and fingertip tight. Do not overtighten. Excessive force may actually prevent the jar from sealing properly.

To keep the jars and product hot, and your processing time accurate, place the jar in the canner after securing the lid.

Place Filled Jar in Canner

Place the jar into the canner immediately after filling and before beginning another one. This important rule helps to reduce jar breakage, and ensure good vacuum seals and safely canned foods:

1. The canner should already contain hot water. Use a jar lifter to place a filled jar into the canner. Make sure to position the lifter securely below the threaded neck of the jar (under the lip, below the screw band). Keep the jar upright at all times; tilting the jar can cause food to seep onto the rim and prevent the jar from sealing properly.

2. If you forget, and start another jar, it's okay to put a closed jar back in the canner if it is still hot.

Again, fill jars one at a time. If you fill all the jars at once, the first jar may cool off too much while waiting for other jars to be filled. The processing time is not accurate for cooler jars, or a cool jar may crack when you put it back into the hot water.

SPOILER ALERT

Do not fill jars all at once and then increase the process time a little to compensate if jars cool off too much. Also, do not start with a cold water bath. You must begin with hot jars and a hot water bath whether you are using the raw-pack or hot-pack method. At best, these little shortcuts can lead to uncertain foods; at worst, the foods may be unsafe and make you sick, or spoil and waste your time and money.

After you have replaced all the jars in the canner, immediately begin processing.

Processing Canned Foods

The processing steps for BWB canning and steam-pressure canning are slightly different. In BWB canning, you cover the jars with boiling water, and then boil them for a specified length of time—it's essentially a one-step process. For pressure canning, the canner must be pressurized before the timing can begin, so it is a two-step process.

BWB Canner Process

After you have filled all of the jars with product and put them in hot water in the canner, you boil them for the time specified in your recipe. These steps describe in detail how to complete the BWB canning process:

1. After all the jars have been filled and placed in the BWB canner, check and adjust the water level. The jars need to be covered with water by 1 to 2 inches above the tops of the jars. If necessary, add hot water to the canner to cover the jars by at least 1 inch. If the processing time will be longer than 20 minutes, use 2 inches to compensate for evaporation. In addition, there needs to be another 1 to 2 inches of space above the water. This extra space allows for a full, rolling boil without too much water being thrown from the pot and uncovering the jars. Canners are designed to allow for this amount of water. If you are using a stockpot, you need to verify sufficient height before you use it for the first time.

2. Place the lid to cover the BWB canner partially. Raise heat to high and bring the water to a full rolling boil. You may lower the heat slightly to reduce boil over, but you must make sure to maintain a full rolling boil for the entire processing time required by the recipe.

3. After the water has come to a full boil, and you have adjusted the heat to maintain it, set a timer for the number of processing minutes called for in the recipe. If you are at an altitude above 1,000 feet, make sure you increase the time correctly. Note: You must follow processing times according to each recipe; they are not interchangeable. Processing time depends on a number of factors, including type of product, food acidity, how the product is packed, and jar size.

4. During processing, check the boiling water every few minutes. It is a good idea to have ready a teakettle of boiling water, in case it is needed:

   - If the water ceases boiling during processing, raise the heat, bring the water back to a full boil, and begin the timing period again.

   - If the water level has dropped to less than 1 inch above the jars, add boiling water slowly to the canner until there is at least 1 inch above the jars. If the water ceases boiling during this time, see the previous step.

After the timer goes off, turn off the heat. The next step is to cool the canner.

Steam-Pressure Canner Process

After you have filled all of the jars with product and put them in the hot water in the canner, you pressurize the canner. Once the canner is pressurized, you process them for the time specified in your recipe. These steps describe in detail how to complete the pressure-canning process:

1. After all of the jars have been filled and placed in the pressure canner, secure the lids. *Note: The canner should already have 2 to 3 inches of hot water (or the level called for in the recipe).* Leave the weight off of the vent port (weighted-gauge model) or open the petcock (dial-gauge model).

2. Raise heat to high until water boils and steam flows freely in a funnel shape from the open vent port or petcock. Leave the heat at its highest setting and set a timer for 10 minutes. Let the steam exhaust for 10 minutes to remove air from the canner and allow the pressure to build.

3. After exhausting the canner, close the petcock (dial-gauge model), or place the correct counter-weight on the vent port (weighted-gauge model). The canner will begin to pressurize.

   - For a dial-gauge model, decrease the heat slightly as the canner comes within 2 pounds of the target pressure, and decrease heat again to maintain the correct pressure when it reaches the desired setting.

   - For a weighted-gauge model, decrease the heat slightly when steam begins to escape or to maintain the jiggle or rocking described by the manufacturer of the canner that the correct pressure has been reached. For some weighted models, this might mean rocking a minimum number of times per minute, and for others it may mean a constant rocking. Check the instructions for your pressure canner.

4. When the correct pressure has been established, set a timer for the time specified in the recipe. *Note: Processing pressure and time must be followed according to each recipe and are not interchangeable. Processing time depends on a number of factors, including type of product, food acidity, how the product is packed, and jar size.*

5. Adjust the heat as needed to maintain, or be slightly above, the correct pressure for the full amount of time required by the recipe. If at any time pressure falls below the required level, raise the heat, bring the canner back up to the required pressure, and begin the timing period again.

After the timer goes off, turn off the heat. The next step is to cool the canner.

Cooling Canners and Jars

Proper canner cooling is part of an accurate canning process. Never shorten the cooling time or try to speed it up by adding cold water or other methods. The procedure for cooling the canner is detailed in the following sections. The steps are different for each type of canner.

Cool a BWB Canner

Cooling a BWB canner is very straightforward. Follow these steps:

1. When the processing time is complete, turn off the heat.

2. Remove the BWB canner cover carefully to avoid being burned. Lift the lid up toward you, using it as a shield between you and the steam rising from the pot.

3. Set a timer for 5 minutes and allow the contents to cool.

After the timer goes off, the next step is to cool the jars.

Cool a Steam-Pressure Canner

Depressurizing is part of the pressure-canning process. Never shorten the cooling time by putting the pressure canner in cold water or any other method. Forced cooling can result in underprocessed, unsafe product, and can seriously damage the pressure canner. Remember: no shortcuts. Follow these steps:

1. When the processing time is complete, turn off the heat. On electric stoves, remove the canner from the burners only if it can be moved safely by lifting, not sliding.

2. Allow the pressure canner to cool naturally.

   • For dial-gauge models, wait until the gauge returns to zero. After depressurization is complete, open the petcock and wait 10 minutes.

   • For weighted-gauge models, wait the amount of time specified in the instructions for your model—which is usually in the range of 30 to 60 minutes and depends on the size of the canner as well as the size of the jars. After the required time has passed, nudge the weighted gauge; if it does not produce any steam or resistance, the pressure has reached zero. Newer models may have pressure indicators or locks that prevent opening canners until they are completely depressurized. If your model is older, proceed carefully. After depressurization is complete, remove the weight from the vent port and wait 10 minutes.

3. Unfasten and remove the cover carefully to avoid being burned. Lift the cover up toward you, using it as a shield between you and any steam rising from the pot.

After opening the steam-pressure canner, the next step is to cool the jars.

Cool the Jars

Proper jar cooling is an important part of the canning process. During cooling, the vacuum seal is formed. A tight seal keeps the product stable at room temperature. Follow these steps:

1. After the canner has cooled properly, you may remove the jars. Transfer jars safely, using a jar lifter. Position the lifter securely below the neck of the jar (under the lip; below the screw band). Keep the jar upright at all times; tilting can cause food to seep into the rim and prevent a seal from forming. Do not be concerned about excess water on the lid, it will usually evaporate completely, or can be wiped away later if it doesn't.

2. Place jars at least 1 inch apart on a dry towel or wood surface away from drafts. Cool the jars naturally for 12 to 24 hours.

3. During the cooling process, you may hear a popping or pinging noise as the jars form a vacuum and seal. However, the seal is not complete until the jars have cooled completely. Let jars cool undisturbed to ensure a complete vacuum seal. *Note: During the cooling process, do not touch the lids, remove the bands, or move or tilt the jars for at least 12 hours—preferably 24 hours.*

After the jars have cooled for 12 to 24 hours, the next step is to check the seal, clean, label, and store the canned foods.

Storing Canned Foods

After the jars have cooled for at least 12 to 24 hours, check the seal on each jar before storing. There are two ways to verify a proper seal. I always do both methods on each jar:

+ Press the center of the lid. A properly sealed lid is tight and does not flex up and down when pressed.

+ Remove the screw band. With the band removed, hold the jar steady and try to lift the lid off using your fingertips. If you cannot lift the lid off by pulling on the lid, the seal is good.

If jars do not have a good seal, you have two choices:

+ Reprocess the jar. To do this, open the jar, use the same raw-pack or hot-pack method with a clean jar, and process the jar again for the full amount of time. Reprocessing runs the risk of overcooking the food.

+ Refrigerate the unsealed jar and use the food promptly.

If you follow procedures carefully, seal failures are relatively rare—perhaps one or two in a busy canning season. If your rate is higher, review the information for buying and preparing lids, as well as filling, cleaning, checking headspace in, and closing the jars.

BEST CANNING PRACTICES

Never take shortcuts and always follow best practices when canning. These steps ensure good vacuum seals and safe canned foods. *Best practices* means to always maintain equipment in good working condition, keep the work area sanitary, use a tested recipe, and follow all instructions. When filling jars, remove trapped air to ensure accurate headspace, clean the rim before adding the lid, properly secure the lid with the screw band (not too tight), process at the right heat or pressure for the full amount of time, and cool jars completely. Finally, store foods properly, and consume them within 1 year.

Once you've checked the seals, it's time to store the jars. If you have not already done so, remove the screw band. Use a clean, damp towel to wipe each jar clean, including the bottom, sides, threads, and lid. If there is a lot of sticky deposit (such as sugar syrup) on the jar threads, it is sometimes easier to rinse it under warm running water. Dry the jar. Label each jar with the product and date (for example, "Peaches V. lt. syrup Aug. 2013"). Alternatively, you can label the storage shelf, and place the relevant jars in a row behind the label.

The ideal location for canned foods is clean, dry, and cool, preferably where the temperature ranges from 50°F to 70°F. Properly stored home canned foods should have a shelf life of 1 year. After 1 year, the quality and nutrition decreases, but the food remains safe as long as it is sealed.

PERFECT PRESERVING

I really encourage you to label your foods with the type of syrup or name of the recipe; otherwise, it's easy to forget exactly what you made or did. A notebook that contains copies of the canning recipes you used, with notes, is another very helpful record when canning season rolls around the next year.

Opening Canned Foods

Before opening a jar, inspect the jar and seal. Only if the jar and seal are good should you open the jar and check the contents. If you suspect a food might be unsafe, never taste it, and follow the directions in the next section to discard it properly.

1. Inspect the jar for signs of spoilage. Here's what to look for:

   - Lid is swollen or bulging.

   - Jar is leaking liquid around the rim.

   - There is fuzzy mold (any color) inside the jar or around the lid.

   - The liquid shows signs of moving bubbles inside the jar.

2. Check the seal by holding the jar steady and trying to lift the lid off using your fingertips.

3. If the jar and seal appear to be good, open the jar. Use a bottle opener to break the vacuum seal, and then lift the lid off the jar. Inspect the contents for signs of spoilage. Here's what to look for:

   - Liquid spurts from the jar when it is opened.

   - There is fuzzy mold (any color) inside the jar or the underside of the lid. The lid often contains harmless food particles or may contain flat dark spots due to chemical reactions in some products. Fuzzy mold indicates spoilage.

   - The food doesn't smell the way it should; it's "off."

If the jar, seal, and contents appear to be good, use or consume the food as you normally would. Do not reuse lids for canning; however, you may use the lids as a temporary closure when storing opened jars of food in the refrigerator, with or without a screw band.

If the jar shows signs of spoilage or is not sealed, do not taste the food. Discard it promptly and safely. Spoiled low-acid foods, including tomatoes as well as vegetables or meat, should be treated as though they contain botulinum toxin. Handle carefully as described in the next section.

Discard Spoiled Foods Properly

If you suspect a food might be unsafe, never taste it, and discard it properly.

SPOILER ALERT

Take extra care to avoid contact with suspect foods (especially low-acid foods like tomatoes, vegetables, or meat) and their liquids. Contact with botulinum toxin can be fatal whether it is ingested or enters through the skin. Always wear heavy rubber (latex) or plastic gloves when handling suspect foods or cleaning up contaminated work surfaces and equipment.

If the lid is swollen (indicating the presence of botulin), but the jar is dry and sealed, place the jar in a heavy garbage bag. Close the bag and place in a regular trash container or dispose in a nearby landfill.

If the jar is leaking, unsealed, or open, then follow disposal steps depending on whether the food is high acid or low acid.

For jars showing signs of spoilage that contain high-acid foods—such as fruit, relish, or jam—you may open to discard the contents and wash the jar and ring for reuse. Dispose of the contents and jar lid in the trash bin. Wash the jar and screw band with hot water and soap. After washing, place the jar and screw band in a pan, cover with water by at least 1 inch, bring to a boil, and boil for 10 minutes to sterilize the jar and ring before storing for reuse.

For jars showing signs of spoilage that contain low-acid foods—such as tomatoes, vegetables, or meat—you must carefully perform detoxification before disposal of all components, including the contents, jar, lid, and ring. Follow these steps:

1. Put on heavy rubber (latex) or plastic gloves.

2. Place the lid and screw band on the jar with the food still inside and place in an 8-quart or larger stockpot.

3. Wash your gloved hands thoroughly after handling the suspect jar.

4. Slowly add water to the pot and avoid splashing water. Fill pot with water to completely cover the jar with a minimum of a 1-inch level above the container.

5. Place a cover on the pot and heat the water to boiling. Boil 30 minutes to ensure detoxifying the food, jar, lid, and ring.

6. Turn off heat and cool until you can safely handle the jar.

7. Place the cooled jar with contents, lid, and screw band still intact, and your gloves in a heavy garbage bag. Close the bag and place in a regular trash container or dispose in a nearby landfill.

After handling and disposing of any spoiled foods, be sure to wash your hands thoroughly, and then sanitize the area as described in the next section.

Cleanup After Handling Spoiled Foods

Use a sanitizing solution to disinfect the area after handling spoiled foods. Follow these steps:

1. Put on a new, clean pair of heavy rubber (latex) or plastic gloves.

2. Prepare a solution of 1 part unscented liquid household chlorine bleach (5 to 6 percent sodium hypochlorite) to 5 parts clean water in a spray bottle. (Note: Bleach is an irritant itself and should not be inhaled or allowed to come in contact with the skin.)

3. Spray contaminated surfaces with the bleach solution, including work area, equipment, and utensils that may have come in contact with suspect food or liquid. Let the sanitizing solution stand for 30 minutes, or until completely dry.

4. If there are contaminated food spills, after 30 minutes, wipe up these now sanitized spills with paper towels, being careful to minimize the spread of the spill. Dispose of paper towels in a plastic bag before putting them in the trash. Retreat this area with sanitizing solution and let stand for an additional 30 minutes, or until completely dry.

When the sanitizing process is complete, you may wish to use soap and hot water to clean all surfaces, equipment, and utensils, especially if surfaces seem sticky or grimy.

If you suspect your clothing has been contaminated, you should soak it in a bleach solution, if possible. Otherwise, boil it for 10 minutes or simply discard it.

When cleanup is complete, discard your gloves, towels, sponges, and clothing (if applicable) in a plastic bag before putting in the trash.

Troubleshooting Canned Foods

Problem: **The jar cracks or breaks during processing.**

Remedy: Food is not safe to eat. Discard the jar and its contents.

Prevention: Examine the jar for cracks or nicks before use. Jars that have been dropped, hit, or bumped are susceptible to breakage. Test jars that may have been mishandled to see if they break; immerse them in room-temperature water, bring to a boil, and boil 15 minutes. Handle jars carefully. Avoid using metal utensils to remove air bubbles. Avoid sudden temperature changes, such as putting hot food in a cold jar, putting a cold jar in hot water, or placing a hot jar on a cold or wet surface. Use a rack in the canner; do not place jars directly on canner bottom. Do not overpack jars with food. Avoid reducing canner pressure under running water or lifting the pressure control or petcock before pressure drops to zero.

Problem: **The jar fails to seal properly.**

Remedy: Reprocess within 24 hours, or simply refrigerate and use within 3 days.

Prevention: Always use new lids. Keep lids hot in hot—never boiling—water. Check jar rims for cracks or chips before using. Use good quality product. Keep equipment and work area sanitary. Use tested recipes. Follow all procedures. Wipe jar rims clean before applying lid. Clean rims with vinegar when canning products with oil or fat. Use correct headspace and adjust properly. Food was underprocessed; use correct timing. Lids were tampered with before sealing was complete; cool jars undisturbed for 12 to 24 hours before testing seal.

Problem: **After I removed the jars of vegetables from the canner, some had lost a lot of liquid and the jars were about half-empty.**

Remedy: Do not open the jars to add more liquid. Refrigerate and use within 3 days.

Prevention: Use correct headspace and adjust properly. Use hot pack rather than cold pack. Do not overpack by packing food too tightly. Tighten screw bands sufficiently, but do not overtighten. Begin with hot jars in hot water for either type of canning. Use correct timing, do not over- or underprocess. Jars not adequately covered in BWB canner, or full boil not maintained. Pressure canner not operated correctly; review procedures for pressurizing and maintaining correct pressure. Jar-cooling period inadequate; do not force cooling. Starchy foods (corn, peas, beans) sometimes absorb all of the liquid. Use hot pack, add adequate liquid, and adjust headspace properly.

Problem: **The jar was cleaned before storing, but now is wet around the rim and shows signs of mold or bubbling.**

Remedy: The jar is not sealed. Do not use. Discard safely. Treat low-acid foods as containing botulinum toxin and dispose properly.

Prevention: Review previous problem for troubleshooting jars that fail to seal properly. Store canned foods at 50°F to 70°F, harmless thermophilic bacteria can grow inside jars at temperatures above 55°F.

Problem: **The jar was sealed when stored but unsealed when I went to use it.**

Remedy: Do not use. Discard contents. Treat low-acid foods as containing botulinum toxin and dispose properly.

Prevention: Review previous problem for troubleshooting jars that fail to seal properly. Store canned foods at 50°F to 70°F in a dry location. In high humidity, lids may rust and break the seal.

Problem: **The jar was sealed, but has a bulging lid, liquid coming out, or food smells bad when the jar is opened.**

Remedy: Do not use. Treat as containing botulinum toxin and dispose properly.

Prevention: Review previous problem for troubleshooting jars that fail to seal properly.

Problem: **The jar was sealed, but the underside of the lid contains smooth or flat, but not fuzzy, black or brown spots.**

Remedy: If the deposits are fuzzy, it is mold and the food is unsafe. Otherwise, if there are no other signs of spoilage, it is probably due to harmless chemical reactions and the food is safe to eat.

Prevention: Use distilled or filtered water. Use pans made of stainless steel or enamel, and utensils made of stainless steel, wood, plastic, or silicone. Avoid other metals such as aluminum, brass, cast iron, copper, zinc, worn tinplate, or chipped enamel.

Problem: **Food at top of the jar has darkened or is floating above liquid.**

Remedy: Food is safe to eat if there are no signs of spoilage.

Prevention: Cover foods completely with liquid when filling jars (solids should be filled to slightly under the headspace). Use hot pack, rather than cold pack. Use sweetened liquids rather than unsweetened liquids or plain water for canning fruit. Use correct headspace and adjust properly. Use a tested recipe. Process foods at correct temperature or pressure, and time.

Problem: **The jars of food froze.**

Remedy: Food is safe to eat if the jars are still sealed and there are no signs of spoilage.

Prevention: Store canned foods at 50°F to 70°F in a dry location.

Problem: **Food darkens or turns black, brown, or gray.**

Remedy: Food is safe to eat if there are no signs of spoilage. Some varieties of sweet corn turn brown. Potatoes may darken if not properly stored before preserving. Hard water or certain metal utensils can cause darkening in all foods.

Prevention: Use mature produce that is neither under- or overripe. Choose potatoes that are not stored below 45°F before canning. Use distilled water or filtered water. Use pans made of stainless steel or enamel, and utensils made of stainless steel, wood, plastic, or silicone. Avoid aluminum, brass, cast iron, copper, zinc, worn tinplate, and chipped enamel. Use whole spices; ground spices can darken or discolor liquids. Remove whole spices; if left inside the jar, they may darken or discolor pickles. Use correct timing; do not over- or underprocess.

Problem: **Light-colored foods or their canning liquid turns pink, red, blue, or purple in the jar.**

Remedy: Food is safe to eat.

Prevention: These colors are natural chemical reactions that may occur in cooked fruit, especially apples, quince, peaches, or pears. Use distilled water, pans made of stainless steel or enamel, and utensils made of stainless steel, wood, plastic, or silicone. Avoid aluminum, brass, cast iron, copper, zinc, worn tinplate, and chipped enamel. Use mature produce that is neither under- or overripe. Do not overprocess—process at correct temperature or pressure, and time. Do not can red varieties of garlic.

Problem: **Crystals, sediment, or glasslike particles in the jar.**

Remedy: Food is safe to eat; crystals are organic acids that are naturally present in some fruits or vegetables. Some fruits, such as blueberry, cranberry, raspberry, strawberry, and grape contain ellagic or tartaric acids that form sediment or crystals. In spinach, calcium and oxalic acids may form crystals. Sediment may simply be unfiltered solids from fruit or vegetables. Starchy foods (corn, peas, beans) naturally contain sediments.

Prevention: Strain berry and grape juices through a fine mesh strainer or cheesecloth. Discard sediment and process only the clear juice. In jam, measure sugar accurately, stir in sugar completely, and boil for the right amount of time. Use distilled water; hard water can increase sediment.

Problem: **Fruit products do not have full fruit flavor.**

Remedy: Products are safe but were poorly processed.

Prevention: Use mature produce that is neither under- or overripe. Do not overcook. Do not overprocess—process at correct temperature or pressure, and time. Do not add excessive water to product. Store canned foods at 50°F to 70°F.

Problem: **Fruit darkens after removing from the jar.**

Remedy: Safety is doubtful. If there are no signs of spoilage, enzymes were probably not deactivated due to underprocessing. Boil fruit for 10 minutes before use or discard.

Prevention: Process at correct temperature or pressure, and time.

Problem: **Fruit juice or jam is full of bubbles.**

Remedy: Product may be fermented (if bubbles are moving), or may simply be trapped air. Safe to eat, but may contain alcohol.

Prevention: Keep equipment and work area sanitary. Use correct headspace and adjust properly. Process at correct temperature or pressure, and time. For jam, cook spread thoroughly, fill jars with hot spread, and adjust headspace accurately.

Problem: **Fruit juice or jam is fermented.**

Remedy: Juice is safe to drink, but contains alcohol.

Prevention: Use correct headspace and adjust properly. Process at correct temperature or pressure, and time.

Problem: **Jam made without commercial pectin (or with natural pectin) won't gel, is runny, or is too soft.**

Remedy: Try remaking the product (reheat and add more fruit, sugar, acid, or natural pectin), or use as a sauce.

Prevention: Overripe produce; use mature produce that is neither underripe or overripe. Use a tested recipe with the right balance of fruit, sugar, acid, and pectin. Measure ingredients accurately. Test that the gel stage has been reached. Test that your natural pectin gels.

Problem: **Jam made with commercial pectin is runny or too soft.**

Remedy: Try remaking the product (heat and add more pectin). Or use as a sauce.

Prevention: Overripe produce; use mature produce that is neither underripe or overripe. Use the recipe that comes with the pectin product. Measure ingredients accurately. Don't double a recipe; if you want more product, make 1 recipe multiple times. Use a full rolling boil for the time specified.

Problem: **Jam is too stiff.**

Remedy: Spread is safe to eat if there are no signs of spoilage.

Prevention: Too much pectin; use a tested recipe, and measure ingredients accurately. Overcooked; follow recipe.

Problem: **Jam weeps or loses liquid upon standing.**

Remedy: Stir to combine.

Prevention: Use mature produce that is neither underripe or overripe. Use a tested recipe with the right balance of fruit, sugar, acid, and pectin. Test that the jam has reached the gel stage before canning. Store canned foods at 50°F to 70°F.

Problem: **Liquid separates at the top of the jar in tomato sauce or juice.**

Remedy: This is natural and harmless. The liquid will recombine when shaken, stirred, or cooked.

Prevention: Use one of the methods described for minimizing separation in tomato sauce or juice in Chapter 16. The basic technique is to heat tomatoes whole or in quarters before chopping or juicing. As soon as you cut tomatoes, enzymes start to break down pectin that holds solids and liquids together. You need to deactivate the enzyme as quickly as possible by heating before or as you are crushing the tomatoes.

Problem: **Liquid separates at the bottom of the jar in tomatoes, sauce, or juice.**

Remedy: This is natural and harmless. The liquid will recombine when shaken or stirred.

Prevention: The sauce or juice was heated too long. Heat no more than 5 minutes, then turn heat low to keep hot while filling jars.

Problem: **Canned tomatoes often spoil.**

Remedy: The jar is not sealed. Do not use. Discard contents. Treat low-acid foods (including tomatoes) as containing botulinum toxin and dispose properly.

Prevention: Acidify tomatoes just before filling each jar in one of the following ways: add 1 (2) table-spoon bottled lemon juice, $\frac{1}{4}$ ($\frac{1}{2}$) teaspoon citric acid powder per pint (quart), or 2 (4) tablespoons vinegar of 5 percent or greater acidity. Use mature tomatoes; never can overripe tomatoes.

Problem: **Tomatoes seemed fine and the jar was sealed, but they taste bitter, sour, or medicinal.**

Remedy: Harmless thermophilic bacteria is the usual cause of sour taste. Boil tomatoes for 10 minutes before use, or discard.

Prevention: Use good quality, fresh tomatoes. Keep your equipment and work area sanitary. Do not underprocess; process at the correct temperature or pressure, and time. Store canned foods at 50°F to 70°F.

Problem: **Tomato products have thin sticks of red floating in the liquid.**

Remedy: Food is safe to eat.

Prevention: Tomato skins roll up into thin sticks and create a rustic texture that you may or may not prefer. To reduce or eliminate, grind very fine, strain, or peel tomatoes before canning or making sauce.

Problem: **Liquid, pickles, or jam is cloudy or color is dull.**

Remedy: Food is safe to eat if there are no signs of spoilage.

Prevention: Use distilled water; hard water can cause cloudy liquids. Use canning salt; table salt contains additives that cause cloudy liquids. Do not add flour or other starches to canning recipes. For pickles, use freshly harvested pickling cucumbers, brine of proper concentration, and complete fermentation. For jam, do not use too green fruit; use mature produce that is neither under- or overripe. Boil quickly, for the right amount of time; overcooking may cloud spreads. Fill jars quickly as soon as spread is cooked; don't hold cooked spread. For juice, chill at least 24 hours and strain to remove sediment before making jelly. Don't press solids to squeeze out more juice. Store canned foods at 50°F to 70°F.

Problem: **Pickles are soft or slippery.**

Remedy: Pickles are spoiled and should be discarded safely.

Prevention: Use tested recipe and measure accurately; brine may be too weak. Use vinegar of at least 5 percent acidity. Cut and discard $\frac{1}{16}$-inch slice from blossom end of cucumbers. Cover fermented pickles completely in brine. Remove scum daily from fermented pickles. Pickles were underprocessed; use correct timing.

Problem: **Pickles are hollow.**

Remedy: Pickles are safe to eat if there are no signs of spoilage. Hollow cucumbers (usually large or over-ripe) cause hollow pickles.

Prevention: Use small, freshly harvested pickling cucumbers. Use large cucumbers for relish, or cut for spears or slices to check interior before canning.

Problem: **Pickles are shriveled.**

Remedy: Pickles are safe to eat if there are no signs of spoilage.

Prevention: Use tested recipe. Pickles were overcooked or overprocessed; use correct timing. Measure salt, sugar, and vinegar accurately. Do not use a too-strong solution at the beginning of the pickling process. Prick whole pickles before canning. Use unwaxed cucumbers for canning.

Problem: **Recipe calls for ladling relish into jars without further processing, and/or turning them upside down.**

Remedy: This method is called "open kettle" and is no longer considered safe.

Prevention: Look for a tested recipe similar to the one you have. You many not alter the proportions of solids, vinegar, water, or other liquids in a recipe. When canning foods with vinegar added the only safe adjustments are to sugar, salt, and spices, which you may freely omit, add, increase, or decrease. You must always process canned food in a BWB or steam-pressure canner using a tested recipe.

Problem: **Pickles or relish have bitter taste.**

Remedy: Relish is safe to eat if there is no sign of spoilage.

Prevention: Use fewer spices and vinegar of no more than 5 percent acidity. Use a tested recipe; do not boil too long. Avoid salt substitutes, especially potassium chloride, because they are naturally bitter.

Problem: **Canned tuna tastes very strong.**

Remedy: Fish is safe to eat if there are no signs of spoilage.

Prevention: The strong flavor of dark tuna flesh affects the delicate flavor of white flesh. Many people prefer not to can dark flesh, or they use it as pet food.

Problem: **Canned smoked salmon is dry or burned.**

Remedy: May be safe, but is not appetizing. Discard if inedible, or feed to animals if not spoiled.

Prevention: Do not oversmoke. Smoke for 30 to 60 minutes. Use brine with sugar and salt. Don't brine longer than 1 hour per pound. Use a rack in the canner; do not place jars directly on canner bottom.

Problem: **I'm not sure whether the food is spoiled or not.**

Remedy: When in doubt, always throw it out.

Prevention: Can jam or pickles, which are inherently safer due to their acid content, before you attempt other types of foods. Take a canning class to get hands-on instruction in proper procedures.

Cellaring Foods   ∞   8

In the broadest sense, cellaring is any form of storage that holds food in optimum condition for an extended period. Today's modern "root cellar" is the refrigerator. However, if you want to maintain a supply of food without the use of electricity, then some knowledge and practice of cellaring methods are useful.

Cellaring methods vary by locale. The tradition of cellaring takes advantage of the climate where you live. Cold climates provide a natural environment to store foods. In temperate locations, storage areas need to be given more thought. Either way, the storage methods you use must provide a controlled environment for the types of foods you wish to keep.

Storage Options

There are a number of options for storing seasonal crops through winter. In the city, you have several options for cellaring food, whether you live in a house, condominium, or apartment. If you garden, you may store crops in outdoor pits, trenches, cold frames, or hotbeds.

Root Cellars and Cold Rooms

Root cellars preserve fresh food by controlling the storage temperature and humidity. The basic difference between a root cellar and a cold room is the construction. Root cellars existed when houses had unfinished basements with dirt floors, making the cellar cool, drafty, and relatively humid. The open, uninsulated root cellar had adequate airflow that, despite the humidity, discouraged condensation on the walls. In contrast, a cold room is a finished but unheated room in an otherwise warm, dry basement.

Any type of indoor cellar requires a method to control air temperature and relative humidity. Depending on the type of food to be stored, cellars and cold rooms need cool temperatures ranging from 32°F to 60°F and higher than average humidity—between 60 to 90 percent relative humidity (RH). To measure temperature and humidity accurately, you may find that a thermometer with a hygrometer is helpful, but it's not required.

Two storage areas with different environments are ideal: one that is cold (32°F to 40°F) and humid (80 to 90 percent RH), and one that is slightly warmer (40°F to 60°F) and drier (60 to 70 percent RH). This is easier than it sounds. Your cold room might be an underground basement, an enclosed but unheated porch, or an outdoor storage shed or room. The warm room could be your attic, an upstairs room or warm closet, or a basement furnace room. A pan of water is often all you need to raise the humidity in an enclosed space that is too dry.

If you have a cold room, or a basement that is partly below ground, you may be able to create a usable cold room by making some modifications. You need to protect both the cold room and the rest of your basement from the increased humidity.

The basic requirements for a basement cold room are to seal the space from water and air leaks using appropriate paint, caulk, and insulation. The trick is to design the room as if it is actually an exterior space. The key element of the construction is to insulate the ceiling and interior walls, but leave the exterior walls uninsulated. In addition, add a vapor barrier on the warm side of the house and an insulated exterior door with weather stripping to the room. Most importantly, add two screened, adjustable vents (easiest to do through a window) that provide a (high) warm-air outlet and (low) cool-air intake. Ensure the floor is a porous material (dirt, cement, or composite deck material are better than wood or linoleum). Finally, build shelving away from the walls to promote air circulation within the room.

Ideally, you want to monitor the cellar environment using a thermometer, as well as a hygrometer that measures relative humidity. For a nominal amount ($10 to $20), you can buy a small digital device that operates on AA batteries. These devices not only display the temperature and relative humidity, but offer features that record minimum and maximum values for the room, as well as the concurrent outdoor readings. Proper temperature and humidity are crucial to reliable long-term storage, and regular monitoring will help you maintain the quality of your food for an entire season of delicious eating.

Here are the guidelines for operating vents to maintain your cellar environment:

- While the weather remains warm in the fall, close both vents during the day and open them at night.

- When the weather becomes more severe, the plan is reversed (open during the day and close at night).

- Close vents tightly whenever the outdoor temperature is higher than the storage temperature (when the outdoor temperature rises above 32°F).

In extended periods of cold weather (10°F to 20°F or less), keep a pail of water in the storage area to help maintain a cellar temperature above freezing (32°F); the water will freeze before the crops do. Very low temperatures can cause injury to some produce, like potatoes, and lead to rapid decay.

Unless you add humidity, basement cold rooms with finished floors are usually drier than true root cellars. Drier rooms are less than ideal for most vegetables, except potatoes, onions, and garlic.

You can use several strategies to raise humidity. Place large pans of water near the fresh-air intake, sprinkle the floor with water, or cover the floor with straw or sawdust. Use a pile of snow if your climate provides it, and you have installed a floor drain. You can store individual crops in a way that enhances their humidity. Layer them in sand, sawdust, sphagnum moss, or well-ventilated plastic bags. If you use plastic bags, routinely examine the bags for condensation and immediately air out bags with visible moisture; mold can quickly make a crop inedible.

In addition to thoughtful design, control of temperature, and humidity, you need to maintain the space properly. Once per year, air out the room and thoroughly clean the walls, floor, and shelves with soap and water, followed by a disinfecting bleach solution of 1 cup of bleach per gallon of water. Proper cleaning kills molds and bacteria that can lie dormant and ruin stored foods the next season. The best time to perform maintenance is in late spring or early summer. In spring, the outside air has warmed up and your cellar contents are usually at their lowest level. You have used most of the storage crops (root crops, onions, etc.). Cold winter air may have condensed on the walls and shelves as the weather warms up. Thorough cleaning prevents mold growth.

Dry Pantry

In modern homes, a pantry is warmer and drier than a cold room with cool room temperature (55°F to 65°F) and dry humidity (45 to 65 percent RH, or less in desert regions). This room is useful for storing dry staples, such as grains, beans, pastas, nuts, dried foods, canned goods, and wines. Lower temperatures are desirable since each rise of 10°F cuts storage time in half. For example, a bag of flour that may go stale in 6 months at 70°F, keeps for 1 year at 60°F, and 2 years at 50°F.

All vegetables prefer humid conditions (60 to 70 percent RH). Therefore, the shelf life of vegetables is shorter in a warm, dry pantry than in a cool, humid cellar or cold room. In a dry pantry, you need to limit produce to vegetables that prefer warm temperatures. These include dried chiles (hot peppers), pumpkins, winter squashes, sweet potatoes, and green tomatoes. Onions and garlic prefer cooler temperatures, but can be stored for a short period.

The pantry is not ideal for long-term storage of many vegetables, including carrots and other root crops; cabbages and greens; warm-weather vegetables such as tomatoes, cucumbers, and peppers; and all types of fruit. However, if the pantry is at least 10°F cooler than your kitchen, then it makes sense to store fruit, potatoes, garlic, and onions there.

Makeshift Cellars

If you don't have a cellar, cold room, or pantry, there are several other ways you can store food:

- Basement utility rooms, especially those with a furnace, tend to be warm and dry. This type of room is suitable for vegetables such as winter squashes and onions, or short-term storage of tomatoes, as well as dried and canned foods.

- Attic rooms, if they are warm and dry, are well suited to curing onions and sweet potatoes, and drying vegetables and herbs. If the attic becomes very cold in severe weather, you will need to rotate food to another location. By summertime, if the weather turns hot and humid, your stored food should be used up.

- Purchase an additional energy-efficient refrigerator to use for long-term storage of seasonal fruits and vegetables.

Regardless of the method used, be sure to monitor these makeshift cellars as you would any other food storage area. Check the produce every month for possible signs of wilting or decay. At least once a year, thoroughly clean and sanitize food storage areas.

Garden Mulching, Trenches, and Pits

Mulching and burying vegetables in pits and trenches are easy and inexpensive methods of keeping them fresh for an extended period. If you have gophers or other rodent problems, then consider a more permanent trench or pit using concrete, rock, or drain tile. Containers or indoor storage may be a better choice.

Mulching (also called *overwintering*) is the technique of simply covering a crop where it grows in the garden. Be sure to wait until the ground is cold, or the vegetables will decay. This technique is useful for root crops such as carrots, parsnips, and turnips. After the ground begins to freeze in the fall, cover with at least 12 inches of mulch, such as hay, straw, or dry leaves.

Select only the highest-quality vegetables for trenches or pits. Do not place any vegetables in storage that are damaged, immature, unripe, or diseased. If you remove only part of the produce from a pit, make sure you check the remaining vegetables and discard any that show signs of decay.

For a trench, dig an oblong pit in a well-drained spot, preferably with sandy soil. Make the pit 1 or 2 feet deep, long, and narrow. This shape makes it easy for you to remove the produce. In addition, you can make partitions in the dirt as you dig, and mark them with stakes. Make an air vent with a tunnel of straw or perforated PVC pipe. To fill the trench, line the bottom of the pit with straw, add a shallow layer of vegetables, cover with 6 inches of straw, and top with 6 inches of soil. Do not crowd the vegetables or they will sweat and ferment. In subzero weather, add another 6 inches of mulch for protection against freezing temperatures.

Rather than a trench, you can use a pit or storage clamp, which is simply a small mound. To create a clamp, place a layer of straw or mulch in a circle. Stand a piece of perforated PVC pipe or mound of straw in the center for a vent. Pile the harvested crop in a conical shape around it (like a mountain). Cover the vegetables with 6 inches of straw. Finally, cover the mound with 6 inches of soil, leaving the pipe or center straw mound open to the air. Dig the soil for the cover from a trench around the crop; this also creates a drainage ditch in the event of rain. For best results, place one type of crop in one clamp and remove all of the vegetables at the same time.

Cold Frames and Hotbeds

Cold frames and hotbeds are covered frames in the garden that collect heat during the day and protect plants from cold temperatures at night. Cold frames use only the sun and some method to trap solar heat. Hotbeds use artificial heat, and are essentially miniature greenhouses. Methods for heating hotbeds include manure, electric cables, light bulbs, and hot water or steam pipes.

The goal is to maintain nighttime temperatures of 60°F or more. On warm or sunny days, you may want to open the cover to provide ventilation and prevent overheating. Water plants early in the day. This will give foliage time to dry before you close the frame at night.

For either type, construct the frame with a higher back than the front, and cover the frame with transparent material. The slope from front to back should increase 1 inch per foot.

Glass is the ideal transparent covering; however, you may also use clear fiberglass or 4 to 6 mil clear polyethylene. Plan for a way to secure or weight the frame to prevent lifting in windy conditions. Construction can be simple, using available materials (such as wood and glass), or elaborate, using lightweight metals and solar collectors.

Position garden frames for a southern exposure (to maximize sunlight) and a north or northwest windbreak (to conserve heat). Create a windbreak by positioning the frame next to a building, solid fence, or evergreen hedge, or constructing a wall with bales of hay.

Buried Containers

If you don't have an indoor cellar and don't garden (or even if you do), buried containers make a convenient cold storage place for root crops. Even if you grow your own vegetables, buried containers are easier to set up and use than trenches and pits.

The container should be new or clean, and should not have previously held nonfood items. Metal containers provide more protection from rodents and other pests than plastic, but either type is acceptable. Suitable containers include new metal or plastic garbage cans and plastic storage bins. Drill holes in the bottom of the container for drainage.

Locate the container in an area convenient to your house, but away from garages and car fumes. Dig a hole just large enough to hold the container, with at least 2 inches sticking out above ground level. Load the container with layers of vegetables, separated by straw. Cover the top of the container with 1 to 2 feet of insulating material.

Storage Strategies

Always choose firm, unblemished fruits and vegetables, and handle them carefully during storage. Place produce gently in clean containers without sharp edges. Fresh fruits and vegetables require separate storage areas. Fruits prefer cool and dry storage, while most vegetables need cold and humid conditions. Furthermore, many fruits give off gases (like ethylene) that will quickly spoil vegetables if cellared together. Potatoes and onions have different storage requirements, too, and don't make good neighbors in your cellar.

SPOILER ALERT

Never place any damaged or decaying produce in a storage room. It can contaminate other items if stored nearby. Immediately use or compost overripe produce.

The following sections detail the ideal storage requirements for different types of foods. This information may help you to choose the products you want to store and design appropriate storage spaces for them.

Vegetables

Most vegetables require high humidity for storage. If you are new to cellaring, you may find that cabbages, onions, potatoes, and root crops are the easiest crops to master. Most vegetables are best stored in baskets or containers that allow for plenty of air circulation.

If you grow your own vegetables, choose varieties recommended for long-term storage. Harvest vegetables early in the morning, on a cold day.

Asparagus can be forced (to grow out of season) in a cellar or hotbed. To cellar, dig roots from the garden in late fall and store in 4 to 6 inches of moist sand at warm (near 60°F) temperatures. For best results, provide some light with a lamp. Cut stems can be cellared in cold (32°F to 40°F), humid (80 to 90 percent RH) conditions for about 2 weeks.

Brussels sprouts are very hardy. You can leave this vegetable in the garden through fall and early winter.

Cabbage keeps best when you invert it and store in a garden pit or trench. You can also store cabbage in-ground with heavy mulching, or in an outbuilding hung upside down by their roots from hooks. Cabbage gives off ethylene gas, so store it away from other crops. Do not store cabbage indoors, because the odor will fill the house. Cabbage prefers cold (32°F to 40°F), humid (80 to 90 percent RH) conditions.

Cauliflower prefers cold (32°F to 40°F), humid (80 to 90 percent RH) conditions. Since it can withstand light frosts (to 34°F), provide heavy mulching in ground, or use cold frames or hotbeds as needed in severe weather. Like cabbage, do not store cauliflower inside.

Celery can be stored in the ground if covered up to the top with soil, or upright in a pit. Store celery in the cellar in cold (32°F to 40°F), humid (80 to 90 percent RH) conditions, in boxes filled with soil, sand, or sphagnum moss. Celery gives off ethylene gas; store it away from other crops.

Chiles (hot peppers) can be strung, dried, and then stored in a cool, dry location, such as an attic, covered porch, or pantry.

Corn can be stored in the field by bundling the stalks into groups called *corn shocks*. Just before the first frost, cut the corn stalks at ground level. Although the leaves are dead, you should see plenty of moisture when you cut the stalk. Stand 20 to 60 stalks together (around a pole if necessary) and tie with rope or twine to create a corn shock. The longer you store corn, the more firm and starchy it becomes. Corn can also be frozen, dried, or canned as whole kernels, creamed, or made into relish.

Greens, including endive, romaine, and kale, may be stored in-ground for several weeks, and can withstand light frosts (to 34°F) with heavy mulching. Leafy greens give off ethylene gas; store them away from other crops.

Onions and garlic should be harvested as soon as their tops fall over and the soil is dry. Before cellaring, condition the onions for long storage by "curing" or drying: Place uprooted bulbs in a well-ventilated place (such as an attic, open shed, or covered porch), protected from sun and rain. Spread in a single layer on newspaper. In 2 to 3 weeks, their outer skins should make a rustling sound, indicating they are sufficiently dry for storage. Before you store onions, sort them for quality. Place those with thin, firm necks in separate containers, and plan to use them last. Cut the tops off before storing in mesh bags, baskets, or other containers that permit free airflow. Medium-size red or yellow onions keep longer than large, white, or sweet varieties. Onions and garlic prefer cool (40°F to 50°F), dry (60 to 70 percent RH) rooms. Onions and garlic (as well as leeks) can also be stored in-ground for several weeks, and can withstand light frosts (to 34°F) with heavy mulching.

Peppers (sweet peppers), cucumbers, summer squashes such as zucchini, and eggplants can be stored as described for firm tomatoes. Choose only perfect, unblemished vegetables for storage and handle them as you would eggs, for they are very delicate.

Potatoes can be placed in storage clamps. Before cellaring, condition potatoes for long storage by "curing": Sort and remove any damaged or suspect potatoes for immediate use. Place firm, unblemished potatoes in a single layer, in the dark (in slightly open paper sacks or loosely covered with newspaper), at 45°F to 60°F for 2 weeks. Store in a cold (32°F to 40°F), dry (60 to 70 percent RH) location. Store potatoes in complete darkness, such as inside paper bags, covered wooden boxes, tin pails, or buried in dry sand. Sprouting indicates the potatoes are too warm, or are stored next to apples or onions.

Pumpkins and winter squashes can be harvested after the vines are killed by a frost. Leave stems on to protect fruit against disease in storage. The best way to store winter squashes is in a cool to warm (40°F to 60°F), dry (60 to 70 percent RH) room. Attics, closets, or near a basement furnace can be excellent alternative locations. Place them individually on shelves or hung in mesh bags.

Root crops, including beets, carrots, celeriac, horseradish, parsnips, rutabagas, salsifies, turnips, and winter radishes, may be stored in-ground for several weeks, and can withstand light freezing (to 28°F) with heavy mulching. You can leave horseradish, parsnip, and salsify in the ground, well mulched until spring; they become sweet in very cold temperatures. All root crops store well in trenches or clamps. Rutabagas, turnips, and winter radishes give off strong odors, so don't store them indoors. In the cellar, store only beets, carrots, horseradish, parsnips, and salsifies. To store in the cellar, cut off the tops, leaving a 1-inch stem, and place in baskets or boxes. To optimize moisture in dry storage rooms, layer the crops with sand or sphagnum moss. Root crops prefer cold (32°F to 40°F), very humid (80 to 90 percent RH or more) conditions.

Sweet potatoes have different requirements than potatoes. Treat them delicately, as you would peppers, cucumbers, and eggplants.

Tomatoes can be stored individually wrapped in tissue paper, or layered in shallow containers with dry sphagnum moss or straw. You may also place ripe, sound tomatoes (free from blemishes) in a crock and cover with strong (10 percent) brine. To use brined tomatoes, soak in fresh, cold water for 12 hours, and then peel and slice. Tomato plants may be pulled from the ground and hung from hooks in the cellar ceiling. For any of these methods, store tomatoes cool (40°F to 50°F) to slightly warm, and dry (60 to 70 percent RH).

Fruits

Most fruits other than apples, grapes, and melons can be stored only for a few weeks, and some fruits for less time than that.

Berries are extremely perishable and keep only a few days even at refrigerator temperatures (32°F to 40°F), so are not suitable for cellaring.

Citrus fruits last longest when stored in cool (40°F to 50°F), dry (60 to 70 percent RH) conditions in baskets or mesh bags to maximize airflow and prevent mold growth. Oranges can be stored closer to freezing (32°F to 34°F).

Figs are very perishable and bruise easily. Store at cold (32°F to 40°F) temperatures up to 1 week. For best results, preserve promptly.

Grapes can be cellared in cold (32°F to 40°F), very humid (80 to 90 percent RH) conditions. Layer in sand, sawdust, or sphagnum moss; pack into well-ventilated plastic bags; or wrap fruits individually in tissue paper. Grapes readily absorb odors; store them away from other crops.

Melons should be stored in cold to cool (32°F to 50°F), humid to very humid (80 to 95 percent RH) conditions. Store in baskets or mesh bags to maximize airflow.

Pome fruits, like apples and pears, need to be stored as near freezing (32°F) as possible, in very humid (80 to 90 percent RH or more) conditions. Layer in sand, sawdust, or sphagnum moss; pack into well-ventilated plastic bags; or wrap fruits individually in tissue paper and layer in boxes. If you use plastic bags, routinely examine the bags for condensation; immediately air out bags with visible moisture, or the crop can quickly become moldy and inedible. Apples and pears give off ethylene gas; you may store them together, but away from other crops.

Rhubarb can be forced (to grow out of season) in a cellar or cold frame. To cellar: Dig roots from the garden in late fall and plant in containers with 3 to 4 inches moist sand or compost. Store outside and allow to freeze several times, and then cellar at cool (near 50°F) temperatures, covered to keep light out and moisture in. Forced rhubarb stalks are small and light pink rather than red.

Stone fruits like apricots, cherries, and peaches can be picked while green and stored in cool to warm (40°F to 60°F), dry (60 to 70 percent RH) conditions to delay ripening for just a few weeks. To ripen, return to room temperature. The best approach is to ripen as soon as possible after picking and then preserve by some other method.

Tropical fruits can be picked while green and stored in cool to warm (40°F to 60°F), dry (60 to 70 percent RH) conditions to delay ripening for just a few weeks. To ripen, return to room temperature. The best approach is to ripen as soon as possible after picking and then preserve by some other method. Bananas are not appropriate for cellaring.

Cheese

Most of us store cheese in the refrigerator, which is a great environment for many types of mass-produced cheese. You can wrap the cheese in parchment, waxed paper, or freezer paper and store it in the meat drawer, or wrap it loosely in plastic wrap and store it on any shelf in the refrigerator.

For ripened cheeses that will continue to age naturally (for example, artisanal or farmstead cheeses), a refrigerator is too cold and too dry. These cheeses prefer temperatures of 48°F to 58°F and relative humidity of 80 to 98 percent. In this case, you have a few options.

✢ Place unwrapped cheese in a covered (plastic, glass, or ceramic) container, and place on a mat or rack that allows air circulation around the cheese. For optimum humidity, fill the container only half-full of cheese, and add a folded, damp towel in one corner of the box. Store the cheese box in a cellar or basement cold room, or in a warmer part of the refrigerator (such as in front on an upper shelf).

✢ Buy a small refrigerator dedicated to cheese storage. Adjust the temperature control as needed and place a container of water on the lower shelf; if necessary, partially cover the water container to maintain ideal humidity.

For best results, do not crowd cheeses and store them without touching each other. If moisture builds up in a container or in a dedicated refrigerator, wipe it down as soon as possible to prevent mold growth.

Wine and Hard Cider

Optimum conditions for long-term storage of bottled wine and hard cider include constant cool temperature, moderate humidity, and darkness.

Consistent temperature is the key issue. The ideal temperature is around 55°F. However, a consistent temperature is better than one that fluctuates even 10 degrees. Therefore, a consistent year-round temperature of either 50°F or 60°F is better than a location where the temperature fluctuates from 50°F to 60°F from summer to winter.

Natural corks expand and contract with temperature changes. If they become dry and brittle, air gets into the bottle, and soon you have a cellar full of vinegar. For this reason, store corked bottles on their sides to keep corks in contact with the liquid, keeping the cork moist and the bottle sealed tight.

Humidity should be moderate (60 to 65 percent RH). If there is too much moisture, mold can grow on the cork and spoil the beverage. If there is too little, the cork can dry out and may lead to oxidization.

Either a dry pantry or not-too-humid area of a cellar can work for wine storage. Other alternatives include a cool, interior closet, a storage area under stairs, an unused fireplace, or an energy-efficient refrigerator with the temperature adjusted upward. Wine refrigerators begin as low as $100 for small countertop or freestanding models.

Canned Foods

Using a permanent marker, label all home and commercially canned food containers with the processing or purchase date (month and year) on the lid. Store all canned foods in a cool, dark, dry place. Here are some other storing tips:

✢ Store away from heat sources and light, such as furnaces, hot water pipes, and windows, or in rooms where the temperature fluctuates, such as uninsulated garages and attics.

✢ Do not allow canned foods to freeze. Freezing changes food textures, and leads to rust, bursting cans, and broken seals.

✢ Store metal cans off the floor; moisture can wick into cans and encourage rusting.

PERFECT PRESERVING

As a rule, use older foods before newer foods, use canned foods within 1 year for best quality, and discard canned foods older than 2 years or that have passed their expiration date.

Cured Meats, Poultry, and Fish

Traditional dry-cure methods use salt and nitrites to produce a shelf-stable sausage that is suitable for cool temperature storage (60°F or less), up to 3 months. This type of sausage continues to dry out, and may become very hard. To prevent this, store the sausage in a plastic bag or airtight container, next to a clean, slightly damp cloth napkin. You may also store dry sausage in the refrigerator for up to 1 year, wrapped in freezer paper or waxed paper. Another good method is to slice all of the sausage, then vacuum seal in small packages for the refrigerator or freezer. Caution: Vacuum-sealed foods must be stored at 40°F or less.

Cured poultry must be stored in the refrigerator, up to 2 weeks, or up to 1 year in the freezer.

Store cured fish about 10 days in the refrigerator, or 2 to 3 months in the freezer. Many modern cured fish products are highly perishable and may not keep longer than raw fish.

Dried Foods

While dried foods such as grains, flours, beans, pastas, and dried fruits and vegetables are shelf stable, insects can invade these products during long-term storage. Here are some tips to safeguard your supply of these foods:

✢ Store dried foods in closed containers, such as heavy zipper-lock plastic bags or airtight plastic, glass, or metal containers.

✢ Inspect dried foods routinely for signs of spoilage. Immediately remove any spoiled food. Clean and sanitize the area before introducing new food.

✢ Keep doors (and windows, if present) closed against unwanted pests.

✢ Keep the storage area (such as pantry or cupboard) well organized. Label all products with a preparation or purchase date. Add new foods behind old foods, and always use older ones first.

✢ At least once a year, clean and sanitize the shelves, walls, and floors. Clean the walls, floor, and shelves with soap and water, followed by a disinfecting bleach solution of 1 cup bleach per gallon of water.

Troubleshooting Cellared Foods

Problem: **Mold in the basement or cold room.**

Remedy: Empty, clean, and sanitize the room. Carefully inspect all food before returning it to the clean cellar; discard any moldy food.

Prevention: Make sure the cold room is sealed from water and air leaks. Caulk and insulate the cold room. Add a vapor barrier. Monitor the temperature and humidity; vent the room properly as needed. Don't crowd shelves. Clean and sanitize the room annually.

Problem: **Strong vegetable odors throughout the house.**

Remedy: Remove fresh cruciferous vegetables including cabbages, cauliflower, turnips, rutabagas, and radishes to a refrigerator or outside storage space. Ferment these vegetables or layer with dry salt if storing in an indoor cellar. Alternatively, blanch and freeze or dry cauliflower and root vegetables.

Prevention: Do not cellar fresh cruciferous vegetables indoors; their odors will fill the rest of the house.

Problem: **Sprouting food in the cellar.**

Remedy: The room could be too warm; vent as needed. Check that incompatible foods are not stored together (for example, fruits with vegetables or potatoes with onions).

Prevention: Monitor the temperature and humidity. Review ideal storage conditions for different types of fresh produce.

Problem: **Moldy food in the cellar.**

Remedy: Discard any moldy food.

Prevention: Monitor the temperature and humidity; vent the room properly as needed. Inspect food monthly and look for condensation; air out food stored in plastic bags.

Problem: **Frozen food in the cellar.**

Remedy: Prepare frozen food promptly; you may need to discard excess frozen food, or cook into soup, if possible.

Prevention: Monitor the temperature and humidity; vent the room properly as needed. During very cold weather (20°F or less), keep a pail of water in the storage area to help maintain a cellar temperature above freezing (32°F).

Problem: **Insects in dry goods.**

Remedy: Small infestations are not unusual; food is usually safe to eat.

Prevention: Place dry goods inside airtight containers.

Problem: **Rodents in the cellar where food is stored.**

Remedy: Foods with scars or near droppings or fecal material should be discarded. Clean and sanitize walls, shelving, or floors as needed.

Prevention: Look for areas of entrance and seal them tight. Store foods in pest-resistant containers.

Problem: **Stored grapes seem fresh, but have an "off" flavor.**

Remedy: They are safe to eat. Soak grapes in a vinegar solution for 10 minutes, then rinse in clean water.

Prevention: Grapes readily absorb odors; store them away from other crops that give off ethylene gas (apples) or strong odors (cabbage).

Problem: **Food in the garden trenches or pits is fermented or rotten.**

Remedy: Discard moldy or decayed food. Fermented foods may be safe to eat; if unpalatable, try using in soups or adding to bread doughs and batters, which is traditional in many cultures throughout the world.

Prevention: Add a vent when building outdoor storage pits. Do not crowd vegetables in pits; place in an even, shallow layer.

Problem: **Food in the garden is frozen.**

Remedy: Prepare frozen food promptly; you may need to discard or compost excess frozen food, or cook into soup, if possible.

Prevention: Mulch garden plants with at least 6 inches of dry material. Increase mulch to 12 inches in severe weather.

Freezing Foods ⌘ 9

Freezing is a very simple form of food preservation and produces a product that is most like fresh food. However, frozen food is dependent on a relatively expensive appliance, a consistent supply of electricity, adequate preparation and packaging, and managing the use of the food.

Freezing temperatures are defined as 0°F or less. Frozen foods maintain best quality and storage life if the freezer is opened infrequently, is full of food (rather than half-empty), is located in a cool place (basement, not a hot garage in summer), and is well insulated. Here are some other general tips for freezing food:

- Freeze only food that is in perfect condition. Freezing does not improve quality. If you freeze overripe or spoiled food, it will still be in the same condition (or worse) when you thaw it.

- Freeze food in small portions to ensure rapid freezing. Smaller pieces freeze faster and result in better quality.

- Use the correct type of packaging or container.

- Wrap or seal food tightly so no air or water can get in or out.

- Maintain a freezer temperature of 0°F to −10°F.

- Do not freeze too many items at one time.

- Leave space around newly introduced packages and do not stack until they are frozen solid.

Equipment and Materials

There is a difference between freezing foods in a dedicated freezer appliance (a deep freezer) and the freezer compartment of your refrigerator. To maximize your food dollar, it is important that you understand the differences in storing frozen foods in these two appliances.

It is also important to understand how to properly prepare and package foods. Packaging is important to prevent freezer burn in all frozen foods. Freezer burn occurs when the packaging is inadequate and not airtight. Therefore, the type of wrapping material and containers must be freezer safe and keep air out.

Not All Freezers Are the Same

An easy way to remember the difference between the freezer compartment of your refrigerator and a deep freeze is that they are a lot like bank accounts:

⚜ A refrigerator freezer is a like a checking account.

⚜ A deep freezer is like a savings account.

In other words, a refrigerator freezer is for short-term storage (up to 1 month) and a deep freezer is for long-term storage (up to 12 months). Manage these resources carefully to derive the most benefit and keep energy costs down.

You get the most benefit from a deep freezer by buying food in quantity at bulk or sale prices. Extend the shelf life and maintain optimal quality by repacking and storing bulk foods in a deep freezer. For most efficient operation, plan meals a week or a month ahead, open the deep freeze infrequently to get products for several meals at a time, and use the refrigerator freezer for short-term storage.

You can purchase meats throughout the year on sale, or in bulk from a local or specialty butcher. Game meat tends to depend on hunting season. Some seafood is seasonal. You can save money on these seasonal foods, as well as bulk grains and nuts.

Locally grown fresh fruits and vegetables have a definite season and short life. You can most easily preserve their fresh qualities by freezing. Supermarket produce is grown primarily for eating when fresh, these varieties are well suited to early, mechanical harvest, and long-distance transportation, but not necessarily for preservation.

Your refrigerator freezer is useful to hold items retrieved from the deep freezer for use during the month, short-term storage of leftovers, or partially cooked foods that you plan to use during the month. For example, I may make a double batch of stew, and freeze the second batch in small amounts for lunches throughout the month (or deep freeze for later consumption). If we won't eat dinner leftovers within 2 or 3 days, I freeze them for later use (usually lunches).

When cooking whole grains or beans, I often cook an entire pound at a time. For example, I will soak beans, boil them until just tender, lightly salt them, and then drain, cool, and freeze them in small packages for use throughout the month. Whole grains can become breakfast cereal, or a side dish pilaf. Beans can be made into dip or spread, or combined with barbecue sauce for baked beans. Precooked grains and beans are healthful additions to any soup, stew, stir-fry, or pasta dish.

I use a similar technique with potatoes and other vegetables. I peel and cut several pounds at one time, blanch, and freeze. Potatoes are ready to sauté for breakfast or with savory seasonings to serve as a side dish. Greens and other vegetables are ready for chunky or creamed soups, stir-fries, or pasta dishes. I like the flexibility that packages of individual vegetables have—it's like your own brand of convenience food without the box or additives that come with commercially prepared packages.

Deep freezers come in two styles: upright and chest. Upright freezers look like a refrigerator and are easier to access, but use more energy. Chest freezers look like a big box whose top opens up. They are more energy efficient but more difficult to load and unload, so they require more attention to organization and management.

In addition, freezers may be manual or automatic defrost (also called *frost free*). Manual defrost freezers maintain better food quality than frost-free ones. Frost-free models utilize a fan to remove excess moisture, which also removes moisture from stored foods, particularly if they are inadequately wrapped. However, manual defrost freezers need to be turned off (or unplugged) and completely defrosted at least once a year or when ice accumulation is more than ¼ inch thick. Defrost when inventory is low for convenience. Temporarily store frozen food in insulated containers. After defrosting, clean the interior before turning the freezer back on, as described in the following sidebar. Frost-free freezers do not need to be defrosted; however, they should be cleaned at least once a year.

CLEANING YOUR FREEZER

Transfer the food temporarily to insulated containers and unplug the freezer. When it is warm, clean the freezer with a solution made of 1 tablespoon baking soda dissolved in 1 quart warm water. Wipe the interior with the cleaning solution using a clean cloth or sponge, then dry with an absorbent cloth. Plug in the freezer, close the door, and allow the freezer to completely chill (30 minutes or longer) before returning the food.

Packaging for the Freezer

Packaging for the freezer includes rigid containers and flexible wraps. Containers and wrapping material for frozen foods must be freezer safe, airtight, leakproof, and hold a maximum of 2 quarts (½ gallon).

Rigid containers may be made of plastic, glass, or wax-coated cardboard. Square containers take up less space than round ones, and therefore maximize your use of freezer space. If covers are not airtight, you should seal them with freezer tape, which sticks even at cold temperatures. Here are some tips for using these containers:

- ❖ Plastic containers need to be freezer-safe material that will not become brittle and crack at cold temperatures.

- ❖ Glass canning jars may be used as freezer containers. However, jars with a narrow or tapered top require extra headspace, or frozen food could expand and break the jar neck. Other types of glass containers can be used, provided they are made from thick, tempered glass that can withstand freezer temperatures. Most jars from previously purchased products are thin, nontempered glass and may crack at cold temperatures. The only way to tell for sure if a glass container is safe for freezing is to purchase glass containers designed specifically for freezing.

- ❖ Wax-coated cardboard boxes are acceptable for some products. Depending on the contents, you may need to line them with freezer-safe plastic wrap or bags, foil, greaseproof paper, or other leakproof materials.

Flexible packaging includes plastic bags, treated freezer paper, and foil. All of these supplies are available at supermarkets or other stores where housewares are sold:

- ✢ Plastic bags should be designed for freezer use. Thin food-storage bags are not airtight and allow air to pass through the bag. Some plastic food wraps are designed only for short-term use (up to 2 weeks) in the freezer.

- ✢ Freezer paper is specially designed with a plastic coating that keeps moisture in and air out.

- ✢ Foil is freezer safe, moisture proof, and airtight.

There are different ways to package the same food (for example, in rigid plastic containers, glass jars, freezer paper, foil, or plastic bags). Which method you use depends on the type of food, and may also be affected by how long you want to store and use the food.

PERFECT PRESERVING

When packaging liquids in narrow-mouth containers, leave 1½ inches of headspace for either pints or quarts. If packaged in wide-mouth containers, leave ½ inch of headspace for pints and 1 inch for quarts.

Freezing Methods

Most foods can be frozen with good results. All frozen products must have packaging that is airtight. Badly packaged foods can lead to loss of color, flavor, texture, nutrients, and possibly of the food itself if there are large areas of freezer burn.

Freezer burn happens when poorly wrapped food loses moisture and dries out during frozen storage. If you have food with freezer burn, you will see gray or white patches on the surface of the food. Freezer burn is not harmful, but the quality of the food is poor. Dehydrated food is dry, tough, and may be inedible. You can prevent freezer burn by wrapping foods airtight and using them within the recommended shelf life.

A Primer on Freezing Foods

Some foods just don't freeze well; when thawed, they may have a different texture that is unappealing or they may separate. Other foods freeze well, but only under certain conditions or if you take some precautions. Here's a list of what does and does not freeze well:

- ✢ Most cheese products change texture when thawed. Natural cheese keeps well in the refrigerator for a few weeks, so freezing is usually not necessary. Hard or semihard cheese is less affected by freezing and can be frozen in ½- to 1-pound pieces. Frozen pieces may become crumbly after thawing but will retain their flavor. Grated cheese freezes very successfully. Cream cheese and cottage cheese can be frozen, but due to texture changes are best if thawed slowly (24 hours) in the refrigerator and then blended for dips and spreads or baked in cheesecakes.

✦ Milk freezes successfully only if homogenized and pasteurized. Freezing may cause some separation; stir well before using. Milk may also become grainy when thawed.

✦ Heavy cream and whipped cream freeze well only if they contain 40 percent or more butterfat. To prevent separation, heat cream to 170°F to 180°F for 15 minutes, and then cool quickly in a shallow pan. Frozen heavy cream will not whip as stiffly after freezing as never-frozen cream. Freeze individual whipped cream garnishes by whipping cream, placing dollops of whipped cream on baking sheet, and freezing. Once solidly frozen, remove dollops and package in rigid containers. Use crumpled parchment paper or wax paper to take up headspace. For storage longer than 2 months, stir in $\frac{1}{3}$ cup sugar per quart of cream.

✦ Sour cream separates when thawed and cannot be blended again.

✦ Eggs in the shell, either raw or hard-cooked, may not be frozen. Raw eggs will crack when frozen, making them unsafe. To freeze raw eggs, crack open and either separate whites and yolks to freeze separately, or blend together before freezing. Hard-cooked eggs become spongy, rubbery, and unappetizing when thawed.

✦ Vegetables that you normally serve raw, such as salad greens, tomato slices, sliced cabbage for coleslaw, cucumbers, and radishes become limp when thawed. However, blanched greens and cabbage and peeled or unpeeled whole or quartered tomatoes can be successfully frozen and used for soups and stews. If unpeeled, tomato skins form thin threads in sauces or stews that are unacceptable to some cooks; peel or purée to avoid this issue.

✦ Vegetables that you normally serve cooked freeze well when properly blanched, cooled, and packaged. Remember that their cooking time will be greatly reduced. Most blanched and frozen vegetables can be heated very briefly for serving, or added at the last minute to soups and stews.

✦ Foods whose flavor intensifies in the freezer may contribute strong or off flavors when added to prepared foods. These include raw garlic or onion, raw chiles or bell peppers, cloves (a spice), and synthetic vanilla. Use these ingredients sparingly when you plan to freeze prepared foods that contain them.

✦ Salt loses intensity in the freezer. Rather than oversalting, cut the measure in half and plan to salt the food during preparation or consumption to return it to full flavor.

✦ Pasta (especially small shapes like elbow macaroni) freezes very successfully if slightly undercooked, chilled quickly in cold water, and drained well before packaging for the freezer. To facilitate use, spread well-drained pasta in a single layer on a paper-lined baking sheet, freeze, and then transfer to a zipper-lock plastic bag.

✦ Rice freezes very successfully if slightly undercooked. Spread in a single layer on a paper-lined baking sheet and chill in the refrigerator before packaging for the freezer.

✦ Crisp fried foods such as fried chicken, french fries, onion rings, or crumb toppings may become soggy when reheated in a moderate oven. Foods dredged in flour or crumbs recrisp more successfully upon reheating than batter-dipped foods. Toppings are best when added before reheating the frozen (or thawed) food in an oven.

⁜ Gravies and white sauces may separate when thawed and cannot be reblended, especially when they contain too much fat. To freeze these sauces successfully, use no more than 1 tablespoon fat (pan dripping or butter) and 1 to 2 tablespoons starch for each cup of liquid (water or stock) in sauce that you want to freeze. The best starches to use are arrowroot and instant tapioca. All-purpose flour and cornstarch can give mixed results, although I've used both successfully. Sauces thickened with potato flour thin out when reheated.

⁜ Mayonnaise and vinaigrette salad dressings separate when thawed and cannot be reblended.

⁜ Gelatin, meringue, custard, and cream fillings or puddings do not freeze well because they become watery or separate when thawed and cannot be blended again.

⁜ Jelly and jam freeze successfully. If freezing PB&J sandwiches, be sure to spread both bread slices with peanut butter to prevent jam from soaking into the bread and making the sandwich soggy when thawed and eaten.

⁜ Frosting made with egg whites thins out when thawed and cannot be rewhipped. However, butter cream, whipped cream, and fudge frostings freeze successfully.

Blanching Fruits and Vegetables

Blanching, or partial cooking, is used to prepare fruits and vegetables for freezing. Blanching helps fruits and vegetables retain color and stay fresh longer while they are frozen. Without blanching, enzymes that are naturally present remain active. Over time, enzyme activity alters the color, flavor, texture, and nutrient content of food.

When to Use Blanching

Blanch all vegetables before freezing, unless you know you will be using them within 1 month. Onions and peppers are two exceptions; these vegetables may be packaged and frozen raw.

Blanch fruits only if they turn brown when cut and you do not wish to control browning by some other method, such as ascorbic acid (see Chapters 2 and 7 for more details on how to prevent browning).

Meats, poultry, seafood, eggs, and dairy do not require blanching before freezing as enzyme activity does not affect their frozen storage life.

Water and Steam Blanching

There are two methods of blanching: water and steam.

Water blanching is a good method to use for large volumes of vegetables that you intend to preserve by freezing. A large stockpot with a basket (such as one used for cooking pasta) is ideal. Alternatively, you can use any large pot (8 to 10 quarts or larger), and a metal sieve or strainer to add and remove vegetables.

To water blanch vegetables, follow these steps:

1. Prepare the vegetables to be blanched by washing, peeling, slicing, and chopping into serving pieces as desired.

2. Prepare a large bowl or sink with water and ice. (If you use the kitchen sink, be sure to wash and sanitize it first.) You will use the ice bath to cool the vegetables quickly and stop the cooking.

3. Set up a colander over a large bowl for draining cooled vegetables.

4. Fill a large pot with water until ¾ full. Bring water to a full, rolling boil over high heat.

   Blanch up to 1 pound of vegetables for every 1 gallon of water. If desired, add 2 tablespoons of salt for every gallon of water. Salt helps retain the color and enhances the flavor of vegetables, but is optional.

5. Plunge vegetables into the boiling, salted water. Begin timing. The length of time you need to blanch vegetables depends on the size and thickness of the pieces; most take between 1 and 5 minutes. Test food frequently to determine whether blanching is sufficient. (See the following section for more information on timing.)

6. Lift vegetables from the boiling water using a basket or sieve, let the hot water drain back into the hot pot, and plunge vegetables into the ice water bath. Soak for the same length of time as the blanching period, or until vegetables are cool to the touch.

7. Remove cooled vegetables to the colander to drain for at least 30 minutes before packaging for frozen storage.

Steam blanching is useful for smaller amounts of chopped vegetables, or larger pieces—particularly slices of food, such as potatoes. Use a steamer or a large pot or wok fitted with a steamer rack, add pieces of food in a single layer, cover, and steam for the recommended period. You need a large pot or wok fitted with a rack that will hold vegetables over, not in boiling water.

To steam blanch vegetables, follow these steps:

1. Prepare vegetables, ice bath, and a colander as described in steps 1 through 3 for water blanching.

2. Bring water to a boil in a pot or wok fitted with a steamer rack; add pieces of food in a single layer, and cover. Steam for the recommended period—generally 1 to 5 minutes depending on the size and thickness of the pieces. You need to develop the skill for judging when blanching is sufficient, which should stop short of cooking the piece all the way through.

3. Remove vegetables from the steamer, cool, and drain as described in steps 6 and 7 for water blanching.

Notes on Blanching Time

Some blanching methods recommend you start timing after the water returns to a boil. However, I find this often leads to overblanching, so I like to start timing immediately. Ideally, you want the water to return to a boil in 1 minute; if it takes much longer, you have too many vegetables in the pot.

PERFECT PRESERVING

Adding salt to the blanching water improves the flavor of frozen vegetables.

Test food for sufficient blanching by cutting through or biting into a piece. It should be tender-crisp—tender on the outside, and firm or crunchy in the center. The vegetable will be translucent near the edge, but still opaque in the center.

Blanching time varies with the size of the vegetable pieces. Thick potato slices will take longer to blanch than small cubes. Leafy greens and small vegetables such as peas and corn kernels can take as little as 1 minute and large corn cobs as long as 10 minutes. The following table lists blanching times for some common vegetables cut in varying sizes. Use this table as a guide.

Blanching Times for Common Vegetables

Vegetable	Water Blanching Time
¼-inch slices or cubes:	1–2 minutes
Cabbage	
Carrots, diced	
Celery, diced	
Collards	
Corn kernels	
Eggplant, cubed	
Kale	
Kohlrabi, cubed	
Mustard and other greens (turnip, beet)	
Onion, diced (can be frozen raw without blanching)	
Peas, shelled	
Peppers, cut into strips or rings (can be frozen raw without blanching)	
Spinach or chard	
1-inch pieces:	2–4 minutes
Broccoli florets	
Brussels sprouts	
Cauliflower	

Vegetable	Water Blanching Time
Sticks or spears:	2–4 minutes
Asparagus, whole spears	
Beans, shelled	
Beans, string	
Carrot sticks	
Okra pods	
Parsnips, sliced or cubed	
Pea pods, edible	
Potatoes, sliced or cubed	
Rutabagas, sliced or cubed	
Squash, summer, sliced or cubed	
Turnips, sliced or cubed	
Large pieces (1–3 inches):	3–6 minutes
Artichoke hearts	
Artichokes, Jerusalem	
Carrots, whole	
Kohlrabi, whole	
Mushrooms, whole	
Onions, sliced	
Parsnips, small whole	
Potatoes, whole	
Rutabagas, small whole	
Squash, summer, small whole	
Turnips, small whole	
Very large pieces:	7–9 minutes
Corn on the cob	
Beets, slices or cubes	Do not blanch; cook until tender
Pumpkin, slices or cubes	
Squash, winter, slices or cubes	
Sweet potatoes, slices or cubes	

Although this table can give you general guidelines, don't rely on it to tell you how long to blanch vegetables before freezing. Blanching time varies with the size and thickness of your pieces and maturity of the vegetables (underripe or ripe). You need to develop the skill for judging when steam blanching is sufficient. Underblanching stimulates, rather than deactivates enzymes, which is the goal of blanching. Overblanching causes loss of flavor, color, and nutrients.

Packing Methods

The methods for freezing fruits and vegetables include dry pack and liquid pack. Dry pack simply means to seal the food in a package and freeze it. Liquid pack immerses the food in liquid and freezes the solids and liquid together. There are variations for each of these basic methods.

Dry Pack and Tray Pack

When using dry pack, you simply place food in a package that will be used all at one time and freeze it. Once frozen, the individual pieces usually form one solid mass. To use the food, you must thaw and use the entire package.

An alternative dry-pack method is tray pack, which prefreezes the food before packaging so the food does not freeze in a block as with dry pack. To use the tray-pack method, spread the food in a single layer on a shallow tray. Place it in the freezer until solid (30 to 120 minutes), and then package. The advantage of tray pack is the pieces stay separate, allowing you to freeze larger quantities, remove part of the contents of a frozen package for use, and return the frozen remainder to the freezer. For example, if you tray pack frozen peas in a 1-quart zipper-lock plastic bag, you can easily pour out 1 cup, reclose the bag, and return it to the freezer.

Tray pack is useful for small, individual pieces of fruits, such as berries and diced vegetables.

Without salt, the flavor of vegetables can be improved by adding lemon juice or spices. Drizzle 1 to 2 tablespoons lemon or orange juice on each quart of vegetables (especially carrots, beets, or asparagus) before packaging. Sprinkle ¼ to ½ teaspoon ground mace, nutmeg, or curry powder per quart of vegetables (especially green beans or peas) before packaging. These small amounts are not intended to add flavor but bring out the natural flavors of the vegetables.

Liquid Packs

Sugar-pack mixes cut fruit with sugar, forming a syrup that protects the color and flavor of fruit during storage. For example, peeled and diced peaches or strawberry halves can be sprinkled with sugar and allowed to stand 30 minutes in the refrigerator, or until syrup forms. Package fruit with syrup in amounts that will be used at one time. Sugar packs freeze like dry packs, in one solid block.

Syrup pack immerses fruit in sugar syrup before packaging. Package fruit with any sugar syrup, pickling syrup, or sugar-free liquid listed in Chapter 7, or use pectin syrup (see the following sidebar).

Plain water or unsweetened liquids such as fruit juice may be used to pack fruits. Sugar-free liquids do not preserve the color, flavor, and texture as well as fruits packed with some sugar (dry or syrup). Plain or salted water may be used to pack vegetables or fruits. Like sugar, salt helps protect color and flavor.

MAKING A PECTIN SYRUP

Pectin pack is an unsweetened alternative to water or fruit juice that better protects the texture of fruit. To make pectin syrup for frozen fruits, stir together 1 (1.75-ounce) package powdered pectin with 1 cup water in a small (1-quart) saucepan. Heat over medium heat to boiling; boil 1 minute. Remove from heat, add 1¾ cups water, and stir until blended. Cool. Add more water if thinner syrup is desired. This makes about 3 cups syrup.

Artificial sweeteners may be used in any unsweetened liquid. However, they will only sweeten the fruit and will not help protect the color and texture like dry sugar or syrup, or the texture like pectin syrup.

Freezer Packing Methods for Fruits and Vegetables

Method	Fruit	Vegetables
Dry pack	Yes	Yes
Tray pack	Yes	Yes
Water/liquid	Yes	Yes
Pectin water	Yes	No
Sugar pack	Yes	No
Syrup pack	Yes	No
Unsweetened juice	Yes	No

Meat and Poultry Packing Methods

Tray-wrapped fresh meats purchased at grocery stores are not meant for long-term freezer storage. Meats in foam trays with overwrap will show freezer burn in just a few weeks. To store them longer, unwrap, and discard the store packaging. Then rewrap the meat in new, flexible wrapping. Meats and poultry purchased already frozen do not need to be rewrapped.

Seafood Packing Methods

There are three packing methods for seafood. Since seafood is highly perishable, using one of these methods will considerably extend the storage life of your fresh fish, protecting the nutrition and flavor:

- **Ice glaze.** Place unwrapped fish in the freezer. As soon as it is frozen 30 to 120 minutes, dip fish in ice water. Place fish again in the freezer a few minutes. When the glaze is hardened (30 minutes), repeat the dipping and freezing process until a uniform cover of ice is formed. Wrap the frozen fish in freezer paper, foil, or heavy plastic wrap.

❧ **Water immersion.** Place fish in a shallow metal, plastic, or foil pan that fits it closely. Cover fish with water and freeze. When the water is frozen solid, remove the ice block with the fish frozen inside, and wrap it in freezer paper, foil, or heavy plastic wrap. Alternatively, the fish can be placed in a zipper-lock plastic freezer bag, filled with water, and placed on a tray until frozen solid.

❧ **Lemon-gelatin glaze.** To prepare glaze, stir together ¼ cup lemon juice with 1¾ cups water. In a small bowl, stir together ½ cup lemon juice–water mixture and 1 (¼-ounce or about 2¼-teaspoon) packet of unflavored gelatin, until dissolved. Heat remaining 1½ cups lemon juice–water mixture to boiling. Stir dissolved gelatin mixture into the boiling liquid. Cool to room temperature before using. Dip cold fish into lemon-gelatin glaze and drain. Wrap fish in freezer paper, foil, or heavy plastic wrap.

Seafood Pretreatment Methods

Fish are categorized as either oily/fatty or white/lean. Oily fish include anchovies, eel, herring, mackerel, orange roughy, salmon, sardines/sprats, swordfish, trout, and fresh tuna. Lean fish include bass, catfish, cod, flounder, grouper, haddock, hake, John Dory, marlin, monkfish, pollack, redfish, snapper, sheepshead, sole, tilapia, turbot, whiting, most freshwater fishes, and most shellfish such as clams, scallops, and shrimp.

Before freezing, pretreat oily fish to decrease rancidity and flavor changes. Treat lean fish to firm fish and decrease moisture loss on thawing.

❧ Dip oily fish in an ascorbic acid solution for 20 seconds. For ascorbic acid, dissolve 2 teaspoons ascorbic acid powder in 1 quart of cold water.

❧ Dip lean fish in a brine for 20 seconds. To make brine: dissolve ¼ cup salt in 1 quart of cold water.

Freezer Packing Methods for Meats, Poultry, and Seafood

Method	Meat	Poultry	Seafood
Dry pack	+	+	+
Tray pack	+	+	+
Ice glaze	-	-	+
Water immersion	-	-	+
Lemon-gelatin glaze	-	-	+
Pretreat	o	o	+

+ = best method, - = limited method, o = not recommended

Wrapping Methods

Flexible wraps include plastic, paper, and foil. Solid pieces of meat, poultry, and seafood freeze best when wrapped in flexible packaging using a method that excludes all possible air. In addition to meats, you may remove frozen blocks of fruits or vegetables from their freezing container, and wrap in flexible materials. This allows you to use the container again for another purpose. Pop the frozen block from the container, wrap, and return to the freezer.

There are two standard wrapping methods: butcher wrap and drugstore wrap.

Butcher wrap rolls freezer paper or foil around a piece of meat or frozen block of food (such as dry-pack vegetables), and tucks in the ends before completing the wrap, and sealing with tape. Here's how to do it:

1. Use a piece of freezer paper, foil, or heavy plastic wrap about 2 to 3 times the size of the food to be wrapped.

2. Place food close to one corner of the wrap; fold the corner flap over the food.

3. Fold the left and right sides over first flap.

4. Roll the package over and over to the opposite edge.

5. Use freezer tape to seal edges.

Drugstore wrap begins by pulling the sides up over the food to be wrapped, folding the sides down until they rest against the product, folding the ends under, and securing with tape. Here are the steps:

1. Use a piece of freezer paper, foil, or heavy plastic wrap about 2 to 3 times the size of the food to be wrapped.

2. Place food in the center of the freezer wrap.

3. Bring the two longest edges together above the food. Fold them down about 1 inch. Continue folding, making a 1-inch fold each time until the fold rests flat against the food.

4. Press out as much air as possible at each end.

5. Fold ends down tightly against the package and use freezer tape to seal.

PERFECT PRESERVING

You can download a PDF file titled *Freezing Animal Products* from the National Center for Home Food Preservation. It contains step-by-step drawings to help you master these two wrapping methods. Go to nchfp.uga.edu/publications/uga/FreezingAnimalProducts.pdf.

Food and Freezer Management

The most important concepts in managing your frozen foods are temperature, rotation, thawing, and power outages. Here are some tips for managing your supply of frozen food:

- Maintain temperatures of 0°F to –10°F in the deep freezer. Freezer compartments in the average refrigerator are not true freezers and should only be used for short-term storage of 1 month or less.

- Chill foods thoroughly before freezing.

- Label and date all foods.

- Freeze no more than 2 pounds of food for every cubic foot of freezer capacity within a 24-hour period. For example, for a 20-cubic-foot freezer, add no more than 40 pounds of food, which is about 10 roasts or whole chickens.

- Freeze new foods in a single layer. Stack them up to conserve space only after they are frozen solid.

- Keep a freezer inventory near the freezer (or taped to the front). Add new foods along with their use-by date. Cross foods off when they are removed. Update the inventory as needed.

- Thaw foods in the refrigerator, never at room temperature. If you must quickly thaw something, place it in a waterproof bag and immerse the bag in a large bowl with cold running water. Thaw in the microwave only if you plan to immediately prepare the food. Microwaving tends to warm the food and promote microbial spoilage.

Cleaning to Remove Odors

If food has spoiled in a freezer because of a power failure or some other reason, it is very important to promptly discard the food and clean the interior of the freezer. Turn off or unplug the freezer, defrost if necessary, and allow it to come to room temperature.

Clean a warm freezer with a solution made of 1 tablespoon baking soda in 1 quart tap water, or 1 cup of white vinegar in 1 gallon tap water. Wipe the interior with the cleaning solution using a clean cloth or sponge. Dry after cleaning with an absorbent cloth. Turn the freezer on, close the door, and allow the freezer to completely chill (30 minutes or longer) before adding food.

If a bad odor from spoiled food persists after cleaning, use activated charcoal. This type of charcoal is extra dry and absorbs odors more quickly than barbecue charcoal. Purchase activated charcoal at a drugstore or pet supplies store. To use it, unplug the freezer. Put the charcoal in shallow containers in the bottom of the freezer for several days. If the odor remains, discard charcoal and replace with fresh. When the odor is gone, clean the freezer as described earlier in the chapter before reloading it. If the odor has moved into the insulation, it may not be possible to remove it and you may have to discard the freezer. Be sure to remove the door and dispose of the appliance properly according to the regulations in your state.

Dealing with a Power Outage

Food in a fully loaded freezer may stay frozen for 2 to 4 days. A half-filled freezer may keep food frozen only about 24 hours. To maximize storage time without power, avoid opening the freezer door and cover the freezer with blankets; however, take care not to cover the compressor, which is usually located in the lower rear of the freezer. If needed, ice may be brought in after 24 hours to maintain cold temperatures.

Food can be safely refrozen if …

- Its color and odor are good.

- It has been kept at a temperature of 40°F or below.

- It still has ice crystals in the package.

SPOILER ALERT

Any food stored for more than 2 hours at temperatures above 40°F could be unsafe and should be discarded.

Troubleshooting Frozen Foods

Problem: **Food has white, gray, or brown areas (known as freezer burn).**

Remedy: Food is probably safe, but may be dry, unappetizing, or inedible.

Prevention: Thaw in refrigerator; trim and discard freezer-burned portions. Cook meats with liquids, such as by stewing, or use to make soup. Pack foods in freezer-safe containers; remove all air from flexible wraps. If food does not fill container, add parchment paper, waxed paper, or foil to take up the extra airspace. Use frozen food within 1 year.

Problem: **Glass jars or plastic containers break or crack in the freezer.**

Remedy: Food may contain small particles of glass or plastic and is not safe to eat. Discard container and food.

Prevention: Be sure your containers are freezer safe. Use adequate headspace, usually ½ to 1 inch. Chill foods before freezing, so outside doesn't freeze before interior.

Problem: **Vegetables are dull in color or turn brown.**

Remedy: Food is safe to eat but may be dry, unappetizing, or inedible. Use in soups.

Prevention: Blanch vegetables adequately, and cool properly before freezing. Pack foods in freezer-safe containers; remove all air from flexible wraps. If food does not fill the container, add parchment paper, waxed paper, or foil to take up the extra airspace, or pack in salted water.

Problem: **Power is out in the freezer.**

Remedy: Keep the door closed; cover the freezer (but not the compressor or any vents) with heavy blankets. Add ice to the freezer or transfer food temporarily to insulated containers until power is restored. Use a thermometer to monitor the storage temperature of the food. Discard foods that have been at 40°F for more than 2 hours. If food is stored at 40°F or lower, and still contains ice crystals, you may refreeze it. Discard foods that have been contaminated by raw meat juices.

Prevention: Have a plan in place in case of a power outage. A freezer full of food will usually keep about 2 days if the door is kept shut; a half-full freezer will last about a day. Will you use ice, ice packs, and picnic coolers? A generator? Do you have shelf-stable foods to eat, so the freezer door can remain closed? Use other shelf-stable methods of preservation, such as drying or canning, for some of your food.

Problem: **Eggs in shell froze and cracked.**

Remedy: Eggs are not safe; discard safely by placing in a plastic garbage bag and disposing in a trash bin or landfill. Uncracked eggs may be used for baking or hard-cooked.

Prevention: Store eggs in a carton to maintain constant temperature and guard against freezing.

Recipes ⚜ 2

A lot of preserving books give you five ways to make berry jam. I wanted to make sure that you knew five different ways to preserve berries, plus suggest ways to use your stash of berries in sauces, snacks, pies, smoothies, and more. Most of the recipes in this book are simple to prepare. In some cases, they feature common, everyday foods in uncommon but tasty recipes from cultures around the world. Many of them include variations, so whether you like things mild or hot, sweet or tart, you'll find many delicious ways to enjoy the foods you "put by." There are treats like Hawaiian dried fruit (called *crack seed*), Thai-style dried beef, citrusy pickled onions, Mexican barbecue sauce … oh, and more than a few ways to make berry jam. Each recipe was chosen to demonstrate one or more of the essential techniques you learned in Part 1.

Dried Foods  10

Drying is the oldest method of food preservation. Almost every type of food can be dried, including fruits, vegetables, herbs, meats, seafood, grains, legumes, nuts, and seeds. There are several methods you can use to dry foods, and some work better than others for specific types of food.

Dried Fruits

Fruits are one of the easiest foods to dry. Berries need no preparation other than washing. You may need to peel and cut other fruits, or treat them to prevent darkening.

Because sugars become concentrated when fruit is dried, most dried fruits are sweeter than their fresh counterparts. However, if mature or underripe fruits are dried, they can become tart. Dried fruits have many uses; use them dried for snacking or rehydrated in recipes—from sauces to baked goods.

Dried Whole Fruits

Fruits such as berries, cherries, and figs are suitable for drying whole—and, of course, dried grapes become raisins. These small fruits require almost no other preparation, so it's very easy to preserve some summer bounty for use throughout the year.

PERFECT PRESERVING

The recipes in this section specify oven or dehydrator drying; however, all fruits may also be dried using sun or solar methods. You'll find instructions for these methods and plenty of other helpful preparation tips in Chapter 2, as well as instruction on how to pretreat fruits and vegetables to prevent browning, inactivate spoilage enzymes, "check" fruit skins to promote complete drying, and prevent the growth of harmful microorganisms. Once your fruits are dried, be sure to also review the information in Chapter 2 about the best ways to cool, package, and store them for longest storage life.

Dried Berries

Dried berries are among the easiest dried foods to prepare and are chock-full of healthful antioxidants. They're wonderful tossed into cereal or yogurt, added to baked goods, combined with nuts in trail mix, or substituted in any recipe calling for raisins.

Yield:	Prep time:	Drying time:	Serving size:
½ to 1 pound	20 to 40 minutes	24 to 36 hours	1 to 2 ounces

3 lb. (about 3 qt.) fresh, whole, soft or firm berries

1. Wash berries. Large strawberries may be halved, quartered, or sliced. Leave all other berries whole. Pretreat firm berries by checking. Spread berries on towel-lined trays to remove excess moisture.

2. Preheat the oven or food dehydrator to 130°F to 140°F. Place berries on the drying trays. Dry until berries have shrunk considerably, are wrinkled and no longer sticky, and there is no visible moisture when squeezed or cut. Dry until pliable for snacking, or until brittle for longer storage.

3. Cool 30 minutes, or until no longer warm. Remove berries from the drying trays. Store berries in an airtight container in a cool, dry place.

Variations: For **Dried Cherries** (any variety, tart or sweet), wash fresh cherries. Pretreat whole cherries by checking or piercing. Drain in a colander, and spread on towel-lined trays to remove water. Pit cherries for the most flexibility in use and faster drying. Pretreat gold cherries for browning. For **Dried Grapes** (raisins), wash grapes. For seeded grapes, cut in half and remove seeds before drying. Pretreat whole grapes by checking or piercing. Place grapes on drying trays (cut side up for halved grapes).

HOW TO PIT CHERRIES

You can pit cherries using a hairpin or paper clip (opened up into an S shape). Push the loop of either one into the stem end of the cherry. Move the loop around and under the pit, and then pull up. Some pits are easier to extract than others! You can also purchase a cherry- or olive-pitting tool at any kitchen supply store. There are several types, including handheld tools and countertop models.

Tart Cherry Crack Seed

Salty dried fruits known as crack seed are popular in Hawaii. Historically, Asian travelers used them for long-distance travel, to restore salt lost from perspiration and reduce muscle cramps. Popular examples include *li hing mui* (traveling plum) and *umeboshi*, both salty dried plums.

Yield:	Prep time:	Drying time:	Serving size:
1 pound	2 hours to 5 days	8 to 24 hours	1 to 2 ounces

1 qt. water

1 cup brown sugar

3 TB. salt

3 medium lemons, juiced

1 tsp. Chinese five-spice powder

3 lb. (6 cups, pitted) fresh cherries (tart, sour, or pie)

1. In a small saucepan, combine water, brown sugar, salt, and lemon juice, and bring to a boil over high heat. Reduce heat to low, and cook 10 minutes, or until brown sugar dissolves.

2. Raise heat to high, add Chinese five-spice powder and cherries, and bring to a boil. Reduce to a simmer, and poach gently for 5 minutes. Remove from heat and allow cherries to cool in syrup up to 2 hours. For additional flavor, cover and refrigerate up to 5 days before drying.

3. Preheat an oven or food dehydrator to 130°F to 140°F. Spread cherries on towel-lined trays to remove moisture before placing on the drying trays. Dry until cherries are pliable, have shrunk considerably, and there is no visible moisture when squeezed or cut. Sweet varieties may remain very slightly sticky.

4. Cool 30 minutes, or until no longer warm. Remove from drying tray. Store in an airtight container in a cool, dry place.

Variations: For **Sweet Cherry Crack Seed,** poach unpitted fresh sweet cherries (such as Bing) in brine before drying. To make brine, combine in a small saucepan over high heat 1 quart water, ½ cup kosher or pickling salt, and 750 milligrams ascorbic acid to preserve color (if desired). Bring to a boil and stir until salt dissolves. Meanwhile, in a large bowl, sprinkle 3 pounds sweet cherries with 1 teaspoon Chinese five-spice powder. Pour hot brine over cherries. Cool 30 minutes, then refrigerate up to 5 days; the longer they soak, the saltier the crack seed will be. Drain and pat dry before placing cherries on the drying trays.

Dried Figs

The Greeks enjoyed succulent figs in ancient times, and they're just as tasty today. Figs are wonderful when stewed with apples and cinnamon, braised with meat, added to poultry stuffing, or substituted in any recipe that calls for prunes.

Yield:	Prep time:	Drying time:	Serving size:
1 pound	40 minutes	8 to 24 hours	1 to 2 ounces

3 lb. (about 36) small fresh figs

1. Wash figs. Pretreat light-colored varieties for browning. Pretreat whole figs by checking or piercing. Spread on towel-lined trays to remove excess moisture.

2. Preheat an oven or food dehydrator to 130°F to 140°F. Place figs on the drying trays. Dry until figs are pliable but no longer sticky, and there is no visible moisture when squeezed or cut.

3. Cool 30 minutes, or until no longer warm. Remove from the drying trays. Store in an airtight container in a cool, dry place.

Variation: For **Dried Italian Prunes or Plums** (any variety, such as greengage, mirabelle, or wild plums), wash fruit. Pretreat by checking when drying plums whole. Drain in a colander, and spread on towel-lined trays to remove most of the water.

PERFECT PRESERVING

The best fig varieties for drying have small seeds and sweet flavor. Select ripe figs that yield to soft pressure for the sweetest dried fruit with no sour taste. Figs have a short shelf life of just 3 days in the refrigerator, so plan to dry them soon after they are ripe. Figs bruise easily, so handle them gently. The smallest figs (less than 2 inches) can be dried whole. Larger fruits may take over 24 hours to dry, so cut into halves or quarters to speed up drying time. If you live in the desert and dry figs in the sun, be sure to cover with cheesecloth to reduce exposure that will make the skins tough and zap the flavor.

Dried Halved, Sliced, or Chopped Fruits

Fruits larger than berries and cherries—like apples and peaches—need to be halved, sliced, or chopped to facilitate drying. Like whole small fruits, dried halves and slices can be enjoyed in many of the same ways, whether used in recipes or just for snacking. They make mouthwatering dried-fruit snacks. They're wonderful blended with equal parts water for quick and yummy sauces and are great for pies and cobblers, too. Just rehydrate and use like you would fresh or frozen fruit.

To cut dried fruit easily, use a clean pair of scissors instead of chopping with a knife. Dip the scissors in hot water as needed to get rid of sticky buildup. If the fruit is very dry, rehydrate before cutting. To rehydrate, soak for 20 to 30 minutes in water, fruit juice, or liquor such as rum, brandy, or wine. Use hot liquid for faster plumping.

Dried Stone Fruits

Brightly colored stone fruits are a delectable way to promote healthful eating of everything from breakfast cereals and yogurts, to salads, to side dishes, to baked goods. These tasty beauties can be used in the same way as raisins or figs.

Yield:	Prep time:	Drying time:	Serving size:
1 pound	20 to 40 minutes	8 to 24 hours	1 to 2 ounces

3 lb. (about 3 pt.) fresh apricots, cherries, nectarines, peaches, or plums

1. Wash fruit. Prepare as desired (see the following sidebar). Pat dry to remove excess moisture.

2. Preheat an oven or food dehydrator to 130°F to 140°F. Place fruit on drying trays. Dry until fruit has shrunk considerably and there is no visible moisture when squeezed or cut. Dry until pliable for snacking, or until crisp for longer storage.

3. Cool 30 minutes, or until no longer warm. Remove from drying trays. Store in an airtight container in a cool, dry place.

Variations: For **Dried Apples, Pears, or Asian Pears,** wash fruit. Peel if desired, core, and slice or chop. Pretreat for browning. Pat dry to remove excess moisture. For **Dried Tropical Fruits,** wash fruit. Peel and remove seeds or cores as needed. Slice fruit thick or paper thin, or dice into ¹/₂-inch pieces, and pat dry to remove excess moisture. For **Candied Fruits,** combine 2 cups sugar and 1¹/₂ cups cup water in a medium (2-quart) saucepan, bring to a boil over high heat, reduce heat to medium-low, and simmer for 10 minutes. Add about 1 pound thick fruit slices, and poach 20 to 30 minutes, or until fruit becomes translucent. Lift fruit from syrup and roll in ¹/₂ cup sugar. Place sugared fruit on drying trays. Reserve syrup for another use. Dry until leathery.

PREPARING STONE FRUITS

The sweetest dried fruits are made from fully ripe stone fruits. Blanch cherries and plums to check their tough, waxy skins when drying halves. Pit cherries and cut in half or chop. Cut apricots, nectarines, and plums in half; remove pits or stones (do not peel); and quarter or chop if desired. Blanch peaches to peel the skins, cut in half or slice, and remove the pits. To remove the pit in stone fruits, look for freestone varieties, whose pits are easier to remove than clingstone varieties. Treat light-colored stone fruits to prevent browning, including gold cherries, apricots, nectarines, and peaches.

Dried Citrus Fruit and Zest

Dried citrus wheels add an exciting flavor accent to many dishes from *kung pao* shrimp to fruit compote. Grind zest to powder to add citrusy notes to baked goods, salad dressings, and spice rubs.

Yield:	Prep time:	Drying time:	Serving size:
¹/₄ to ¹/₂ pound	10 minutes	6 to 24 hours	1 to 2 ounces

3 lb. (about 12 medium) fresh citrus fruit (any variety)

1. Wash citrus fruit. Either slice whole fruits for drying, leave peel on, remove any pits, and pat dry to remove excess moisture; or remove peel from citrus, using a small, sharp knife or potato peeler. When peeling, trim off the outer colored portion of the citrus peel, as if you were peeling an apple. Try not to include any of the white pith, which is bitter. You can buy a zesting tool that trims peel off in thin strips. Use the fruit for juice or fresh eating.

2. Preheat an oven or food dehydrator to 130°F to 140°F. Place fruit or zest slices on drying trays. Dry until crisp.

3. Cool 30 minutes, or until no longer warm. Remove from drying trays. Store in an airtight container in a cool, dry place.

Variation: For **Candied Citrus,** slice 3 whole citrus or cut the peels from 6 fruits into ¼-inch slices. In a small (1-quart) saucepan, cover citrus or peels with cold water, and bring to a boil over high heat. Pour off water. Repeat boiling process two more times to remove bitter qualities, and then set the citrus aside in a small bowl. Combine 2 cups sugar and 1½ cups water in a medium (2-quart) saucepan, and bring to a boil over high heat. Reduce heat to medium-low, and simmer for 10 minutes. Add boiled citrus or peels, and poach 20 to 30 minutes, or until fruit becomes translucent. Lift fruit from syrup and roll in ½ cup sugar. Place sugared fruit on drying trays. Reserve syrup for another use. Dry until leathery.

PERFECT PRESERVING

Dry almost any variety of citrus, including grapefruit, kumquat, lemon, lime, orange, or tangerine. Dry ¼-inch slices with or without peels, as desired. Some peels contribute more bitter flavors than others. When choosing a variety, remember that flavors intensify when dried; bitter citruses such as Seville oranges will become more bitter. Choose thick peels to peel for zest; they're easier to prepare. Choose organic fruit for peels without chemical residues (organic citrus fruits may not have bright colors because they aren't injected with artificial dyes). Fresh citrus can be stored at room temperature or loose in the refrigerator crisper, and stay fresh for about 2 weeks.

Dried Melon

Dried melon—which Marco Polo once described as "sweet as honey"—makes a melt-in-your-mouth snack. Drying intensifies their aromatic, musky flavors. Cantaloupe, honeydew, and watermelon in particular provide distinctive, ethereal tastes.

Yield:	Prep time:	Drying time:	Serving size:
½ to 1 pound	20 minutes	4 to 20 hours	1 to 2 ounces

3 lb. (1 medium) fresh melon (any variety)

1. Wash melon. Peel, seed, and slice melon thick or paper thin, and pat dry to remove excess moisture.

2. Preheat an oven or food dehydrator to 130°F to 140°F. Place melon on drying trays. Dry thick slices until pliable and no moisture is visible when squeezed or cut. Dry paper-thin slices until crisp.

3. Cool 30 minutes, or until no longer warm. Remove from drying trays. Store in an airtight container in a cool, dry place.

Variation: For **Dried Melon Seeds,** place melon seeds in a large bowl of water. Rub seeds to loosen stringy fibers. Discard any seeds that float to the top. Remove seeds from water and rinse in a sieve. Repeat soaking, rubbing, and rinsing in several changes of water, until seeds are clean. Place seeds in a small saucepan, and add 2 cups water and 1 tablespoon salt for every cup of seeds. Bring to a boil, reduce heat to medium-low, and simmer for 10 minutes. Drain seeds and place on drying trays. Dry thoroughly until they rattle.

PERFECT PRESERVING

Melons are usually enjoyed as a refreshing fruit in late summer when they are in season. Fermented into wine, watermelon juice is a wonderful beverage to be enjoyed long after summer has faded. Smooth melon rinds can be pickled or made into jam. Dried melon can be enjoyed as a sweet snack all year; the seeds can also be dried and are said to treat impotence. Add dried melon seeds as a substitute in any recipe calling for pumpkin seeds or simply for crunchy texture. Toast the seeds and use them to make nut brittle, or grind them finely using a coffee grinder and use them to thicken soups or stews.

Fruit Leathers or Fruit Rolls

Fruit leathers are made from fruit purées that are spread thin, and then dried until they become supple, leatherlike sheets of chewy fruit. The sheets are usually rolled up and individually wrapped for storage.

The best fruit rolls are made from apples, apricots, cherries, mangos, nectarines, peaches, pineapples, and plums. Combine other fruits with these "best" options for optimal results:

- Combine watery fruit purées such as citrus or melon with purée from one of the best fruits.

- Sweeten tart fruits such as crabapple, cranberry, and quince by combining with a very sweet fruit such as apple or pineapple. Alternatively, add ½ cup honey or corn syrup, or saccharin-based artificial sweetener to taste.

- Strain berry seeds from purée before combining with other fruits.

- Combine bananas, berries, dates, figs, guavas, and grapes with another fruit for best results.

Use your imagination and combine fruits you and your family love. Here are a few ideas to get your creative juices flowing: apple-quince-honey, apricot-fig, cherry-rhubarb, mango-guava, nectarine-blueberry, peach-raspberry, pineapple-orange-banana, and plum-pear.

Apple Leather

Leathers concentrate flavors into a chewy, satisfying snack. They're the best way to get a fruit fix during winter or to have a summer reverie anytime.

Yield:	Prep time:	Drying time:	Serving size:
8 rolls	10 to 20 minutes	4 hours to 2 days	1 fruit roll

> 1½ lb. fresh apples (4 to 5 medium), 2½ cups frozen apple slices, 2 cups drained canned apples, 2 cups apple purée, or 2 cups applesauce

1. Wash fresh apples. Peel if desired, core, and cut in chunks. Including skins is optional for fruits that are often eaten fresh without peeling (such as apples and peaches). Pretreat for browning. In a blender or food mill, process fruit chunks or slices to a smooth purée.

2. Preheat an oven or food dehydrator to 130°F to 140°F. Using plastic wrap or parchment paper, line the dehydrator trays. Spread purée ¼ to ½ inch thick on the liner. Dry leather until evenly pliable and firm; there should be no soft spots when pressed in the center.

3. Peel leather from the liner while still warm. Cut or roll into serving pieces. Cool 30 minutes, or until no longer warm. Wrap individually, and store in an airtight container in a cool, dry place.

Variations: For **Spiced Apple Leather,** add ¼ teaspoon ground cinnamon, ⅛ teaspoon ground nutmeg, and ⅛ teaspoon ground cloves to the purée and stir until well combined. For **Nut-and-Honey Apple Leather,** add ½ cup honey, ½ cup finely chopped toasted almonds, and ⅛ teaspoon almond extract to the purée and stir until well combined. For **Quince Leather (Quince Paste),** use 4 pounds quince, 2 tablespoons honey (or to taste), and 1 tablespoon fresh or bottled lemon juice (or to taste). Wash and quarter quince. In a large (4-quart) saucepan, cover quince with water, and bring to a boil over high heat. Reduce heat to medium-low, cover, and simmer 1 hour, or until very soft. Press quince through a sieve or food mill to remove seeds and skin. In a small (1-quart) saucepan, add quince purée. Cook over medium heat 1 hour, until reduced to 2 cups thick purée. Add honey (flavor concentrates after drying). Add lemon juice to brighten flavor. Dry as directed.

PERFECT PRESERVING

Making fruit leather is a good way to use culls, ripe fruit, slightly bruised fruit, or fruit left over from making jam or other preparations. If needed, add a small amount of water to facilitate puréeing. Embellish flavor by adding spices, extracts, nuts, seeds, coconut, or finely chopped dried fruits. Leathers studded with solid pieces (like nuts, dried fruits, or coconut) may not roll up without breaking; cut these leathers into strips without rolling. Typical drying times for leathers are 4 to 8 hours in a food dehydrator, 12 to 20 hours in an oven, or 1 to 2 days in the sun. Fruit leathers stick together; be sure to wrap individually for storage.

Strawberry-Rhubarb Leather

This sweet-tart leather combines the succulent flavor of strawberries with tart and spicy rhubarb.

Yield:	Prep time:	Drying time:	Serving size:
8 rolls	10 to 20 minutes	4 hours to 2 days	1 fruit roll

1 lb. (about 6 medium stalks) fresh rhubarb

2 TB. water

¾ lb. (about 1¾ cups) fresh whole strawberries

2 TB. honey, or to taste

1 TB. fresh or bottled lemon juice, or to taste

1. Trim rhubarb leaves, wash stalks, and cut into ½-inch slices. In a small (1-quart) saucepan, add water and rhubarb. Cook over medium heat until rhubarb starts to soften. Remove from heat and cool 10 minutes. Purée softened rhubarb in a food mill, sieve, blender, or food processor. It should make about 1 cups purée.

2. Mash strawberries into a purée by hand using a fork, by processing in a food processor or blender to leave the seeds in, or by pressing strawberries through a sieve or food mill to remove seeds. Any of the methods should make about 1 cup. In a small bowl, stir together rhubarb and strawberry purées. Add honey (flavor concentrates after drying). Add lemon juice to brighten flavors and protect color.

3. Preheat an oven or food dehydrator to 130°F to 140°F. Using plastic wrap or parchment paper, line the dehydrator trays. Spread purée ¼ to ½ inch thick on the liner. Dry until leather is evenly pliable and firm; there should be no soft spots when pressed in the center.

4. Peel from the liner while still warm. Cut or roll into serving pieces. Cool 30 minutes, or until no longer warm. Wrap individually, and store in an airtight container in a cool, dry place.

Variations: For **Strawberry-Banana Leather,** purée 3 bananas with 1 tablespoon fresh or bottled lemon juice to make 1 cup banana purée. Combine with 1 cup strawberry purée. Dry as directed. For **Berry Leather,** purée 4 cups of any soft or firm berries; remove seeds in a food mill or sieve (if desired). Add optional honey or lemon juice. Dry as directed.

Dried Vegetables and Herbs

Drying vegetables is almost as easy as drying fruits. Most vegetables need to be blanched before drying in order to deactivate enzymes that cause foods to spoil; string bean britches are one exception. (See Chapter 2 for more on blanching.) Dried britches, *ristras* (a Spanish word meaning *rope*), and herb bunches are best suited to dry climates. If you live where there is more humidity, plan to use these attractive vegetables and herbs first, before using frozen and canned foods. Like some fruits, a few vegetables such as potatoes and eggplant need to be treated to prevent darkening (see Chapter 2).

Dried Whole Vegetables and Herbs

A few vegetables can be dried whole, including string beans, okra pods, chiles, and herb bunches. These dried vegetables have various uses, which are described in each recipe.

Dried String Bean Britches

Slow simmered with onions, tomatoes, and herbs, dried snap beans make a comforting, mellow side dish. For more complexity, toss them with butter, toasted nuts, dried fruits, or crisp bacon.

Yield:	Prep time:	Drying time:	Serving size:
¼ to ⅓ pound	20 minutes	3 to 4 days	½ to 1 ounce

2 lb. (about 2 dry pt.) fresh, tender stringless beans (or remove strings before drying)

1. Wash beans. Using a large needle and heavy-duty thread (upholstery or buttonhole type), fishing line, or any other twine or cord, thread each bean near the stem end; knot the thread around the end of each vegetable (to keep it from sliding). Create 3-foot lengths, or enough beans for one meal. Leave 6 to 12 inches string at either end for hanging.

2. If desired, treat beans with a salt solution for longer storage. Soak in a 10 to 15 percent cold salt solution for 15 minutes.

3. Hang in a shaded area with good air circulation, such as a covered porch or an attic. Dry until leathery.

4. Store in place or in an airtight container in a cool, dark, dry place.

Variations: For **Dried Okra,** string okra pods in the same manner as green beans. For **Dried Chile Pepper Pods,** thread ripe, red chiles to create a ristra and dry in full sun. A simple though not traditional method for creating a ristra uses the threading process described in the recipe to create a bunch, rather than a single line of vegetables. Let chiles rest for 2 to 3 days after harvesting to age the stems slightly; fresh stems break more readily. Thread the first chile through the stem and tie a knot to anchor the bunch. Thread additional chiles in an alternating starburst pattern up the line to create a tight bunch. Create 3-foot lengths, with 12 inches at the top for hanging. Do not dry immature green chiles; they will shrivel and turn a dull orange color.

PERFECT PRESERVING

Thread string beans, herbs, or chiles to hang and dry in bunches, or hang on a line—like socks or trousers (*britches*) on a clothesline. Dried chiles make an attractive display in the winter kitchen. Use these dried vegetables by snipping them from the line, leaving the remaining vegetables hanging in place. Toss beans into soups or rehydrate to serve as a side dish. Toast and grind dried chiles to season any dish, or rehydrate for sauces. Pull leaves off dried herb bunches and let their heady fragrance brighten a winter day and your cooking.

Dried Herb Bunches

Dried herb bunches are beautiful to look at, provide delectable accents for any dish, and impart herbaceous aromas in the winter kitchen.

Yield:	Prep time:	Drying time:	Serving size:
1 bunch	5 minutes	3 to 4 days	1 teaspoon crushed

1 bunch fresh herbs with firm stems (such as lavender, mint, or thyme)

1. For best results, dry one type of herb per bunch. Tie bundle using lightweight cotton cord or twine. Wrap the cord several times around the base. Form a loop for hanging.

2. Hang upside down in a shaded area with good air circulation. Do not dry herbs in full sun. Dry until brittle.

3. Store in place or in an airtight container in a cool, dark, dry place.

Dried Halved, Sliced, or Chopped Vegetables

Dried vegetables can be great time-savers when it comes to meal preparation. Small pieces are ideal for use in warm and comforting soups and stews. Slices layered and baked with sauce, cheese, and herbs make fabulous *gratins*. Vegetable halves, such as small eggplant and zucchini, are convenient containers for stuffing and baking. Stuff them with grain pilafs to serve as a side dish, or stuff with meat fillings for a hearty main dish.

Dried Tomatoes

The intense herbal notes of dried tomatoes add piquancy to everything from pizza to soups, to salads, to stews. Grind into powder and add water for sauce. Drizzle with olive oil to serve as antipasto.

Yield:	Prep time:	Drying time:	Serving size:
15 to 20 ounces	20 minutes	4 to 20 hours	½ to 1 ounce

> 15 to 20 (about 5 lb.) medium fresh ripe tomatoes, preferably no larger than 3 in. in diameter

1. Peel and seed tomatoes, if desired. Core, halve, or quarter small tomatoes up to 3 inches in diameter; slice large tomatoes ⅛ to ⅜ inch thick. (For more information, see the following sidebar.)

2. Preheat an oven or food dehydrator to 130°F to 140°F. Place tomatoes on drying trays. Dry tomatoes for 2 to 4 hours or until tomatoes have begun to shrivel but are still quite moist and bright red. Peel them from the trays and turn over.

3. Continue to dry until tomatoes have flattened completely, shrunk greatly in size, deepened in color to a dark red, and are no longer plump or sticky. Dry until pliable, or crisp and brittle for longer storage.

4. Cool 30 minutes, or until no longer warm. Remove tomatoes from drying trays. Store in an airtight container in a cool, dry place.

Variations: For **Seasoned Dried Tomatoes,** sprinkle tomato slices sparingly with ¼ to 1 teaspoon each sugar, salt, ground black pepper or crushed red pepper, and dried oregano or Italian seasonings blend before drying. Try the lower amount on a small batch and check for flavor before seasoning a large batch. All flavors intensify in dried foods. Use seasoned tomatoes in the same way as plain dried tomatoes, and place on drying trays. For **Roasted Dried Tomatoes,** prepare roasted tomatoes by one of the following methods before drying, and then place on drying trays: 1) Grill whole tomatoes on a barbecue over medium-high heat, turning every few minutes, until charred in spots and skins loosen. 2) Roast tomatoes one at a time by turning with a fork over a gas flame; cool, remove skins, and cut in halves or quarters. 3) Place quartered fresh tomatoes on a rimmed baking sheet and roast in a preheated 450°F oven for 40 to 50 minutes; remove skins and seeds if desired.

PREPARING TOMATOES FOR DRYING

Whether to peel and seed tomatoes or season them before drying is a matter of personal preference. Peels and seeds are more noticeable in dishes that don't receive long cooking; however, some people like the textural interest. Plum tomatoes have fewer seeds and less liquid, so they are a good choice for drying. Removing seeds and juice speeds up drying time. Remove peels before or after drying tomatoes. Remove before drying by blanching; remove after drying by rehydrating dried tomatoes in hot water. Scoop out seeds after cutting in halves or quarters. For sliced tomatoes, seeds are difficult to remove, so feel free to leave them in. Some cooks season tomatoes before drying, but plain dried tomatoes offer the most flexibility.

Dried Chopped Vegetables

What could be better than a colorful cache of vegetables, ready to toss into warm and comforting winter soups and stews?

Yield:	Prep time:	Drying time:	Serving size:
⅛ to ⅓ pound	20 minutes	4 to 20 hours	½ to 1 ounce

2 lb. (about 2 dry pt.) fresh vegetables (such as carrots, peas, or broccoli)

1. Wash vegetables. Peel and trim as needed. Cut in serving-size pieces and blanch. Spread on towel-lined trays to remove excess moisture.

2. Preheat an oven or food dehydrator to 130°F to 140°F. Place vegetables on drying trays. Dry until vegetables are shriveled and leathery, or brittle for longer storage.

3. Cool 30 minutes, or until no longer warm. Remove from drying trays. Store in an airtight container in a cool, dry place.

Dried Veggie Chips

These thin, crunchy snack chips are as beautiful as they are healthful. Herbs or seasonings add zest and spice to complement the vegetal flavors. There's no need to eat just one.

Yield:	Prep time:	Drying time:	Serving size:
⅛ pound	20 minutes	4 to 20 hours	½ to 1 ounce

2 lb. fresh vegetables from the following list:
  Carrots (3 to 4 large per pound): peel and water blanch 4 minutes
  Potatoes (2 medium per pound): peel and water blanch 8 minutes
  Beets (5 medium per pound): roast until tender and peel
Salt or other seasonings to taste (optional)

1. Cool vegetables in ice water to stop cooking. Drain and pat dry. Use a mandoline to slice vegetables paper thin. Sprinkle slices sparingly with salt or seasonings, if using (flavor intensifies when dried).

2. Preheat an oven or food dehydrator to 130°F to 140°F. Place vegetable slices on drying trays. Dry until brittle. Dried chips will be denser and not crisp like fried chips.

3. Cool 30 minutes, or until no longer warm. Remove from drying trays. Store in an airtight container in a cool, dry place.

Variations: For **Dried Taro Chips,** dry land varieties are best for chips. Use gloves since taro can irritate the skin. Remove tough outer skin, and cut large taro in halves or quarters. Water blanch 8 minutes or until just tender, cool, and slice thinly. Season if desired. For **Seasoned Kale Chips,** wash 1 bunch large kale leaves and cut with scissors or tear to remove tough stems. Pat dry with paper towels or spin in a salad spinner. Toss kale with 3 tablespoons olive oil and 1 teaspoon sea salt or 2 tablespoons soy sauce, 2 tablespoons sesame seeds, and 1 tablespoon vinegar.

Dried Protein Foods

Cultures around the world prepare dried meat in various forms. Beef, venison, and wild game are most common. For drying, choose lean meat from the loin, flank, or round that is free from visible fat. Most poultry is not used for dried meat due to undesirable flavor and texture. However, smoked turkey leg meat and seasoned ground poultry turn out acceptable dried meats. Many types of fish make excellent dried products. Other protein foods such as nuts and seeds are dried to improve their storage life.

SPOILER ALERT

Be sure to give full attention to sanitation steps when you prepare dried meats. Most incidences of food-borne illness are due to improper procedures or inappropriate cure for the drying method. See Chapter 2 for a full discussion on precautions to take when working with dried meats.

Dried Meat and Seafood

Recipes in this section include the American snack food beef jerky, prepared and seasoned in several ways. Hunters like to make jerky with wild game, especially venison.

Beef or Venison Jerky

Beef jerky is a convenient oven-dried meat product. This basic marinade makes a lightly seasoned jerky flavored with pepper and smoke.

Yield:	Prep time:	Drying time:	Serving size:
½ to 1 pound	2 to 9 hours	10 to 24 hours	1 to 2 ounces

½ cup kosher salt, ¼ cup table salt, or ¼ cup curing salt

¼ cup granulated sugar

2 qt. water

3 TB. liquid smoke

½ tsp. ground black pepper

2 lb. lean meat, sliced

1. In a large bowl, mix together kosher salt and sugar. Heat 1 quart water to boiling, and pour over mixture. Stir until salt and sugar dissolve completely. Add remaining 1 quart water, liquid smoke, and pepper. Refrigerate brine until completely chilled.

2. Place strips of meat in a marinating container. Pour cold brine over meat, cover, and refrigerate 1 to 8 hours.

3. If desired, precook meat before drying to an internal temperature of 160°F (165°F for poultry).

4. Preheat an oven or food dehydrator to 185°F. Remove meat strips from marinade and drain on clean, absorbent towels. Place meat on drying trays. Dry until internal temperature is 160°F and meat cracks when bent but does not break.

5. Remove from drying trays. Remove any oil beads by patting jerky with towels. Cool 30 minutes, or until no longer warm. Store in an airtight container in a cool, dry place.

Variations: For **Ground Meat Jerky,** mix together 2 pounds lean ground beef or venison, 2 teaspoons sugar, 1 teaspoon ground black pepper, 1 teaspoon garlic powder, and 1½ tablespoons table or curing salt. Press mixture between two pieces of plastic wrap or parchment paper and use a rolling pin to flatten to a thickness of ¼ to ⅓ inch. Use a knife to cut meat into strips 1 to 2 inches wide and any length. Place meat on drying trays. For **Teriyaki Beef Jerky,** make a marinade using ⅓ cup soy sauce, 1½ teaspoons onion powder, ½ teaspoon salt, and ½ teaspoon ground black pepper. Marinate 1 hour.

Thai-Style Dried Beef

Slightly sweet and garlicky, this peppered dried beef is usually made in winter to perk up a cold day.

Yield:	Prep time:	Drying time:	Serving size:
½ to 1 pound	2 to 9 hours	10 to 24 hours	1 to 2 ounces

2 qt. water

⅔ cup table salt or pickling salt

⅓ cup soy sauce or fish sauce

16 cloves garlic, minced

1 cup finely minced shallot, leek (white part), or green onion

2 TB. minced fresh ginger, peeled

2 TB. palm sugar, brown sugar, or honey

2 TB. chopped fresh cilantro leaves with stems (optional)

2 tsp. freshly ground white pepper

2 lb. lean beef, sliced

1. In a large bowl, combine water, salt, soy sauce, garlic, shallot, minced ginger, palm sugar, cilantro (if using), and white pepper. Stir until sugar and salt dissolve completely. Place strips of meat in a marinating container. Pour marinating liquid over meat, cover, and refrigerate 1 to 8 hours.

2. If desired, precook meat before drying to an internal temperature of 160°F (165°F for poultry).

3. Air-, sun-, or solar-dry meat, or preheat an oven or food dehydrator to 185°F. Remove meat strips from marinade and drain on clean, absorbent towels. Place meat on drying trays. Dry until internal temperature is 160°F, or meat cracks when bent but does not break.

4. Remove from drying trays. Remove any oil beads by patting dried beef with towels. Cool 30 minutes, or until no longer warm. Store in an airtight container in a cool, dry place.

Variation: For **Mexican-Style Dried Beef (*Carne Seca*)**, use 1- to 1¼-pound piece of beef and slice ⅛ inch thick, using the accordion method. Slice thin (⅛ inch) with the grain, cut across the block of meat and stop ⅛ inch from end, turn 180°, slice in the opposite direction, stop ⅛ inch from end, turn, and continue to slice entire block into one long piece ⅛ inch thick. Mix together 1 tablespoon freshly squeezed lime juice, 1½ teaspoons dried oregano, and 1½ teaspoons table or pickling salt. Rub marinade evenly on all sides of meat. Cover and refrigerate for 2 days. Dry by any method—air, sun/solar, oven, or dehydrator.

SPOILER ALERT

Air-dried meat is popular in many cultures. However, air-dried meat is traditionally cooked before eating, rather than used as snack food as we do in the United States. For snacking, be sure to precook or fully cook your dried meat. Otherwise, cook your dried meat as they do in other countries. For example, Thai-Style Dried Beef is deep-fried for 2 to 3 minutes or until crispy, and served with sticky rice. Mexican-Style Dried Beef is shredded and sautéed, perhaps with onions or chiles, to make a filling for tacos or burritos.

Smoked Salmon

Sweet and briny smoked salmon adds zip to cream cheese spread or creamy potato chowder.

Yield:	Prep time:	Drying time:	Serving size:
1 pound	1 day	30 minutes	2 to 3 ounces

1 qt. water

⅓ cup canning, pickling, or kosher salt

½ cup brown sugar

1 1b. salmon fillet, skin on

1. In a medium bowl, stir water, salt, and brown sugar until dissolved. Place salmon fillet in a container large enough to hold brine. Pour brine over salmon, cover, and marinate 1 hour in the refrigerator.

2. Drain salmon and pat dry with paper towels. Place on a rack over a baking sheet and refrigerate overnight.

3. Hot smoke salmon 30 minutes, or to an internal temperature of 160°F in the thickest part of fillet. Serve immediately or refrigerate for up to 3 days. Freeze for longer storage.

BEST WOODS FOR SMOKING FISH

Alder is traditional for smoking wild salmon. However, any light, sweet wood works well for fish, such as ash or fruit trees (especially guava, peach, plum, and nectarine), as well as corncobs, grapevines, and seaweed. Mesquite and Kiawe have a strong flavor that is recommended by some people. Pimento wood and leaves (from allspice trees), the traditional wood used for Jamaican Jerk barbecue, also works well for fish. When using stronger woods, limit fish smoking time to 10 or 20 minutes.

Dried Nuts and Seeds

Like most fruits and vegetables, nuts should be preserved within 24 hours after harvest. Drying and roasting are two different methods of preparing nuts and seeds.

Dried Peanuts

Most nuts are dried at 100°F. However, peanuts are actually a legume, so they are dried at a higher temperature. Peanuts are popular for snacks, grinding into butter, or added to stir-fries.

Yield:	Prep time:	Drying time:	Serving size:
2½ pounds	30 minutes	8 hours to 4 weeks	3 ounces (½ cup)

3 lb. (about 6 cups) peanuts in the shell, dried on the vine in full sun for 4 to 10 days

1. To air-dry (preferred method), spread peanuts in a single layer on drying trays or newspaper in a warm, dry area for 2 to 4 weeks. To dry small amounts using a dehydrator, wash nuts by rubbing vigorously in several changes of water until water is clear. Drain and pat dry. Preheat a food dehydrator to 120°F to 130°F. Place nuts on drying trays and dry for 8 to 10 hours. Dry until shells are brittle and nuts rattle in their shells.

2. Cool nuts to room temperature before testing. Crack several shells and check for adequate dryness. Peanuts should be tender. Package nuts in metal or glass containers to protect from insects and rodents. Store several months in a cool, dry location. Boil and can, or freeze for longer storage. Nuts that turn brown and darken are scorched and bitter.

Variation: For **Roasted Peanuts in the Shell,** preheat an oven to 300°F. Place peanuts in shell on baking sheets and roast, stirring occasionally, for 30 to 40 minutes or until aromatic and slightly crunchy.

Dried Pumpkin Seeds

Besides snacks, pumpkin seeds add nutty goodness to baked goods. Ground pumpkin seeds make a flavorful thickener in soups and stews.

Yield:	Prep time:	Drying time:	Serving size:
1 cup	30 minutes	1 hour to 2 days	2 to 3 tablespoons

1 cup pumpkin seeds

1. Wash pumpkin seeds in several changes of water to remove fibrous material. Spread on towel-lined trays to remove excess moisture.

2. Preheat a dehydrator to 100°F to 120°F, an oven to its lowest setting, or sun-dry. Spread pumpkin seeds evenly on drying trays. Dry until shells are brittle. Package seeds in metal or glass containers to protect from insects and rodents. Store several months in a cool, dry location.

Variation: For **Roasted Pumpkin Seeds,** preheat an oven to 250°F. Toss pumpkin seeds with vegetable oil and salt (if desired), spread on baking sheets, and roast for 15 to 20 minutes or until just beginning to brown. If desired, remove hulls after roasting: Spread seeds on a baking sheet or parchment paper. Roll seeds lightly back and forth with a rolling pin to crack the hulls, without crushing the inner seeds. Immerse seeds in water; the hulls will float to the top.

PERFECT PRESERVING

Parboil pumpkin seeds in their hulls before drying to produce crispier dried and toasted pumpkin seeds for snacking. In a small saucepan, add pumpkin seeds, and add 2 cups water for every 1 cup pumpkin seeds. Add 1½ teaspoons salt for every 1 cup water, or to taste, and bring to a boil over high heat. Reduce heat to medium-low, and simmer for 10 minutes. Remove from heat and drain. If desired, remove hulls after boiling; pinch the narrow end of each seed, and squeeze until the seed slips out of the hull.

Fermented Foods  11

There are many different ways to categorize fermented foods—for example, by type of fermentation (such as alcoholic or lactic), by method used to control fermentation (such as salting or culturing), or by the type of food (fruits or dairy).

Until the widespread adoption of refrigeration in the last hundred years, fermenting was the preservation method used for centuries by people around the world. In many countries, fermenting is still widely used. Wine and yeasted breads are two of the oldest forms of fermented foods.

Hard Cider, Wine, and Vinegars

Hard cider and wine is the anaerobic (without air) fermentation of fruit, and vinegar is the aerobic fermentation of cider or wine. While you can leave fruit juice and wine to ferment naturally, it takes a while. Using a controlled process that introduces a yeast starter is not only faster, it gives better and more consistent results.

Grapes are the most common fruit used to make wine. In the United States, commercially bottled wine that is not made with grapes must be labeled with the type of fruit, for example pineapple wine. However, you can make "country" wines from just about any fresh or dried fruits.

There is some confusion over cider terminology. Not everyone agrees, and the meaning of various terms is different from state to state, and outside of the United States. Following are some common definitions for apple juice, cider, hard cider, and apple wine:

- Apple juice is squeezed from fresh apples.

- Sweet cider is the same as apple juice.

- Cider usually means apple juice in the United States; everywhere else, it means hard cider. In the United States, we specify "hard cider" when we mean fermented juice.

- Hard cider is a fermented beverage that you can make from apples or other orchard fruit (such as peaches or pears). Hard cider is lower in alcohol (about 2 to 7 percent) than apple wine (about 10 to 12 percent).

- Apple cider may refer to apple juice, sweet cider, or hard cider. It depends on the context and who is saying it. In some locations, apple juice means filtered juice and apple cider means unfiltered juice.

- Apple wine has sugar added before fermentation in order to raise the alcohol content. When allowed to ferment naturally, apples do not have enough natural sugar to produce an alcohol content higher than 7 percent.

The following recipes all feature apples made into hard cider, wine, and vinegar. If you try each of these recipes, you will have a solid understanding of how alcohol and acetic fermentation plays out.

Hard Cider

Like wine and beer, cider can range in style from light, dry, and sparkling to dark, fruity, and creamy. This simple recipe is a good choice if you are new to home brewing. Fermented apple juice is the easiest alcoholic drink you can make.

Yield:	Prep time:	Fermenting time:	Serving size:
1 gallon	60 to 90 minutes	1 to 6 weeks	12 ounces

   1 gal. (4 qt.) unfiltered freshly pressed apple juice, or pasteurized commercial apple juice or sweet cider, plus more as needed

   2 cups brown sugar or honey (optional)

   ½ packet (5 to 15 g or 0.176 to 0.52 oz.) wine or beer yeast (see following sidebar)

1. (Optional pasteurization) Heating kills any wild yeasts and bacteria that are present in fresh or unpasteurized cider. Omitting this step may or may not improve the flavor and quality. When working with fermentation, it's all a bit of a gamble. To pasteurize, add cider to a large (2-gallon) saucepan, and stir in brown sugar or honey (if using). (Adding sugar tends to increase the alcohol content and make dry rather than sweet cider.) Bring to a simmer over medium heat. Do not allow cider to boil at any time, or you will activate apple pectin

and cause the final product to become cloudy. Reduce heat to medium-low to maintain a simmer (180°F to 190°F) for 45 minutes. Turn off the heat and let cider cool to room temperature.

2. Dissolve wine yeast in a small amount of tepid water (or according to package directions). Wait at least 10 minutes to ensure yeast is beginning to foam. (If it does not, discard and start with a new packet of yeast.)

3. Pour yeast solution into a sanitized 1-gallon jug. Add 2 quarts room-temperature apple juice. Cap it and shake to mix thoroughly. Remove the cap and add more juice, up to the top of the jug. Refrigerate any remaining juice and save for step 5.

4. Secure an airlock to the top of the jug. Let juice ferment undisturbed at room temperature (68°F to 72°F). Bubbles appear in the airlock within 24 to 48 hours. They eventually subside when fermentation is complete, usually in 1 to 2 weeks.

5. (Optional) When the airlock bubbles have slowed to about 1 per minute (anywhere from 4 days to 2 weeks; it's faster when there is added sugar), an intermediate racking may be performed to clarify cider and improve the flavor. In this case, be sure you still have extra reserved juice for topping off the jug. Remove the airlock; clean and sanitize it. Using ¼-inch or larger food-grade plastic tubing, siphon cider into another clean and sanitized 1-gallon jug. Leave behind the sediment in the bottom; it is composed of apple sediment and yeast that will cloud the cider. Top the new jug with reserved juice from step 3 (or buy additional pasteurized commercial juice). Secure the airlock to the top of the jug. Let cider sit undisturbed at room temperature (68°F to 72°F) for another 2 to 4 weeks, or until clear.

6. Siphon cider into clean and sanitized glass bottles. Leave behind the sediment in the bottom of the jug. Cap the bottles tightly. Store in a cool (50°F to 60°F) location, or refrigerate. Cider is best when consumed within 6 months.

YEAST OPTIONS

When making hard cider or wine, the choice of yeast is subjective. Champagne or sparkling wine yeast will produce a fermented beverage that is dry to very dry, and white-wine yeast will make one that is softer, fruitier, and less tart. Ale, cider, and mead yeasts produce fruitier ciders, but are not usually used for wine. Wild yeast from unpasteurized juice may also be used as a starter for hard cider, but it can be unpredictable. When making cider vinegar, use wine, ale, cider, or mead yeast. Bread yeast does not produce a good hard cider, wine, or vinegar.

Apple Wine

Like hard cider, apple wine can be fruity or dry. It has about twice the amount of alcohol as hard cider and uses the same basic process, plus a few additional ingredients. Use this recipe to make country wine from pear, peach, or other fruits, too.

Yield:	Prep time:	Fermenting time:	Serving size:
1 gallon	60 to 90 minutes	4 to 10 months	4 ounces

12 lb. (about 36 medium) mature apples (see following sidebar)

2½ qt. distilled water

1 Campden tablet, crushed and dissolved in ¼ cup water

1½ tsp. pectic enzyme

1 tsp. yeast nutrient

1 package (5 g or 0.176 oz.) wine yeast (see previous "Yeast Options" sidebar)

2 lb. superfine sugar

Pasteurized apple juice, as needed

1. Wash apples well, especially if using fallen fruit. Trim and discard any bruised areas. Do not peel; remove cores and seeds. Treat for browning. Chop apples into small pieces. Clean and sanitize a primary fermentation bucket. Place apple pieces, distilled water, and dissolved Campden-tablet water into the fermentation bucket. (The distilled water will not cover apples.) Cover with a clean towel. Stir every 2 hours to rotate apples from top to bottom.

2. After 12 hours, stir in pectic enzyme and yeast nutrient. Cover with a clean towel. Stir every 2 hours to rotate apples from top to bottom.

3. After another 12 hours, dissolve wine yeast in a small amount of tepid water (or according to package directions). Wait at least 10 minutes to ensure wine yeast is beginning to foam. (If it does not become active, discard and start with a new packet of yeast.) Stir wine yeast into apple mixture. Cover with a clean towel. Stir twice a day for 7 to 10 days, or until vigorous fermentation subsides.

4. Clean and sanitize a large stainless-steel bowl. Strain pulp in a nylon straining bag over the bowl, pressing to extract as much juice as possible. Add superfine sugar slowly to juice, stirring continuously until dissolved completely.

5. Clean and sanitize a 1-gallon glass jug. Pour juice into the jug. Refrigerate any leftover juice to use for topping off later. Secure airlock to the top of the vessel. Let juice ferment undisturbed at warm room temperature (70°F to 75°F) for 60 days, or until clear.

6. Remove the airlock; clean and sanitize it. Clean and sanitize a second 1-gallon glass jug. Using 3 feet of ¼-inch or larger food-grade plastic tubing, siphon wine into the second jug. Leave behind the sediment in the bottom of the first jug; it is composed of apple sediment and yeast that will cloud the wine. If needed, top the new jug with reserved juice from the previous step (or buy pasteurized apple juice). Secure the airlock to the top of the jug. Let wine sit undisturbed at warm room temperature (70°F to 75°F) for 60 days.

7. Clean and sanitize glass bottles. Siphon wine into bottles. Leave behind the sediment in the bottom of the jug. Cap the bottles tightly. Store in a cool (50°F to 60°F) location. Wine is best when aged 6 to 12 months before consuming. Drink within 2 to 3 years.

Variation: For **Pear Wine,** use 12 pounds mature pears, mixing sweet and tart flavors as for apples. Remove seeds and cores; treat for browning. Juice or freeze pear flesh to help break down cellular walls. Proceed as for apple wine. Apple-pear blends are possible; however, most people report better results by fermenting fruits separately and blending wines before bottling.

CHOOSING APPLES FOR WINE MAKING

When selecting apples for wine making, it is best to choose several different varieties of mature fruits. For example, McIntosh and Red or Golden Delicious apples are fruity and aromatic, crab apples are tart, and Jonathan and Winesap apples have high acid. Combining apples with a range of these qualities is more likely to yield a pleasing wine. The general recommendation is to use more tart cooking apples than sweet eating apples. If using freshly squeezed cider or frozen juice concentrate, choose one with rich apple flavor, good color, and a balance of sweetness and astringency. For your first wine, start with what's readily available in your area. There are over 2,000 varieties of apples. Feel free to experiment and adjust to your taste. Raisins, lemon juice, and spices can also enhance apple flavors.

Apple Cider Vinegar

Good vinegar is pleasantly tart and redolent of the raw material used to make it (such as grapes, apples, or pineapple).

Yield:	Prep time:	Fermenting time:
1 quart	30 to 60 minutes	2 to 4 weeks

¼ packet (5 to 15 g or 0.176 to 0.52 oz.) wine or beer yeast (see previous "Yeast Options" sidebar)

1 qt. pasteurized apple juice (without sorbate or other preservatives)

1 mother from unpasteurized vinegar (optional)

1. Dissolve yeast in a small amount of tepid water (or according to package directions). Wait at least 10 minutes to ensure yeast is beginning to foam. (If it does not, discard and start with a new packet of yeast.)

2. Pour yeast solution into a clean and sanitized 1-quart glass jar. Add 2 cups room-temperature apple juice. Cap it and shake to mix thoroughly. Add more juice, filling the jar no more than ¾ full. Cover the jar with a clean piece of cheesecloth (or a towel).

3. Store at warm room temperature (70°F to 75°F), away from light (for example, in a cupboard). Full acetic fermentation usually takes 2 to 4 weeks. Near the end of this period, you should notice a vinegar smell. Taste a small sample daily until the desired strength is reached.

4. (Optional) If the acetic fermentation is slow, or after at least 2 weeks with yeast, strain juice through a fine-mesh sieve or cheesecloth. Add mother to a clean and sanitized 1-quart glass jar. Pour in strained juice. Cover the jar with a clean piece of cheesecloth (or towel). Store at room temperature (68°F to 72°F), away from light, for 7 to 10 days, or until pleasantly tart.

5. If desired, filter vinegar through a coffee filter, or 2 to 3 layers of damp cheesecloth. Reserve mother, if desired, for the next batch of vinegar. Pour vinegar into a clean jar and cap tightly. Use unpasteurized vinegar within 12 months.

6. Pasteurize vinegar for longer storage. To pasteurize, pour filtered vinegar into a stainless-steel or enamel saucepan, and place over medium heat until vinegar reaches 140°F to 160°F. Cool to room temperature before bottling. Pasteurized vinegar keeps indefinitely.

"MOTHER" OF VINEGAR

Vinegar "mother" is a floating, gelatinous blob that may be found only in unpasteurized vinegar. It contains favorable *Acetobacter* plus cellulose, a type of soluble fiber. Don't mistake the gray powdery sediment at the bottom of a bottle of vinegar for the mother. The sediment is composed of bits of source material (such as apples or grapes), along with enzymes, pectin, amino acids, vitamins, and minerals. The sediment is healthful but isn't important in helping you get an acetic fermentation started. If you can't find a mother, use wine, ale, or mead yeast.

Potato-Peel Vinegar

Vinegar heightens flavor by adding tart accents to many recipes from salad dressings and marinades, to soups, to beverages.

Yield:	Prep time:	Fermenting time:
1 quart	30 to 60 minutes	2 to 4 weeks

1 packet (5 to 15 g or 0.176 to 0.52 oz.) wine or beer yeast (see previous "Yeast Options" sidebar)

4 cups distilled water

½ cup granulated sugar

1 cup clean, thinly sliced potato peels

1 "mother" from unpasteurized vinegar (optional)

1. Dissolve wine yeast in a small amount of tepid water (or according to package directions). Wait at least 10 minutes to ensure yeast is beginning to foam. (If it does not, discard and start with a new packet of yeast.)

2. In a clean and sanitized 1½-quart or larger glass or stoneware container, stir distilled water and sugar, until sugar dissolves. Stir in yeast mixture and potato peels. Cover the jar with a clean piece of cheesecloth (or towel).

3. Store at warm room temperature (70°F to 75°F), away from light (for example, in a cupboard). Full acetic fermentation usually takes 2 to 4 weeks. Near the end of this period, you should notice a vinegar smell. Taste a small sample daily until the desired strength is reached.

4. (Optional) If the acetic fermentation is slow, or after at least 2 weeks with yeast, strain vinegar through a fine mesh sieve or cheesecloth. Add mother to a clean and sanitized jar. Pour in strained vinegar. Cover the jar with a clean piece of cheesecloth (or towel). Store at room temperature (68°F to 72°F), away from light, for 7 to 10 days, or until pleasantly tart.

5. If desired, filter vinegar through a coffee filter, or 2 to 3 layers of damp cheesecloth. Reserve mother, if desired, for the next batch of vinegar. Pour vinegar into one or more clean and sanitized jars and cap tightly. Use unpasteurized vinegar within 12 months.

6. Pasteurize vinegar for longer storage. To pasteurize, pour filtered vinegar into a 2-quart or larger stainless-steel or enamel saucepan, and place over medium heat until vinegar reaches 140°F to 160°F. Cool to room temperature before bottling. Pasteurized vinegar keeps indefinitely.

Variation: For **Fruit Vinegar,** use culls, seconds, or overripe or fallen fruit, or peelings from apples, oranges, or pineapples. Remove fruit stems and leaves. Wash thoroughly, trim well any bruised or moldy spots, and remove any seeds. Chop fruit finely or slice peels thinly. Treat for browning, if needed. Proceed as for potato vinegar, omitting sugar if fruit is sweet and ripe.

PERFECT PRESERVING

Making vinegar is a good way to use peels and trimmings from just about any produce. People around the world make vinegar from a variety of ingredients, including coconut water, palm tree sap, or cane juice.

Yeast Starters and Yeasted Breads

Bread is an ancient food, and the oldest form is flatbread. The early inhabitants of Africa, western Asia, and parts of Europe made flatbread from local grains or legumes ground into flour. There are many types of flatbread still made and enjoyed using a wide variety of flours, such as Greek *pita* bread (made with wheat flour), Mexican *tortillas* (corn), Ethiopian *injera* (teff), French *socca* (chickpea), and Indian *dosa* (rice and lentil).

One day as I was making flatbread, a thought occurred to me: Where would I get yeast if I couldn't buy it at the store? I know that yeast is all around, but how do I get it to land on my dough?

I don't necessarily recommend that you make your own yeast. Tap water, commercially farmed products, and central heating or air-conditioning are not conducive to growing wild yeast. Trying to harness wild yeast is like trying to catch fireflies. Like all wild beings, yeast is unpredictable; its erratic behavior is precisely why people started to package it. However, there are a couple of ways you can try to make your own baking yeast. One method is to ferment fruit or grain in water. You will have the most success using fresh, organic, or wild fruits that have not been cleaned commercially. Another way is to ferment flour, yeast (dried homemade or commercial), and water to make a "sponge" or soft dough. You use the sponge to make yeasted bread, but save a little to use as a starter for your next loaf.

The following recipes illustrate the ways you can start a yeast culture and make simple breads from yeast water or sponge.

Sponge Starter

Sponge starters are convenient money savers if you bake bread at least twice a week. Purchased starters provide great flavor and predictable results. However, it is fun to make your own.

Yield:	Prep time:	Fermenting time:
3 cups	30 minutes	2 to 7 days

   1 cup organic whole-wheat or rye berries
   1 cup distilled or potato cooking water, at room temperature
   ½ tsp. honey or pinch granulated sugar
   Pinch salt

1. Crush or grind berries finely using a mortar and pestle, coffee grinder, grain grinder, or heavy-duty blender. Alternatively, use whole-grain wheat or rye flour; however, freshly ground berries tend to give better results. Add ½ cup distilled water to a 1-quart jar, followed by ½ cup ground berries, honey, and salt. Cover the jar with a lid, and shake vigorously to blend the ingredients. Uncover, place cheesecloth over the jar, and secure with a screw band or a rubber band.

2. Ferment at warm room temperature (75°F to 90°F), stirring twice a day, for 2 to 4 days, or until the mixture becomes foamy. When using flour and water as a yeast starter, lactic acid bacteria (LAB) often become active before yeast. LAB create a lot of gas, which may smell very sour and increase the volume as much as three times. Stir it down frequently, as needed. As the acidity increases, LAB become inactive and yeast take over. The volume drops, and mixture may appear inactive. Wait another day or two and starter will expand again with yeast activity, though not as much as the first time. The odor becomes faintly sour and breadlike.

3. Add remaining ½ cup distilled water and remaining ½ cup ground berries, and stir vigorously to combine. Place cheesecloth over the jar, and secure with a screw band or a rubber band. Store at warm room temperature (75°F to 90°F) for 24 hours, or until starter is foamy again. At this point, you can use starter to make bread.

4. If you are not making bread right away, cover the jar with a lid, store starter in the refrigerator, and "feed" it once a week. To feed your starter, add an equal volume of distilled water and organic whole grain flour, and stir vigorously to combine. For example, if you have 1 cup starter, stir in 1 cup flour and 1 cup water (if you do this, you need a container bigger than 1 quart). Store it at room temperature for 24 hours, and then use it for baking, or return it to the refrigerator. If starter decreases in volume or separates (solids on the bottom and yellowish liquid on top), it is running out of food. Stir it together, and then use it to make bread or feed it. Over time, using and feeding starter regularly will improve its flavor and performance in baked bread.

5. To freeze starter, make sure starter is at peak activity. Feed it ¼ of the normal amount. For example, if you have 1 cup of starter, add ¼ cup flour and ¼ cup water. Transfer to an airtight container, cover, and freeze up to 6 months. To use, defrost at room temperature. Feed, and wait until the mixture is bubbly and active before using.

6. To dry starter, line a rimmed baking sheet with parchment paper, and spread starter in a thin layer. Dry at room temperature for 2 to 3 days (or in a food dehydrator at 100°F or less for several hours), or until crumbly. Store in an airtight container up to 3 months. To restart, crumble dried starter in enough warm water to cover completely, and begin regular feedings.

SECRETS FOR YEAST STARTERS

Chlorine kills yeast, so always use distilled or filtered water, or leave tap water open to the air for 24 hours to evaporate the chlorine. If no activity appears in your starter in the first 2 to 5 days, discard it and begin again. After the first two to three feedings using ground wheat or rye berries or organic whole grain flour, you can switch to bread flour or all-purpose flour for subsequent feedings. If the starter smells strange or stinky, is any color other than creamy white or slightly yellow, or has a furry growth (indicating mold), throw it out. Before placing starter in the refrigerator, feed it and beat it vigorously to incorporate lots of air. To reduce the amount of starter, use it to bake bread, or discard half the volume.

Yeast Water

If you don't make bread at least twice a week but want to explore the use of starters, try yeast water. It can be frustrating when it doesn't work, but that's really part of the fun. It's what wild yeast is all about.

Yield:	Prep time:	Fermenting time:
3 cups	30 minutes	2 to 7 days

¼ cup organic raisins or whole rye berries

Pinch granulated sugar

Pinch salt

3 cups distilled water, at room temperature

1. Put organic raisins, sugar, and salt in a 1-quart sanitized jar, and add distilled water. Place cheesecloth over the jar, and secure with a screw band or a rubber band.

2. Store at warm room temperature (75°F to 90°F) for 3 to 4 days, or until bubbles appear around edge of liquid, solids float, and mixture smells faintly sweet—like wine or bread. In warm summer months, this may take 1 to 2 days, and in winter, this can take up to 7 days. In a cool kitchen, turn on the oven light, and place the jar on a folded towel on the oven rack. (Attach a note to the oven door, so the oven is not inadvertently turned on with the jar still inside.) If nothing happens within 1 week, discard and start again.

3. Once bubbles appear, use yeast water to make bread or a sponge starter, or cover the jar with a lid and store in the refrigerator up to 1 month.

Variations: For **Apple Yeast Water,** use 1 medium organic apple, cut in quarters to remove seeds, and then finely chop. For **Potato Yeast Water,** use 1 medium organic potato, washed and finely chopped. For **Fruit-Pulp Yeast Water,** use 1 cup fruit pulp left over from juicing. Note for the recipe and any of the variations: soaked raisins, grains, potatoes, or apples may be added to dough when making bread.

Focaccia with Herbs

Garlicky, fresh herb topping accents this soft, billowy Italian flatbread. It is exceptionally easy to make.

Yield:	Prep time:	Fermenting time:	Baking time:
1 loaf	30 to 60 minutes	2 hours	30 to 35 minutes

1 cup active Sponge Starter (recipe earlier in this chapter), at room temperature

¾ cup tepid tap water

1 tsp. granulated sugar

1 tsp. salt

2 to 2½ cups unbleached all-purpose flour, or as needed

3 TB. olive or vegetable oil

1 TB. yellow cornmeal

2 cloves garlic, chopped

1 TB. coarsely chopped fresh parsley

1 TB. coarsely chopped fresh rosemary

1 TB. coarsely chopped fresh oregano, or 1 teaspoon dried

3 TB. extra-virgin olive oil

½ tsp. coarse kosher salt

1. Always feed starter within 8 hours prior to making bread to make sure it is at its peak. In a large (4- to 6-quart) bowl, stir together Sponge Starter, tepid water, sugar, salt, and 1 cup all-purpose flour. Cover with plastic wrap and set aside for 1 hour, or until foamy and active.

2. Lightly oil a large bowl and a 12-inch pizza pan with ½ to 1 teaspoon olive oil. Sprinkle the pizza pan with yellow cornmeal, and shake off excess.

3. Add remaining 8 teaspoons olive oil and 1 cup all-purpose flour to foamy starter mixture, and beat until well blended. Continue to add flour until soft dough is formed that is slightly sticky.

4. Turn dough out onto a lightly floured surface and knead by hand for 5 minutes. If dough sticks to the work surface or your hands, sprinkle with additional flour.

5. Place kneaded dough in the oiled bowl, turning it over once to coat lightly with oil. Cover with plastic wrap and let rise until doubled, about 1 hour.

6. While dough is rising, prepare topping. In a small bowl, combine garlic, parsley, rosemary, oregano, and extra-virgin olive oil.

7. When dough has doubled, carefully turn it onto the prepared pizza pan. Press dough—deflating it as little as possible—to fill the pan. Gently brush surface with herbed garlic-oil topping, and sprinkle with coarse kosher salt. Cover lightly with a piece of plastic wrap and let rise 20 minutes.

8. Preheat the oven to 425°F. After dough has risen, press the top in 15 places with your fingers to create dimples.

9. Bake dough on the center rack for 20 minutes. Rotate the pan, and bake for another 10 to 15 minutes, or until focaccia is golden. Remove from the oven and let cool in the pan for 10 to 15 minutes before cutting into 12 squares or wedges. Serve warm.

Variation: For **Focaccia Using Dry Yeast,** omit Sponge Starter. Dissolve 1 packet (0.75 ounce) dry baking yeast in ¼ cup water and add a pinch of granulated sugar. When yeast is foamy, add ¾ cup water, 1 teaspoon sugar, 1 teaspoon salt, and 1 cup all-purpose flour. Cover with plastic wrap and set aside for 1 hour, or until foamy and active. Continue with step 2. Up to 1 cup additional all-purpose flour will be needed, or 3 to 3½ cups total.

Flatbread with Seeds (*Lavash*)

Make lavash with basic yeast dough that you roll thin and bake until crisp. Serve as a cracker, or soften with water and use as a wrap with your favorite sandwich ingredients.

Yield:	Prep time:	Cook time:	Serving size:
3 11×17-inch crackers	5 minutes	20 to 22 minutes	⅛ cracker

1 cup Yeast Water (recipe earlier in this chapter)

1 tsp. granulated sugar

1 cup whole-wheat flour

¼ cup drained potato or rye grains from Yeast Water (optional)

2 cups unbleached all-purpose flour, or as needed

½ tsp. sea salt

3 TB. Dried Pumpkin Seeds (recipe in Chapter 10), or sesame or poppy seeds

1 tsp. vegetable oil or softened butter

1 tsp. salt stirred into 1 TB. water to brush over dough before baking

1. In the bowl of an electric mixer, or a large bowl by hand, stir together Yeast Water, sugar, and whole-wheat flour. Cover with plastic wrap and set aside for 1 hour, or until foamy and active.

2. Add potato or rye grains (if using), 1 cup all-purpose flour, and sea salt to foamy starter mixture. Beat until well combined.

3. Gradually add more flour until soft dough forms that is slightly sticky. If using an electric stand mixer, switch to the dough hook. Stir in remaining 1 cup flour, a little at a time, until a soft dough forms that is only slightly sticky. Too soft is generally better than too stiff. If you add too much flour, stir in water 1 tablespoon at a time.

4. Turn dough out onto a lightly floured surface. Form dough into a smooth ball and then flatten it. Sprinkle Dried Pumpkin Seeds evenly over flattened dough. Knead dough by hand for 5 minutes, or until a smooth, round dough forms that is still very soft and only slightly sticky. Use additional flour as needed only when dough is sticky. Cover with a towel or plastic wrap.

5. Coat the sides of a large mixing bowl lightly with vegetable oil. Uncover kneaded dough and place in the bowl, turning it over once to coat lightly with fat. Cover the bowl with a towel or plastic wrap and let dough rise in a warm place, free from drafts, until doubled, about 1 hour.

6. Preheat oven to 350°F. Uncover the bowl and press dough all over to deflate it. Divide dough in thirds. Roll out one portion at a time and keep remaining dough covered while you work.

7. Sprinkle the working surface with a little flour. Roll one portion thinly into a rough rectangle approximately 10×14 inches. Transfer to a baking sheet. Brush lightly and evenly with salted water. Bake at 350°F for 20 to 22 minutes, or until lightly browned in spots. Bread will puff and brown unevenly. Remove to a rack to cool. Repeat rolling and baking with remaining dough.

8. Store crisp lavash in an airtight container. Because it is made without eggs, butter, or oil, lavash will keep almost indefinitely. Break into irregular pieces to serve as crackers, or rinse lightly under water and cover with a towel until softened.

Variations: For **Lavash Using Dry Yeast,** omit Yeast Water. Dissolve 1 packet (0.75 ounce) dry baking yeast in ¼ cup water and add a pinch of granulated sugar. When yeast is foamy, add ¾ cup water, 1 teaspoon granulated sugar, ½ teaspoon salt, and 1 cup whole-wheat flour. Cover with plastic wrap and set aside for 1 hour, or until foamy and active. Continue with step 2 of preceding recipe.

ABOUT LAVASH

Flatbreads are the world's oldest breads. One of the most ancient forms is Armenian flatbread known as lavash. Lavash is usually made from wheat flour in countries throughout southwestern Asia, including Azerbaijan, Iran, Turkey, Georgia, Lebanon, Syria, and Afghanistan. Many regional variations exist, and lavash recipes include unleavened dough as well as versions using yeast or baking powder to raise the dough. Traditionally, Armenians make lavash in autumn, stretch the dough very thin, bake it until crisp in clay ovens called *tonirs,* and then stack them to store and use throughout winter. Before serving, lavash may be softened with water or oil and used as a wrapper for cheese and barbecued meats, as a utensil to scoop up stew, or to soak up sauce or soup.

Cultured Milk Products

The recipes in this section show you how easy it is to make cultured milk products, by simply heating milk with acid. The acid coagulates the milk proteins, which separate into curds. The curds float in a thin, clear, yellow liquid known as whey. You can use whey to make pickles, or substitute for liquids in baked goods recipes.

Fresh Goat Cheese

This soft cheese could not be easier to make. Lemon juice makes a mild, slightly earthy cheese, while vinegar adds more tang. Use fresh goat cheese for spreads, dips, or lasagna.

Yield:	Prep time:	Culturing time:	Serving size:
¼ pound	90 minutes	1 day	1 ounce

1 qt. goat milk or whole milk

1 TB. freshly squeezed lemon juice or vinegar

¼ to ½ tsp. salt, or to taste

1. In a medium (2-quart) nonreactive (stainless-steel or enamel) saucepan, stir together goat milk, lemon juice, and salt. Place over medium heat. When mixture comes to a boil, reduce heat to medium-low and simmer slowly for 30 minutes. Remove from heat and let stand undisturbed for 30 minutes.

2. Line a colander or sieve with two layers of damp cheesecloth, and place over a large bowl. Slowly pour milk into the colander. Place in the refrigerator overnight.

3. Spoon cheese into a storage container. Stir in additional salt to taste. Cover, refrigerate, and use within 10 days. Refrigerate whey indefinitely; it can be used for baking or pickling, or enjoyed as a beverage.

Yogurt

Whole milk makes creamy yogurt with a subtle tang, while low-fat or nonfat milk creates slightly textured, tart yogurt. That's the beauty of homemade yogurt; you can make it in any style.

Yield:	Prep time:	Culturing time:	Serving size:
4 cups	60 to 90 minutes	3 to 7 hours	1 cup

1 qt. cold, pasteurized whole, low-fat, or nonfat milk
2 to 4 TB. plain yogurt with live active cultures

1. Place milk in a heavy-bottomed saucepan or on the top of a double boiler. Heat milk to 180°F to 200°F; stir occasionally to prevent scorching. Do not allow milk to boil at any time.

2. Place the pan or top of the double boiler in a pan of clean, cold water to cool milk rapidly to 115°F to 130°F. Remove the pan from cold water bath.

3. In a small bowl, stir together yogurt with about ½ cup of warm milk. Stir yogurt mixture into remaining milk, mixing until well blended. Pour into a sanitized and warmed 1-quart jar.

4. Incubate (culture) yogurt between 110°F to 122°F for 3 to 7 hours, or until set. (See Chapter 3 for ways to incubate yogurt.) Do not allow the temperature to drop below 98°F, or pathogens may take hold; letting the temperature go above 130°F kills bacteria. Some people report they achieve more consistent results at 115°F to 120°F than 110°F to 115°F.

5. Cover and refrigerate yogurt. Use within 3 weeks.

Variation: For **Greek Yogurt** (also known as yogurt cheese), line a colander or mesh sieve with several layers of damp cheesecloth, and place it over a bowl. Add 1 cup yogurt for every ⅓ cup yogurt cheese you wish to make. Refrigerate and allow to drain 1 to 12 hours. The liquid draining into the bowl should be clear; if it contains thick, white liquid, you need more layers of cheesecloth. The longer it drains, the thicker the cheese will be. Use yogurt cheese like you would sour cream or cream cheese. Use the whey as a substitute for milk or water in bread, muffin, and cake recipes.

Cream Cheese

Homemade cream cheese is creamier and less firm than commercial brands, which often add thickeners. Use it as a spread with sweet or savory toppings such as jam or relish, or mix it with dried herbs to serve with crackers.

Yield:	Prep time:	Culturing time:	Serving size:
¼ pound	30 to 60 minutes	2 days	1 ounce

    3½ qt. pasteurized whole milk

    1 pt. whipping cream

    1 cup sour cream

    ¼ rennet tablet, dissolved in ¼ cup water

    1 tsp. salt, or to taste

1. In a medium (2-quart) nonreactive (stainless-steel or enamel) saucepan, stir together whole milk, whipping cream, and sour cream. Place over medium heat and warm milk to 90°F to 95°F.

2. Add dissolved rennet tablet to warm milk and stir 2 to 3 minutes to blend well. Remove from heat. Cover the pan and let stand undisturbed at room temperature (65°F to 70°F) overnight, or until a soft curd forms. Cut across the curds in two directions at ½-inch intervals.

3. Line a colander with 3 to 4 layers of damp cheesecloth, and place over a bowl. Ladle curds into the colander. Strain whey into a separate container and refrigerate. Add contents of the strainer to curds. Place in the refrigerator overnight.

4. Spoon cream cheese into a storage container. Stir in salt to taste. Cover, refrigerate, and use within 10 days. Refrigerate whey indefinitely. It can be used for baking or pickling, or enjoyed as a beverage.

Variation: For **Low-Fat Neufchâtel Cheese,** substitute 1 gallon low-fat milk for whole milk and whipping cream, and 1 cup cultured buttermilk in place of sour cream. Proceed with recipe for Cream Cheese.

Lacto-Fermented Vegetables

These fermented pickles use salt or whey to establish LAB that help preserve the vegetables. They offer a wide range of sweet, sour, salty, and spicy flavors to complement any meal.

Half-Sour Pickles in Brine

Half-sour pickles are satisfying in every way: quick and easy to make, pretty to look at, and supremely crunchy, with a light, crisp, not-very-sour flavor that's similar to fresh cucumbers.

Yield:	Prep time:	Fermenting time	Serving size:
1 quart	30 to 60 minutes	3 to 5 days	1 pickle

3 cups distilled or filtered water

3 TB. sea salt

1½ pounds unwaxed organic cucumbers, small to medium size

1 head fresh dill or 1 TB. dill seed

1 to 3 cloves garlic, peeled

1. In a medium (3-quart) saucepan over high heat, bring distilled water to a boil. Add sea salt and stir until dissolved. Turn off heat and let brine cool to room temperature.

2. Wash cucumbers well. If possible, leave ¼ inch of stem attached, but trim and discard ¹⁄₁₆ inch from blossom end. Set aside in a clean bowl.

3. Place dill and garlic in the bottom of a sterilized, 1-quart canning jar. Add prepared cucumbers.

4. Pour cooled brine over cucumbers up to the rim of the jar. If needed, hold cucumbers under brine using a wooden bamboo skewer. If brine doesn't completely cover the cucumbers, prepare more brine, using 2¼ teaspoons salt for each cup boiling water. Cover the jar loosely, place on a plate (to catch fermenting brine), and set aside in a cool place (64°F to 72°F).

5. Taste a pickle after 3 days. If you are satisfied with the texture and flavor, cover the jar and refrigerate (usually no more than 5 days, about half the time it takes for cucumbers to ferment completely). Refrigerate up to 1 month.

Sauerkraut (Fermented Cabbage)

Salted cabbage goes by different names around the world: sauerkraut in Germany, *kimchi* in Korea, and *curtido* in El Salvador. For best results, choose firm heads of young, fresh cabbage and prepare within 48 hours after harvest.

Yield:	Prep time:	Fermenting time:	Serving size:
2 to 3 quarts	60 to 90 minutes	2 to 4 weeks	½ cup

2 to 3 medium heads (about 6 lb. total*) green cabbage

2½ oz.* (¼ cup) canning or pickling salt (do not use table, sea, or iodized salt)

*Adjust this recipe to any amount of cabbage, using 1½ tablespoons salt to every pound of cabbage, or 5¾ ounces (¾ cup) salt for 25 pounds cabbage. A 1-quart container will hold 2 to 2½ pounds cabbage, a 1-gallon container will hold 5 pounds cabbage, and a 5-gallon container will hold 25 pounds cabbage. Fill container no more than ¾ full to allow room for fermentation activity.

1. Wash cabbage and discard outer leaves. Tip: Slice off stem end to use as a cover inside the jar to keep cabbage submerged. Cut heads in quarters, remove core, and shred or slice cabbage thinly (¹⁄₁₆ to ⅛ inch). Weigh 5 pounds of shredded cabbage.

2. In a large bowl, toss together cabbage and canning salt until evenly mixed. Pack firmly into a clean, dry, 1-gallon crock (or use 4 or 5 sterilized 1-quart, wide-mouth canning jars), pressing each layer to draw out juices. Leave 4 to 5 inches headspace in a large crock, or 2 to 3 inches in 1-quart jars. If juices do not cover cabbage, prepare a very weak brine using 1½ tablespoons pickling salt per quart of boiling water. Cool and pour enough brine over cabbage to cover completely. Cover and weight cabbage.

3. During fermentation, store container at 64°F to 72°F. If you use a brine-filled bag to seal the crock completely, do not disturb sauerkraut until fermentation is complete. If you use another type of weight, check and remove any white scum at least every other day. If brine level drops, add fresh brine of 2½ percent strength as needed.

4. Fermentation is complete when the bubbling stops, cabbage is pale and transparent, and sauerkraut tastes pleasantly tart. Cabbage usually ferments in 2 to 4 weeks.

5. Cover and store sauerkraut in the fermenting container or other clean containers, in the refrigerator up to 6 months. As during fermentation, remove any scum that forms. For shelf-stable storage, pack fermented sauerkraut into clean pint (quart) canning jars, leaving ½ inch headspace, and process in a boiling water bath for 25 (30) minutes.

Variations: For **Kimchi (Korean Sauerkraut),** use 3½ pounds shredded Chinese (napa) cabbage; 1 small white onion, thinly sliced; 1 large peeled carrot, shredded; 1 cup peeled and shredded daikon; 5 green onions, thinly sliced; 2 to 4 cloves garlic, minced; ¼ cup pickling salt; 2 tablespoons raw, organic sugar; 1 tablespoon minced fresh ginger; ¼ cup Korean chili powder; and 1 tablespoon soy sauce. Toss ingredients together until evenly mixed, pack, and ferment as for Sauerkraut. For **Curtido (Latino Sauerkraut),** use 3½ pounds shredded green cabbage; 1 pound onions, thinly sliced; 1 large peeled carrot, shredded; 2 to 4 jalapeños or habaneros, stemmed, seeded, and finely chopped (or ½ teaspoon crushed red pepper); ¼ cup pickling salt; 1 teaspoon dried oregano; and 1 teaspoon raw, organic sugar (or to taste). Toss ingredients together until evenly mixed, pack, and partially ferment, about 3 to 7 days. For **Sour Turnips (*Kisla Repa* or *Sauer Ruben*),** substitute 5 pounds shredded turnips for cabbage. Central and East European cultures enjoy salt-fermented turnips as much as cabbage is enjoyed elsewhere.

Red Pickled Daikon

Whey gives these brightly colored daikon pickles a clean, slightly tangy flavor that complements beef, seafood, and vegetarian meals.

Yield:	Prep time:	Fermenting time:	Serving size:
1 quart	30 to 60 minutes	3 days to 3 weeks	¼ cup

2 cups distilled or filtered water, at room temperature

½ cup whey, at room temperature (see following sidebar)

1 TB. kosher or sea salt

1 to 2 cloves organic garlic, thinly sliced (optional)

1 tsp. black peppercorns or crushed red pepper (optional)

1 lb. organic daikon, peeled, halved, and thinly sliced

1 lb. organic red or yellow beets, peeled, halved, and thinly sliced

1. In a small bowl, stir together distilled water, whey, and kosher salt.

2. Add garlic (if using) and black peppercorns (if using) to a sterilized 1-quart canning jar. Pack daikon and red beets into the jar, leaving at least 1 inch headspace.

3. If necessary, stir liquid until salt is completely dissolved. Pour over vegetables to cover completely. If there is not enough liquid, prepare more using the ratio of ½ cup distilled water, 2 tablespoons whey, and ¾ teaspoon kosher salt.

4. Weight vegetables to keep them submerged in liquid. Cover and let stand at warm room temperature (68°F to 72°F) for at least 3 days, or up to 3 weeks. Vegetables are ready when they have a pleasant salty and sour flavor. If liquid stops bubbling, fermentation is complete, and they should be immediately moved to the refrigerator. Refrigerate up to 1 month.

Variation: For **Pickled Daikon and Carrots,** substitute 1 pound carrots for the beets. Cut the daikon and carrots into sticks. Omit garlic and black peppercorns. Add 2 to 4 tablespoons granulated sugar, or to taste, to whey solution.

MAKING WHEY

It's easy to make whey. In a sieve set over a bowl, drain 2 cups of any type of plain yogurt for at least 30 minutes, or until you have ½ cup drained liquid. The liquid that drains into the bowl is whey.

Whey Bread-and-Butter Pickles

This fast and easy version of bread-and-butter pickles uses whey and honey. They are "whey" good!

Yield:	Prep time:	Fermenting time:	Serving size:
1 pint	30 to 60 minutes	2 weeks	¼ cup

> 1 cup thinly sliced, small organic cucumbers (preferably 1½ in. or less in diameter), end slices discarded
>
> ⅔ cup thinly sliced organic onions
>
> ⅓ cup thinly sliced organic red bell pepper strips
>
> 1 TB. pickling salt
>
> ½ tsp. mustard seed
>
> ½ tsp. celery seed
>
> ¼ tsp. ground turmeric
>
> ½ cup whey
>
> ½ cup raw honey

1. In a large bowl, toss together cucumbers, onions, and red bell pepper strips.

2. Add pickling salt, mustard seed, celery seed, and turmeric to a 1-pint sterilized canning jar. Pack vegetables tightly into the jar, leaving at least 1 inch headspace.

3. In a small bowl, stir together whey and honey. Pour over vegetables to cover completely. Cover and refrigerate for 2 weeks, shaking the jar every other day. Use within 1 month.

Whey-Pickled Kimchi

This recipe makes tangy, spicy-hot, and delicious kimchi quickly.

Yield:	Prep time:	Fermenting time:	Serving size:
1 quart	60 to 90 minutes	3 days to 2 weeks	½ cup

1½ lb. Chinese (napa) cabbage

½ cup peeled daikon, cut in sticks

1 small peeled and shredded carrot

¼ red bell pepper, stemmed, seeded, and cut in sticks

1 to 2 green onions, thinly sliced

1 to 2 cloves garlic, minced

¼ cup whey

1 tsp. soy sauce, or to taste

2 to 3 tsp. Korean chili powder, or to taste

2 to 3 tsp. kosher or sea salt, or to taste

1 to 2 tsp. raw organic sugar, or to taste

1 to 2 tsp. minced fresh ginger, or to taste

1. Discard outer leaves of Chinese cabbage. Wash cabbage. Tip: Slice off stem end to use as a cover inside the jar to keep cabbage submerged. Quarter, trim core and discard, and then shred or slice cabbage thinly (¹⁄₁₆ to ⅛ inch).

2. In a large bowl, toss shredded cabbage, daikon sticks, shredded carrots, red bell pepper sticks, green onions, garlic, whey, soy sauce, Korean chili powder, kosher salt, sugar, and ginger until evenly mixed. Taste and adjust seasonings; the mixture should taste slightly salty. It can be as hot or sweet as you like.

3. Pack mixture firmly into the jar, pressing or gently tamping each layer to draw juices from cabbage, leaving 1 inch headspace. If juices do not cover cabbage completely, add more whey to the top of the jar.

4. Cover the jar with a lid and let stand at warm room temperature (68°F to 72°F) for 3 days. Refrigerate at least 2 weeks before using. Use within 1 month.

Pickled Foods ❧ 12

Cultures around the world pickle foods as a way to add interest to meals, as well as to preserve foods. Pickled foods may be salted, dried, fermented, and immersed in vinegar or other acids. They can be salty, bitter, sour, sweet, or fiery hot.

Preserved citrus such as lemons and limes are found in Morocco and India. Pepper relish known as *ajvar* is made throughout the Balkan Peninsula from Slovenia to Turkey, while *achar* adds excitement and interest to an Indian *thali*. Called *tsukemono* in Japan, pickles may be quick cucumbers dressed with vinegar, as well as more assertive pickles featuring soy (*Shoyuzuke*) and miso (*Misozuke*). *Escabeche* is found around the Mediterranean and uses vinegar to preserve meats or fish, accented with herbs and spices. In this chapter, you'll find recipes for these and many other interesting pickled foods.

Salted Foods

Salted foods have a long history. It's an easy and inexpensive way to preserve vegetables. Every country, every heritage has their specialty. The fast and easy recipes in this chapter come from nearly every corner of the globe. Some are pungent, salty, and sour, and some will make you sweat. Sugar is always optional if you like your pickles to be sweet. Be sure to use clean containers and the best fresh produce you can find.

Salted Green Beans

Many people consider salted green beans far superior in taste and texture to canned or frozen beans. Their fresh, earthy flavor adds interest to salads and side dishes.

Yield:	Prep time:	Pickling time:	Serving size:
3 to 4 quarts	60 to 90 minutes	2 to 4 weeks	¼ cup

5 lb. green or wax beans

1 lb. (3¼ cups) fine- or coarse-grain pickling or kosher salt (do not use table, sea, or iodized salt)

1. Use only young, tender, very fresh beans. Wash, trim ends, and weigh beans to determine how much salt to use (see following sidebar). Measure the correct amount of salt. Beans may be left whole, sliced lengthwise (*frenched*), or cut in 1- or 2-inch lengths, as desired. Steam-blanch beans, cool, and pat dry.

2. In a large bowl, toss beans and pickling salt until evenly mixed. Pack beans and salt into a sterilized 1-gallon crock or four 1-quart canning jars, leaving 1 to 2 inches headspace. Cover and weight the beans. Set aside in a cool, dark place.

3. In 24 hours, if the juices do not cover the food completely, prepare a 20 percent brine using 7.7 ounces (¾ cup) pickling salt per quart of water. Add enough brine to cover the beans generously. Cover and weight the beans to keep them submerged.

4. Cure the vegetables 2 to 4 weeks. Store in a cold cellar or refrigerator up to 6 months. Check twice a week for scum or mold.

Variation: For **Salted Cauliflower,** substitute cauliflower florets for the beans. Wash, trim, cut into florets, and weigh to determine how much salt to use. Steam-blanch florets, cool, pat dry, and proceed with preceding recipe for Salted Green Beans.

> **PERFECT PRESERVING**
>
> This recipe uses 20 percent salt by weight. Adjust this recipe to any amount of beans, using 3.2 ounces (⅓ cup) pickling salt for every pound of beans. This amount of salt will prevent the beans from fermenting. To make fermented or soured beans (like sauerkraut), shred or french the beans, and use only 1.6 ounces (2½ tablespoons) salt for every pound of beans. A 1-quart container will hold about 1½ pounds green beans, a 1-gallon container will hold 6 pounds, and a 5-gallon container will hold 30 pounds. Fill the container no more than ¾ full to allow room for fermentation activity.

Moroccan Preserved Lemons

Add these salty, tangy pickled lemon slivers to spicy meat stews, sautéed greens, or lemonade for a surprising zing. Combine with green olives for an appetizer, or dress up mayonnaise for a citrusy aioli to pair with seafood.

Yield:	Prep time:	Pickling time:	Serving size:
2 to 3 cups	30 to 60 minutes	1 to 4 weeks	1 to 2 tablespoons

1 lb. medium lemons (about 4 to 6), preferably organic Meyer

4 TB. pickling salt, or more as needed

3 to 6 coriander seeds (optional)

1 to 3 whole cloves (optional)

1 to 3 black peppercorns (optional)

1 small bay leaf (optional)

½ cinnamon stick (optional)

¼ teaspoon fennel seeds (optional)

Additional freshly squeezed lemon juice, as needed

1. To extract the maximum amount of juice from a lemon, roll it on the countertop several times to soften, microwave for 15 to 30 seconds, or blanch in boiling water for 3 to 5 minutes and then cool before handling.

2. Cut a cross in each lemon from the top to within ½ inch of the base (i.e., quarter the lemons lengthwise without cutting all the way through). Sprinkle inside of each lemon generously with pickling salt, using about 3 tablespoons total, and close lemons again.

3. Place remaining 1 tablespoon pickling salt and optional coriander seeds, whole clove, black peppercorns, bay leaf, cinnamon stick, and fennel seeds (if using) on the bottom of a sterilized 1-quart canning jar. Pack lemons tightly into the jar, adding more salt between each layer. Press lemons to release their juices. If juice released from pressing does not cover lemons completely, add freshly squeezed juice. (Do not use bottled lemon juice or water.) Fill the jar no more than ¾ full.

4. Cover the jar with a lid or plastic wrap and let lemons stand in a warm place (80°F to 100°F). Lemons are ready to use in 1 to 4 weeks and improve over time. Cover and refrigerate. Preserved lemons usually keep for up to 1 year.

5. To use: Rinse lemons under running water. Remove peel and discard lemon pulp. Slice or chop the peel.

Variation: For **Preserved Oranges,** substitute 3 to 4 medium oranges for lemons. Preserved oranges are wonderful in lemonade or rice pilaf.

Indian-Style Hot Lime Pickles

These blazing hot-and-tangy pickles are a devilishly spiced version of preserved lemons. Traditionally served as a small meal or snack with rice or bread, they also pair nicely with grilled foods.

Yield:	Prep time:	Pickling time:	Serving size:
1 quart	60 to 90 minutes	2 to 6 weeks	1 to 2 pieces

1½ tsp. mustard seeds

1 tsp. fenugreek seeds

2 TB. crushed red pepper or cayenne

1 TB. turmeric powder

½ tsp. *asafetida,* garlic, or onion powder

1 lb. (6 to 8) medium limes

⅓ cup pickling salt (do not use table, sea, or iodized salt)

1 cup neutral oil, such as untoasted sesame, peanut, or canola oil

1. Measure all spices before beginning. Heat a small frying pan over medium heat. When it is hot, add mustard seeds and fenugreek seeds. Toast seeds, tossing occasionally, for 5 minutes, or until mustard seeds turn gray. All at once, add crushed red pepper, turmeric powder, and asafetida. Continue to toss in the hot pan for 10 to 15 seconds, or until spices are lightly toasted. Transfer spice mixture to a small bowl and allow to cool.

2. Wash limes and dry thoroughly with a clean towel; any residual water will cause pickles to spoil quickly. Cut each lime in half, and each lime half in quarters (8 pieces per lime). In a small bowl, toss lime pieces with pickling salt.

3. Using a spice grinder or mortar and pestle, grind cooled spice mixture into a fine powder.

4. In a large skillet over medium heat, add sesame oil. When oil is hot, turn off the heat, and then add spice mixture. Stir for 10 to 15 seconds and then add salted lime pieces. Stir to coat all of lime pieces evenly with spiced oil.

5. Transfer limes and spiced oil to a sterilized 1-quart canning jar. Cool, cover, and refrigerate. Lime pickles are ready to use in 2 weeks and improve over time. Preserved lime pickles usually keep for up to 1 year.

ASAFETIDA

Asafetida is used in Indian cooking especially to flavor legumes (*dal*), where it aids in digestion and imparts a slight onion-garlic flavor. It is sold in lump or powdered form. The powder has a powerful odor that disappears during cooking, but be aware that a jar of powder can take over your whole kitchen. So buy a small amount of powder, or use the lump form, which lasts indefinitely with no odorous drawback.

Brined Raw Eggs (*Xiandan*)

Chinese salted eggs have a very liquid white and a bright orange-red, firm yolk. When cooked, these eggs are salty and flavorful and lend a pleasing contrast to bland foods such as plain rice, noodle soups, salad greens, or toast. Duck eggs, which are traditional, have larger yolks than chicken eggs.

Yield:	Prep time:	Pickling time:	Serving size:
1 dozen	30 to 60 minutes	3 to 6 weeks	1 egg

¾ cup sea salt

3 cups boiling water

2 star anise

2 dried red chiles

2 tsp. Sichuan or black peppercorns

12 medium duck or large chicken eggs

2 TB. rice wine

1. Place sea salt in a large bowl and pour boiling water over it, stirring until dissolved. Allow water to cool to room temperature.

2. Add star anise, red chiles, and Sichuan peppercorns to a sterilized wide-mouth, 1-quart canning jar with a screw-top lid. Carefully inspect duck eggs, discarding any that are cracked. Using tongs, gently and carefully place each egg into the jar.

3. When brine is cool, add rice wine to the jar and pour in salted water to completely cover eggs. Save leftover brine for future use. Carefully cover and weight eggs. A yogurt or other lid that fits inside the jar works well; if necessary, add some wadded-up waxed or parchment paper (do not use aluminum foil), and then screw on the jar lid. The goal is to keep eggs submerged. Set aside in a cool place.

4. After 3 weeks, crack 1 egg into a bowl. Yolk should be a dark orange and firm; white will appear unchanged. If eggs haven't cured completely, leave in brine and test again every 3 to 7 days. Depending on size of egg or thickness of shell, some eggs can take 6 weeks to cure completely.

5. When eggs are cured, remove from brine, place in a covered container, and refrigerate up to 3 weeks. Prepare or cook salted eggs the same way you would fresh eggs, by pickling, poaching, steaming, or boiling. Serve for breakfast, in salads, or as a snack.

6. Strain brine through a fine mesh sieve. Transfer to a sterilized jar, cover, and refrigerate. Bring to a boil again before using for the next batch.

Vinegared Foods

When salted foods ferment, they create lactic acid. In these recipes, you add acid directly. Vinegar contains mostly acetic acid.

Original Bread-and-Butter Pickles

Here is an easy, no-canning recipe for a classic sweet pickle that is a real crowd pleaser. Serve them at your next backyard barbecue and watch them disappear!

Yield:	Prep time:	Pickling time:	Serving size:
1 pint	6 to 8 hours	1 to 30 days	¼ cup

1 cup thinly sliced small cucumbers (preferably 1½ in. in diameter or less), ends trimmed and discarded

⅔ cup thinly sliced onions

⅓ cup thinly sliced green bell pepper strips

1 TB. pickling salt

2 qt. ice cubes, or as needed for icing vegetables

½ cup white vinegar (5 percent)

⅔ cup granulated sugar

½ tsp. mustard seeds

½ tsp. celery seeds

¼ tsp. ground turmeric

1. Combine sliced cucumbers, onions, and green bell pepper strips in a large bowl. Add pickling salt. Cover with 2 inches of ice cubes. Refrigerate 4 hours, replenishing ice if needed. Drain, rinse, and drain again.

2. In a medium saucepan, combine white vinegar, sugar, mustard seeds, celery seeds, and turmeric. Cover and cook over high heat to boiling; reduce heat to medium-low and simmer 10 minutes.

3. Raise heat to high, and add drained cucumbers, onions, and peppers to saucepan. As soon as mixture returns to a boil, remove from heat. Uncover and cool 30 minutes.

4. Transfer pickles to a sterilized 1-pint canning jar. Cool, cover, and refrigerate. Use within 1 month.

Variations: For **Zucchini or Yellow Squash Bread-and-Butter Pickles,** substitute 1¼ cups slender, sliced zucchini or yellow summer squash for cucumbers. Proceed in step 1 with salting and draining. For **Lemon-Honey Bread-and-Butter Pickles,** omit white vinegar and granulated sugar and substitute ¼ cup fresh lemon juice, ¼ cup whey (or more fresh lemon juice), and ¼ cup honey.

Easy Pickled Carrots

This pickle recipe takes just 30 minutes to prepare. In summer, these carrots provide a refreshing, toothsome accompaniment to barbecued foods. In winter, serve them with roast meats, stews, beans, and grains.

Yield:	Prep time:	Pickling time:	Serving size:
1 pint	30 minutes	3 days	¼ cup

1 lb. (5 to 7) medium carrots

¾ cup cider vinegar

¼ cup tap water

½ cup packed brown sugar

2 tsp. salt

2 to 3 cloves garlic

1 tsp. black peppercorns

1 tsp. crushed red pepper

1. Wash and peel carrots; cut into sticks or slices (leave whole if small). Steam-blanch for 3 minutes, or until tender-crisp. Place carrots in a sterilized 1-pint canning jar.

2. In a small saucepan, stir cider vinegar, water, brown sugar, salt, garlic, black peppercorns, and crushed red pepper, and bring to a boil over high heat. Reduce heat to medium-low and simmer 2 minutes, or until sugar and salt have dissolved.

3. Pour hot liquid over carrots. Cool, cover, and refrigerate. Pickled vegetables may be served within 1 to 2 hours, but are best after at least 3 days. Use within 1 month.

Variations: For **Minted Carrots,** omit garlic, black peppercorns, and crushed red pepper. Add 2 tablespoons freshly chopped mint to vinegar mixture. For **Lemon-Honey Carrot Pickles,** omit garlic. Substitute 1 cup fresh lemon juice or 1 cup whey (or a combination) for cider vinegar and water, and substitute ¼ cup honey for brown sugar, or to taste (honey is sweeter than sugar).

Roasted Pepper Relish (*Ajvar*)

The smoky pepper relish known as ajvar (*EYE-vahr*) is a staple in Slovenia, Croatia, Serbia, and other countries. There are several styles using red or green peppers. This recipe uses a mix of red and green.

Yield:	Prep time:	Pickling time:	Serving size:
1 quart	90 to 120 minutes	1 to 30 days	¼ cup

5 medium red bell peppers or mild red peppers (such as Marconi)

5 medium green bell peppers or mild green peppers (such as poblano)

1 (about 1 lb.) medium eggplant

2 cloves garlic, minced

2 TB. extra-virgin olive oil

¼ cup red wine vinegar or fresh lemon juice, or to taste

1 tsp. salt, or to taste

1 tsp. granulated sugar, or to taste

⅛ tsp. cayenne or crushed red pepper, or to taste

1. Roast red bell peppers, green bell peppers, and eggplant over a charcoal or gas flame, or bake in a preheated oven at 475°F, and turn until skins are blistered. Place roasted peppers and eggplant in a paper bag or wrap loosely in aluminum foil for 10 minutes, to steam and loosen skins. Peel, stem, and seed bell peppers. Peel and stem eggplant. Roughly chop bell pepper and eggplant pulp.

2. Place bell peppers and eggplant in the bowl of a food processor. Add garlic, extra-virgin olive oil, red wine vinegar, and salt. Pulse until mixture is chunky or smooth, as desired. Transfer relish to a small bowl.

3. Combine relish with sugar, cayenne, and additional vinegar or salt to taste. Transfer to a sterilized 1-quart glass jar. Cover and refrigerate. Use within 1 month. Serve as an appetizer with bread and feta cheese, an accompaniment to grilled meats, or a relish for burgers and hot dogs.

Indian-Style Pickled Vegetables (*Achar*)

The nutty overtones of this spicy, crunchy vegetable will keep you coming back for more. *Achar* refers to pickled and salted vegetables that may be sweet, sour, salty, or hot.

Yield:	Prep time:	Pickling time:	Serving size:
1 quart	90 to 120 minutes	1 to 30 days	¼ cup

⅓ cup coarsely chopped onion

2 TB. roasted, salted peanuts

½ tsp. crushed red pepper

1 cloves garlic, roughly chopped

1 tsp. grated fresh peeled ginger

¾ cup white vinegar

¼ cup jaggery or lightly packed brown sugar

1¾ tsp. pickling salt

¾ tsp. ground turmeric

4 to 5 cups vegetables from the following list:

   Carrots cut in 1-in. diagonal slices (1 lb. carrots makes 2 to 3 cups sliced)

   Cauliflower cut in 1-in. florets (1 medium head makes about 6 cups florets)

   Salad cucumber cut in 1-in. diagonal half slices (1 medium makes 1 to 1½ cups seeded, halved, and sliced)

   Radish halves (1 lb. globe radishes make 2 to 3 cups halved)

   Green or red ripe tomato quarters (1 medium makes about 1 cup quartered)

1. Using a mortar and pestle, or in the bowl of a food processor, grind together onion, peanuts, crushed red pepper, garlic, and fresh ginger to make a paste.

2. In a large stockpot, stir together paste, white vinegar, jaggery, pickling salt, and turmeric. Bring to a boil over high heat, stirring frequently to prevent scorching. Reduce heat to medium-low, cover, and simmer gently for 5 minutes.

3. Add vegetables, and return to a boil over high heat. Simmer 5 minutes, or until vegetables are heated through. Cool, cover, and refrigerate. Achar may be served within 1 to 2 hours, but is best after at least 3 days. Use within 1 month.

INDIAN-STYLE PICKLES

Serve achar as an accompaniment to grilled foods or vegetarian meals, or as part of a relish tray. In India, pickles are made from local fruits, including green mango, eggplant, lemon, lime, onion, chiles, and berries, as well as meats and seafood. Happily, the flavors and spices of achar translate to vegetables commonly found in the Western Hemisphere. You can use other types of nuts in this recipe, such as almonds, hazelnuts, macadamias, or pine nuts.

Quick Japanese Pickles (*Tsukemono*)

These slightly sweet, mild pickles provide a crisp, refreshing complement to any meal.

Yield:	Prep time:	Pickling time:	Serving size:
about 1 quart	30 minutes	1 to 3 hours	¼ cup

6 Chinese or green cabbage leaves, cut into bite-size pieces

3 young turnips, peeled, cut into wedges

1 carrot, peeled and sliced thin

1 red bell pepper or other sweet red pepper, quartered, stemmed, seeded, and sliced ¼ in.

1 Japanese cucumber, sliced ¼ in.

⅓ cup rice vinegar

2 TB. water

1 TB. sake

1 tsp. salt

½ tsp. granulated sugar

1. In a medium (2-quart) bowl, toss cabbage, turnips, carrot, red bell pepper, and Japanese cucumber. Pack vegetables into a sterilized 1-quart canning jar.

2. In a small bowl, stir rice vinegar, water, sake, salt, and sugar until sugar dissolves.

3. Pour dressing over vegetables. Cover jar and shake until vegetables are thoroughly coated with dressing. Refrigerate 1 to 3 hours before serving. Pickles are best when eaten within a few hours. Use within 3 days.

Variations: For **Mild Chinese-Style Pickled Vegetables,** omit cabbage, turnips, carrots, and bell peppers; substitute 2 additional sliced Japanese cucumbers and add 1 thinly sliced garlic clove, 1 tablespoon snipped chives, and 1 sliced green onion. Dress with ⅓ cup rice vinegar, 2 tablespoons water, 1 tablespoon soy sauce, and salt to taste. For **Lemon-Pickled Vegetables with Cumin,** omit turnips, carrots, and bell peppers; substitute ½ small onion, quartered and thinly sliced, and ½ pound green beans, blanched and sliced ¼ inch. Use Persian cucumber in place of the Japanese cucumber, if available (or any burpless variety). Prepare a dressing of ¼ cup lemon juice, 1 teaspoon salt, ½ teaspoon toasted and ground cumin seed, ½ teaspoon granulated sugar (optional), and ¼ teaspoon cayenne.

Haitian *Pikliz*

Like a zesty coleslaw or hot Italian *giardiniera*, this spicy, mildly sour vegetable relish from Haiti dresses up any meal or sandwich with delicious results.

Yield:	Prep time:	Pickling time:	Serving size:
about 1 quart	30 to 60 minutes	1 to 3 days	¼ cup

¼ head green or Chinese cabbage, cored and thinly sliced or shredded

1 large carrot, peeled and thinly sliced

1 small onion, peeled, halved, and thinly sliced

2 to 3 cloves garlic, minced

1 to 2 serranos or habaneros, stemmed, seeded, and minced

1 cup mild vinegar (such as cane, palm, or rice)

1 tsp. salt

½ tsp. cracked black peppercorns

1. In a medium (2-quart) bowl, toss cabbage, carrot, onion, garlic, and serranos. Pack vegetables into a sterilized 1-quart canning jar.

2. In small bowl, combine mild vinegar, salt, and cracked black peppercorns.

3. Pour dressing over vegetables. Cover jar and shake until vegetables are thoroughly coated with dressing. Refrigerate 24 hours before serving. Use within 3 days.

PERFECT PRESERVING

I like to add individual spices rather than buying prepared mixes. For pickling spice, I use 1 cinnamon stick; 2 to 3 bay leaves; 2 to 3 whole cloves; and 1 teaspoon each allspice, coriander seeds, mustard seeds, and black peppercorns. If I want more heat, I may add fresh slices of ginger and a few dried red chiles. Whole spices last longer, and they're easy to grind yourself for other recipes; just buy an inexpensive coffee grinder and reserve it for grinding your whole spices.

Pickled Game Birds (Escabeche)

In Spain and Portugal, they like to preserve small game birds or fish in vinegar, to serve cold. Escabeche has origins in ancient Persia, Arabia, and Greece—everywhere that Spanish explorers went. It's simple, delicious hot-weather food. Use chicken, Cornish hen, or game birds such as pheasant, partridge, or quail.

Yield:	Prep time:	Cooking time:	Serving size:
2½ to 3½ pounds	2 to 3 hours	25 to 35 minutes	6 to 7 ounces

½ cup olive oil

3½ to 4½ lb. bone-in poultry, dressed and cut into 6 to 8 serving pieces

½ cup cider vinegar, sherry vinegar, or red wine vinegar

½ cup hard cider, medium-dry sherry, or dry red wine

½ cup water, or as needed

1 large onion, peeled, halved, and thinly sliced

12 garlic cloves, peeled and halved

6 dried bay leaves, crumbled

3 sprigs fresh thyme

12 black peppercorns

1 TB. hot paprika

1 tsp. salt

½ tsp. freshly ground black pepper

¼ cup freshly chopped parsley

1. In a large (4- to 6-quart) saucepan, add olive oil and heat over medium until hot. Brown poultry pieces in hot oil, about 2 to 3 minutes per side.

2. Add cider vinegar, hard cider, water, onion, garlic, bay leaves, thyme, black peppercorns, hot paprika, and salt, and bring to a boil. Reduce heat to low, cover, and simmer for 25 to 35 minutes, or until chicken is cooked through. Keep liquid at a bare simmer—do not boil or meat will be tough.

3. Transfer mixture to a shallow, nonreactive pan (such as glass or glazed pottery) and cool 30 minutes. Refrigerate until cold; cover after chicken is completely chilled. Prepare and store up to 3 days ahead.

4. About 30 minutes before serving, remove escabeche from the refrigerator to allow it to come to room temperature. Arrange meat on a serving platter, pour liquid over it, and sprinkle with pepper and parsley.

Variation: For **Duck** or **Turkey Escabeche,** use 3½ to 4½ pounds turkey or bone-in duck legs in place of poultry, and substitute white wine vinegar for cider vinegar, and white wine for hard cider. Increase cooking time to about 1 hour, or until internal temperature is 165°F.

PAPRIKA

Paprika is made from ground red peppers (*Capsicum annum*), usually a variety that is milder than hot chile peppers but stronger than sweet red bell peppers. There are three basic styles of paprika: sweet, hot, and smoked. Paprika sold in grocery stores is usually mild, earthy, and slightly sweet. Higher-quality paprika is prepared from specially grown pepper varieties, ground after removing the seeds and pith, and packaged without additives. Hungarian paprika represents the classic hot paprika with a rich fruity flavor, but comes in styles ranging from delicate and sweet to pungent and hot. Spanish paprika is the classic smoked paprika, prepared by smoking the peppers before grinding, and comes in a range of sweet (dolce) to hot (picante) styles.

Pickled Fish (Escabeche)

Spiked with herbs, citrus, and sweet spices, this typical Spanish escabeche makes wonderful warm-weather fare.

Yield:	Prep time:	Cooking time:	Serving size:
1 pound	2 days	15 minutes	¼ pound

¼ cup flour or cornmeal (or a combination)

¾ tsp. salt, or as needed

⅛ tsp. freshly ground black pepper

1 lb. fish fillets, skin on (trout, mackerel, or sardines)

¾ cup olive oil

2 peeled garlic cloves, crushed

1 small red or white onion, halved lengthwise and thinly sliced

½ medium red or green bell pepper, sliced into thin rings or strips

1 medium carrot, peeled, and thinly sliced

1 tsp. sweet (dolce) smoked paprika

½ tsp. dried oregano

1 cup dry white wine

½ cup sherry vinegar

1 (3-in.) cinnamon stick

1 (3×½-in.) strip orange zest

1 (3×½-in.) strip lemon zest

1. Whisk together flour, ¼ teaspoon salt, and pepper. Pat fish fillets dry and sprinkle lightly with a big pinch of salt. Dredge in seasoned flour and shake off excess.

2. In a 12-inch heavy skillet over medium-high heat, add olive oil. When oil is hot, add garlic and brown for 1 minute. Remove garlic with a slotted spoon. Working in batches, fry fillets—turning once—for 2 to 3 minutes total, or until cooked through. Transfer to a shallow dish. When all of fish has been cooked, strain the oil to remove any bits.

3. Wipe the pan clean, return strained oil to it, and place over medium heat. Add red onion, red bell pepper, and carrot to the hot oil. Cook, stirring occasionally, for 3 to 5 minutes, or until onion is translucent. Add sweet smoked paprika and

oregano, and stir for 1 minute. Add white wine, sherry vinegar, cinnamon stick, orange zest, lemon zest, and ½ teaspoon salt. Raise heat to high, bring to a simmer, reduce heat to medium-low, and simmer for 15 minutes, or until liquid is reduced slightly. Turn off heat and cool sauce to room temperature. Pour over fish, cover, and refrigerate. Marinate at least 2 days, or up to 1 week.

4. Bring fish to room temperature before serving. Taste sauce and season with additional salt, if necessary.

Fruit Juice–Pickled Foods

Lemon juice is commonly used instead of vinegar to pickle foods. Other tart juices also make refreshing, zesty pickles that are usually less tart than those made with vinegar.

Persian Eggplant Relish (*Nazkhatun*)

This succulent relish uses tart pomegranate juice or verjuice to balance the sweetness of the eggplant.

Yield:	Prep time:	Pickling time:	Serving size:
1 quart	90 to 120 minutes	1 to 30 days	¼ cup

1 (1 lb.) medium eggplant

2 TB. olive oil

1 small onion, finely chopped

3 medium tomatoes, blanched, peeled, seeded, and finely chopped

⅓ cup pomegranate juice, whey, or verjuice

1 tsp. dried marjoram, or 1 TB. chopped fresh basil

½ tsp. salt, or to taste

¼ tsp. freshly ground black pepper, or to taste

1. Preheat the oven to 350°F. Prick eggplant in several places with a fork. Place on a baking sheet and bake for 40 to 50 minutes, or until tender. Cool eggplant for 30 minutes, or until comfortable to handle, and then cut off stem, cut in half, and scoop out flesh. Chop eggplant finely.

2. In a large skillet over medium heat, add olive oil and onions and sauté 5 to 8 minutes, or until onions begin to brown lightly. Add eggplant, tomatoes, pomegranate juice, marjoram, salt, and pepper, and bring to a boil. Reduce heat to medium-low, and simmer slowly for 30 to 40 minutes, or until thick. Turn off heat and cool to room temperature.

3. Add additional salt and pepper to taste. Transfer pickles to a sterilized 1-quart canning jar. Cool, cover, and refrigerate. Use within 1 month. Serve cold or at room temperature as an appetizer drizzled with olive oil and yogurt.

Variation: For **Eggplant Spread with Lemon Juice (*Baba Ghanoush*),** omit onion, tomatoes, pomegranate juice, and dried marjoram. In a food processor or mortar and pestle, mash to a smooth paste baked eggplant flesh, 1 to 2 cloves mashed garlic, ⅓ cup fresh lemon juice, and ⅓ cup *tahini* (sesame seed paste). Season to taste with ground cumin seed, dried mint, salt, and pepper. Serve as a spread for pita bread or Lavash (recipe in Chapter 11) along with olives.

HOW TO MAKE VERJUICE (GREEN JUICE)

Choose underripe fruit—such as seeded red or green grapes, cored crabapples, or pitted plums—or even sorrel leaves. Coarsely chop raw fruit or sorrel and press through a fine mesh sieve to extract juice, refrigerate, and use within 3 days. Another old French method macerates fruit with sugar and alcohol: place ½ cup coarsely chopped fruit in a sterilized 1-quart jar. Chop and press 1 pound fruit, or enough to make 1 cup juice, and add to the jar with ¼ cup granulated sugar, 2 cups 80-proof vodka, and ½ cup white wine vinegar. Cover and refrigerate 2 months. Strain liquid and transfer to a sanitized container. Discard solids. This verjuice keeps indefinitely. Use to deglaze pan sauces for poultry or ham.

Citrus-Pickled Onions

Bright, fresh, and spicy, use these onions on everything from sandwiches to grilled fish.

Yield:	Prep time:	Pickling time:	Serving size:
1 pint	30 to 60 minutes	1 to 30 days	⅛ cup

10 allspice berries

2 bay leaves

1 habanero, stemmed, seeded, and cut in strips

2 large sweet onions, thinly sliced

¼ cup orange juice

¼ cup lime juice

¼ cup malt vinegar

1 tsp. granulated sugar, or to taste

½ tsp. salt

1. Place allspice berries, bay leaves, habanero, and sweet onions in a warm, sterilized 1-pint jar.

2. In a small saucepan over high heat, bring orange juice, lime juice, malt vinegar, sugar, and salt to a boil. Reduce heat to medium-low, stir, and simmer 2 minutes, or until salt and sugar dissolve completely.

3. Pour hot liquid over onions and spices. Cool, cover, and refrigerate. Use within 1 month.

Soy-Pickled Foods

Naturally brewed soy sauce helps to preserve foods because it is salty, slightly acidic (with a pH of about 4.8), and contains lactic acid as well as other organic acids.

Good Fortune Pickles (*Fukujinzuke*)

Referring to a popular group of Japanese deities—the Seven Lucky Gods (*Shichi Fukujin*)—this eclectic blend of sweet, savory, and crunchy vegetables is a popular accompaniment to rice and curry dishes.

Yield:	Prep time:	Pickling time:	Serving size:
1 quart	90 to 120 minutes	1 to 2 weeks	¼ cup

3 lb. (about 6 cups) of any of the following vegetables (or enough to make 1 quart):

Daikon, peeled, thinly sliced, and quartered

Turnip, peeled, thinly sliced, and quartered

Lotus root, peeled, thinly sliced, and quartered

Japanese eggplant, trimmed, and thinly sliced

Japanese cucumber, peeled, and thinly sliced

Carrot, peeled, and thinly sliced

Fresh shiitake mushrooms, stemmed, and cut in thin strips

Fresh enoki mushrooms, roots trimmed and discarded

1 TB. grated fresh ginger, peeled

1 TB. kosher or sea salt

⅓ cup brown sugar

¼ cup soy sauce

¼ cup sake

¼ cup mirin

¼ cup rice vinegar

3 to 5 shiso leaves (optional)

1. In a large bowl, toss vegetables, shiitake mushrooms, enoki mushrooms, ginger, and kosher salt until evenly mixed.

2. In a medium (2- to 3-quart) saucepan, stir together brown sugar, soy sauce, sake, and mirin, and bring to a boil over high heat. Add vegetables, and return to a boil for 5 minutes. Turn off heat. Add rice vinegar, and toss vegetables well. Cool to room temperature.

3. Layer vegetables in a sterilized 1-quart canning jar with shiso leaves (if using). Cover and refrigerate at least 24 hours before serving. Full flavor develops after 1 to 2 weeks. Use within 1 month.

> **PERFECT PRESERVING**
>
> Always start with fresh produce and quality ingredients when making pickles. As a rule, you should not save and reuse pickling liquids to make another batch. However, pickling liquids may be reused in sauces, soups, stir-fries, and salad dressings.

Cucumbers in Mustard Soy Sauce (*Shoyuzuke*)

A zesty east-meets-west pickle, accented with toasted sesame.

Yield:	Prep time:	Pickling time:	Serving size:
1 pint	30 minutes	1 hour	⅛ cup

3 small Japanese, Persian, or English cucumbers

3 tsp. salt

¾ cup soy sauce

2 tsp. granulated sugar

1 tsp. Dijon-style mustard

¼ cup toasted sesame seeds

1. Cut Japanese cucumbers in half lengthwise and scoop out seeds. Cut diagonally into ½-inch-thick slices. Sprinkle with 1 teaspoon salt and set aside for 10 minutes. Place cucumbers in a sieve and rinse under running water. Drain and pat dry.

2. In a small bowl, combine remaining 2 teaspoons salt, soy sauce, sugar, and Dijon-style mustard.

3. In a medium bowl, toss cucumber and dressing until well blended.

4. Refrigerate 1 hour before serving. Garnish with sesame seeds before serving. Best when eaten within a few hours; use within 3 days.

Miso-Pickled Vegetables (*Misozuke*)

Misozuke is the oldest known variety of Japanese pickles. Naturally fermented soybean paste (miso) is ideal for making easy, crunchy vegetable pickles. Try white miso for mild, sweet flavor, or red miso (akamiso) for more assertive pickles.

Yield:	Prep time:	Pickling time:	Serving size:
1 to 2 cups	30 to 60 minutes	1 to 30 days	⅛ cup

1 lb. total of any of the following vegetables:

Daikon, peeled, sliced ¼ in., and then halved (half-moons)

Japanese eggplant, trimmed, and sliced ¼ in.

Japanese cucumber, peeled, seeded, and sliced ¼ in.

Carrot, peeled, cut in spears, and blanched for 1 minute

Asparagus, cut in 2-in. lengths, and blanched for 1 minute (use shorter marinating time for asparagus)

1 cup white miso (*shiromiso*) or red miso (*akamiso*)

¼ cup mirin

1 TB. granulated sugar

1 tsp. soy sauce

1. Place vegetables in a shallow dish.

2. In a small bowl, stir together white miso, mirin, sugar, and soy sauce. Pour over vegetables, making sure to cover vegetables completely. Cover and refrigerate up to 1 month.

3. Rinse pickles under running water before serving.

Macerated Foods

The word *macerate* comes from the Latin *macerare*, which means "to soften or soak." The technique infuses flavor into either the solids or the liquid by soaking. Macerating uses alcohol and sugar to draw out the juices in fruit, as you'll see in the following recipes.

Limoncello (Lemon-Steeped Vodka)

This intensely flavored, sweet lemon liqueur comes from Sorrento, the Italian town justly famous for this refreshing beverage.

Yield:	Prep time:	Pickling time:	Serving size:
1½ quarts	30 to 60 minutes	4 to 30 days	1 to 2 ounces

14 to 16 large lemons
750 mL 100-proof vodka
3 cups water
1½ lb. (3 cups) granulated sugar

1. Remove zest from lemons and reserve, and then juice lemons. Discard lemon rinds. Combine lemon zest, lemon juice, and 100-proof vodka in a clean and sterilized nonreactive container, preferably glass or stoneware. Cover, place in a cool location, and let stand 4 days or up to 30 days. After 4 days, strain and reserve lemon vodka. Discard solids.

2. While vodka is infusing, in a medium saucepan, stir together water and sugar. Bring to boil over high heat, stirring occasionally. Reduce heat to low and simmer 2 minutes. Remove saucepan from heat and cool syrup to room temperature. Store syrup in a bottle in the refrigerator until ready to use.

3. Combine strained lemon vodka and simple syrup in a sterilized 2-quart glass bottle or jar. Store in the refrigerator. Keeps indefinitely.

Variations: For *Fragole Cello* **(Strawberry Liqueur),** use 2 pints fresh strawberries. Wash, hull, and halve strawberries, and then combine with vodka. Proceed with the recipe for Limoncello. For *Ciliegia Cello* **(Cherry Liqueur),** use 2 pounds fresh cherries. Wash, stem, and crush cherries, and combine with vodka. Proceed with the recipe for Limoncello. For *Rabarbarcello* **(Rhubarb Liqueur),** use 2 pounds fresh rhubarb. Wash and slice rhubarb into ½-inch pieces, and combine with vodka. Proceed with the recipe for Limoncello, substituting honey for sugar syrup; stir together ¾ cup honey and ¼ cup hot water until well blended.

SERVING LIMONCELLO

Enjoy limoncello cold, served "straight up" in a shot glass, as a digestive after dinner. Prepare a refreshing cocktail by pouring 2 ounces limoncello over ice in a tall glass, top with club soda, and garnish with a sprig of mint. Make a limoncello martini with 1½ ounces limoncello, 1 ounce plain or lemon vodka, ½ ounce fresh lemon juice, and ½ ounce simple (very heavy) syrup, or to taste. Shake with ice, strain into a sugar-rimmed glass, and garnish with a lemon twist.

Macerated Cherries

Serve these scented cherries with buttery shortbread cookies for a simple yet sophisticated dessert. Use the syrup as a sauce over ice cream or cheesecake, or as a refreshing cocktail, topped off with club soda.

Yield:	Prep time:	Pickling time:	Serving size:
1 quart	30 minutes	3 to 5 days	¼ cup

2 TB. granulated sugar, or to taste

1½ cups gold rum

4 cups fresh, sweet, unpitted cherries (such as Bing)

3 pieces star anise

3 whole cloves

1 cinnamon stick

1. In a small saucepan, stir together sugar and gold rum. Place over medium heat and stir until sugar dissolves completely. Cool to room temperature.

2. Wash cherries, remove stems, and drain well. Prick cherries with a fork to pierce their skins.

3. Add star anise, cloves, and cinnamon stick to a sterilized 1-quart canning jar, and fill with cherries. Pour cooled syrup over the fruit. Cover and refrigerate. Best after 3 to 5 days. Use within 6 months.

Variations: For **Macerated Pineapple,** substitute 4 cups fresh pineapple chunks for cherries. Add 3 slices peeled, fresh ginger to the jar with the spices. For **Macerated Pink Grapefruit,** substitute 4 cups fresh grapefruit sections for cherries. Substitute gin for the rum. Omit spices. Add 2 tablespoons Campari liqueur to the jar before adding fruit and syrup. For **Macerated Melon,** substitute 4 cups melon balls for cherries. (Use any type of fresh melon, such as cantaloupe, honeydew, casaba, or watermelon.) Substitute plain vodka for the rum. Omit spices. Add 15 to 20 fresh mint leaves, 2 tablespoons melon liqueur (optional), and 2 tablespoons lemon or orange zest (optional) to the jar before adding fruit and syrup.

Cured Meat and Fish  13

Curing is a form of pickling and preserves by soaking meats and fish in salt. There may be additives such as nitrites or acid to supplement the salt cure. You apply meat and fish cures by dry-salting or brining. In addition, complementary methods such as drying and smoking may be used.

Good sanitation is paramount; your hands are loaded with bacteria and touching food that is being cured can introduce the very pathogens you are trying to control. So keep this in mind as you work through these recipes. Wash your hands thoroughly, and use sanitized tools or disposable gloves when handling your products.

The recipes in this chapter span a wide range of techniques from all around the globe. Some recipes use nitrites and others don't; in some recipes its use is optional. Some recipes prepare well-cured meats for long storage, and a few have short shelf lives. Perhaps more than any other method of preservation, curing is more art than science. You can make brine weak or strong, and cure for a short or long time. You can make full-flavored foods, or lightly seasoned ones.

So dive in, put some pork belly in brine, fire up your smoker, rub a salmon with some love, and get excited about curing meats and fish.

Dry-Cured Foods

Most of the recipes in this section are very easy. They offer you a nice introduction to dry-salting methods. As you see, you can cure many kinds of meat and fish, including beef, pork, duck, and salmon. Curing salt is available from retailers of sausage-making supplies (see Chapter 5 for more information).

Italian-Style Air-Dried Beef (*Bresaola*)

The flavor of air-dried beef is like butter, clean and rich. Enjoy thin slices with simple accompaniments such as pickles, fresh cheese, bread, and wine.

Yield:	Prep time:	Curing time:	Serving size:
1½ pounds	30 minutes	5 weeks	1 ounce

> 1 (2¼ to 2½ lb.) beef top round or eye-of-round roast
> 1½ TB. kosher salt
> 1½ TB. granulated sugar
> 1 TB. dried Italian seasonings blend
> 1½ tsp. ground black pepper
> ½ tsp. curing salt #2

1. Cures cannot penetrate connective tissue or fat, so trim meat of all visible fat and silver skin (the thin, tough membrane on some cuts of meat such as loin and ribs). Mix together kosher salt, sugar, Italian seasonings blend, pepper, and curing salt #2; reserve half of cure for step 2. Evenly rub meat with remaining cure on all sides, seal in a zipper-lock plastic bag, and refrigerate 7 days, rotating bag ¼ turn daily.

2. Remove meat from the bag. Do not rinse, but dry thoroughly with paper towels. Rub with reserved cure. Place meat in a clean zipper-lock plastic bag and refrigerate again for 7 days, rotating bag ¼ turn daily.

3. Remove meat from the bag, rinse thoroughly under cold running water, and dry thoroughly with paper towels. Set on a rack to dry at room temperature for 2 hours. Using cotton butcher's twine, tie around width of meat at 1-inch intervals. Tie around length of meat once, creating a loop for hanging at one end. Record weight of meat.

4. Hang in a cool (60°F) place with high humidity (60 to 70 percent) for 3 weeks. Check daily. If signs of mold appear, wash rind with 5 percent vinegar using a clean piece of muslin. Bresaola is ready when it feels firm and has lost 30 percent of its weight.

5. Wrap cured bresaola loosely in plastic, store in the refrigerator, and consume within 6 months.

BRESAOLA

Italian-style air-dried beef or *bresaola* is treated with a "slow cure," and then dried in circulating air with no cooking step. Bacterial control is achieved by curing with nitrates and by drying to reduce the moisture content of the meat. Air-dried meat is made in many cultures, and is sometimes dried in thin pieces that are more like jerky. The color of bresaola is a deep, rich, burgundy red; the texture is silky when thinly sliced.

Oven-Smoked Cured Pastrami

Pastrami is cured, spice-rubbed beef (brisket or round) that is often smoked. Slice for sandwiches (hot or cold). If you have a smoker, go for it—or use this easy oven-smoking method.

Yield:	Prep time:	Curing time:	Serving size:
4 pounds	60 minutes	3 to 4 days, plus cooking	3 to 4 ounces

3 TB. black peppercorns

3 TB. coriander seeds

1 TB. mustard seeds

1 TB. paprika

2 tsp. garlic powder

¼ cup Morton Tender Quick

¼ cup brown sugar, loosely packed

1 (5 to 6 lb.) beef brisket, flat cut (see following sidebar)

¼ cup liquid smoke

3 TB. coarsely ground black pepper

1. In a coffee grinder or using a mortar and pestle, coarsely grind black peppercorns, coriander seeds, and mustard seeds. Add paprika and garlic powder and grind until evenly mixed. In a small bowl, stir spice mixture, Morton Tender Quick, and brown sugar until well blended.

2. Evenly rub brisket with cure on all sides. Seal in a zipper-lock plastic bag, and refrigerate 3 to 4 days, flipping the bag over and massaging brisket every 12 hours. By the end of the first day, you will notice liquid collecting in the bag. This is normal.

3. Remove brisket from bag and rinse under cold running water, while rubbing surface to remove most seasoning. Dry thoroughly with paper towels.

4. Preheat oven to 350°F. Place brisket on a piece of heavy-gauge aluminum foil large enough to wrap brisket completely. Sprinkle brisket with liquid smoke and massage to distribute evenly. Wrap tightly in the foil. Place the foil packet in a heavy casserole dish or roasting pan. Pour in 1½ cups water. Cover pan with a lid or another piece of foil. Bake for 2 to 2½ hours, or until brisket is very tender.

5. Unwrap brisket and discard the foil. Place brisket on a clean baking sheet and sprinkle evenly on both sides with pepper. Place brisket, uncovered, in the 350°F oven for 30 minutes to form a peppered crust. Slice while still warm; or cool, wrap, and chill in the refrigerator to serve cold the next day.

PERFECT PRESERVING

Select a flat-cut brisket weighing 5 to 6 pounds that is thick and rectangular, with even thickness. A point-cut brisket is too thin and tapered; it becomes dried meat at the edges when traditionally smoked. Oven-smoking is more forgiving, however, when your meat is an irregular shape.

Salt-Cured Bacon

Home-cured bacon is easy to make and a good first project. Like the previous recipe for pastrami, you can "smoke" your bacon in the oven or use your favorite smoking method.

Yield:	Prep time:	Curing time:	Serving size:
4 pounds	60 minutes	6 to 7 days, plus cooking	2 ounces

1 (5 lb.) trimmed, fresh pork belly

¼ cup kosher salt

1 tsp. pink curing salt #1

½ cup brown sugar, packed

1. Square sides and trim pork belly to fit in a large zipper-lock plastic bag. If skin is intact, leave it on during curing and smoking. Use trimmed meat for cooking, meatloaf, or meatballs.

2. In a small bowl, stir kosher salt, pink curing salt #1, and brown sugar until evenly mixed. Evenly rub pork belly with cure on all sides. Seal in a zipper-lock plastic bag.

3. Refrigerate 6 to 7 days, flipping the bag over and massaging pork belly every 12 hours. By the end of the first day, you will notice liquid collecting in the bag. This is normal.

4. Remove bacon from the bag and rinse thoroughly under cold running water. Dry thoroughly with paper towels.

5. Preheat a smoker or oven to 200°F. Place bacon in the smoker or oven for 2 hours, or until the internal temperature reads 150°F.

6. If skin is still on, pull it off while still warm. Cool bacon to room temperature. Wrap and refrigerate up to 10 days or freeze up to 3 months.

Variations: For **Maple-Flavored Breakfast Bacon,** substitute ½ cup maple sugar or maple syrup (or a combination) for brown sugar. Syrup makes more of a paste to rub over meat. For **Pepper-Herb Bacon,** reduce brown sugar to ¼ cup and add 3 tablespoons freshly ground black pepper, 1 tablespoon dried thyme, and 1 tablespoon dried sage or rosemary.

PERFECT PRESERVING

If you have a large piece of pork belly, you may want to cure a smaller portion and freeze the rest. Frozen uncured pork maintains its quality longer than cured bacon. So feel free to cut a fresh pork belly into 2½- to 5-pound portions. Wrap and freeze up to 6 months. Just remember to adjust the amount of cure. Make up a batch of cure for 5 pounds pork belly, and use 50 percent for 2½ pounds pork belly. Save remaining cure for your next batch.

Duck Prosciutto

Duck prosciutto is another easy-to-make cured meat. This straightforward recipe cures a breast half in salt, and then dries it slowly. The result is firm, rich meat with distinctive flavor—perfect for hors d'oeuvres, salads, or pasta.

Yield:	Prep time:	Curing time:	Serving size:
about 5 ounces	30 minutes	1 to 3 weeks or more	½ ounce

2 cups coarse kosher salt, or as needed

1 (6 to 8 oz.) boneless duck breast half, skin on

¼ tsp. ground white pepper

1. Cover the bottom of a glass or ceramic bread pan with a ½-inch layer kosher salt. Handling duck with gloved or very clean hands, or tongs, dry it thoroughly with paper towels. If tenderloin is not securely attached, remove it, and reserve for another use. Place duck breast on salt layer, flesh side down (skin side up). Pour in enough salt to cover sides and top by ½ inch. Cover tightly with plastic wrap, and place in the refrigerator to cure for 24 hours.

2. Remove duck from salt, rinse under cold running water, and dry thoroughly with paper towels. Breast meat will be firm. Weigh duck breast, and multiply weight by 0.7. Write down both numbers, along with today's date, on a sticky note and attach to the refrigerator door. Sprinkle duck meat on both sides with white pepper. Wrap in a single layer of cheesecloth, and tie the ends with cotton butcher's twine. Discard curing salt.

3. Suspend duck breast so that air can circulate all around. For example, tape the ends of the cheesecloth securely to suspend duck over a bread pan, hang meat from a coat hanger, suction cup hook, or use duct tape or some other method that allows air to circulate freely around the wrapped duck.

4. Refrigerate for 1 to 3 weeks, or until duck has lost 30 percent of its weight (check the sticky note on your refrigerator door). When squeezed, breast should feel firm and stiff, not soft or spongy. The color should be deep red. For serving, place skin side up, and use a very sharp knife to cut paper-thin slices at a 45-degree angle. Refrigerate up to 14 days, or freeze for 6 months.

Variation: For **Spiced Duck Prosciutto**, combine 2 tablespoons granulated sugar, 2 tablespoons garlic powder, 1 tablespoon ground black pepper, 1 tablespoon crushed red pepper, and 1 tablespoon dried oregano with 2 cups coarse kosher salt until well blended. Proceed with preceding recipe substituting spice mix for kosher salt.

CURING MEAT IN THE REFRIGERATOR

In a normal refrigerator, the temperature ranges from 32°F to 40°F, and the humidity from 10 percent relative humidity (RH) in the main compartment (with lots of circulating air) to 80 to 90 percent RH in the produce drawers (with little air circulation). If dried in conditions that are too cold and dry, the outside meat may dry out before the interior, causing a condition known as case-hardening. Case-hardening prevents meat from drying completely, and may allow too much bacteria to grow. If conditions are too humid, mold may grow. In your kitchen refrigerator, place curing meat on a high shelf toward the front, with a pan of water nearby to increase humidity. For frequent curing, buy a small refrigerator, increase the temperature, and add a pan of water to increase humidity.

Salted Salmon (*Shiozake*)

Salted salmon has a fresh, clean flavor and is popular in Hawaiian and Japanese cuisines. The salt makes the flesh firm and extends its shelf life in the refrigerator or freezer. Soak salmon in water to remove excess salt before eating or cooking.

Yield:	Prep time:	Curing time:	Serving size:
1½ pounds	30 to 60 minutes	1 to 3 days	3 ounces

1 (2-lb.) salmon fillet, skin on

4 TB. coarse kosher or sea salt (do not use table salt)

1. Pat salmon dry with paper towels. Rub kosher salt evenly over both sides of salmon. Wrap in several layers of paper towels. Place in a plastic (not metal) colander and then place colander in a shallow container to catch any liquid. Refrigerate for 1 to 3 days.

2. Rinse salmon under cold running water. Pat salmon dry with paper towels. If desired, cut salmon into serving-size pieces. Place salmon on a drying rack over a baking sheet and refrigerate uncovered for 8 hours, or until dry and firm. Wrap in plastic wrap and refrigerate for 2 weeks, or freeze up to 2 months.

3. To prepare salted salmon for use, soak in cold water for 3 to 6 hours, changing water every hour.

IDEAS FOR USING SALTED FISH

Several cultures around the world enjoy salted salmon. Hawaiians make Lomilomi salmon, an appetizer commonly served at luau. The Japanese enjoy salted salmon in several ways: sprinkle it with lemon juice and crushed red pepper, stuff it inside sushi rice balls (*onigiri*), or add to fried rice with peas, carrots, green onion, and egg. Make an impressive savory Russian pie called *pirog* (not to be confused with Polish *pierogi*) with layers of rice, salmon, hard-cooked eggs, and sautéed mushrooms wrapped in pastry and baked until golden. Other types of fish that may be salted in this way include mackerel, halibut, and cod.

Gravlax

Gravlax is salt-cured raw salmon with an incredibly silky texture and clean flavor. It means "buried salmon," which was the traditional method of preparation in Scandinavian countries.

Yield:	Prep time:	Curing time:	Serving size:
1½ pounds	30 to 60 minutes	1 to 3 days	3 ounces

> 1 (2-lb.) salmon fillet, skin on
>
> ¼ cup brown sugar
>
> 2 TB. coarse kosher or sea salt (do not use table salt)

1. Pat salmon dry with paper towels. In a small bowl, stir together brown sugar and kosher salt. Rub mixture evenly over both sides of salmon.

2. Wrap salmon tightly in several layers of plastic wrap. Place in a shallow pan. Weight down with a cutting board and several books or cans of food. Refrigerate for 1 to 3 days.

3. Rinse salmon under running water and pat dry with paper towels. Use a very sharp knife to cut paper-thin slices at a 45-degree angle. Serve on bread, with sour cream, chopped red onion, and capers or pickles. Consume within 5 days. Freezing ruins the texture but otherwise doesn't harm the product.

Variation: For **Gravlax with Dill and Pepper,** use 2 tablespoons granulated sugar and ¼ cup kosher salt. Cut salmon fillet in half lengthwise before rubbing with salt mixture. Place one piece skin side down on the plastic wrap. Top with several sprigs fresh dill and 1 tablespoon coarsely ground white pepper. Place second piece salmon, flesh side down, over top of dill. Wrap tightly in plastic wrap and continue at step 2 for preceding recipe. Flip over wrapped salmon 3 to 4 times each day while curing.

SPOILER ALERT

It is rare—but not impossible—to find worms in seafood. Although it's not usually life threatening unless you have a weakened immune system, eating live worms can make you sick. Salt and acid offer only slight protection; however, heating or freezing readily kills the parasites. Cook fish to an internal temperature of at least 140°F to kill parasites. In the United States, seafood to be served raw in restaurants (such as *sushi*) is required to be previously frozen. For safety at home, prefreeze fish that will be prepared and served raw, such as the recipes in this chapter for salted salmon and gravlax. You could also purchase sushi-grade fish; however, it is considerably more expensive.

Wet-Cured Foods

Dry-salting and brining are more or less interchangeable. There are some guidelines but no hard-and-fast rules. As you can see, there is a recipe in this section for brine-cured bacon, which isn't all that much different from the previous one for salt-cured bacon. These other recipes represent broad cross sections of the many ways different cultures preserve meats and fish by pickling.

Korean Salty Beef (*Jangjorim*)

This intensely flavored, shredded beef is infused with soy and garlic. The salty flavor comes only from soy sauce; no other salt is added in the traditional preparation, and none is needed.

Yield:	Prep time:	Cooking time:	Serving size:
about 1 pound	30 minutes	2 hours	¼ cup

1 (1½ lb.) beef flank steak or brisket

2 qt. water, or as needed

1 cup soy sauce

2 cups water

12 cloves garlic, peeled

3 shishito, serrano, or jalapeño chiles, seeded and sliced lengthwise

3 green onions, cut in 2-in. lengths

1 TB. grated fresh ginger, peeled

¼ cup brown sugar

½ tsp. ground black pepper

1. Cut meat into 2-inch cubes. Place in a pot, cover with cold water, and bring to a boil over high heat. Reduce heat to medium-low and simmer, skimming and discarding any foam that rises to the surface. Simmer meat for 10 to 15 minutes, or until no more foam appears.

2. Add soy sauce, water, garlic, shishito chiles, green onions, ginger, brown sugar, and pepper. Partially cover and continue to simmer for 1 to 1½ hours, or until meat is fork-tender and liquid has reduced by about half. Turn off heat, uncover, and let meat cool in broth for 1 hour.

3. Remove meat from broth and shred into long pieces. Return meat to broth and refrigerate up to 1 month, or freeze for longer storage.

PERFECT PRESERVING

Korean salty beef is strongly flavored. A popular lunch food, it is served in small portions. Accompaniments include hard-cooked eggs, simmered in the same broth, and fresh hot chiles. Add it to stir-fries, sandwich wraps, or salads; serve it with rice; or make a soup with it.

Smoked Turkey Hindquarters

This easy recipe turns out moist, smoky, flavorful meat.

Yield:	Prep time:	Curing time:	Serving size:
5 pounds	60 minutes	4 days, plus smoking time	⅓ pound

4 qt. water

½ cup (5 oz.) pickling salt

½ cup packed brown sugar

1 tsp. pink curing salt #1 (optional)

5 lb. bone-in turkey hindquarters (legs and thighs)

1. In a medium (3- to 4-quart), nonreactive (stainless-steel or enamel) saucepan, add 2 quarts water, pickling salt, and brown sugar, and bring to a boil over high heat. Reduce heat to medium-low and simmer, stirring constantly, until salt and sugar are completely dissolved. Turn off heat and add remaining 2 quarts water.

2. When brine has cooled to room temperature, add pink curing salt #1 (if using) and stir until completely dissolved. (Curing salt enhances the flavor and delays spoilage.) Transfer brine to a container large enough to hold brine and turkey. Refrigerate until well chilled.

3. When brine has cooled to 38°F to 40°F, add turkey pieces; if necessary, weight with a plate to keep meat completely submerged in brine. Soak for 3 to 4 days, preferably at 36°F to 38°F, turning over every 12 hours. Note: curing activity stops below 34°F and under no circumstance should rise above 40°F.

4. Remove turkey from brine and rinse thoroughly under cold running water. Dry thoroughly with paper towels.

5. Preheat a smoker or oven to 200°F. Place turkey in the smoker or oven for 2 hours, or until the internal temperature reads 165°F.

Variation: For **Brine-Cured Bacon (Wiltshire Cure),** increase salt to 1 cup (10 ounces). Square sides and trim a 5-pound piece of pork belly to fit in a brining container. If skin is intact, leave it on during curing and smoking. Use trim for cooking, or making meatloaf or meatballs. After curing, bacon is ready to use; smoking is optional.

Salted Salmon Roe (*Ikura*)

If you fish—or know someone who does—try your hand at making this salmon caviar. The briny flavor is reminiscent of the open ocean and complements everything from omelets to soup.

Yield:	Prep time:	Curing time:	Serving size:
about 1 pint	60 minutes	20 minutes	2 tablespoons

4 cups water

⅞ cup (1 cup, minus 2 TB.) pickling salt

1 roe skein from wild salmon

1. In a medium (3- to 4-quart), nonreactive saucepan, add 2 cups water and pickling salt, and bring to a boil. Reduce heat to medium-low and simmer, stirring constantly, until salt dissolves completely. Turn off heat, and add remaining 2 cups water. Transfer to a storage container and refrigerate until well chilled.

2. Rinse roe skein under cold running water. Add skein to brine, making sure it is completely submerged. Refrigerate for 10 minutes; the membrane and eggs will become cloudy. Remove skein and return brine to the refrigerator.

3. Handling gently, hold skein over a mesh strainer set in a bowl. Rinse skein under hot tap water to shrink membrane and release eggs into the strainer. Discard membrane. Rinse eggs in several changes of cool water, removing all pieces of membrane. Return eggs to brine, and refrigerate for 10 minutes, or until eggs turn clear. Place eggs in a mesh strainer set over a bowl, and drain in the refrigerator for 1 hour.

4. Without rinsing, pack eggs into one or more sterilized jars, and refrigerate as cold as possible, preferably 30°F to 34°F. Use within 2 weeks. Eggs shouldn't taste salty; if they do, next time decrease the brining time.

Sealed Foods ∼ 14

Although cultures around the world have sealed foods by various methods for centuries, modern recipes often omit important aspects of traditional preparations. Traditional methods prepared food for storage without refrigeration. They routinely used game meat and fat, and large amounts of salt, or preservatives such as saltpeter (potassium nitrate). Without refrigeration, these products ferment during storage, resulting in robust (some may say putrid) flavors.

Modern fat-sealed foods tend to have clean (some may say bland) flavors compared to old-fashioned methods. Fat-sealed foods may also be a difference between having plenty and facing near starvation. Historically, sealed foods are often used to sustain cultures in times of calamity.

Fat-Sealed Foods

The kind and amount of fat in the American diet has been the center of controversy since the mid-twentieth century, waged between U.S. government agencies, the medical community, health practitioners, and popular media. Dietary fat carries some benefits and important nutrients. Also, eating fat helps to curb hunger. Unless you have health issues that dictate otherwise, moderate consumption of fat can be a delicious treat, as the recipes in this chapter show you.

Regardless of your dietary practices, fat-sealed foods are a fun way to occasionally use and preserve expensive protein foods like meats, poultry, and seafood. Like many other preservation methods, some of these methods have been used for centuries by cultures around the world.

Pork *Rillettes*

Meats simmered in fat until tender and shredded produce a rich, creamy spread for wintertime enjoyment. While the name means "little strips of pork," you can make rillettes with any type of poultry or rabbit.

Yield:	Prep time:	Cook time:	Serving size:
2 to 3 pints	60 to 90 minutes	4 to 6 hours	¼ cup

> 2 lb. lean boneless pork, preferably belly or shoulder (butt)
>
> 2 lb. pork fat (trimmed from the meat used in recipe, or use leaf lard)
>
> ¼ cup water
>
> 1 tsp. salt, plus additional to taste
>
> ½ tsp. ground black pepper, plus additional to taste
>
> ⅛ tsp. ground allspice, plus additional to taste
>
> 1 bay leaf
>
> 6 sprigs thyme
>
> 6 whole garlic cloves

1. Cut boneless pork and pork fat into 1-inch cubes. In a large (6-quart) heavy casserole dish with a lid, add pork, pork fat, water, salt, pepper, and allspice. Toss mixture to distribute seasonings evenly. Add bay leaf, thyme, and garlic. Place over low heat (or bake in the oven at 300°F) for 4 to 6 hours, or until pork is very tender and falling apart. Remove casserole dish from heat, uncover, and let meat cool for 30 minutes.

2. Remove and discard bay leaf and thyme. Using a slotted spoon, transfer garlic to a small dish, and mash with a fork. Transfer pork to a large bowl. Using a fine mesh strainer or cheesecloth, strain melted fat to remove large particles.

3. Using 2 forks, shred pork into fine strands. Stir in 1 cup strained, melted fat. Add additional salt, pepper, and allspice to taste until mixture is well seasoned.

4. Pack pork into sterilized 1 cup or smaller jars or ramekins. Pour melted fat over pork to cover completely in a thin ⅛-inch or thick ½-inch layer. Store in the refrigerator for up to 2 weeks if a thin layer of fat is used, or up to 6 months if a thick layer of fat is used. When fat is cold, press a piece of aluminum foil or waxed paper over the top to protect it from air. Any leftover fat may be refrigerated or frozen and used for sautéing or frying.

5. Serve rillettes at room temperature with bread, pickles, and beer.

Variation: For *Confit* **Meat Patties,** prepare 8 meat patties from 2 pounds ground beef or ground pork sausage, seasoned as desired. Sauté or grill 4 to 5 minutes per side, or until the internal temperature is at least 160°F. Cool and pack into containers with melted tallow (beef fat) or lard (pork fat).

Duck Confit

Confit meat is redolent with spices and richly flavored, comparable to a dry-aged ham or smoked turkey. This modern recipe prepares confit with minimal salt and optional cure, requiring storage in the refrigerator.

Yield:	Prep time:	Cook time:	Serving size:
2 to 2¼ pounds	1 to 2 days	1½ to 3 hours	⅓ to ½ pounds

2½ TB. salt

1 tsp. curing salt #1 (optional)

2 bay leaves, crumbled

½ tsp. dried thyme

¼ tsp. ground black pepper

Pinch ground cloves

2 to 2¼ lb. duck legs and thighs

1 lb. duck fat or pork lard cut in ½-in. cubes, or as needed

1. In a small bowl, stir together salt, curing salt #1 (if using), bay leaves, thyme, pepper, and cloves until well combined. Rub duck pieces evenly all over with salt mixture. Place in shallow dish, cover with plastic wrap, and refrigerate for 24 to 48 hours.

2. Rinse salt from duck under running water and pat pieces dry with paper towels.

3. Place duck fat in a fireproof casserole large enough to hold duck pieces comfortably and melt fat over medium heat. When fat is hot and melted, add duck legs and thighs, overlapping slightly. If meat is not completely submerged, add additional fat as needed. Reduce heat to medium-low and cook confit uncovered at a very slow simmer (only an occasional bubble) for 1½ to 2 hours, or until meat is very tender and pulls easily from the bone. Larger Muscovy duck pieces may take up to 3 hours. Note that meat may still look pink if curing salt is used.

Alternatively, to ensure even, slow heat, cook duck in a slow cooker on low heat or in the oven at 250°F for 2 to 3 hours, or until very tender. Make sure meat is completely submerged in fat and leave the slow cooker or casserole dish uncovered during cooking.

4. Using a slotted spoon, transfer duck to a large platter. Using a fine mesh strainer or cheesecloth, strain melted fat to remove large particles.

5. Add at least ½ inch melted fat to each sterilized jar; chill until fat has completely solidified. Pack meat into sterilized 1 cup or smaller jars or ramekins, making sure it does not touch the sides. Pour melted fat over meat to cover completely in a thin ⅛-inch layer. Store in the refrigerator up to 1 month. If curing salt was used and longer storage is desired (up to 6 months), the next day, add another ½-inch layer of fat. When fat is cold, press a piece of aluminum foil or waxed paper over the top to protect it from air.

6. To prepare for serving, in a skillet over medium heat, melt a thin layer of fat. Brown duck pieces on all sides, about 15 minutes total, or until heated through. Alternatively, shred meat for salads or soup. Fat may be refrigerated or frozen and reused for another confit, or for sautéing or frying.

Potted Salmon

Potting is the English term for meat or fish preserved by layering in a container with fat. It is equivalent to French confit and rillettes. Shrimp, trout, anchovies, and salmon are some common fish preserved by this method.

Yield:	Prep time:	Cook time:	Serving size:
1 pound	30 minutes	10 minutes	3 to 4 ounces

1 lb. salmon fillet, skin removed

1 tsp. sea salt, or to taste

¼ tsp. ground white pepper, or to taste

¼ tsp. paprika

8 oz. (2 sticks) unsalted butter, melted

Grated zest of 1 lemon

2 TB. lemon juice

2 TB. snipped chives or dill

1. Preheat the oven to 375°F. Place salmon in a baking pan just large enough to hold it. Sprinkle with sea salt, white pepper, and paprika. Pour melted unsalted butter (leaving behind milk solids) over salmon. Place in the oven and bake for 8 to 10 minutes, or until cooked through.

2. Transfer hot salmon to a large bowl. Pour in half of butter from baking pan and add lemon zest, lemon juice, and chives. Mash with a large fork or spoon until salmon breaks up, butter starts to solidify, and mixture becomes very smooth. Add additional salt or white pepper to taste.

3. Pack mixture into small ramekins, smoothing the tops. Pour remaining butter from the baking pan over tops to cover salmon paste. Refrigerate until butter is hard, and then press a piece of aluminum foil or waxed paper over the top to protect it from air. Refrigerate up to 1 week, or freeze for up to 2 months.

4. Let potted salmon come to room temperature before serving. Serve with toast as an appetizer or light supper dish.

Traditional *Pemmican*

Pemmican is one of the original "superfoods," a nutritious survival and trail food dating back hundreds of years. This traditional preparation comes from the North American Cree tribe, who made it from dried meat, such as buffalo or elk.

Yield:	Prep time:	Serving size:
8 to 20 ounces	60 to 90 minutes	1 to 1½ ounces

2 cups (4 oz.) shredded, dried lean meat or jerky*

¼ to 2 cups tallow (rendered suet), lard, or clarified butter (ghee)

¼ tsp. salt, or to taste** (optional)

¼ cup honey or brown sugar, or to taste** (optional)

Use jerky from any dried, fully cooked meat such as beef, buffalo, bison, caribou, moose, elk, or deer.

**Although neither salt nor sugar is traditional, current tastes sometimes prefer them. If seasoned jerky is used, additional salt is not usually desirable.*

1. Line a rimmed baking sheet with parchment paper, waxed paper, or plastic wrap.

2. Grind meat into a powder with a traditional method—such as using a heavy rock pounder and placing meat inside a canvas cloth—or a modern method—such as using a large mortar and pestle, a food processor, or a blender. Place powder in a large bowl.

3. In a saucepan over medium heat, heat tallow for 10 to 15 minutes, or until completely melted.

4. Pour melted fat onto meat powder. Add salt (if using) and honey (if using). Stir until fat congeals and mixture is well coated, sticks together, and is smooth.

5. Spread mixture on the lined baking sheet, about ½ inch thick, and allow to cool. When mixture is firm, cut into small bars. Wrap bars in aluminum foil, waxed paper, or plastic wrap. Store in an airtight container. If kept cool (40°F to 70°F), pemmican can be stored for several years. It may also be frozen. Be sure to store in the refrigerator if the temperature rises above 70°F.

Variations: For **Dried Fruit Pemmican,** substitute up to 1 cup shredded meat with an equal amount of dried berries. Grind berries into a powder and combine with powdered meat before adding seasonings and fat. For **Vegan Fruit-and-Nut Pemmican,** substitute 2 cups roasted nuts and dried fruits for meat. Grind to a powder, and combine with ¼ to 2 cups melted, refined coconut oil. Add salt, sugar, or spices to taste.

Canned Fruits ∾ 15

The recipes in this chapter include basic canning methods for fruits and berries. The first set of recipes is grouped by type of fruit: berries, stone fruits, pomes (like apples and pears), citrus, tropical, and specialty fruits. You may pack any of these fruits in liquid, or prepare them as purée, juice, or syrup. Following the recipes for basic fruits, there are instructions for sauces, pie fillings, and ice cream toppings.

Some of these recipes include processing time for a pressure canner, which results in a higher quality product.

General Procedure for Canning Fruits

For more details on the steps to prepare, process, and store canned foods, see Chapter 7. Use the following general procedure for all of the recipes in this chapter:

1. Prepare boiling water–bath or pressure canner, jars, and lids. Before proceeding, review your recipe; preparing the canner and jars is usually the first step, unless the recipe preparation is very lengthy.

2. Prepare fruit and hot canning liquid as directed in each recipe. For hot-packed fruits, use any type of canning liquid, including plain water, unsweetened fruit juice, sugar syrup, honey syrup, or pickling syrup. For raw-packed fruits, the best results are achieved by using sweetened canning liquids, such as light to medium sugar syrups. See Chapter 7 for how to make different canning syrups.

3. Fill hot jars by the hot-pack or raw-pack method as allowed in the recipe. Use the following general packing instructions, unless recipe directs otherwise.

- Hot pack: *Method 1 (using canning liquid):* Bring a large pot of canning liquid to a boil. Add prepared fruit in one layer. Cook 1 to 2 minutes for cubes or slices, or up to 5 minutes for halves or small whole fruits (like figs), until hot throughout. Fill the hot jar with hot fruit; pack tightly without crushing. Add hot canning liquid, adjusting headspace as directed in recipe. *Method 2 (using sugar):* Instead of canning liquid, cook fruit and sugar until sugar completely dissolves. Ladle hot product into the hot jar. If there is not enough liquid to cover fruit, add boiling water. Adjust headspace as directed in recipe. *Method 3 (uniform product such as juice, pie filling, or sauce):* Ladle hot product into the hot jar, adjusting headspace as directed in recipe.

- Raw pack: Bring canning liquid to a boil, and then reduce heat and keep hot while filling jars. Ladle a small amount of hot canning liquid into the hot jar. Add raw fruit; pack tightly without crushing, and add hot liquid to cover, adjusting headspace as directed in recipe.

4. Clean the rim and secure the lid. Use process time as directed in recipe. Properly cool, and store the jars up to 1 year for best flavor.

You should use only the packing methods, jar sizes, headspace, and processing times specified in the recipe. These requirements are not interchangeable from one recipe to another.

Fruits and Berries

Most fruits are suitable for canning, including soft and firm berries, stone fruits such as cherries and peaches, apples and other pome-type fruits, citrus fruits, tropical fruits, rhubarb, and figs. There are a few fruits you should not can. Overripe fruits are low in acid and may not be safe; turn them into frozen purée or fruit leather. There are no tested canning recipes for bananas; try drying or freezing. Melons are low acid, so these fruits must be pickled.

Whole, Half, and Sliced Fruits

You may preserve berries and fruits in sweetened or unsweetened liquids; it is mostly a matter of preference. If you aren't sure which method will work best for you, review the information in Chapter 7 about ingredients and preparation.

Berries

Canned berries are appetizing fruit bombs. They're packed with healthful antioxidants, too, so spoon them over hotcakes, stir them into plain yogurt, or use them in family favorite recipes from cranberry sauce to berry crisp.

Yield:	Prep time:	Process time:	Headspace:
1 to 14 quarts	60 to 90 minutes	8 to 20 minutes	½ inch

Berries, Hot Pack or Raw Pack

1 Quart*	7 Quarts*	14 Quarts*	Ingredient
2¼ lb.	15¾ lb.	31½ lb.	Berries
¼ cups	1¾ cups	3½ cups	Canning liquid (hot pack, Method 1)
½ cup	3½ cups	7 cups	Sugar (hot pack, Method 2)
1½ cups	10½ cups	5¼ qt.	Canning liquid (raw pack)

Estimated at an average of 2¼ pounds fruit and 1½ cups canning liquid per quart.

1. Review the section "General Procedure for Canning Fruits" at the beginning of the chapter.

2. Wash berries; pick over and remove stems or moldy berries. Large strawberries may be halved, quartered, or sliced. Leave all other berries whole. Prepare any canning liquid.

3. Fill hot jars by the hot-pack or raw-pack method using the following procedure.

   • Hot pack: Keep all products hot while filling jars. *Method 1 (using canning liquid):* For each quart of berries, use only ¼ cup canning liquid, or enough to prevent sticking while heating the berries for 1 to 2 minutes. *Method 2 (using sugar):* For each quart of berries, add ¼ to ½ cup sugar. Let stand 2 hours in a cool place, and then heat over medium until sugar dissolves and berries are hot throughout.

   • Raw pack: Pretreat firm berries by checking. (See Chapter 7).

Process time for berries (at 0 to 1,000 feet), in minutes:

- **Boiling water, hot pack:** pints or quarts, 15

- **Boiling water, raw pack:** pints, 15; quarts, 20

- **Dial gauge at 6 pounds, hot pack:** pints or quarts, 8

- **Dial gauge at 6 pounds, raw pack:** pints, 8; quarts, 10

- **Weighted gauge at 5 pounds, hot pack:** pints or quarts, 8

- **Weighted gauge at 5 pounds, raw pack:** pints, 8; quarts, 10

Variation: For **Pickled Berries,** prepare a tart or tangy fruit-pickling syrup (see Chapter 7). For each cup Tart Syrup, add 6 allspice berries, 6 whole cloves, 1 cinnamon stick, ½ teaspoon fennel seeds, and ½ teaspoon black peppercorns. Simmer, covered, for 10 to 15 minutes. Remove spices before using syrup to pack jars by either method.

HOW TO HULL STRAWBERRIES

Wash strawberries before hulling. To *hull* a strawberry means to remove the hull or calyx (the green leafy portion). To remove the strawberry hull, insert the point of a small paring knife at an angle next to the hull, and then twist the knife in a circular motion while pulling. This technique easily removes the green calyx along with any white core. A special strawberry hulling tool is also available; some cooks use a star-shaped pastry tip to extract the strawberry hull easily.

Stone Fruit

The muted flavors of canned stone fruits offer comfort in a jar. Dress them up if you like with the warm, spicy aromas of cinnamon and brandy or the freshness of lemon and orange.

Yield:	Prep time:	Process time:	Headspace:
1 to 14 quarts	2 to 3 hours	8 to 30 minutes	½ inch

Stone Fruit, Hot Pack or Raw Pack

1 Quart*	7 Quarts*	14 Quarts*	Ingredient
2½ lb.	17½ lb.	35 lb.	Stone fruit
1½ cups	10½ cups	5¼ qt.	Canning liquid

Estimated at 2½ pounds fruit and 1½ cups canning liquid per quart.

1. Review the section "General Procedure for Canning Fruits" at the beginning of the chapter.

2. Wash stone fruit. Peel, pit, halve, or slice, and treat against darkening as needed. Prepare any canning liquid.

Process time for apricots, nectarines, and peaches (at 0 to 1,000 feet), in minutes:

- **Boiling water, hot pack:** pints, 20; quarts 25
- **Boiling water, raw pack:** pints, 25; quarts 30
- **Dial gauge at 6 pounds, hot or raw pack:** pints or quarts, 10
- **Weighted gauge at 5 pounds, hot or raw pack:** pints or quarts, 10

Process time for cherries (at 0 to 1,000 feet), in minutes:

- **Boiling water, hot pack:** pints, 15; quarts 20
- **Boiling water, raw pack:** pints, 25; quarts 25
- **Dial gauge at 6 pounds, hot pack:** pints, 8; quarts, 10
- **Dial gauge at 6 pounds, raw pack:** pints or quarts, 10
- **Weighted gauge at 5 pounds, hot pack:** pints, 8; quarts, 10
- **Weighted gauge at 5 pounds, raw pack:** pints or quarts, 10

Process time for plums (at 0 to 1,000 feet), in minutes:

- **Boiling water, hot or raw pack:** pints, 20; quarts 25
- **Dial gauge at 6 pounds, hot or raw pack:** pints or quarts, 10
- **Weighted gauge at 5 pounds, hot or raw pack:** pints or quarts, 10

Variations: For **Pickled Pears,** prepare sweet fruit-pickling syrup (see Chapter 7). For each cup sweet pickling syrup, add 1 cinnamon stick, 1 teaspoon whole cloves, and 1 teaspoon allspice berries; simmer, covered, for 10 to 15 minutes. Remove spices before using syrup to pack jars. For **Sweet Spiced Fruit,** prepare a medium to heavy syrup. For each cup of syrup, add 1 cinnamon stick, 1 allspice berry, 1 whole clove, and 1 ½-inch slice fresh ginger; simmer, covered, for 10 to 15 minutes. Remove spices before using syrup to pack jars.

PREPARE STONE FRUITS FOR CANNING

Leave cherries whole or remove pits; if whole, prick with a small knife or fork to prevent bursting. Blanch plums to check their waxy skins; leave whole and prick to prevent bursting, or cut in half and remove pits. Cut apricots and nectarines in half, remove pits or stones, and do not peel. Blanch peaches to peel skins, cut in halves or slices, and remove pits. To remove the pit easily in stone fruits, select freestone varieties, whose pits are easier to pull off than clingstone varieties. Treat light-colored stone fruits to prevent browning, including gold cherries, apricots, nectarines, and peaches.

Apples and Other Pomes

Capture the crisp, refreshing flavor of apples by packing in a light syrup or unsweetened apple juice. Add canned apples to yogurt, use them to make apple crisp, or serve with slow-cooked pork chops for a comforting midwinter dinner.

Yield:	Prep time:	Process time:	Headspace:
1 to 14 quarts	2 to 3 hours	8 to 25 minutes	½ inch

Apples and Other Pomes, Hot Pack Only

1 Quart*	7 Quarts*	14 Quarts*	Ingredient
2½ lb.	17½ lb.	35 lb.	Pome fruit
1½ cups	10½ cups	5¼ qt.	Canning liquid

Estimated at 2½ pounds fruit and 1½ cups canning liquid per quart.

1. Review the section "General Procedure for Canning Fruits" at the beginning of the chapter.

2. Wash fruit. Peel, core, and cut into halves, slices, or wedges as desired. Pretreat for browning. Loquats may be left whole, peeled or unpeeled, but seeds must be removed; some varieties are better for freezing or jelly. All pome-type fruits will float unless hot packed in light or medium sugar syrup. The mayhaw fruit is a small berrylike pome popular in southeastern states that contains several seeds, so has not been tested for canning wholes or halves; the fruit is always strained to make pulp or juice for sauce or jelly.

3. Acidify Asian pears before packing jar by adding 2 tablespoons bottled lemon juice to each quart (or 1 tablespoon to each pint).

Process time for apples or crabapples (at 0 to 1,000 feet), in minutes:

- **Boiling water, hot pack:** pints or quarts, 20
- **Dial gauge at 6 pounds, hot pack:** pints or quarts, 8
- **Weighted gauge at 5 pounds, hot pack:** pints or quarts, 8

Process time for acidified Asian pears (at 0 to 1,000 feet), in minutes:

- **Boiling water, hot pack:** pints, 20; quarts, 25
- **Pressure canner:** not safe

Process time for loquats (at 0 to 1,000 feet), in minutes:

- **Boiling water, hot pack:** pints, 15; quarts, 20
- **Pressure canner:** not safe

Process time for pear or quince (at 0 to 1,000 feet), in minutes:

- **Boiling water, hot pack:** pints, 20; quarts, 25
- **Dial gauge at 6 pounds, hot pack:** pints or quarts, 10
- **Weighted gauge at 5 pounds, hot pack:** pints or quarts, 10

Variations: For **Minted Fruit,** for each pound of fruit, add 1 teaspoon coarsely chopped fresh mint to simmering syrup before adding fruit. For **Honeyed Wine– Soaked Fruit,** make a medium honey syrup (see Chapter 7). Combine 2 parts (2 cups) honey syrup with 1 part (1 cup) light, slightly sweet white wine such as

Riesling, gewürztraminer, or chenin blanc. Poach fruit in hot honeyed-wine syrup and pack as directed. For **Pickled Quince or Crabapple,** prepare a very sweet fruit-pickling syrup (see Chapter 7). For each cup of syrup, add 1 cinnamon stick, 1 strip of fresh orange peel, 1 small bay leaf, ½ teaspoon coriander seeds, ¼ teaspoon whole cloves, and ¼ teaspoon black peppercorns, and simmer, covered, for 10 to 15 minutes. Remove spices and add peeled, cored, and quartered quince. Simmer, covered, for about 2 hours, or until soft and red. Don't overcook or they'll disintegrate. For best flavor, store 4 to 6 weeks before using.

SPOILER ALERT

Pits and seeds of many common fruits contain cyanide-releasing chemicals. These include kernels inside the pits of stone fruits like apricots, cherries, peaches, and plums, and the seeds of apples and pears, as well as raw cassava root. Avoid crushing and chewing the pits and seeds from these fruits to prevent accidental cyanide poisoning. Parents should teach their children not to eat fruit pits and seeds. The kernels of specific varieties of *Prunus* stone fruits have been developed for edible pips that are used in some types of commercial crack seed dried fruits.

Grapefruit and Other Citrus

Tree-ripened citrus fruits in light syrup make a refreshing finish to any meal. You can use them in Chinese orange beef or spicy curries, or as a topping for spinach. Create a festive beverage from citrus canning liquid, topped with club soda or sparkling wine.

Yield:	Prep time:	Process time:	Headspace:
1 to 14 quarts	2 to 3 hours	8 to 10 minutes	½ inch

Grapefruit and Other Citrus, Raw Pack Only

1 Quart*	7 Quarts*	14 Quarts*	Ingredient
2 lb.	14 lb.	28 lb.	Citrus fruit
1½ cups	10½ cups	5¼ qt.	Canning liquid

Estimated at 2 pounds fruit and 1½ cups canning liquid per quart.

1. Review the section "General Procedure for Canning Fruits" at the beginning of the chapter.

2. Wash citrus fruit. Peel fruits, making sure to remove all white pith, which will add bitterness to canned citrus. Peels may be candied or used for marmalade. Peel by hand to pull apart citrus sections with the membranes intact, discarding the white core and any other white spongy or stringy material. Alternatively, peel fruits to remove all white pith and section with a knife to extract fruit from membranes. This method creates citrus juice to use as part of the canning liquid.

    Raw pack results in a product with a flavor closer to fresh citrus fruit. See the following sidebar for more tips on preserving citrus fruits successfully.

Process time for citrus fruit (at 0 to 1,000 feet), in minutes:

- **Boiling water, raw pack:** pints or quarts, 10

- **Dial gauge at 6 pounds, hot pack:** pints or quarts, 8

- **Dial gauge at 6 pounds, raw pack:** pints, 8; quarts, 10

- **Weighted gauge at 5 pounds, hot pack:** pints or quarts, 8

- **Weighted gauge at 5 pounds, raw pack:** pints, 8; quarts, 10

Variations: For **Citrus in Orange Liqueur,** substitute ⅓ of plain or honey syrup with Cointreau or Grand Marnier liqueur. For **Honeyed Citrus Slices,** make a medium honey syrup (see Chapter 7). Citrus juice may be used in place of water in the syrup. For **Spiced Citrus,** prepare medium to heavy plain or honey syrup. For each cup of syrup, add 1 cinnamon stick, 2 allspice berries, and 2 whole cloves; simmer, covered, for 10 to 15 minutes. Remove spices before using syrup to pack jars.

Tropical Fruits

Preserve tropical fruits at the height of their season, like any other fruits. Canned tropical fruits taste like paradise in smoothies, salads, baked goods, entrées, and desserts; add to cabbage slaws and seafood salads, bake in muffins and cakes, grill or roast with seafood or chicken, or turn them into refreshing sorbets.

Yield:	Prep time:	Process time:	Headspace:
1 to 14 quarts	60 to 120 minutes	15 to 20 minutes	½ inch

Tropical Fruit, Hot Pack Only

1 Quart*	7 Quarts*	14 Quarts*	Ingredient
3 lb.	21 lb.	42 lb.	Slightly underripe tropical fruit
1½ cups	10½ cups	5¼ qt.	Canning liquid

Estimated at 3 pounds fruit and 1½ cups canning liquid average per quart.

1. Review the section "General Procedure for Canning Fruits" at the beginning of the chapter.

2. Wash fruit; scrub pineapple using a stiff brush. Peel pineapple, mango, or papaya; core or seed; and cut into slices, wedges, or cubes. (Green mango can irritate the skin, so be sure to wear heavy plastic or rubber gloves when cutting it.) Guava can be canned with or without peel and seeds; peel, if desired; cut in half or quarter; and scoop out seeds, if desired.

   All tropical fruits require hot pack and will float unless packed in light or medium (or heavier) sugar, honey, or pickling syrup.

Process time for tropical fruits (at 0 to 1,000 feet), in minutes:

- **Boiling water, hot pack:** pints, 15; quarts, 20

- **Pressure canner:** not safe

Variations: For **Tropical Fruit Cocktail,** for each quart use 3 pounds mixed tropical fruits; cut into cubes. Poach fruit cubes in light or medium syrup for 3 minutes before packing hot into hot jars, leaving ½ inch headspace. For **Spicy Pickled Pineapple,** prepare a delicate fruit-pickling syrup (see Chapter 7) substituting

pineapple juice for water. For each cup of syrup, add 3 slices fresh ginger, 1 dried red chile, and 1 tablespoon cider or palm vinegar; simmer, covered, for 10 to 15 minutes. Remove spices before using syrup to pack jars.

SPOILER ALERT

Not all tropical fruits are suitable for canning. There are no tested canning recipes for banana, banana blossom, coconut, longan, lychee, passion fruit, or pomegranate. Use other methods of preservation to preserve these fruits, such as drying or freezing.

Rhubarb

Mouth-puckering rhubarb is prized for pies, pastries, and tangy sweet or savory sauces.

Yield:	Prep time:	Process time:	Headspace:
1 to 14 quarts	30 to 60 minutes	8 to 15 minutes	½ inch

Rhubarb, Hot Pack Only

1 Quart*	7 Quarts*	14 Quarts*	Ingredient
1¾ lb.	12¼ lb.	24½ lb.	Rhubarb
½ cup	3½ cups	7 cups	Sugar
As needed	As needed	As needed	Water

Estimated at an average of 1¾ pounds rhubarb and ½ cup sugar per quart.

1. Review the section "General Procedure for Canning Fruits" at the beginning of the chapter.

2. Wash rhubarb. Trim and discard leaves, and slice stalks into 1-inch pieces.

3. Rhubarb requires hot pack, using Method 2. In a large saucepan or stockpot, measure and add rhubarb and sugar to taste. Let stand 3 to 4 hours in a cool place. Heat rhubarb over medium heat for 5 minutes, or until sugar dissolves and mixture boils. Boil for 30 seconds. When filling jars, use boiling water to adjust headspace, if needed.

Process time for rhubarb (at 0 to 1,000 feet), in minutes:

- **Boiling water, hot pack:** pints or quarts, 15

- **Dial gauge at 6 pounds, hot pack:** pints or quarts, 8

- **Weighted gauge at 5 pounds, hot pack:** pints or quarts, 8

Variation: For **Pickled Rhubarb,** prepare a mellow to very sweet fruit-pickling syrup (see Chapter 7). For each cup of syrup, add 6 slices fresh ginger, ½ teaspoon whole cloves, and ¼ teaspoon crushed red pepper. Simmer, covered, for 10 to 15 minutes. Remove solids.

SPOILER ALERT

Never use rhubarb leaves, which contain toxic levels of oxalic acids.

Figs

Figs have clean, honey and nut flavors that accent sweet or savory dishes. Try figs over ice cream, paired with fresh goat cheese, or turned into a sauce for grilled steak or lamb.

Yield:	Prep time:	Process time:	Headspace:
1 to 14 quarts	60 to 90 minutes	45 to 50 minutes	½ inch

Figs, Hot Pack Only

1 Quart*	7 Quarts*	14 Quarts*	Ingredient
2½ lb.	17½ lb.	35 lb.	Figs
1½ cups	10½ cups	5¼ qt.	Canning liquid
1 TB.	7 TB. (less than ½ cup)	14 TB. (less than 1 cup)	Bottled lemon juice

Estimated at an average of 2½ pounds figs and 1½ cups canning liquid per quart.

1. Review the section "General Procedure for Canning Fruits" at the beginning of the chapter.

2. Wash figs under running water. Water-blanch whole figs for 2 minutes. Drain.

3. Acidify figs before packing jar by adding 1 tablespoon bottled lemon juice to each quart jar (or 1½ teaspoons to each pint).

Process time for figs (at 0 to 1,000 feet), in minutes:

- **Boiling water, hot pack:** pints, 45; quarts, 50
- **Pressure canner:** not safe

Spring Compote with Strawberries and Rhubarb

Compote is simply stewed fruit, gently poached in sugar syrup, and may have added spices or liqueur. This compote is a pleasant sauce for breakfast over yogurt, as well as a dessert sauce for ice cream, pound cake, or tart shells.

Yield:	Prep time:	Process time:	Headspace:
1 to 14 pints	60 to 90 minutes	15 minutes	½ inch

Strawberry Rhubarb Compote, Hot Pack Only

1 Pint	7 Pints	14 Pints	Ingredient
2 medium	12 medium (about 2 lb.)	24 medium (about 4 lb.)	Rhubarb stalks
3 cups	6 cups (1½ lb.)	3 qt. (3 lb.)	Strawberries
2½ TB.	1¼ cups	2½ cups	Granulated sugar
2¼ tsp.	⅓ cup	⅔ cup	Fresh orange juice
2 tsp.	1½ TB.	3 TB.	Grated orange zest

1. Review the section "General Procedure for Canning Fruits" at the beginning of the chapter.

2. Trim and discard rhubarb leaves, wash, and cut into ½-inch slices. Wash strawberries, hull, and cut in half or slice if large. In a large saucepan, add sugar, orange juice, orange zest, and rhubarb slices. Bring to a boil over high heat, stirring occasionally. Reduce heat to medium-low and simmer 5 to 8 minutes, or until rhubarb is tender but not falling apart. Add strawberries and return to a boil, skimming foam if necessary. Reduce heat to medium, or as needed to prevent compote from sticking, but keep it hot while filling jars.

Process time for compote (at 0 to 1,000 feet), in minutes:

- **Boiling water, hot pack:** half-pint or pints, 15
- **Pressure canner:** not safe

COMPOTES VS. PRESERVES

Compotes differ from preserves in the size of fruit pieces, amount of sugar, and density of liquid. In compotes, fruit halves or slices are poached in lightly sweetened syrup. Serve compotes as a fruit side dish for breakfast, alongside roasted meats, or as a dessert. Preserves are thicker and sweeter than compotes. Small whole fruits or large pieces of fruit are cooked in a sweet jelly. Serve preserves like jam as a toast spread, or use as an ingredient in tarts and cookies.

Fresh Fruit Purées

You can preserve fruit purée made from most of the preceding types of fruit. However, see the sidebar after the following recipe for fruit purées that you cannot safely can.

Fruit Purée

Mouthwatering fruit purées are easy to preserve. Use them for yogurt smoothies, sauces, and fillings. Popular fruits to purée include strawberries, blueberries, pears, peaches, cherries, and pineapples.

Yield:	Prep time:	Process time:	Headspace:
1 to 14 quarts	2 to 3 hours	8 to 15 minutes	¼ inch

Fruit Purée, Hot Pack Only

1 Quart*	7 Quarts*	14 Quarts*	Ingredient
6 cups	10½ qt.	21 qt.	Chopped fresh fruit
1 cup	7 cups	3½ qt.	Water
¼ cup	1¾ cups	3½ cups	Granulated sugar, or to taste
1 TB.	7 TB. (less than ½ cup)	14 TB. (less than 1 cup)	Fresh or bottled lemon juice

Estimated at an average of 4 pounds fruit per quart of purée.

1. Review the section "General Procedure for Canning Fruits" at the beginning of the chapter.

2. Measure chopped fruit into a large saucepan and crush slightly using a potato masher or the back of a large spoon. Add 1 cup water for each quart of fruit and cook over medium heat, stirring frequently, for 10 to 15 minutes, or until fruit is soft. Purée fruit using a wire mesh strainer, food mill, food processor, or hand blender. Add sugar to taste. Fresh or bottled lemon juice may be added to enhance flavor, using about 1 tablespoon per quart of finished purée. (Lemon juice is used to enhance flavor, not raise acidity, so fresh lemon juice is acceptable in this recipe only.) Reheat purée to a boil; if sugar was added, continue to cook until sugar is completely dissolved. Reduce heat to medium, or as needed to prevent purée from sticking, but keep it hot while filling jars.

Process time for fruit purée (at 0 to 1,000 feet), in minutes:

- **Boiling water, hot pack:** pints or quarts, 15
- **Dial gauge at 6 pounds, hot pack:** pints or quarts, 8
- **Weighted gauge at 5 pounds, hot pack:** pints or quarts, 8

Variations: For **Spiced Purée,** add spices after fruit has cooked and before puréeing. For each quart use 1 teaspoon pumpkin pie spice; or use ½ teaspoon ground cinnamon, ¼ teaspoon ground cloves, and ¼ teaspoon ground allspice. For **Chunky Purée,** purée half of either Fruit Purée or Spiced Purée, then combine with unpuréed half and heat to boiling before packing into hot jars.

> **SPOILER ALERT**
>
> There are no safe home canning recommendations available for purées made from low-acid fruits, including bananas, figs, Asian pears, cantaloupe and other melons, ripe papayas, ripe mangos, and coconuts, as well as tomatoes, pumpkin, and winter squash. For these fruits and vegetables, try freezing the purée or drying the fruits. Dried fruits can be rehydrated in water and blended into a purée.

Applesauce

Applesauce needs no introduction. As American as apple pie, this basic fruit sauce can be made from any of the 2,000 available varieties of apples, for sauce that is anything from sweet and succulent to crisp and spicy.

Yield:	Prep time:	Process time:	Headspace:
1 to 14 quarts	2 to 3 hours	8 to 20 minutes	½ inch

Applesauce, Hot Pack Only

1 Quart*	7 Quarts*	14 Quarts*	Ingredient
2½ lb.	17½ lb.	35 lb.	Apples
⅛ cup	⅞ cup	1¾ cups	Granulated sugar, or to taste

Estimated at an average of 2½ pounds apples and ⅛ cup sugar per quart.

1. Review the section "General Procedure for Canning Fruits" at the beginning of the chapter.

2. Wash apples. Peel, core, and cut into quarters. In a large saucepan, add apples, cover, and cook over medium heat 10 to 15 minutes, or until apples are soft. Add water if needed, to prevent sticking. Purée apples using a wire mesh strainer, food mill, food processor, or hand blender. Add ⅛ cup sugar per quart, or to taste. Reheat applesauce to a boil; if sugar was added, continue to cook until sugar is completely dissolved. Reduce heat to medium, or as needed to prevent applesauce from sticking, but keep it hot while filling jars.

Process time for applesauce (at 0 to 1,000 feet), in minutes:

- **Boiling water, hot pack:** pints, 15; quarts, 20
- **Dial gauge at 6 pounds, hot pack:** pints, 8; quarts, 10
- **Weighted gauge at 5 pounds, hot pack:** pints, 8; quarts, 10

Variations: For **Cinnamon Applesauce,** add 1 to 2 teaspoons ground cinnamon for each quart after fruit has cooked and before puréeing. For **Chunky Applesauce,** purée half of either Applesauce or Cinnamon Applesauce, then combine with unpuréed half and heat to boiling before packing into hot jars.

Fruit Juice

Fruit juice requires more preparation than purée. For clear juice, it can take up to 2 days for the solids to settle out for filtration. But that's the beauty of preserving your own food; whether your style is rustic and country or refined and elegant, you can make it the way you and your family like best.

Apple Juice

Apples from different heirloom varieties provide you the opportunity to make juice in any style you prefer—from bracing and acidic to sublimely soft and mellow—using a single variety or a custom blend.

Yield:	Prep time:	Process time:	Headspace:
1 to 14 quarts	3 hours to 2 days	10 minutes	¼ inch

Apple Juice, Hot Pack Only

1 Quart*	7 Quarts*	14 Quarts*	Ingredient
4 lb.	28 lb.	56 lb.	Apples
1⅓ cups	9¼ cups	18½ cups	Water

Estimated at an average of 4 pounds apples per quart.

1. Review the section "General Procedure for Canning Fruits" at the beginning of the chapter.

2. Wash apples. Remove stems and coarsely chop apples. In a large saucepan, combine apples along with peels, cores, and seeds and water, and bring to a boil over medium-high heat. Reduce heat to medium and boil gently for 10 to 15 minutes, or until apples are tender. Transfer apples to a colander lined with a double layer of dampened cheesecloth and set over a large bowl. (Work in batches, if needed.) Let drain undisturbed for at least 2 hours. Proceed immediately to the next step, unless a clearer juice is desired. For clearer juice, drained juice may be refrigerated for 24 to 48 hours, then carefully strained again, leaving behind solids at the bottom of the container.

3. Pasteurize juice before filling jars by the hot-pack method. In a large saucepan over medium-high heat, heat juice to 190°F. Do not boil; adjust heat as needed and keep juice at 190°F for 5 minutes. Keep juice hot while filling jars.

Process time for apple juice (at 0 to 1,000 feet), in minutes:

- **Boiling water, hot pack:** pints or quarts, 10; half-gallons, 10
- **Pressure canner:** not safe

Berry, Cherry, Cranberry, Grape, or Rhubarb Juice

Turn luscious berries into a yummy tonic for breakfast or a festive ingredient for cocktails. Note: you must pasteurize (heat) freshly squeezed juices before canning.

Yield:	Prep time:	Process time:	Headspace:
1 to 14 quarts	3 hours to 2 days	10 to 15 minutes	¼ inch

Berry Juice, Hot Pack Only

1 Quart*	7 Quarts*	14 Quarts*	Ingredient
3½ lb.	24½ lb.	49 lb.	Berries, cherries, etc.
1 cup	7 cups	3½ qt.	Hot water
1 to 4 TB.	7 TB. to 1¾ cups	1¾ to 3½ cups	Granulated sugar, or to taste (optional)

Estimated at an average of 3½ pounds fruit and 1 to 4 tablespoons sugar per quart.

1. Review the section "General Procedure for Canning Fruits" at the beginning of the chapter.

2. Wash fruit. Be sure to look for and discard any berries that are moldy or soft from rotting. Stem or hull, pit, and crush berries, cherries, and grapes. If using rhubarb, cut in ½-inch slices. Measure fruit into a large saucepan and crush slightly. Add 1 cup hot water for each quart of fruit. Cook over medium heat, stirring frequently, for 10 to 15 minutes or until fruit is soft. Transfer to a juice strainer or large colander lined with a double layer of dampened cheesecloth and set over a large bowl. (Work in batches, if needed.) Let drain undisturbed for at least 2 hours. Discard solids in the strainer. In a large saucepan, combine juice with sugar (if using). Sugar may be omitted but helps juice hold its color and flavor; try 1 tablespoon sugar per quart of sweet juice or up to ¼ cup sugar for tart juices such as rhubarb.

3. Pasteurize juice before filling jars by the hot-pack method. In a large saucepan over medium-high heat, heat juice to 190°F. Do not boil; adjust heat as needed and keep juice at 190°F for 5 minutes. Keep juice hot while filling jars.

Process time for juice (at 0 to 1,000 feet), in minutes:

- **Hot pack:** pints or quarts, 15

- **Boiling water, hot pack:** pints or quarts, 10; half-gallons, 10

- **Pressure canner:** not safe

PERFECT PRESERVING

Some fruits contain acids that can crystallize or form sediment in juices made from them. Berries that are high in these acids and more susceptible to crystal and sediment formation include blueberries, cranberries, raspberries, strawberries, and grapes. The sediment is safe to drink; filter it to obtain a clear juice. To filter these juices, refrigerate drained juice from step 3 for 24 to 48 hours; clear juice will float above the sediment. Carefully strain juice again through a fine mesh strainer or cheesecloth, leaving behind sediment. Process the clear juice.

Fruit Nectar

Golden nectar made from stone fruits or pears provides honey-sweet refreshment. Like berry juice, enjoy these pleasing beverages from breakfast to the cocktail hour.

Yield:	Prep time:	Process time:	Headspace:
1 to 14 quarts	2 to 3 hours	15 minutes	¼ inch

Fruit Nectar, Hot Pack Only

1 Quart*	7 Quarts*	14 Quarts*	Ingredient
3½ lb.	24½ lb.	49 lb.	Pears, apricots, cherries, peaches, etc.
1 cup	7 cups	3½ qt.	Hot water
2 TB.	14 TB. (less than 1 cup)	1¾ cups	Fresh or bottled lemon juice
1 to 4 TB.	7 TB. to 1¾ cups	1¾ to 3½ cups	Granulated sugar, or to taste (optional)

*Estimated at an average of 3½ pounds fruit per quart and sugar to taste.

1. Review the section "General Procedure for Canning Fruits" at the beginning of the chapter.

2. Wash fruit. Peel, pit, and coarsely chop. Treat with ascorbic acid to prevent darkening. Measure fruit into a large saucepan and crush slightly. Add 1 cup hot water for each quart of fruit. Cook over medium heat, stirring frequently, for 10 to 15 minutes or until fruit is soft. Purée fruit using a wire mesh strainer, food mill, food processor, or hand blender. Add lemon juice and sugar (if using) to taste. (Lemon juice is used to enhance flavor, not raise acidity, so fresh lemon juice is acceptable in this recipe.) If sugar is added, reheat purée to a boil. Reduce heat to medium and continue to simmer until sugar is completely dissolved. Keep nectar hot while filling jars.

Process time (at 0 to 1,000 feet), in minutes:

- **Boiling water, hot pack:** pints or quarts, 15
- **Pressure canner:** not safe

Sweetened Fruit Sauces

Fruit sauces are essentially sweetened fruit purées. In this chapter, we provide several specific recipes for pie fillings, ice cream toppings, and cranberry sauce.

Pie Fillings

The first several pie fillings require that you use a thickening agent called ClearJel (see the sidebar after the following recipe). There is no substitution for ClearJel; if you cannot locate ClearJel, choose another recipe or another method of preservation, such as freezing apple or peach slices, whole blueberries, or pitted cherries. Delicious pies can also be made from canned or dried fruit or jam.

Fruit Pie Fillings Using ClearJel

These pie fillings bake into scrumptious, mouthwatering pies.

Yield:	Prep time:	Process time:	Headspace:
1 or 7 quarts	2 to 3 hours	25 minutes	1 inch

Apple Pie Filling, Hot Pack Only

1 Quart	7 Quarts	Ingredient
$3\frac{1}{2}$ cups	6 qt.	Fresh peeled, sliced apples*
$\frac{1}{2}$ cup	$3\frac{1}{2}$ cups	Granulated sugar
$\frac{1}{4}$ cup	$1\frac{3}{4}$ cups	Brown sugar, loosely packed
$\frac{1}{4}$ cup + 1 TB.	2 cups	Regular (not instant) ClearJel
$\frac{1}{2}$ tsp.	1 TB.	Cinnamon
$\frac{1}{8}$ tsp.	1 tsp.	Nutmeg (optional)
$\frac{1}{2}$ cup	$2\frac{1}{2}$ cups	Apple juice
$\frac{3}{4}$ cup	5 cups	Cold water
2 TB.	$\frac{3}{4}$ cup	Cider vinegar

Treat for browning while slicing, and then drain before blanching.

1. Review the section "General Procedure for Canning Fruits" at the beginning of the chapter.

2. In a large pot with 1 gallon boiling water over high heat, add $3\frac{1}{2}$ to 6 cups apples and blanch for 2 minutes. Drain, transfer to a large bowl, and keep covered. Repeat for any remaining apples. In a large pot, combine granulated sugar, brown sugar, ClearJel, cinnamon, and nutmeg (if using). Add apple juice, cold water, and cider vinegar. Place over medium-high heat; cook and stir until mixture thickens and begins to bubble. Fold drained fruit into the hot liquid. Reduce heat to medium, or as needed to prevent pie filling from sticking, but keep it hot while filling jars.

Variations: For Peach Pie Filling, substitute peeled, pitted, sliced, pretreated, and blanched peaches for blanched apples. Increase granulated sugar from ½ to ¾ cup for 1-quart recipe or from 3½ to 5¼ cups for 7-quart recipe. Reduce cinnamon from ½ to ⅛ teaspoon (for 1 quart) or 1 tablespoon to a scant ½ teaspoon (for 7 quarts). Omit apple juice. Add ⅛ or 1 teaspoon almond extract with water for 1- or 7-quart recipe, respectively (optional). If desired, substitute fresh or bottled lemon juice for the cider vinegar. **For Cherry Pie Filling,** substitute washed, pitted, and halved fresh sour cherries or thawed frozen sour cherries for blanched apples. Omit brown sugar and increase granulated sugar from ½ to 1 cup (1-quart recipe) or 3½ to 7 cups (7-quart recipe). Reduce cinnamon from ½ to ⅛ teaspoon (1-quart recipe) or 1 tablespoon to a scant ½ teaspoon (7-quart recipe). Add 2 tablespoons or ⅞ cups water for 1- and 7-quart recipes, respectively. Add ⅛ or 1 teaspoon almond extract with water (optional). If desired, substitute fresh or bottled lemon juice for cider vinegar.

Process time for apple pie filling (at 0 to 1,000 feet), in minutes:

- **Boiling water, hot pack:** pints or quarts, 25

- **Pressure canner:** not safe

Process time for peach, blueberry, or cherry pie filling (at 0 to 1,000 feet), in minutes:

- **Boiling water, hot pack:** pints or quarts, 30

- **Pressure canner:** not safe

ABOUT CLEARJEL

ClearJel is modified cornstarch used commercially in baked goods and frozen foods because it is more stable than regular cornstarch or flour. ClearJel works with acidic ingredients and does not thicken excessively. It allows thorough heat penetration in thick fillings, withstands high heat, and does not separate or thin out during storage. There are two formulas: regular and instant. Use only the regular formula in home canning. Use tested recipes to make fruit pie fillings, fruit sauces, and jam; there is no substitution for ClearJel. If there is no local retail source selling ClearJel, try searching online. Otherwise, make pie filling and sauce in some other way, such as with frozen, canned, or dried fruits, or make jam using another recipe.

Lemon or Lime Curd

You can turn piquant lemon or lime juice into puddinglike curd to fill a baked pie shell or serve with sweet fruit sauce and whipped cream for a mouthwatering dessert.

Yield:	Prep time:	Process time:	Headspace:
2 or 4 half-pints	2 to 3 hours	15 minutes	½ inch

Lemon or Lime Curd, Hot Pack Only

2 Half-Pints	4 Half-Pints	Ingredient
4 large	7 large	Egg yolks
2 large	4 large	Whole eggs
1¼ cups	2½ cups	Superfine sugar
¼ cup	½ cup	Bottled lemon or lime juice
¼ cup	½ cup	Fresh lemon or lime juice
6 TB.	¾ cup	Unsalted butter, chilled and cut into approximately ½-inch pieces
¼ cup	½ cup	Freshly grated lemon or lime zest

1. Review the section "General Procedure for Canning Fruits" at the beginning of the chapter.

2. In a large bowl, whisk egg yolks, whole eggs, superfine sugar, bottled lemon or lime juice, and fresh lemon or lime juice until thoroughly blended.

3. Transfer mixture to a double boiler over—but not touching—gently simmering water. Stir curd with a wooden spoon for 10 to 15 minutes, or until it reaches a temperature of 170°F using a food thermometer. Pour curd through a wire mesh strainer to remove any bits of cooked egg.

4. Return curd to the top of the double boiler. Add butter a few pieces at a time, stirring thoroughly after each addition until butter is incorporated. Stir in lemon or lime zest. Continue to stir for 5 minutes, or until curd thickens. Keep curd warm while you fill the jars.

Process time for lemon or lime curd (at 0 to 1,000 feet), in minutes:

- **Boiling water, hot pack:** half-pints, 15
- **Pressure canner:** not safe

SPOILER ALERT

While other canned foods can be stored for 1 year, the flavor of lemon or lime curd made with eggs begins to deteriorate after just 4 months.

Rum-Raisin Pie Filling

This raisin pie filling with spices and rum is a fresh take on old-fashioned mincemeat pie.

Yield:	Prep time:	Process time:	Headspace:
1 to 7 quarts	90 to 120 minutes	30 minutes	½ inch

Rum-Raisin Pie Filling, Hot Pack Only

1 Quart	7 Quarts	Ingredient
3 cups	5 qt.	Peeled and chopped tart apples
1 cup	2 qt.	Cranberries
¼ cup	1 lb.	Dark seedless raisins
¼ cup	1 lb.	Golden raisins
1 tsp.	¼ cup	Freshly grated lemon zest
1 TB.	1½ cups	Water
½ cup	2½ cups	Brown sugar
¾ cup	2½ cups	Granulated sugar
2 TB.	1 cup	Dark rum (or ¾ tsp. or 1½ TB. rum extract plus water to make 2 TB. or 1 cup total liquid)
3 TB.	1 cup	Bottled lemon juice
1 tsp.	2 TB.	Ground cinnamon
¼ tsp.	1 tsp.	Ground nutmeg

1. Review the section "General Procedure for Canning Fruits" at the beginning of the chapter.

2. In a large pan, combine tart apples, cranberries, dark raisins, golden raisins, lemon zest, water, brown sugar, granulated sugar, dark rum (or water flavored with rum extract), bottled lemon juice, cinnamon, and nutmeg. Heat over medium heat 30 to 40 minutes or until fruit is tender and mixture is slightly thickened. Keep pie filling hot while filling jars.

Variation: For **Green Tomato Pie Filling,** substitute chopped green tomatoes for apples, peeled and chopped tart apples for cranberries, orange zest for lemon zest, 1 tablespoon cider vinegar for water, and 2 tablespoons water for rum. Add ¼ teaspoon ground cloves.

Process time for rum-raisin pie filling (at 0 to 1,000 feet), in minutes:

- **Boiling water, hot pack:** pints or quarts, 30

- **Pressure canner:** not safe

Process time for green tomato pie filling (at 0 to 1,000 feet), in minutes:

- **Boiling water, hot pack:** pints or quarts, 15

- **Pressure canner:** not safe

Other Fruit Sauces

These toppings prepared from fresh, seasonal fruits can be used as sweet treats as well as accompaniments to savory foods.

Ice Cream Topping

Classic flavors for ice cream toppings include strawberry, blackberry, peach, cherry, mango, and pineapple.

Yield:	Prep time:	Process time:	Headspace:
1 to 14 pints	90 to 120 minutes	10 minutes	¼ inch

Ice Cream Topping, Hot Pack Only

1 Pint*	7 Pints*	14 Pints*	Ingredient
1½ lb. (3 cups)	10½ lb. (5¼ qt.)	21 lb. (10½ qt.)	Whole fresh fruit as purchased or picked (or prepared and chopped fresh or frozen fruit)
¼ cup	1¾ cups	3½ cups	Granulated sugar, or to taste
1 TB.	7 TB.	Less than 1 cup	Fresh lemon juice, or to taste

Estimated at an average of 1½ pounds fruit and ¼ cup sugar per pint.

1. Review the section "General Procedure for Canning Fruits" at the beginning of the chapter.

2. Wash fresh fruit. Stem or hull, peel or pit, and chop fruits. Treat susceptible fruits for browning.

3. In a large saucepan, stir together fruit and sugar. Taste and add additional sugar or lemon juice to taste. Heat over medium heat and crush fruit as it cooks; stir constantly to prevent sticking. Bring topping to a full boil; raise heat to high, if needed. Reduce heat and simmer 5 minutes, stirring constantly to prevent burning; skim foam, if necessary. Keep topping hot while filling jars.

Process time for ice cream topping (at 0 to 1,000 feet), in minutes:

- **Boiling water, hot pack:** half-pints or pints, 10
- **Pressure canner:** not safe

Cranberry Sauce

A holiday favorite, tangy cranberry sauce is easy to make and preserve at home. Make it chunky or smooth, with sweet or spicy accents.

Yield:	Prep time:	Process time:	Headspace:
1 to 14 pints	60 minutes	15 minutes	¼ inch

Cranberry Sauce, Hot Pack Only

1 Pint*	7 Pints*	14 Pints*	Ingredient
2 cups	3½ qt.	7 qt.	Fresh cranberries
¼ cup	1¾ cups	3½ cups	Water
1 cup	7 cups	3½ qt.	Granulated sugar, or to taste

Estimated at an average of 2 cups cranberries and 1 cup sugar per pint.

1. Review the section "General Procedure for Canning Fruits" at the beginning of the chapter.

2. Wash cranberries; pick over and remove stems or moldy berries. In a large saucepan, measure cranberries and add water. Cook over medium heat for 10 to 15 minutes or until skins split. Leave berries whole, or purée to desired consistency in a food processor or hand blender. If smooth sauce is desired, strain through a wire mesh strainer or food mill. Return sauce to the pan, add sugar, and bring to a boil over high heat. Boil for 3 minutes. Reduce heat to medium, or as needed to prevent sauce from sticking, but keep it hot while filling jars.

Process time for cranberry sauce (at 0 to 1,000 feet), in minutes:

- **Boiling water, hot pack:** half-pints or pints, 15

- **Pressure canner:** not safe

Variation: For **Orange-Cranberry Sauce,** to either puréed or whole berry sauce, add 1 teaspoon freshly grated orange zest for each pint of sauce and substitute freshly squeezed orange juice for water. Add zest with juice, and cook as directed.

Fruit Syrup

Seductive fruit syrups tempt you with ripe, luscious flavors. Don't we all need a little guilty pleasure?

Yield:	Prep time:	Process time:	Headspace:
1 to 14 pints	2 to 3 hours	15 minutes	½ inch

Fruit Syrup

1 Pint*	7 Pints*	14 Pints*	Ingredient
1 lb. (2 cups)	7 lb. (3½ qt.)	14 lb. (7 qt.)	Fresh fruit (or frozen chopped fruit or fruit juice)
¼ cup	1¾ cups	3½ cups	Water
¾ cup	5¼ cups	10½ cups	Granulated sugar, or to taste
1 TB.	7 TB.	Less than 1 cup	Fresh lemon juice, or to taste

Estimated at an average of 1 pounds fruit, ¼ cup water, and ¾ cup sugar per pint.

1. Review the section "General Procedure for Canning Fruits" at the beginning of the chapter.

2. Wash fresh fruit. Stem or hull, peel or pit, and chop fruits. Treat susceptible fruits for browning. In a large saucepan over medium-high heat, bring chopped fruit and water to a boil. Reduce heat, and simmer 5 to 10 minutes or until soft. Drain hot fruit in a colander set over a large bowl; let sit 30 minutes or until cool enough to handle. Press solids gently to extract more juice; excessive pressing will create cloudy syrup. Discard fruit pulp. Combine juice, sugar, and lemon juice in a large saucepan over high heat, and bring to boil. Boil 1 minute, skimming foam if necessary. Reduce heat to medium, or as needed to prevent sauce from sticking, but keep it hot while filling jars.

Process time fruit syrup (at 0 to 1,000 feet), in minutes:

- **Boiling water, hot pack:** half-pints or pints, 15

- **Pressure canner:** not safe

Variation: For **Syrup with Whole Fruit Pieces,** add ¼ to ⅓ cup crushed fresh fruit for each pint of syrup. Add crushed fresh fruit to juice, sugar, and lemon juice and simmer as when making regular syrup.

MAKING AND USING FRUIT SYRUPS

Make fruit syrups from almost any fruits, especially berries, cherries, peaches, oranges, pomegranates, mangos, and pineapples. Use fruit syrups on pancakes or waffles, over ice cream, mixed with sparkling wines or club soda, or in cocktails. Make a fruit vinaigrette for green salads with nuts and cheese, glaze ham or roast chicken, serve it as a dipping sauce for grilled meats, or drizzle over sautéed root vegetables or sweet potatoes. Heat it up with plain gelatin and chill for a fun treat.

Canned Tomatoes

The following recipes include techniques for canning whole or cut tomatoes in water, their own liquid, or tomato juice. There is a complete range of tomato products, including plain and seasoned tomato sauces, pasta and other cooking sauces, salsa, and ketchup. These recipes add adequate acid to make them safe for boiling water canning. Some of these recipes include processing time for a pressure canner, which results in a higher quality product.

General Procedure for Canning Tomatoes

For more details on the steps to prepare, process, and store canned foods, see Chapter 7. Use the following general procedure for all of the recipes in this chapter:

1. Prepare boiling water–bath or pressure canner, jars, and lids. Before proceeding, review your recipe; preparing the canner and jars is usually the first step, unless the recipe preparation is very lengthy.

2. Prepare tomatoes or tomato product as directed in each recipe.

3. Acidify all tomatoes just before filling each jar, unless recipe directs otherwise.

   - Quart jars: Add ¼ cup cider vinegar, 2 tablespoons bottled lemon juice, or ½ teaspoon citric acid powder per quart. To counteract acid flavors or as a matter of preference, add 2 teaspoons granulated sugar and/or 1 teaspoon salt per quart.

   - Pint jars: Add 2 tablespoons cider vinegar, 1 tablespoon bottled lemon juice, or ¼ teaspoon citric acid powder. To counteract acid flavors or as a matter of preference, add 1 teaspoon granulated sugar and/or ½ teaspoon salt per pint.

- Half-pint jars: Add 1 tablespoon cider vinegar, 1½ teaspoons bottled lemon juice, or ⅛ teaspoon citric acid powder. To counteract acid flavors or as a matter of preference, add ½ teaspoon granulated sugar and/or ¼ teaspoon salt per half-pint.

4. Fill hot jars by the hot-pack or raw-pack method as allowed in the recipe. Use the following general packing instructions, unless recipe directs otherwise.

   - Hot pack: Ladle hot product into hot jars, adjusting headspace as directed in recipe.

   - Raw pack: Bring canning liquid to a boil, and then reduce heat and keep hot while filling jars. Ladle a small amount of hot liquid into the hot jar. Add raw tomatoes; pack tightly without crushing, and add hot liquid to cover, adjusting headspace as directed in recipe.

5. Clean the rim and secure the lid. Use process time as directed in recipe. Properly cool, and store the jars up to 1 year for best flavor.

You should use only the packing methods, jar sizes, headspace, and processing times specified in the recipe. These requirements are not interchangeable from one recipe to another.

Guidelines for Adjusting Canned Tomatoes and Tomato Sauce Recipes

The unbreakable rule for canning acidified foods (like tomato sauces in the second recipe section of this chapter) is *never alter the proportions of solids, vinegar, water, or other liquids in a recipe.* When canning foods with vinegar added, the only safe adjustments are to sugar, salt, and spices, which you may freely omit, add, increase, or decrease.

Other ingredient substitutions vary, and you should proceed with extreme caution. The following tested recipes are safe for canning, if you carefully measure all ingredients and follow all instructions. Some recipes list safe substitutions, should you wish to make any adjustments.

Tomatoes, Purée and Juice

Canned tomatoes in various forms offer a great deal of flexibility and can be used in everything from soups and stews to sauces and salsa.

Whole or Cut Tomatoes

The following recipes include tomatoes canned whole, halved, quartered, and crushed. Canning liquids may be water, their natural juices, or added tomato juice (commercial or homemade). Several recipe variations offer seasoning options for different cooking styles and cuisines.

Whole, Cut, or Crushed Tomatoes in Water (Raw or Hot Pack)

Small or medium tomatoes may be canned whole, otherwise plan to halve or quarter tomatoes. Canned tomatoes can be used in many recipes from tomato soup and beef stew to marinara sauce, tomato salsa, chicken *cacciatore*, and seafood creole.

Yield:	Prep time:	Process time:	Headspace:
1 to 14 quarts	2 to 3 hours	10 to 45 minutes	½ inch

Tomatoes in Water, Hot or Raw Pack

1 Quart*	7 Quarts*	14 Quarts*	Ingredient
3 lb.	21 lb.	42 lb.	Ripe tomatoes
1½ cups	2½ qt.	5 qt.	Water
2 TB.	14 TB. (less than 1 cup)	28 TB. (1¾ cups)	Cider vinegar **OR**
1 TB.	7 TB. (less than ½ cup)	14 TB. (less than 1 cup)	lemon juice **OR**
½ tsp.	3½ tsp.	2⅓ TB.	citric acid
1 TB.	7 TB. (less than ½ cup)	14 TB. (less than 1 cup)	Granulated sugar (optional)
1 tsp.	7 tsp. (2⅓ TB.)	14 tsp. (4⅔ TB.)	Salt (optional)

*Estimated at 3 pounds per quart. Tomatoes may also be packed in pint jars, yielding 2 pints, 14 pints, or 28 pints.

1. Review the section "General Procedure for Canning Tomatoes" at the beginning of the chapter.

2. Wash tomatoes. Peel skins (see the following sidebar) and remove cores. Leave tomatoes whole, or cut into halves or quarters. In a saucepan or teakettle, heat water to boiling. Reduce heat to low and keep tomatoes hot while filling jars.

Process time for tomatoes in water (at 0 to 1,000 feet), in minutes:

- **Boiling water, hot or raw pack:** pints, 40; quarts, 45

- **Dial gauge at 6 pounds, hot or raw pack:** pints or quarts, 15

- **Dial gauge at 11 pounds, hot or raw pack:** pints or quarts, 10

- **Weighted gauge at 5 pounds, hot or raw pack:** pints or quarts, 15

- **Weighted gauge at 10 pounds, hot or raw pack:** pints or quarts, 10

Variations: For **Crushed Tomatoes** (hot pack only), quarter tomatoes and crush with a potato masher or large spoon as they cook for 5 minutes. For **Herb-Seasoned Tomatoes,** add 1 tablespoon dried seasonings blend to each quart before filling with tomatoes. Several commercial spice manufacturers offer a variety of dried seasonings blends that pair well with tomatoes, such as Italian, Mexican, Greek, Mediterranean, or Cajun. Be sure to acidify variations as directed in the section "General Procedure for Canning Tomatoes" at the beginning of this chapter.

HOW TO PEEL TOMATOES

Using a small, sharp knife, cut a shallow X in the blossom end (opposite the brown-core or stem end). Drop the tomato into a pot of unsalted boiling water; wait 10 to 60 seconds, or just until skin wrinkles or splits. Ripe tomatoes will take a few seconds; less ripe ones take longer. Don't heat too long, or they will start to cook. Use a slotted spoon to transfer tomato to a bowl of ice water. To peel, grasp a flap of skin at one corner of the X and pull. The skins should pull off easily; peel with a knife if they don't, and blanch the next tomato a little longer.

Whole, Cut, or Crushed Tomatoes in Tomato Juice (Raw or Hot Pack)

For the most concentrated flavor, pack tomatoes in tomato juice (either commercial or homemade). These full-flavored tomatoes have the same uses as water-packed ones.

Yield:	Prep time:	Process time:	Headspace:
1 to 14 quarts	2 to 3 hours	15 to 85 minutes	½ inch

Tomatoes in Tomato Juice, Hot or Raw Pack

1 Quart*	7 Quarts*	14 Quarts*	Ingredient
3 lb.	21 lb.	42 lb.	Ripe tomatoes
1½ cups	2½ qt.	5 qt.	Commercially made or homemade tomato juice
2 TB.	14 TB. (less than 1 cup)	28 TB. (1¾ cups)	Cider vinegar **OR**
1 TB.	7 TB. (less than ½ cup)	14 TB. (less than 1 cup)	lemon juice **OR**
½ tsp.	3½ tsp.	2⅓ TB.	citric acid
1 TB.	7 TB. (less than ½ cup)	14 TB. (less than 1 cup)	Granulated sugar (optional)
1 tsp.	7 tsp. (2⅓ TB.)	14 tsp. (4⅔ TB.)	Salt (optional)

Estimated at 3 pounds per quart. Tomatoes may also be packed in pint jars, yielding 2 pints, 14 pints, or 28 pints.

1. Review the section "General Procedure for Canning Tomatoes" at the beginning of the chapter.

2. Wash tomatoes. Peel skins and remove cores. Leave tomatoes whole, or cut into halves or quarters. In a saucepan, heat tomato juice to boiling. Reduce heat to low and keep tomatoes hot while filling jars.

Process time for tomatoes in tomato juice (at 0 to 1,000 feet), in minutes:

- **Boiling water, hot or raw pack:** pints or quarts, 85

- **Dial gauge at 6 pounds, hot or raw pack:** pints or quarts, 40

- **Dial gauge at 11 pounds, hot or raw pack:** pints or quarts, 25

- **Weighted gauge at 5 pounds, hot or raw pack:** pints or quarts, 40

- **Weighted gauge at 10 pounds, hot or raw pack:** pints or quarts, 25

- **Weighted gauge at 15 pounds, hot or raw pack:** pints or quarts, 15

Variations: For **Crushed Tomatoes in Tomato Purée** (hot pack only), quarter tomatoes and crush with a potato masher or large spoon as they cook for 5 minutes. For **Tomatoes Packed in Their Own Juice** (raw pack only), omit tomato juice. Pack raw tomatoes tightly into jars, pressing tomatoes to extract juice, leaving ½ inch headspace. Remove trapped air and adjust headspace by adding additional tomatoes or a small amount of boiling water. For **Herb-Seasoned Tomatoes** (raw or hot pack), add 1 tablespoon dried seasonings blend to each quart. Several commercial spice manufacturers offer a variety of these seasonings blends that pair well with tomatoes, such as Italian, Mexican, Greek, Mediterranean, or Cajun. Be sure to acidify variations as directed in the section "General Procedure for Canning Tomatoes" at the beginning of the chapter.

AVERAGE TOMATO YIELD

The average yield for canned tomatoes is 3 pounds tomatoes per quart jar. However, actual yield can vary from 1½ to 4 pounds tomatoes per quart jar. Yield depends on several factors. Whole tomatoes give lower yields; cut or crushed tomatoes give higher yields. Raw pack gives lower yields than hot pack. Tomatoes processed with added water or tomato juice give lower yields, and those in their own liquid give higher yields. The lowest yield tends to be for whole tomatoes canned in water using raw pack. The highest yield is achieved with crushed tomatoes canned in their own liquid using hot pack. Actual yields also tend to increase with experience in the canning process.

Fresh Tomato Purée

For a modern method of sauce making, the first step is to crush or purée fresh tomatoes. You can prepare purée by hand or using any of several methods, summarized in the following table and detailed later in this section. Each one has advantages, disadvantages, and required tools. Which method you use depends on personal preference.

Advantages and Disadvantages of Tomato Purée Methods

Method	Advantages	Disadvantages
By hand	Makes the chunkiest purée	Time consuming for large batches
Using a food processor or blender	Easy	Requires additional equipment
		Time consuming for large batches
		Requires separate step to remove skin and seeds
Using a food mill or food grinder	Easiest	Requires additional equipment
	Removes skins and seeds in one step	Slightly less yield
	Fast for large batches	
From roasted tomatoes	Adds a roasted flavor	Requires additional equipment and time
	Suitable for large batches	
From frozen tomatoes	Easy	Requires additional equipment and time
	Removes skins easily	Requires separate step to remove seeds

Use fresh tomato purée to produce a wide variety of seasoned cooking sauces—from thin to thick—as well as homemade salsa, ketchup, and tomato juice. Whether or not to peel and seed the tomatoes depends on several factors. See the sidebar "Do You Need to Peel and Seed Tomatoes?" later in this chapter.

Yields for Purée and Sauce from Fresh Tomatoes

Fresh Tomatoes (in Pounds)	Purée*	Juice	Thin Sauce	Thick Sauce	Paste
1	1½ cups	1⅓ cups	1 cup	¾ cup	½ cup
2	3 cups	2¾ cups	1 pint	1½ cups	1 half-pint
4	3 pints	5 cups	1 quart	3 half-pints	2 half-pints
6	9 cups	2 quarts	3 pints	2 pints	3 half-pints
8	3 quarts	10 cups	2 quarts	3 pints	4 half-pints
10⅔	4 quarts	14 cups	5 pints	4 pints	5 half-pints
12	9 pints	4 quarts	3 quarts	9 half-pints	6 half-pints
13⅓	5 quarts	9 pints	3 quarts	5 pints	6 half-pints
21	8 quarts	7 quarts	5 quarts	8 pints	10 half-pints
28	10½ quarts	9 quarts	7 quarts	5 quarts	14 half-pints
37	13¾ quarts	12 quarts	9 quarts	7 quarts	18 half-pints
40	15 quarts	13 quarts	10 quarts	15 pints	19 half-pints
53	20 quarts	17 quarts	13 quarts	10 quarts	26 half-pints

Based on an average yield of 1½ cups purée per pound of tomatoes reduced by ⅓ for thin sauce, by ½ for thick sauce, and by ⅔ for paste.

Fresh Tomato Purée by Hand

1. When making purée by hand, peel tomatoes before cutting and chopping. Without the aid of a food processor or food mill to grind skins very finely, hand-chopped tomatoes will reveal fine slivers of skin in tomato preparations. For more information, see the sidebar "How to Peel Tomatoes" earlier in this chapter.

2. Cut out brown core by piercing tomato just outside brown edge and cutting in a circular motion. Cut deep enough to remove any hard white, yellow, or green portion along with brown core.

3. Optionally, remove seeds before chopping. Cut tomato in half horizontally, hold a tomato half (cut side down) over a strainer set over a bowl, and squeeze tomato firmly to extract seeds and liquid. If needed, coax seeds out using your fingers or a butter knife; leaving in a few seeds is also acceptable. Press seeds

with a large spoon to extract as much liquid as possible. Add strained liquid to chopped tomatoes, or reserve for another use such as soup, stock, or juice.

4. Cut tomatoes into quarters or chop in large or small pieces on a cutting board using a large chef's knife.

BLANCHING LARGE VOLUMES OF TOMATOES

To handle a large volume of tomatoes for peeling, use a stockpot or pasta pot fitted with a wire basket. Use the basket to add and remove tomatoes from boiling water to an ice water bath. To cool tomatoes, use the kitchen sink and add cold water and ice or reusable ice packs. Just make sure to clean and sanitize the kitchen sink and ice packs before use. To sanitize, spray or wipe the cleaned sink and packs with sanitizing solution (see Chapter 1), then rinse with clean water.

Fresh Tomato Purée Using a Food Processor or Blender

1. Trim and discard stem end, including any white, green, or yellow hard core. Cut tomatoes into quarters.

2. Fill the bowl of the food processor or blender no more than ⅔ full. Process on high until well blended, stopping the motor and scraping the sides of the bowl with a spatula two or three times until mixture is smooth.

3. If desired, pass purée through a strainer to remove larger bits of seed or peel that were not finely chopped. See the sidebar "Do You Need to Peel and Seed Tomatoes?" later in this chapter for reasons to keep or remove peels and seeds.

Fresh Tomato Purée Using a Food Mill or Food Grinder

1. Cut tomatoes into quarters; it is not necessary to core tomatoes, but cut out any damaged areas. Press tomatoes through a fruit and vegetable strainer such as a manual food mill or chinois with pestle. Alternatively, use a food grinder appliance (such as those made by Victorio or Roma) or a food grinder attachment (KitchenAid, for example).

2. If desired, recover additional tomato essence from skins and seeds discarded by the tool by transferring discarded tomato bits to a bowl and mixing with ¼ cup water per pound of tomatoes. Press this mixture through a fine mesh strainer or chinois. Discard solid waste and add strained liquid to fine purée.

CHOOSING A FOOD GRINDER APPLIANCE

Consider these factors when purchasing a food grinder appliance. *Type of food:* Can the appliance remove tomato skins without binding, create thin or chunky purées, strain small berry seeds, or grind tough skins such as grapes? *Model:* Frequent, large batches more than 10 pounds justify an electric rather than a hand model. *Material:* Metal is more expensive but more durable than plastic. Stainless steel doesn't react with acidic foods such as apples and tomatoes. Tin plate and aluminum are less expensive options for meat grinding. *Replacement parts:* Less expensive appliances are not economical if there are no replacement parts. *Cost:* Cheap models are cost effective for infrequent use or to try new methods.

Fresh Tomato Purée from Roasted Tomatoes

1. Trim and discard stem end, including any white, green, or yellow hard core.

2. Grill whole tomatoes on a barbecue over medium-high heat, turning every few minutes, until charred in spots and skins loosen; or roast tomatoes one at a time by turning with a fork over a gas flame. Cool and cut in halves or quarters. Alternatively, place quartered fresh tomatoes on a rimmed baking sheet and roast in a preheated 450°F oven for 40 to 50 minutes; cool. Remove skins and seeds if desired.

3. Purée using one of the preceding methods: by hand with a knife, using a food processor or blender, or using a food grinding tool. If desired, remove seeds and/or peels as directed by each method.

Fresh Tomato Purée from Frozen Tomatoes

1. Trim and discard stem end, including any white, green, or yellow hard core. Leave tomatoes whole, or cut into quarters.

2. Optionally, peel tomatoes before freezing. Place tomatoes on cookie sheets and freeze 30 to 120 minutes, or until firm. Rinse frozen tomatoes under warm water and skins should slip off easily.

3. Fill zipper-lock plastic bags or airtight plastic or glass containers with unpeeled or peeled tomatoes, expelling as much air as possible. Pack in portions that you plan to use at one time, since you'll need to thaw the entire container for use.

4. Frozen raw tomatoes turn mushy in the freezer. Thaw or partially thaw before using in recipes. If frozen tomatoes are unpeeled, rinse off under warm water and skins should slip off easily.

DO YOU NEED TO PEEL AND SEED TOMATOES?

Whether to leave peels and seeds in tomato preparations is a matter of personal preference. Traditional recipes for tomato sauce and ketchup specify peeling and seeding to make a sauce with smooth texture and sweet flavor. Some cooks like to cook whole tomatoes to capture additional flavors, and then strain the pulp to remove skins and seeds before adding other ingredients to finish the sauce. Many believe the tomato water surrounding the seeds is highly flavorful and like to include it, even if it takes longer to reduce. Those who like the bitterness of tomato seeds like to leave them in while others may strain them out but add some back for textural interest. Still others prefer simply to finely purée whole tomatoes—skins, seeds, and all.

Tomato Juice

Tomato juice is easy to make from any type of sun-ripened tomato. Traditional tomato juice recipes cook and crush fresh tomatoes in small batches, and then strain the hot mixture to produce a silky liquid that does not separate in the jar. If separation is not a concern, use the faster, modern way and prepare juice from fresh tomato purée.

Tomato Juice from Fresh Tomatoes or Purée

Using either fresh tomatoes or purée produces full-flavored tomato juice that is a refreshing reminder of summer. Juice made using the quick method will separate; just shake it up before using it.

Yield:	Prep time:	Process time:	Headspace:
1 to 14 quarts	60 to 90 minutes	10 to 40 minutes	¼ inch

Tomato Juice, Hot or Raw Pack

1 Quart*	7 Quarts*	14 Quarts*	Ingredient
3 lb.	21 lb.	42 lb.	Ripe tomatoes
2 TB.	14 TB. (less than 1 cup)	28 TB. (1¾ cups)	Cider vinegar **OR**
1 TB.	7 TB. (less than ½ cup)	14 TB. (less than 1 cup)	lemon juice **OR**
½ tsp.	3½ tsp.	2⅓ TB.	citric acid
1 TB.	7 TB. (less than ½ cup)	14 TB. (less than 1 cup)	Granulated sugar (optional)
1 tsp.	7 tsp. (2⅓ TB.)	14 tsp. (4⅔ TB.)	Salt (optional)

Estimated at 3 pounds per quart. Tomato juice may also be packed in pint jars, yielding 2 pints, 14 pints, or 28 pints.

1. Review the section "General Procedure for Canning Tomatoes" at the beginning of the chapter.

2. Prepare juice by one of the following methods.

   - Purée method (juice may separate in jar): Prepare purée by any of the preceding methods. Place purée in a heavy stockpot and bring to a boil. Reduce heat to medium and boil gently for 5 minutes. Reduce heat to low and keep juice hot while filling the jars, but do not allow juice to boil longer than 5 minutes. Overheating increases the likelihood of separation in the jar.

   - Traditional method (to prevent juice from separating): Cut 1 pound fresh, ripe tomatoes into quarters and place in a large saucepan. Heat over medium-high heat until boiling; crush tomatoes as they heat with a potato masher or large spoon. Continuing to work with 1 pound tomatoes at a time, cut each batch into quarters, and slowly add to boiling mixture. Maintain a boil at all times, crushing each new batch of tomatoes as they cook. When all tomatoes have been added, simmer 5 minutes. Purée and strain tomatoes by pressing mixture through a food mill, or purée until smooth using a food processor or blender and then press through a sieve to remove seeds and peel. Heat strained juice to boiling and keep hot while filling jars.

Process time for tomato juice (at 0 to 1,000 feet), in minutes:

- **Boiling water, hot or raw pack:** pints, 35; quarts, 40
- **Dial gauge at 6 pounds, hot or raw pack:** pints or quarts, 20
- **Dial gauge at 11 pounds, hot or raw pack:** pints or quarts, 15
- **Weighted gauge at 5 pounds, hot or raw pack:** pints or quarts, 20
- **Weighted gauge at 10 pounds, hot or raw pack:** pints or quarts, 15
- **Weighted gauge at 15 pounds, hot or raw pack:** pints or quarts, 10

Variations: For **Low-Salt Tomato Juice,** omit salt and, if desired, add any type of commercially available salt-free seasoning to taste before reheating juice for packing. For **Spicy Tomato Juice,** add 1 teaspoon salt and several dashes each hot pepper sauce, cayenne, and ground black pepper when reheating juice before packing per quart (or to taste). For **Bloody Mary Mix,** add 2 tablespoons chopped celery, 2 tablespoons chopped green bell pepper, 1 tablespoon chopped onion, and ½ clove minced garlic per quart (or to taste); simmer 20 minutes, stirring occasionally to prevent sticking. Before reheating juice for packing, add 1 tablespoon Worcestershire sauce, 1¼ tea-spoons celery salt, and 1 teaspoon hot pepper sauce per quart (or to taste); taste before heating. After heating, stir in 1 teaspoon prepared commercial horseradish or fresh grated horseradish, or to taste. Be sure to acidify variations as directed in the section "General Procedure for Canning Tomatoes" at the beginning of the chapter.

PERFECT PRESERVING

Tomatoes contain enzymes that break down pectins in the fruit, causing home-made tomato sauce and juice to separate. This has no effect on overall quality. The simplest solution to the issue of separation is simply to stir together the liquid with the solids after opening the canned product for use. Another easy solution is to pour off the tomato liquid and use only the solids.

Tomato-Based Sauces and Tomato Paste

The following recipes include tomato sauces prepared from fresh tomato purée, as well as traditional methods that crush and strain cooked tomatoes. Traditional methods crush the tomatoes in small batches while quickly cooking (to inactivate enzymes that cause separation), then infuse the sauce with whole seasonings, and strain after boiling sauce. The traditional method produces a silky sauce free of seeds that does not separate in the jar. Contemporary methods save time by starting with a fresh tomato purée, cooking the entire batch of tomatoes at once, and using ground seasonings to flavor the sauce. These sauces may separate in the jar.

You may peel tomatoes by hand, or use a tool or appliance like a food mill or food grinder to do most of the work. Some cooks prefer to grind the tomato skins fine and leave them in the sauce for a coarse texture. Other cooks like to leave in some or all of the tomato seeds. Which method to use is a matter of personal preference, the available tools, and the recipe.

Basic Tomato Sauces

The following recipes and their variations provide you with the ability to make a wide range of tomato sauces in various seasonings styles, from chunky to smooth.

Tomato Sauce from Fresh Tomato Purée

Antioxidant rich and bursting with sun-ripened flavor, tomato sauce has many wonderful and delicious uses in sauces, soups, and stews.

Yield:	Prep time:	Process time:	Headspace:
1 to 14 quarts	2 to 3 hours	10 to 40 minutes	¼ inch

Tomato Sauce from Tomato Purée, Hot Pack Only

1 Quart*	7 Quarts*	14 Quarts*	Ingredient
4 or 5½ lb.	28 or 38 lb.	56 or 77 lb.	Ripe tomatoes
2 TB.	14 TB. (less than 1 cup)	28 TB. (1¾ cups)	Cider vinegar **OR**
1 TB.	7 TB. (less than ½ cup)	14 TB. (less than 1 cup)	lemon juice **OR**
½ tsp.	3½ tsp.	2⅓ TB.	citric acid
1 TB.	7 TB. (less than ½ cup)	14 TB. (less than 1 cup)	Granulated sugar (optional)
1 tsp.	7 tsp. (2⅓ TB.)	14 tsp. (4⅔ TB.)	Salt (optional)

Estimated at 4 pounds per quart for thin sauce and 5½ pounds per quart for thick sauce. Tomato sauce may also be packed in pint jars, yielding 2 pints, 14 pints, or 28 pints.

1. Review the section "General Procedure for Canning Tomatoes" at the beginning of the chapter.

2. Prepare tomato purée by any of the preceding methods. Place tomato purée in a large, heavy stockpot and bring to a simmer; check heat and stir occasionally to prevent sticking. Continue to cook and stir, until reduced to desired consistency—reduce by about ⅓ for thin sauce or by ½ for thick sauce. Keep sauce hot while filling jars, but do not boil. Overheating increases the likelihood of separation in the jar.

Process time for tomato sauce from fresh tomato purée (at 0 to 1,000 feet), in minutes:

- **Boiling water, hot pack:** pints, 35; quarts, 40

- **Dial gauge at 6 pounds, hot pack:** pints or quarts, 20

- **Dial gauge at 11 pounds, hot pack:** pints or quarts, 15

- **Weighted gauge at 5 pounds, hot pack:** pints or quarts, 20

- **Weighted gauge at 10 pounds, hot pack:** pints or quarts, 15

- **Weighted gauge at 15 pounds, hot pack:** pints or quarts, 10

Variations: For **Chunky Tomato Sauce,** after peeling and coring tomatoes by hand, remove seeds if desired, then cut tomatoes into quarters before cooking. After cooking, purée ⅓ of sauce. Combine purée with cooked tomatoes, then cook and reduce to desired consistency. For **Herb-Seasoned Tomato Sauce,** add 1 tablespoon dried seasonings blend to each quart before filling with sauce. Several commercial spice manufacturers offer a variety of these blends such as Italian, Mexican, Greek, Mediterranean, or Cajun. For **Spicy Tomato Sauce,** add 1 teaspoon salt and 1 teaspoon cayenne per quart (or to taste) when reheating sauce before packing. Be sure to acidify variations as directed in the section "General Procedure for Canning Tomatoes" at the beginning of the chapter.

WHAT TYPE OF TOMATO MAKES THE BEST SAUCE?

When making tomato sauces and ketchup, the type of tomato can make the difference between a good sauce and a great one. For best results, use a paste- or sauce-tomato variety, rather than a salad tomato. Paste-type or sauce-type tomatoes include varieties such as roma, plum, Napoli, or San Marzano and may be either heirlooms or hybrids. Sauce tomatoes contain more flesh, less liquid, fewer seeds, and are often higher in pectin. These attributes help make a creamy, thick sauce with the least amount of cooking or reducing. Salad tomatoes like beefsteak, Big Boy, Early Girl, and most hothouse grown tomatoes, intended for fresh eating, have more seeds and more liquid, which would require longer cooking and result in lower yields.

Traditional Tomato Sauce from Fresh Tomatoes

This traditional method prepares sauce from fresh tomatoes in small batches. It is the most time-consuming but produces the smoothest sauce, with a silky texture that is unlikely to separate in the jar.

Yield:	Prep time:	Process time:	Headspace:
1 to 14 quarts	3 to 5 hours	10 to 40 minutes	¼ inch

Traditional Tomato Sauce from Fresh Tomatoes, Hot Pack Only

1 Quart*	7 Quarts*	14 Quarts*	Ingredient
4 or 5½ lb.	28 or 38 lb.	56 or 77 lb.	Ripe tomatoes
2 TB.	14 TB. (less than 1 cup)	28 TB. (1¾ cups)	Cider vinegar **OR**
1 TB.	7 TB. (less than ½ cup)	14 TB. (less than 1 cup)	lemon juice **OR**
½ tsp.	3½ tsp.	2⅓ TB.	citric acid
1 TB.	7 TB. (less than ½ cup)	14 TB. (less than 1 cup)	Granulated sugar (optional)
1 tsp.	7 tsp. (2⅓ TB.)	14 tsp. (4⅔ TB.)	Salt (optional)

Estimated at 4 pounds per quart for thin sauce and 5½ pounds per quart for thick sauce. Tomato sauce may also be packed in pint jars, yielding 2 pints, 14 pints, or 28 pints.

1. Review the section "General Procedure for Canning Tomatoes" at the beginning of the chapter.

2. Wash tomatoes thoroughly under running water. Dip in boiling water for 30 to 60 seconds or until skins split; dip in ice water. Remove skins and cores. Prepare tomatoes using one or more of the following methods and keep sauce hot while filling jars.

   - Traditional method (to prevent sauce from separating): Cut 1 pound tomatoes into quarters and place in a large saucepan over medium-high heat until boiling; as they heat, crush tomatoes with a potato masher or large spoon. Continuing to work with 1 pound of tomatoes at a time, cut into quarters, and slowly add to boiling mixture. Maintain a boil at all times, crushing each new batch of tomatoes as they cook. When all tomatoes have been added, simmer 5 more minutes.

   - Quick method (sauce may separate in jar): Quarter tomatoes and place in a large saucepan. As they heat, crush tomatoes with a potato masher or large spoon. Bring to a boil, reduce heat, and simmer 5 minutes.

   - Optionally, for a smooth sauce by either of the previous methods, purée heated sauce in a food mill, food processor, or blender. If desired, strain to remove seeds and peel. Return sauce to a heavy pan and bring to a simmer over high heat; check heat and stir occasionally to prevent sticking.

   - Optionally, reduce the sauce to thicker consistency. Continue to cook and stir, until reduced by ⅓ for thin sauce, or by ½ for thick sauce.

Process time for traditional tomato sauce (at 0 to 1,000 feet), in minutes:

- **Boiling water, hot pack:** pints, 35; quarts, 40
- **Dial gauge at 6 pounds, hot pack:** pints or quarts, 20
- **Dial gauge at 11 pounds, hot pack:** pints or quarts, 15
- **Weighted gauge at 5 pounds, hot pack:** pints or quarts, 20
- **Weighted gauge at 10 pounds, hot pack:** pints or quarts, 15
- **Weighted gauge at 15 pounds, hot pack:** pints or quarts, 10

Tomato Paste

Tomato paste is a very thick, usually unseasoned sauce made by reducing tomato purée by over half of the original volume. Prepare tomato purée using any of the methods described in the section "Fresh Tomato Purée" earlier in this chapter.

Tomato Paste

Tomato paste offers the most concentrated tomato flavor. Use it to intensify tomato and meat flavors in your recipes.

Yield:	Prep time:	Process time:	Headspace:
1 to 14 half-pints	3 to 6 hours	45 minutes	¼ inch

Tomato Paste, Hot Pack Only

1 Half-Pint*	7 Half-Pints*	14 Half-Pints*	Ingredient
2⅔ lb.	14¼ lb.	28½ lb.	Ripe tomatoes
1 TB.	14 TB. (less than 1 cup)	28 TB. (1¾ cups)	Cider vinegar **OR**
1½ tsp.	3½ TB.	7 TB. (less than ½ cup)	lemon juice **OR**
⅛ tsp.	⅞ tsp.	1¾ TB.	citric acid
¾ tsp.	1½ TB.	3 TB.	Granulated sugar (optional)
¼ tsp.	1¾ tsp.	3½ tsp.	Salt (optional)

Estimated at 2⅔ pounds per half-pint for tomato paste.

1. Review the section "General Procedure for Canning Tomatoes" at the beginning of the chapter.

2. Prepare tomato purée by any of the preceding methods. Place purée in a large, heavy saucepan and bring to a simmer over high heat; stir occasionally to prevent sticking. Continue to cook and stir for 2 to 2½ hours, reducing by ⅔, or until paste is very thick. Reduce heat to low and keep paste hot while filling jars, but do not boil.

Process time for tomato paste (at 0 to 1,000 feet), in minutes:

- **Boiling water, hot pack:** half-pints or pints, 45
- **Pressure canner:** not safe

REDUCING TOMATO PASTE

Reducing tomato purée by ⅔ to a thick tomato paste may take 6 hours or more depending on the volume you are reducing, the amount of water in the tomato variety you are using, and the method used. As sauce thickens, you usually want to reduce the heat and stir more often to prevent sticking and burning. A slow cooker set on high and left uncovered can help you to reduce sauce unattended with only occasional stirring, but can also take a very long time to reduce—some users report up to 12 hours or more.

Pasta, Pizza, and Barbecue Sauces

Pasta, pizza, and barbecue are household standards today. With homemade sauces as their base, these simple cuisines can become something very special.

Italian-Style Pasta or Pizza Sauce

This classic sauce is infused with Italian flavors of basil and crushed red pepper. It's suitable for many pasta dishes or as a base for pizza toppings. Substitute equal quantities of different vegetables and change the seasonings for Greek or Creole recipes.

Yield:	Prep time:	Process time:	Headspace:
3 or 12 pints	2 to 3 hours	35 minutes	½ inch

Italian Pasta Sauce, Hot Pack Only

3-Pint Batch	12-Pint Batch	Ingredient
2 qt. (about 4½ lb.)	2 gal. (about 18 lb.)	Fresh plum tomato purée
⅔ cup	2¾ cups	Chopped onion
⅔ cup	2¾ cups	Chopped celery
½ cup	2 cups	Chopped carrots
2 medium	8 medium	Minced garlic cloves
¼ cup	1 cup	Bottled lemon juice
2 tsp.	2 TB. + 2 tsp.	Salt
1 tsp.	2 tsp.	Dried basil
½ tsp.	2 tsp.	Crushed red pepper

1. Review the section "General Procedure for Canning Tomatoes" at the beginning of the chapter.

2. In a large, heavy, nonreactive (stainless-steel or enamel) saucepan, combine 1 cup plum tomato purée, onions, celery, carrots, and minced garlic. Bring to a boil over medium-high heat, stirring occasionally to prevent sticking. Reduce heat to medium-low and simmer 8 to 10 minutes, or until vegetables are tender. Raise heat to high and bring back to a boil. Add remaining tomato purée 1 cup at a time, maintaining a boil the entire time. Stir in lemon juice, salt, basil, and crushed red pepper. Cook mixture at a full rolling boil for 15 minutes, or until reduced by ⅓. Reduce heat to low and keep sauce hot while filling jars.

This sauce needs no additional acidification.

Process time for Italian-style pasta sauce (at 0 to 1,000 feet), in minutes:

- **Boiling water, hot pack:** half-pints or pints, 35

- **Pressure canner:** not safe

Variations: For **Greek-Style Tomato Sauce,** substitute chopped red bell pepper for celery, chopped green bell pepper for carrots, dried oregano for basil, and ground black pepper for crushed red pepper. Add ½ teaspoon ground cinnamon per quart (or to taste). For **Creole-Style Tomato Sauce,** substitute chopped green onions (white and light green parts only) for onions, chopped green bell pepper for carrots, and dried oregano for basil. Add 2 tablespoons red wine vinegar and 1½ tablespoons Worcestershire sauce per quart (or to taste).

American Barbecue Sauce

Among barbecue aficionados, debate rages over the best sauce. Whether you like yours sweet, smoky, or spicy, there's a sauce here for you.

Yield:	Prep time:	Process time:	Headspace:
3 or 12 pints	2 to 3 hours	20 minutes	½ inch

Sweet and Smoky Barbecue Sauce, Hot Pack Only

3-Pint Batch	12-Pint Batch	Ingredient
3 qt. (about 6⅓ lb.)	3 gal. (about 25¼ lb.)	Fresh plum tomato purée
1½ cups	6 cups	Chopped onion
1½ cups	6 cups	Chopped celery
1 cup	4 cups	Chopped red bell pepper
2 small	6 medium	Minced garlic cloves
¾ cup	3 cups	Brown sugar
1½ TB.	⅓ cup	Worcestershire sauce
1½ tsp.	2 TB.	Liquid smoke
2¼ tsp.	3 TB.	Dry mustard
2¼ tsp.	3 TB.	Paprika
2¼ tsp.	3 TB.	Pickling or canning salt
¾ tsp.	1 TB.	Ground black pepper
1⅛ cup	4½ cups	White vinegar (5%)

1. Review the section "General Procedure for Canning Tomatoes" at the beginning of the chapter.

2. In a large, heavy, nonreactive (stainless-steel or enamel) saucepan, combine plum tomato purée, onion, celery, red bell pepper, and garlic. Bring to a boil over medium-high heat, stirring occasionally to prevent sticking. Reduce heat to medium-low, cover, and simmer 30 minutes, or until vegetables are soft. Using

a hand blender, or working in batches using a food processor, purée sauce to desired consistency (smooth or chunky). Stir in brown sugar, Worcestershire sauce, liquid smoke, dry mustard, paprika, pickling salt, black pepper, and white vinegar and return to a boil. Reduce heat to maintain a slow boil, stirring occasionally to prevent sticking, and cook 45 minutes, or until reduced by ⅓ to ½, or to desired consistency (thin to thick). Reduce heat and keep sauce hot while filling jars.

This sauce needs no additional acidification.

Process time for American barbecue sauce (at 0 to 1,000 feet), in minutes:

- **Boiling water, hot pack:** half-pints or pints, 20
- **Pressure canner:** not safe

Variations: For **Hot-and-Spicy Barbecue Sauce,** omit Worcestershire sauce and liquid smoke. Replace some or all of the red bell pepper with hot chile peppers, and/or add 2 tablespoons hot pepper sauce to the 3-pint batch and ½ cup hot pepper sauce to the 12-pint batch. For **Honey Bourbon–Barbecue Sauce,** omit brown sugar, Worcestershire sauce, and liquid smoke. Add ½ cup honey, ¼ cup light molasses, and 2 tablespoons bourbon to the 3-pint batch; and 2 cups honey, 1 cup light molasses, and ½ cup bourbon to the 12-pint batch. Reduce sauce by ⅓ to ½ instead of by ¼.

HANDLING HOT CHILES

Be sure to wear plastic or rubber gloves while handling or cutting hot chiles such as jalapeños. If you do not wear gloves, wash hands thoroughly with soap and water, and do not touch your face or eyes for at least 3 days. Oil from hot chiles lingers on the skin for several days.

Mexican Barbecue Sauce (*Adobo*)

If you prefer the Latin flavors of toasted cumin and oregano, this is the barbecue sauce for you. Don't miss the variations at the end for a Tex-Mex–style enchilada sauce or red mole with cinnamon and cocoa.

Yield:	Prep time:	Process time:	Headspace:
3 or 12 pints	2 to 3 hours	20 minutes	½ inch

Mexican Barbecue Sauce, Hot Pack Only

3-Pint Batch	12-Pint Batch	Ingredient
3 qt. (about 6⅓ lb.)	3 gal. (about 25¼ lb.)	Fresh plum tomato purée
3 cups	12 cups	Chopped onion
1 cup	4 cups	Chopped mild pepper (such as poblano or red bell), roasted, peeled, cored, and seeded
2 medium	8 medium	Stemmed, seeded if desired, and chopped hot chiles (such as habanero, jalapeño, or chipotle)
2 small	6 medium	Minced garlic cloves
¼ cup	¾ cup	Brown sugar, or to taste
1 to 2 TB.	3½ oz.	*Achiote* paste (see following sidebar)
2¼ tsp.	3 TB.	Pickling or canning salt
1½ tsp.	2 TB.	Ground toasted cumin seeds
1½ tsp.	2 TB.	Ground toasted oregano
¾ tsp.	1 TB.	Crushed red pepper
1⅛ cup	4½ cups	White vinegar (5%)

1. Review the section "General Procedure for Canning Tomatoes" at the beginning of the chapter.

2. In a large, heavy, nonreactive (stainless-steel or enamel) saucepan, combine plum tomato purée, chopped onion, mild pepper, hot chiles, and garlic. Bring to a boil over medium-high heat, stirring occasionally to prevent sticking. Reduce heat to medium-low, cover, and simmer 30 minutes, or until vegetables are soft. Using a hand blender, or working in batches using a food processor, purée sauce to desired consistency (smooth or chunky). Stir in brown sugar, achiote paste, pickling salt, cumin seeds, oregano, crushed red pepper, and white vinegar and return to a boil. Reduce heat to medium and maintain a slow boil, stirring occasionally to prevent sticking. Cook about 45 minutes, or until reduced by ⅓ to ½ or to desired consistency (thin to thick). Reduce heat to low and keep sauce hot while filling jars.

This sauce needs no additional acidification.

Process time for Mexican barbecue sauce (at 0 to 1,000 feet), in minutes:

- **Boiling water, hot pack:** half-pints or pints, 20

- **Pressure canner:** not safe

Variations: For **Enchilada Sauce,** omit achiote paste. Add 1 tablespoon chili powder to 3-pint batch or ¼ cup chili powder to 12-pint batch. For **Red Mole Sauce,** omit achiote paste. Add 1 teaspoon ground cinnamon and 1 tablespoon unsweetened cocoa powder to 3-pint batch or 4 teaspoons ground cinnamon and ¼ cup unsweetened cocoa powder to 12-pint batch.

ACHIOTE PASTE

Red achiote paste is a spiced seasoning and marinating mix made from ground annatto seeds combined with spices, salt, vinegar, garlic, and other ingredients. Deep red annatto seeds provide rich orange-yellow color and earthy flavor to sauces, while other ingredients in different brands provide savory, zesty flavor. You can make sauces without it, but a good *recado rojo* or *recado colorado* lends authentic flavor to many Latino recipes. Buy it from retailers selling Mexican groceries. Blend achiote with orange and lime juices for grilled chicken or pork marinade with a south-of-the-border flair. Chili powder is an acceptable although less interesting substitute.

Tomato Ketchup

Make this small batch of ketchup in much less time than traditional methods. This efficient recipe uses a food processor or blender to purée the tomatoes with other vegetables before cooking, and uses ground rather than whole spices to flavor the sauce. Reduce the ketchup in two stages; the second and longer stage can be completed the regular way on the stovetop, or in a slow cooker for slower, unattended cooking.

Easiest Tomato Ketchup

This easy recipe offers several flavor variations, from spicy to sweet, as well as tangy green tomato ketchup.

Yield:	Prep time:	Process time:	Headspace:
4 or 7 pints	3 to 5 hours	15 minutes	⅛ inch

Easiest Tomato Ketchup, Hot Pack Only

4-Pint Batch	7-Pint Batch	Ingredient
16 cups	28 cups	Fresh plum tomato purée
2 cups	3½ cups	Chopped onion
1½ cups	2½ cups	Stemmed, seeded, and chopped bell pepper
3 cups	5¼ cups	Cider vinegar (5%)
1 cup + 2 TB.	2 cups	Brown sugar
¼ tsp.	½ tsp.	Ground cloves
⅛ tsp.	¼ tsp.	Ground allspice
⅛ tsp.	¼ tsp.	Ground cinnamon
⅛ tsp.	¼ tsp.	Ground black pepper
⅛ tsp.	¼ tsp.	Cayenne
4 tsp.	2 tsp.	Celery salt

1. Review the section "General Procedure for Canning Tomatoes" at the beginning of the chapter.

2. Working in batches, fill the food processor bowl or blender jar half full with plum tomato purée, onion, and bell pepper. Blend at high speed until smooth. Pour into a large stockpot as each batch is finished. Repeat until all vegetables are puréed. Bring mixture to a boil over high heat. Reduce the heat to a simmer, and cook gently for 1 hour. Check and stir sauce every 10 minutes to prevent sticking or burning.

3. Add cider vinegar, brown sugar, cloves, allspice, cinnamon, black pepper, cayenne, and celery salt. Stir until well blended. Continue to boil gently, stirring frequently. Alternatively, transfer sauce to a slow cooker to cook unattended on low heat and cover the slow cooker with a splatter screen or cheesecloth to allow ketchup to reduce to the desired consistency. By either method, cook sauce until volume is reduced by ½, or until ketchup rounds up on a spoon with no separation of liquid. Keep ketchup hot while filling jars.

This sauce needs no additional acidification.

Process time for easiest tomato ketchup (at 0 to 1,000 feet), in minutes:

- **Boiling water, hot pack:** half-pints or pints, 15
- **Pressure canner:** not safe

Variations: For **Spicy Ketchup,** replace ½ cup red bell pepper with coarsely chopped jalapeños or other hot chiles. Add 2 large cloves chopped garlic. For **Green Tomato Ketchup,** substitute green tomatoes in this recipe or any of its variations. These variations need no additional acidification.

Traditional Tomato Ketchup

This classic ketchup recipe offers intense tomato flavor, accented with sweet spices.

Yield:	Prep time:	Process time:	Headspace:
7 or 14 pints	5 to 8 hours	15 minutes	⅛ inch

Traditional Tomato Ketchup, Hot Pack Only

7-Pint Batch	14-Pint Batch	Ingredient
3 cups	6 cups	Cider vinegar (5%)
3 sticks	6 sticks	Cinnamon, crumbled
1 TB.	2 TB.	Whole cloves
3 TB.	⅓ cup	Celery seeds
1½ tsp.	1 TB.	Allspice berries
24 lb.	48 lb.	Ripe tomatoes
3 cups	6 cups	Chopped onion
1 medium	2 medium	Minced garlic cloves
¾ tsp.	1½ tsp.	Cayenne
1½ cups	3 cups	Brown sugar
¼ cup	½ cup	Canning or pickling salt

1. Review the section "General Procedure for Canning Tomatoes" at the beginning of the chapter.

2. In a small (1-quart) saucepan, heat cider vinegar to boiling over high heat. Place cinnamon, cloves, celery seeds, and allspice in a spice bag (or wrap in cheesecloth and tie with cotton butcher twine). Add spice bag to vinegar. Turn off heat, cover, and let steep with spices for 25 minutes. Remove and discard the spice bag after 25 minutes.

3. Wash tomatoes. Dip in boiling water for 30 to 60 seconds or until skins split; dip in ice water. Remove skins and cores, and cut in quarters.

4. Place tomatoes, onion, garlic, and cayenne in a 16-quart or larger stockpot. Heat over high heat, until mixture comes to a boil. Reduce heat slightly and boil gently, uncovered, for 20 minutes. Add spiced vinegar and continue to boil gently for 30 minutes, or until vegetables are very soft and mixture begins to thicken.

5. Strain mixture through a food mill or sieve, working in small batches if needed. Discard solids and return liquid to the stockpot. Stir in brown sugar and canning salt, and bring back to a boil over medium heat. Boil gently until reduced by half, or until mixture mounds on a spoon without separating. Keep ketchup hot while filling jars.

This sauce needs no additional acidification.

Process time for traditional tomato ketchup (at 0 to 1,000 feet), in minutes:

- **Boiling water, hot pack:** half-pints or pints, 15
- **Pressure canner:** not safe

Tomato Salsa

Tomato salsa is the condiment of choice in many households for everything from nachos to scrambled eggs to salad dressing. It's easy to make simple, classic salsa from local sun-ripened tomatoes and just as much fun to preserve. Opening a jar of homemade salsa lets you enjoy a taste of summer any time of year.

You can trade one type of tomato for another (green, mature, tomatillo, etc.). Paste-type tomatoes such as roma tomatoes will make a thicker salsa. Slicing or salad tomatoes such as beefsteak, Big Boy, or Early Girl make thin, watery salsa. Likewise, you can trade one type of chile for another.

Exercise caution when trying to make other recipe changes. The only changes you can safely make in tested salsa recipes are to substitute bottled lemon or lime juice for vinegar (but not the other way around), and to change the amount of seasonings (including salt and pepper). Here are some other cautions:

- Do not increase the amount of vegetables (including tomatoes, tomatillos, onions, garlic, and chiles).

- Do not decrease the amount of acid.

- Do not substitute fresh lemon or lime juice in place of bottled lemon or lime juice.

- Do not substitute vinegar in place of bottled lemon or lime juice.

- Do not used untested recipes; freeze salsas made with these recipes instead.

- Do not use quart jars; use only half-pints or pints.

If you have a family-favorite recipe, it's best to can whole or cut tomatoes and then make your special salsa fresh each time using these products.

Tomato Salsa

Make this salsa as fiery or as mild as you like by using different types of chiles from hot habaneros to smoky poblanos.

Yield:	Prep time:	Process time:	Headspace:
3 or 12 pints	30 to 60 minutes	15 minutes	½ inch

Tomato Salsa, Hot Pack Only

3-Pint Batch	12-Pint Batch	Ingredient
5 cups	5 qt. (20 cups)	Fresh tomato purée
3 cups	3 qt. (12 cups)	Hot or mild chiles
2 cups	2 qt. (8 cups)	Chopped onion
½ cup	2 cups	White vinegar (5%)
1½ tsp.	2 TB.	Pickling or canning salt
¼ tsp.	1 tsp.	Ground black pepper

1. Review the section "General Procedure for Canning Tomatoes" at the beginning of the chapter.

2. In a large, heavy, nonreactive (stainless-steel or enamel) saucepan, combine tomato purée, chiles, onion, white vinegar, pickling salt, and pepper, and bring to a boil over medium-high heat, stirring occasionally to prevent sticking. Reduce heat to maintain a slow boil and cook 10 minutes. Reduce heat and keep salsa hot while filling jars.

   This sauce needs no additional acidification.

Process time for tomato salsa (at 0 to 1,000 feet), in minutes:

- **Boiling water, hot pack:** half-pints or pints, 15

- **Pressure canner:** not safe

Variations: For **Roasted-Tomato Salsa,** substitute roasted tomato purée for fresh tomato purée. For **Chunky Tomato Salsa,** prepare fresh tomato purée by hand and coarsely chop tomatoes.

HOT AND MILD CHILE PEPPERS

Chiles come in red or green varieties, from mild chiles such as ancho (poblano), Italian frying pepper, New Mexico chile, Spanish Spice pepper, and Marconi pepper, to hot chiles such as hot yellow Hungarian or banana pepper, green jalapeño or serrano, orange habanero, and red tabasco or Thai (bird's eye) chiles.

Green Tomatillo Salsa (Salsa Verde)

The bright, citrusy flavor of tomatillos shines through in this appealing green sauce. Control the heat by the type of chiles you use and the amount of cayenne you add. It's great as either a chip dip or cooking sauce, especially for chicken and pork.

Yield:	Prep time:	Process time:	Headspace:
1 to 14 pints	90 to 120 minutes	15 minutes	½ inch

Tomatillo Salsa, Hot Pack Only

1 Pint	14 Pints	Ingredient
1½ cups	5½ quarts	Chopped tomatillos (about 4½ pounds)
¼ cup	4 cups	Chopped white onions
¼ cup	4 cups	Chopped green or yellow chiles, seeded*
1 medium	16 medium	Chopped garlic cloves
1½ tsp.	½ cup	Chopped fresh cilantro
2 TB.	2 cups	White vinegar (5%)
1½ TB.	1 cup	Bottled lime juice
¼ tsp.	4 tsp.	Ground cumin, or to taste
⅛ tsp.	2 tsp.	Salt, or to taste
⅛ tsp.	½ tsp.	Cayenne, or to taste

Use any variety mild chile, such as Anaheim, ancho, Hungarian yellow wax, or poblano; or any variety hot chile, such as jalapeño, serrano, or habanero.

1. Review the section "General Procedure for Canning Tomatoes" at the beginning of the chapter.

2. In a heavy, stainless-steel or enamel saucepan, stir together tomatillos, white onions, chiles, garlic, cilantro, white vinegar, lime juice, cumin, salt, and cayenne, and bring to a boil over high heat. Reduce heat to simmer, and stirring occasionally, cook for 20 minutes. Reduce heat and keep salsa hot while filling jars.

   This sauce needs no additional acidification.

Process time for green tomatillo salsa (at 0 to 1,000 feet), in minutes:

- **Boiling water, hot pack:** half-pints or pints, 15

- **Pressure canner:** not safe

ABOUT TOMATILLOS

The tomatillo or Mexican husk tomato is native to Central America. This fruit-cum-vegetable looks like a small green tomato (to which they are distantly related) but has a papery covering, or husk, that is peeled off and discarded. Tomatillos stay fresh when stored in a plastic bag in the refrigerator for 3 to 4 weeks. Tomatillos may also be frozen for longer storage. For canning, be sure to use green tomatillos, which have the higher acidity needed for the boiling water process. Yellow tomatillos are ripe and may be softer and less tart than green tomatillos. Use tomatillos in many of the same ways as tomatoes: eat fresh, fry, stew (*chile verde*), or make into soup, jam, or this lovely salsa verde.

Canned Pickled Vegetables  17

Many Americans think of pickles as a garnish to a hamburger or sandwich, but they can be so much more. Pickles are a welcome respite if you are committed to eating locally. They add interest to salads as well as meat and poultry dishes. Pickles also pair well with vegetarian meals composed of grains and legumes. Pickling is a satisfying way to preserve vegetables from one growing season to the next. Adding vinegar to vegetables raises acidity and makes them safe for boiling water canning. You can make pickles from many kinds of vegetables or fruits. You are limited only by the bounty in your garden, what's at the farmers' market, and your sense of adventure.

For best flavor, store all pickles for 4 or 6 weeks before using. This gives vegetables time to absorb the pickling liquid and for the sharp flavors to mellow to a pleasant tang.

The recipes in this chapter are suitable for canning and include classic dill pickles, individual pickled vegetables, and a few favorite pickled dishes from cultures around the world. Find recipes for naturally fermented half-sour pickles in Chapter 11, for several types of pickled foods in Chapter 12, and for pickled fruits in Chapter 15.

General Procedure for Canning Pickled Vegetables

For more details on the steps to prepare, process, and store canned foods, see Chapter 7. Use the following general procedure for all of the recipes in this chapter:

1. Prepare boiling water–bath canner, jars, and lids. Before proceeding, review your recipe; preparing the canner and jars is usually the first step, unless the recipe preparation is very lengthy.

2. Prepare pickled vegetables as directed in each recipe.

3. Fill hot jars by the hot-pack or raw-pack method as allowed in the recipe. Use the following general packing instructions, unless recipe directs otherwise.

- Hot pack: Ladle hot product into hot jars, adjusting headspace as directed in recipe.

- Raw pack: Bring pickling liquid to a boil, and then reduce heat and keep hot while filling jars. Ladle a small amount of hot liquid into the hot jar. Add raw vegetables; pack tightly without crushing, and add hot liquid to cover, adjusting headspace as directed in recipe.

4. Clean the rim and secure the lid. Use process time as directed in recipe. Properly cool and store the jars up to 1 year for best flavor.

You should use only the packing methods, jar sizes, headspace, and processing times specified in the recipe. These requirements are not interchangeable from one recipe to another.

Guidelines for Adjusting Canned Pickle Recipes

The unbreakable rule for canning pickled foods is: *Never alter the proportions of solids, vinegar, water, or other liquids in a recipe.* When canning foods with vinegar added, the only safe adjustments are to sugar, salt, and seasonings, which you may freely omit, add, increase, or decrease.

Other ingredient substitutions vary, and you should proceed with extreme caution. The following tested recipes are safe for canning, if you carefully measure all ingredients and follow all instructions. Some recipes list safe substitutions, should you wish to make any adjustments.

Classic Cucumber Pickles

For many Americans, the word *pickles* refers specifically to cucumbers preserved in brine or vinegar. Here are recipes for two of the most common types: dill pickles and sweet pickles (also known as *bread-and-butter pickles*).

If you like firm pickles, you may use low-temperature pasteurization on these two recipes. To low-temperature pasteurize: Place prepared pickles in canning jars, and add boiling pickling liquid to cover pickles completely. Close the jars tightly with lids and screw bands. Place the jars in the canner and add hot (120°F to 140°F) tap water to cover lids by at least 1 inch. Place the pan over high heat, and heat the water to

180°F to 185°F. Reduce the heat to maintain this temperature range for 30 minutes. Lower temperatures will not adequately heat-treat pickles, and higher temperatures may cause softening of pickles.

Fresh-Pack Dill Pickles (Whole)

Fresh-pack pickles are unfermented. This classic recipe is sour, salty, and tart, the pickle commonly used for hamburgers and sandwiches. Flavored simply with dill and a hint of zesty black pepper, you can make them as hot as you like.

Yield:	Prep time:	Process time:	Headspace:
1 to 14 quarts	14 hours	10 to 15 minutes	½ inch

Fresh-Pack Dill Pickles, Raw Pack Only

1 Quart	7 Quarts	14 Quarts	Ingredient
For 12-hour soak:			
2 lb.	14 lb.	28 lb.	Cucumbers
¼ cup	2¼ cups	4½ cups	Pickling salt
2 qt.	3½ gal.	7 gal.	Water
For pickles:			
1½ cups	2½ qt.	5 qt.	White vinegar (5%)
2 tsp.	¼ cup + 2 tsp.	9 TB. + 1 tsp.	Granulated sugar
2 cups	3½ qt.	7 qt.	Water
2 tsp.	¼ cup + 2 tsp.	9 TB. + 1 tsp.	Dill seeds
2 tsp.	¼ cup + 2 tsp.	9 TB. + 1 tsp.	Black peppercorns or mustard seeds
1½ tsp.	3½ TB.	7 TB.	Pickling spice (optional)
1 head	14 heads	28 heads	Fresh dill head, in flower (optional)

1. Review the section "General Procedure for Canning Pickled Vegetables" at the beginning of the chapter.

2. Wash cucumbers. Trim ¹⁄₁₆ inch from blossom end. Dissolve pickling salt in water. Pour over cucumbers and let stand 12 hours. Drain, cover, and refrigerate until ready to fill jars.

3. In a saucepan, combine white vinegar, sugar, and water, cover, and heat to boiling. Reduce heat to low and keep liquid hot while filling jars.

4. Before filling a hot jar with cucumbers, add dill seeds, black peppercorns or mustard seeds, pickling spice (if using), and fresh dill head (if using). For pint jars, use ¹⁄₂ the amounts listed for a 1 quart jar.

Process time for fresh-pack dill pickles (at 0 to 1,000 ft.):

- **Boiling water, raw pack:** pints, 10 minutes; quarts, 15 minutes

Variations: For **Hot-Garlic Dill Pickles,** add 2 to 4 cloves garlic and 2 to 4 small hot red chiles to each quart jar. For **Spears, Chunks, or Slices,** in step 1, wash and trim cucumbers. Cut lengthwise into quarters, or crosswise into 1-inch chunks or ¹⁄₄-inch slices. Skip soaking step and pack into jars. Adjust to ¹⁄₄ inch headspace. For **Green Tomato Pickles,** wash small green tomatoes and cut into quarters. Skip soaking step and pack into jars with garlic and hot red chiles, if desired. Adjust to ¹⁄₄ inch headspace.

MAKING CRISP PICKLES

Blossom ends on cucumbers may contain an enzyme that causes softening, so be sure to trim it away before making pickles. Calcium chloride may also be added to quick-process pickles to help ensure firm texture. Look for a product such as Ball Pickle Crisp where canning supplies are sold. When making fermented cucumbers, different crisping methods are used. Fresh-pack pickles receive a short soak in brine before you process them for canning. Fresh-pack is a quick process compared to naturally fermented pickles. However, the flavor of fresh-pack pickles continues to develop in the jar, and the pickles taste better after 4 to 6 weeks.

Bread-and-Butter Pickles

This divine sweet-and-sour pickle can deliciously adorn any meal but has a special affinity for pork, beans, potato salad, and deviled eggs.

Yield:	Prep time:	Process time:	Headspace:
1 to 14 quarts	6 hours	10 minutes	½ inch

Bread-and-Butter Pickles, Hot Pack Only

1 Quart	7 Quarts	14 Quarts	Ingredient
2½ cups	11 lb.	22 lb.	Cucumbers
1½ cups	5 lb.	10 lb.	Sliced onions
2 TB.	¾ cup + 2 TB.	1¾ cups	Pickling salt
1 qt.	2 qt.	3 qt.	Ice cubes, or as needed
1 cup	7 cups	14 cups	White vinegar (5%)
1 cup	8 cups	16 cups	Granulated sugar
1½ tsp.	3½ TB.	7 TB.	Mustard seeds
½ tsp.	3½ tsp.	2 TB. + 1 tsp.	Celery seeds
½ tsp.	3½ tsp.	2 TB. + 1 tsp.	Ground turmeric

1. Review the section "General Procedure for Canning Pickled Vegetables" at the beginning of the chapter.

2. Wash cucumbers. Trim ¹⁄₁₆ inch from blossom end. Cut crosswise into ¼-inch slices. Combine cucumbers, onions, and pickling salt in a large bowl. Cover with 2 inches of ice cubes. Refrigerate 4 hours, replenishing ice as needed. Drain, rinse in a colander under cold running water, and drain again.

3. In a saucepan, combine white vinegar, sugar, mustard seeds, celery seeds, and turmeric; cover, and heat to boiling over high heat. Reduce heat to medium-low and simmer 10 minutes. Uncover, raise heat to high, add drained cucumbers and onions, and reheat to boiling. Reduce heat to low and keep mixture hot while filling jars.

Process time for bread-and-butter pickles (at 0 to 1,000 ft.):

- **Boiling water, hot pack:** pints or quarts, 10 minutes

Variation: For **Zucchini or Yellow Squash Bread-and-Butter Pickles,** wash zucchini or yellow squash and cut crosswise into ¹/₂-inch chunks. Proceed in step 1 with salting and draining.

ABOUT BREAD-AND-BUTTER PICKLES

Omar A. Fanning applied for the trademark "FANNING'S BREAD AND BUTTER PICKLES" in 1923. Omar made sweet-and-sour pickles using an old family recipe from the culls (small cucumbers) on his farm. His wife Cora traded the pickles with her local grocer for staples such as bread and butter. The pickles became popular in their local Illinois community and spread to the South. The mark has changed hands a few times, and is currently owned by GFA Brands, Inc., in New Jersey. The original recipe may have contained green pepper rings (find a recipe for this traditional version in Chapter 12).

Vegetable Pickles

Early American history is rife with many types of pickled foods other than cucumbers. In fact, the H.J. Heinz Company became famous by offering 57 varieties of pickled foods for sale to grocery stores. The following recipes feature some of the most popular pickled vegetables.

Pickled Asparagus

Although it retains little of the grassy flavor of the fresh vegetable, salty, tangy pickled asparagus still satisfies with its meaty texture.

Yield:	Prep time:	Process time:	Headspace:
1 to 14 tall pints	60 to 90 minutes	10 minutes	¹/₂ inch

Pickled Asparagus, Raw Pack Only

1 Tall Pint	7 Tall Pints	14 Tall Pints	Ingredient
1 lb.	3¹/₂ lb.	7 lb.	Fresh asparagus
¹/₃ cup	1¹/₃ cups	2²/₃ cups	White vinegar (5%)

1 Tall Pint	7 Tall Pints	14 Tall Pints	Ingredient
⅓ cup	1⅓ cups	2⅔ cups	Water
2¼ tsp.	⅓ cup	⅔ cup	Pickling salt
1 clove	7 cloves	14 cloves	Garlic, peeled
¼ tsp.	1¾ tsp.	3½ tsp.	Crushed red pepper (optional)

1. Review the section "General Procedure for Canning Pickled Vegetables" at the beginning of the chapter.

2. Wash asparagus. Trim spears from the bottom, in lengths to fit the canning jar, leaving a little more than ½ inch headspace.

3. In a saucepan, combine white vinegar, water, and pickling salt. Bring to a boil. Reduce heat and keep liquid hot while filling jars.

4. Before filling a hot pint jar with asparagus, add 1 garlic clove and ¼ teaspoon crushed red pepper. Pack asparagus spears into jar with the tips up and blunt ends down.

Process time for pickled asparagus (at 0 to 1,000 ft.):

- **Boiling water, raw pack:** pints, 10 minutes

PERFECT PRESERVING

A *tall pint* is a narrow 12-ounce jar that is great for asparagus spears, whole green beans, and carrot spears. Use wide-mouth pints if you can't find tall pints.

Variations: For **Hot Pickled Dill Beans,** substitute green or wax beans for asparagus and add 1 teaspoon dill seeds and 1 fresh dill head to each jar. For **Sweet Pickled Dill Beans,** substitute green or wax beans for asparagus. Omit garlic and crushed red pepper. Add 1 teaspoon dill seeds and 1 fresh dill head to each jar. Add to white vinegar equal parts granulated sugar (for 1-pint batch, add ⅓ cup granulated sugar). Boil and stir pickling solution until sugar completely dissolves.

Pickled Carrots

Sweet and tangy pickled carrots really satisfy with a pleasing crunchy bite.

Yield:	Prep time:	Process time:	Headspace:
1 to 14 pints	60 to 90 minutes	15 minutes	½ inch

Pickled Carrots, Raw Pack Only

1 Pint	7 Pints	14 Pints	Ingredient
1 lb.	7 lb.	14 lb.	Carrots
1⅓ cups	9½ cups	19 cups	White vinegar (5%)
¼ cup	1¾ cups	3½ cups	Water
½ cup	3½ cups	7 cups	Granulated sugar
½ tsp.	3½ tsp.	2 TB. + 1 tsp.	Pickling salt
2 tsp.	About 5 TB.	Scant ⅔ cup	Mustard seeds
1 tsp.	2⅓ TB.	About 5 TB.	Celery seeds

1. Review the section "General Procedure for Canning Pickled Vegetables" at the beginning of the chapter.

2. Wash carrots. Peel and slice on the diagonal into ¼-inch slices, or cut carrots into lengths to fit the canning jar, leaving a little more than ½ inch headspace. Cut carrots lengthwise in quarters for spears.

3. In a saucepan, combine white vinegar, water, sugar, and pickling salt, and bring to a boil. Reduce heat to low and keep liquid hot while filling jars.

4. Before filling a hot pint jar with carrots, add 2 teaspoons mustard seeds and 1 teaspoon celery seeds. When packing spears, alternate thin and thick ends to achieve a tight fit.

Process time for pickled carrots (at 0 to 1,000 ft.):

- **Boiling water, raw pack:** pints, 15 minutes

Pickled Red-Beet *Pkhali*

These sweet-and-zesty pickled beets form the base of pkhali, a Russian vegetable salad or dip. Enjoy as is, or add chopped walnuts, onions, and cilantro. Serve with lavash (see recipe in Chapter 11), or as an accompaniment to any meal.

Yield:	Prep time:	Process time:	Headspace:
1 to 14 pints	90 to 120 minutes	30 minutes	½ inch

Pickled Red-Beet Pkhali

1 Pint	7 Pints	14 Pints	Ingredient
1 lb.	14 lb.	14 lb.	Beets
½ cup	3½ cups	7 cups	White vinegar (5%)
¼ cup	1¾ cups	3½ cups	Water
¼ cup	1¾ cups	3½ cups	Granulated sugar
¼ tsp.	1¾ tsp.	3½ tsp.	Ground coriander
¼ tsp.	1¾ tsp.	3½ tsp.	Ground cumin
⅛ tsp.	1¼ tsp.	2½ tsp.	Pickling salt
⅛ tsp.	1¼ tsp.	2½ tsp.	Dried thyme

1. Review the section "General Procedure for Canning Pickled Vegetables" at the beginning of the chapter.

2. Scrub beets under running water with a vegetable brush. Cover with boiling water and bring to a boil over high heat. Reduce heat to medium-low and simmer 15 to 20 minutes, or until tender. Drain and discard liquid. Cool beets. Trim roots and stems, and then slip off skins. Cut into ¼-inch cubes. Set aside until ready to fill jars.

3. In a saucepan, combine white vinegar, water, sugar, coriander, cumin, pickling salt, and thyme, and bring to a boil. Add beets, and return to a boil; boil 5 minutes. Reduce heat and keep mixture hot while filling jars.

Process time for pickled red-beet pkhali (at 0 to 1,000 ft.):

- **Boiling water, hot pack:** pints, 30 minutes

Pickled Yellow Beets with Fennel and Thyme

Yellow beets mellow to a lovely fawn color and the fennel accents the musky beet flavor. These pickles are a pleasant departure from more common pickled beets, flavored with cinnamon and other sweet spices.

Yield:	Prep time:	Process time:	Headspace:
1 to 14 pints	90 to 120 minutes	30 minutes	½ inch

Pickled Yellow Beets, Hot Pack Only

1 Pint	7 Pints	14 Pints	Ingredient
¾ lb.	5 lb.	10 lb.	Yellow beets
¼ lb.	2 lb.	4 lb.	Fennel bulb with leaves
¾ cup	5 cups	2½ qt.	White vinegar (5%)
¼ cup	1¾ cups	3½ cups	Water
¾ tsp.	5¼ tsp.	3½ TB.	Pickling salt
1 clove	7 cloves	14 cloves	Garlic, halved
¼ tsp.	1¾ tsp.	3½ tsp.	Dried thyme
1 to 3	7 to 21	14 to 42	Fennel sprigs

1. Review the section "General Procedure for Canning Pickled Vegetables" at the beginning of the chapter.

2. Scrub yellow beets under running water with a vegetable brush. Cover with boiling water and bring to a boil over high heat. Reduce heat to medium and boil 15 to 20 minutes, or until tender. Drain and discard liquid. Cool beets. Trim roots and stems, and then slip off skins. Cut beets in half; lay each half flat and cut into 6 to 8 wedges, or about ¼ inch thick.

3. Separate fennel leaves. Cut off and reserve fennel sprigs as needed. Slice fennel bulb into ¼-inch strips.

4. In a saucepan, combine white vinegar, water, and pickling salt, and bring to a boil. Add beets, fennel bulb strips, garlic, and thyme, and return to a boil; boil 5 minutes. Reduce heat and keep hot while filling jars.

5. Add fennel sprigs to each jar before filling with beets and hot pickling liquid.

Process time for pickled yellow beets (at 0 to 1,000 ft.):

- **Boiling water, hot pack:** pints, 30 minutes

Pickled Marinated Mushrooms

Well-seasoned mushrooms in a vinegar and oil marinade are a sure hit on your next relish tray.

Yield:	Prep time:	Process time:	Headspace:
1 to 14 half-pints	90 to 120 minutes	20 minutes	½ inch

Pickled Marinated Mushrooms, Raw Pack Only

1 Half-Pint	7 Half-Pints	14 Half-Pints	Ingredient
¾ lb.	5½ lb.	11 lb.	Small, whole button mushrooms (domestically grown only)
2½ tsp.	6 TB.	¾ cup	Bottled lemon juice
1 qt.	2 qt.	4 qt.	Water, or as needed
3½ TB.	1½ cups	3 cups	Olive or salad oil
4½ TB.	2 cups	4 cups	White vinegar (5%)
2½ tsp.	6 TB.	¾ cup	Finely chopped onions
1¼ tsp.	3 TB.	6 TB.	Diced red bell peppers or hot chiles
¼ tsp.	2¾ tsp.	2 TB.	Oregano leaves
¼ tsp.	2¾ tsp.	2 TB.	Dried basil leaves
¼ tsp.	2¾ tsp.	2 TB.	Pickling salt
3 each	21 each	42 each	Black peppercorns
¼ clove	2 cloves	4 cloves	Garlic, cut in quarters

1. Review the section "General Procedure for Canning Pickled Vegetables" at the beginning of the chapter.

2. Select fresh, unopened mushroom caps less than 1¼ inches in diameter. Wash in several changes of water until no more grit remains. Trim stems, leaving ¼ inch attached to cap.

3. In a saucepan, combine mushrooms, bottled lemon juice, and water to cover, and bring to a boil. Reduce heat and simmer 5 minutes, then drain mushrooms.

4. In another saucepan, combine mushrooms, olive oil, white vinegar, onions, red bell peppers, oregano, basil, and pickling salt, and bring to a boil. Reduce heat and keep mixture hot while filling jars.

5. Before filling a hot jar with mushrooms, add 3 black peppercorns and 1 piece garlic.

Process time for pickled marinated mushrooms (at 0 to 1,000 ft.):

- **Boiling water, hot pack:** half-pints, 20 minutes

PERFECT PRESERVING

When canning pickled mushrooms and other vegetables, be sure to distribute the oil-and-vinegar marinade evenly in the jars. Use only fresh oil in the amount specified in this tested recipe. Take extra care to adjust the headspace and carefully clean the rim, to guarantee a good seal. Ensure that no liquid gets on the flat lid; the oil tends to soften the natural rubber-based lining and may result in loosening of the seal over time. Canning with oil is tricky, but the delicious results are worth the effort.

Pickled Jalapeño Slices

Hot and fruity when made with sun-ripened jalapeños, these piquant rings can go on nachos, in scrambled eggs, and anywhere you need a little zing.

Yield:	Prep time:	Process time:	Headspace:
1 to 14 pints	90 to 120 minutes	10 minutes	½ inch

Pickled Jalapeño Slices, Raw Pack Only

1 Pint	7 Pints	14 Pints	Ingredient
¾ lb. (10 to 15)	5½ lb. (70 to 105)	1 lb. (140 to 210)	Jalapeños
9 TB.	4 cups	8 cups	White vinegar (5%)
5¼ tsp.	¾ cup	1½ cups	Water
½ tsp.	1 TB.	2 TB.	Pickling salt
¼ tsp.	1½ tsp.	1 TB.	Granulated sugar
1 slice	7 slices	14 slices	Peeled and sliced carrot
1 small	7 small	14 small	Onion strips (3 in. long by ¼ in. wide)
⅛ tsp.	⅞ tsp.	1¾ tsp.	Ball Pickle Crisp granules (optional)

1. Review the section "General Procedure for Canning Pickled Vegetables" at the beginning of the chapter.

2. Wash jalapeños. Slice into ¼-inch-thick slices. Discard stem ends.

3. In a saucepan, combine white vinegar, water, pickling salt, and sugar, and bring to a boil over high heat. Keep liquid hot while filling jars.

4. Before filling a hot jar with pepper slices, add 1 carrot slice, 1 onion strip, and rounded ⅛ teaspoon Ball Pickle Crisp granules (if using).

Process time for pickled jalapeño peppers (at 0 to 1,000 ft.):

- **Boiling water, raw pack:** half-pints, 10 minutes

> **PERFECT PRESERVING**
>
> Canned pickled jalapeños—whole or sliced—tend to be soft. If you want to maintain crispness, pierce whole jalapeños and soak in a solution of ½ cup salt for every 1 quart water for 12 to 18 hours. Drain and proceed with step 1. Alternatively, purchase pickling lime or a calcium-chloride crisping product such as Ball Pickle Crisp and use according to package directions. Personally, I like the soft texture of canned jalapeños and appreciate fresh, raw, crisp jalapeños. But when fresh ones are out of season, I look forward to pretty jars of tangy, hot beauties on everything from omelets to tacos.

Sweet-and-Sour Red Cabbage

Sweet, savory, and sour, this unadorned cabbage is a great side dish for braised meats in winter, especially pork and lamb.

Yield:	Prep time:	Process time:	Headspace:
1 to 14 pints	2 days	20 minutes	½ inch

Sweet-and-Sour Red Cabbage, Raw Pack Only

1 Pint	7 Pints	14 Pints	Ingredient
¾ lb.	4½ lb.	9 lb.	Red cabbage
1½ TB.	⅓ cup	⅔ cup	Pickling salt
¾ cup	5½ cups	10½ cups	Red wine vinegar (5%)
1 TB.	½ cup	1 cup	Lightly packed brown sugar
⅛ tsp.	¾ tsp.	1½ tsp.	Ground black pepper
½ lb. (2 medium)	1¼ lb. (4 to 5 medium)	2½ lb. (8 to 10 medium)	Tart apples
¼ cup (¼ medium)	1¾ cups (2 medium)	3½ cups (4 medium)	Chopped onions

1. Review the section "General Procedure for Canning Pickled Vegetables" at the beginning of the chapter.

2. Remove and discard bruised outer red cabbage leaves. Quarter, core, and slice cabbage ½ inch. In a large bowl, toss cabbage with pickling salt until well combined, cover, and let stand in cool location for 24 hours. Rinse cabbage, drain, and dry thoroughly on several layers of paper towels for 6 hours.

3. In a large stockpot, combine red wine vinegar, brown sugar, and pepper; cover, and bring to a boil over medium-high heat. Reduce heat and simmer gently 5 minutes, or until brown sugar dissolves. Keep liquid hot while filling jars.

4. Just before filling jars, peel, core, and shred apples; treat to prevent browning. In a large bowl, toss together red cabbage, apples, and onions.

Process time for sweet and sour red cabbage (at 0 to 1,000 ft.):

- **Boiling water, raw pack:** pints, 15 minutes

Pickled Melon with Ginger

Refreshing, sweet, and zesty bites of pickled melon are a wonderful accompaniment to barbecue and spicy foods. Make them hot, or not.

Yield:	Prep time:	Process time:	Headspace:
7 pints	2 days	15 minutes	1 inch

Pickled Melon with Ginger

1 Pint	7 Pints	14 Pints	Ingredient
1 lb. (about $\frac{1}{3}$)	8 lb. (2 to 3 medium)	16 lb. (4 to 6 medium)	Melon, such as honeydew or cantaloupe
$1\frac{1}{8}$ cups	2 qt.	1 gal.	Cider vinegar (5%)
$\frac{1}{2}$ cup	$3\frac{1}{2}$ cups	7 cups	Water
1 oz.	$\frac{1}{2}$ lb.	1 lb.	Fresh ginger, peeled and sliced paper thin
$5\frac{1}{2}$ TB.	$2\frac{1}{2}$ cups	5 cups	Granulated sugar
$5\frac{1}{2}$ TB.	$2\frac{1}{2}$ cups	5 cups	Packed brown sugar
$\frac{1}{4}$ tsp.	$1\frac{3}{4}$ tsp.	$3\frac{1}{2}$ tsp.	Crushed red pepper (optional)

1. Review the section "General Procedure for Canning Pickled Vegetables" at the beginning of the chapter.

2. Select melons that are full size but green and firm to the touch, including stem area. Wash, halve, and scoop out seeds. Cut into 1-inch slices, remove peel, and cut into 1-inch cubes, or use a melon baller to scoop out balls of melon.

3. In a medium (3- to 4-quart) saucepan, combine cider vinegar, water, and ginger slices, and bring to a boil. Reduce heat, and simmer 5 minutes. Pour hot liquid over melon cubes. Cover and refrigerate melon for 12 to 18 hours.

4. Strain vinegar solution into a large saucepan. Stir in granulated sugar, brown sugar, and crushed red pepper (if using), and bring to a boil. Add melon and ginger slices, and return to a boil. Reduce heat, and simmer 1 hour, or until melon turns translucent. Keep mixture hot while filling jars.

Process time for pickled melon (at 0 to 1,000 ft.):

- **Boiling water, hot pack:** pints, 15 minutes

Canned Savory Sauces, Relishes, and Chutneys 18

People everywhere have been making pickles since ancient times. Fermenting vegetables in salt brine is a common method used around the world to preserve fresh produce for use through the winter. In modern times, you also have the option of acidifying food directly by adding vinegar, and then canning pickled vegetables for long-term storage.

The first rule in any canning recipe is: *Never adjust the recipe.* If you cannot get the ingredients to make a recipe exactly, then consider whether you can freeze the product rather than can it. Alternatively, you might make a small amount of your altered recipe, refrigerate it, and eat it within a month. Otherwise, you should choose another recipe.

In practical terms, substitutions are sometimes desirable. However, it is wise to become familiar with safe substitutions, should you decide to experiment.

The pickle recipes in this chapter are suitable for canning and include classic dill pickles, individual pickled vegetables, and a few favorite pickles from cultures around the world.

General Procedure for Canning Savory Sauces, Relishes, and Chutneys

For more details on the steps to prepare, process, and store canned foods, see Chapter 7. Use the following general procedure for all of the recipes in this chapter:

1. Prepare boiling water–bath canner, jars, and lids. Before proceeding, review your recipe; preparing the canner and jars is usually the first step, unless the recipe preparation is very lengthy.

2. Prepare sauce, relish, or chutney as directed in each recipe.

3. Fill hot jars by the hot-pack method as allowed in the recipe. Use the following general packing instructions, unless recipe directs otherwise.

   - Hot pack: Ladle hot product into hot jars, adjusting headspace as directed in recipe.

   - Do not use raw pack. All sauces, relishes, and chutneys are filled into jars using hot pack only.

4. Clean the rim and secure the lid. Use process time as directed in recipe. Properly cool and store the jars up to 1 year for best flavor.

You should use only the packing methods, jar sizes, headspace, and processing times specified in the recipe. These requirements are not interchangeable from one recipe to another.

Guidelines for Adjusting Canned Sauce Recipes

The unbreakable rule for canning acidified foods is: *Never alter the proportions of solids, vinegar, water, or other liquids in a recipe.* When canning foods with vinegar added, the only safe adjustments are to sugar, salt, and seasonings, which you may freely omit, add, increase, or decrease.

Other ingredient substitutions vary, and you should proceed with extreme caution. The following tested recipes are safe for canning if you carefully measure all ingredients and follow all instructions. Some recipes list safe substitutions, should you wish to make any adjustments.

Savory Sauces

Fruity condiments pair wonderfully with many savory foods. They're a great way to use a bounty of summer produce in new and different ways. Serve these sauces as exciting accents for everything from appetizers, to soup, to entrées.

Pineapple-Chile Salsa

This sweet and fruity salsa pairs well with grilled seafood. To increase heat, substitute hot chiles—such as jalapeños—for some or all Anaheim pepper, or increase cayenne to taste.

Yield:	Prep time:	Process time:	Headspace:
7 half-pints	90 to 120 minutes	15 minutes	½ inch

7 cups chopped pineapple (about 1 pineapple, peeled and cored)

1⅛ cups chopped white onion (about 3 medium)

⅔ cup stemmed, seeded, and chopped Anaheim peppers (about 2 medium)

2 TB. chopped cilantro

2 TB. chopped mint

1⅛ cups bottled lime juice

⅔ cup bottled lemon juice

⅔ cup unsweetened, canned pineapple juice

2 TB. packed brown sugar, or to taste

½ tsp. cayenne, or to taste

1. Review the section "General Procedure for Canning Savory Sauces, Relishes, and Chutneys" at the beginning of the chapter.

2. In a heavy stainless-steel or enamel saucepan, stir together pineapple, white onion, Anaheim peppers, cilantro, mint, lime juice, lemon juice, pineapple juice, brown sugar, and cayenne; bring to a boil over high heat. Reduce heat to medium-low and simmer 10 minutes, stirring occasionally. Keep mixture hot while filling jars.

SALSA RECIPE SUBSTITUTIONS

Substituting ingredients can lead to unsafe products. If you choose alternate fruits for your salsa, consider whether the replacement is of equal or higher acidity (lower pH). The maximum pH for papaya is 5.7, pineapple is 5.2, and mango is 4.6. Therefore, pineapple or mango might replace papaya, but it would not be safe for papaya to replace pineapple. Raisins have a pH of 4.0. Fruits with a lower pH include cranberries, tart apples, and dried apricots. You may safely exchange one variety of pepper or chile for another, from mild bell peppers to hot jalapeños. You may substitute one herb for another, such as mint or oregano for cilantro; add spices such as cumin; increase or decrease the sugar; or add salt.

Peach Salsa

This fruity salsa can be tangy or sweet and as hot as you like. Peach salsa pairs well with pork and lamb.

Yield:	Prep time:	Process time:	Headspace:
7 half-pints	60 minutes	10 minutes	½ inch

7 cups diced hard, unpeeled, unripe peaches (about 3 lb.)

1¾ cups diced red bell pepper (about 4 medium)

½ cup finely chopped red onion (1 medium)

2 TB. chopped fresh cilantro

2 tsp. finely chopped garlic

1½ cups cider vinegar (5%)

½ cup fresh orange juice

½ cup packed brown sugar, or to taste

½ tsp. cayenne, or to taste

1. Review the section "General Procedure for Canning Savory Sauces, Relishes, and Chutneys" at the beginning of the chapter.

2. In a heavy stainless-steel or enamel saucepan, stir together peaches, red bell pepper, red onion, cilantro, garlic, cider vinegar, orange juice, brown sugar, and cayenne; bring to a boil over high heat. Reduce heat to medium-low and simmer, stirring occasionally, for 5 minutes, or until sugar dissolves. Keep mixture hot while filling jars.

Variations: For **Papaya Salsa,** substitute peeled and chopped underripe, green papaya for chopped peaches. For **Mango Salsa,** substitute peeled and chopped underripe, green mango for chopped peaches. Be sure to wear heavy plastic or rubber gloves when cutting green mango, which irritates the skin in some people.

PERFECT PRESERVING

The skin of bell peppers can be tough, so it's a good idea to remove it. Use a vegetable peeler, just as you would on a potato or carrot. You can roast a bell pepper to blister the skin and peel it off. However, roasted pepper will tend to overwhelm the peach flavor in this salsa. I recommend peeling bell pepper raw.

Jalapeño Pepper Sauce

This surprisingly fruity hot pepper sauce provides a bold accent for grilled meats, as well as soups, stews, or eggs.

Yield:	Prep time:	Process time:	Headspace:
7 half-pints	120 minutes	10 minutes	½ inch

6 cups chopped jalapeños, stems removed and seeds intact (3 to 4 lb.)

1¾ cups chopped onions (about 3 medium)

18 cloves garlic, coarsely chopped

9½ cups distilled white or cider vinegar (5%)

2 TB. dried oregano

1½ TB. pickling salt

1½ TB. cumin seeds

½ cup granulated sugar, or to taste

1. Review the section "General Procedure for Canning Savory Sauces, Relishes, and Chutneys" at the beginning of the chapter.

2. In a large saucepan, stir together jalapeños, onions, garlic, white vinegar, oregano, pickling salt, cumin seeds, and sugar; bring to a boil over high heat. Reduce heat to medium, cover, and cook at a slow boil for 30 minutes, stirring frequently to prevent scorching. Strain mixture through a fine mesh strainer. Return strained sauce to pan and return to a boil over high heat. Keep mixture hot while filling jars.

Variations: For **Hot Red Pepper Sauce,** use 5 cups any fresh red chiles—such as habanero—or any dried red chiles—such as (hot) chile de árbol or (mild) New Mexico. Be sure to wear heavy plastic or rubber gloves when cutting hot chiles; chile oil lingers on the skin for several days. For **Asian Pepper Sauce,** use serranos in place of jalapeños, and add 1 to 2 teaspoons curry powder. Omit oregano. Increase or decrease granulated sugar or pickling salt, if desired. However, do not increase amount of chiles, onions, or garlic, and do not decrease amount of cider vinegar.

Relishes

When you make your own relish, you can be confident in the quality of the ingredients. Vegetable relish is a great way to preserve a bounty of produce at the end of the growing season. Using relish goes way beyond burgers and hot dogs. Combine it with yogurt for vegetable dip, blend it with vinegar and oil for flavorful salad dressing, or add it to mayonnaise for sandwich spread. Serve vegetable relish as an accompaniment to grilled or roasted meats and seafood, as well as vegetarian meals.

Combination pickled vegetables fall somewhere between a pickle and relish. You can serve some of them as a winter salad; stronger pickles make great accompaniments to plain foods, including roasted or braised meats, and vegetarian meals based on grain and legumes. These recipes make great use of vegetables that are available in late summer.

Mixed Vegetable Pickles

Use this basic recipe to pickle any variety of vegetables, cut into pieces 1 inch or smaller. Make them sweet or hot, or add seasonings as suggested. Add more sugar for sweeter pickles, less for sour pickles. The main difference between this and the preceding relish recipe is the size of the vegetable pieces.

Yield:	Prep time:	Process time:	Headspace:
7 pints	8 to 24 hours	15 minutes	¼ inch

4 qt. (16 cups) vegetables in 1-in. or smaller pieces from the following list:

Carrots (1 medium carrot makes about ½ cup chopped)

Cauliflower (1 medium head makes about 3 cups chopped)

Celery (2 to 3 medium ribs make about 1 cup chopped)

Cucumbers (1 medium makes 1 to 1½ cups chopped)

Onions (1 medium makes about ½ cup chopped)

Green or red bell peppers (1 medium makes about ½ cup chopped)

Green or red ripe tomatoes (1 medium makes about ½ cup chopped)

Zucchini or summer squash (1 medium makes about 1 cup chopped)

Brining method:

1¼ cups canning or pickling salt

5 qt. cold water

Icing method:

7 TB. canning or pickling salt

2 to 3 qt. cubed or crushed ice, or as needed

Pickling solution:
2 qt. white vinegar (5%)
2 cups granulated sugar
¼ cup mustard seeds
2 TB. celery seeds

1. Review the section "General Procedure for Canning Savory Sauces, Relishes, and Chutneys" at the beginning of the chapter.

2. Toss together vegetables in a large bowl. Prepare by either the brining or icing method:

   • Brining method (crunchier pickles): Dissolve canning salt in cold water. Pour over prepared vegetables. Soak vegetables in the refrigerator for 12 to 18 hours. Drain, rinse, and drain again thoroughly. In a large (8- to 10-quart) stockpot, combine white vinegar, sugar, mustard seeds, and celery seeds; bring to a boil; boil 3 minutes. Add drained vegetables; heat 5 minutes, or until hot throughout. Keep mixture hot while filling jars.

   • Icing method (softer pickles): Toss vegetables with canning salt and cover with 2 inches cubed or crushed ice. Refrigerate 3 to 4 hours. Drain thoroughly. In a large (8- to 10-quart) stockpot, combine white vinegar, sugar, mustard seeds, and celery seeds; bring to a boil; boil 3 minutes. Add drained vegetables, and bring to a boil. Reduce to medium-low heat and simmer 15 minutes. Keep hot while filling jars.

Variation: For **Mustard Pickles (Chow Chow),** substitute cider vinegar for white vinegar, and packed brown sugar for granulated sugar. Omit celery seeds. To spice mixture, add 2 tablespoons mustard powder mixed with 2 tablespoons water, and 1 teaspoon ground turmeric.

PERFECT PRESERVING

When preparing mixed vegetable pickles, select mature vegetables without blemishes or mold. Wash thoroughly. Peel any vegetable that has been waxed. Trim and discard ¹⁄₁₆ inch from each end of cucumbers. Cut pieces to the same uniform size, in ½- to 1-inch pieces.

Mixed Vegetable Relish

Use this colorful relish to preserve a variety of vegetables. It makes a large batch that will last until spring. The spices are deliciously complex: bold, earthy, and sweet.

Yield:	Prep time:	Process time:	Headspace:
7 pints	7 to 9 hours	15 minutes	½ inch

21 cups chopped vegetables from the following list:

Green, Savoy, or Chinese cabbage (1 small head makes about 4 cups chopped)

Cauliflower (1 medium head makes about 3 cups chopped)

Celery (2 to 3 medium ribs make about 1 cup chopped)

Corn (2 medium ears make about 1 cup corn kernels)

Cucumbers (1 medium makes 1 to 1½ cups chopped)

Onions (1 medium makes about ½ cup chopped)

Green or red bell peppers (1 medium makes about ½ cup chopped)

Green or red ripe tomatoes (1 medium makes about ½ cup chopped)

Zucchini or summer squash (1 medium makes about 1 cup chopped)

½ cup canning or pickling salt

7 cups cider vinegar (5%)

3½ cups brown sugar

2 cloves garlic, minced

1 TB. celery seeds

1 TB. mustard seeds

½ tsp. ground allspice

½ tsp. ground cinnamon

½ tsp. ground cloves

1. Review the section "General Procedure for Canning Savory Sauces, Relishes, and Chutneys" at the beginning of the chapter.

2. In a large bowl, toss together chopped vegetables and canning salt. Cover and refrigerate 12 to 18 hours. Drain thoroughly in a colander.

3. In a large stockpot, stir together cider vinegar, brown sugar, garlic, celery seeds, mustard seeds, allspice, cinnamon, and cloves; bring to a boil over high heat. Reduce heat to medium-low and simmer 10 minutes. Add vegetables, raise heat to high, return to a boil, and simmer an additional 30 minutes. Keep mixture hot while filling jars.

Variation: For **Green Tomato Relish (*Piccalilli*),** use 3 quarts chopped green tomato, 3 cups chopped green, Savoy, or Chinese cabbage or cucumber, 3 cups chopped red or green bell pepper, and 3 cups chopped onion.

RELISH-RECIPE SUBSTITUTIONS

Substituting ingredients can lead to unsafe relish. If you choose alternative vegetables, make sure the replacement has equal or higher acidity (lower pH). Tomato has a maximum pH of 4.9, cabbage 6.8, onion 5.9, celery 6.0, bell pepper 5.9, cauliflower 5.6, and cucumber 5.8. If a recipe calls for cabbage, you can substitute any of these vegetables for some or all of the cabbage because they all have lower pH. You may safely exchange one variety of chile for another, from mild bell peppers to hot chiles. You may substitute one type of sugar for another (such as granulated for brown) and any spice for another (such as turmeric for cayenne). You may increase or decrease the sugar, salt, or spices. Never decrease the vinegar.

Indian-Style Pickled Cauliflower (*Achar*)

The nutty overtones of this spicy, crunchy vegetable will keep you coming back for more. *Achar* refers to pickled and salted foods that may be sweet, sour, salty, or hot.

Yield:	Prep time:	Process time:	Headspace:
7 pints	60 to 90 minutes	15 minutes	½ inch

> 1⅓ cups coarsely chopped onion
>
> 7 TB. roasted, salted peanuts
>
> 1 tsp. dried crushed red pepper
>
> 4 cloves garlic, roughly chopped
>
> 1 (1-in.) piece fresh ginger root, peeled and coarsely chopped
>
> 2½ cups white vinegar
>
> 1 cup granulated sugar
>
> 2 TB. pickling salt
>
> 1 TB. ground turmeric
>
> 4 qt. (16 cups) 1-in. cauliflower florets (5 medium heads)

1. Review the section "General Procedure for Canning Savory Sauces, Relishes, and Chutneys" at the beginning of the chapter.

2. Using a mortar and pestle, or in the bowl of a food processor, grind together the onion, peanuts, crushed red pepper, garlic, and fresh ginger root to make a paste.

3. In a large stockpot, stir together paste, white vinegar, sugar, pickling salt, and turmeric. Bring to a boil over high heat, stirring frequently to prevent scorching. Reduce heat to medium-low, cover, and simmer gently 5 minutes. Add the cauliflower, return to a boil over high heat, and simmer 5 minutes, or until the vegetables are heated through. Keep mixture hot while filling jars.

Pickled Corn Salad

This sweet-and-sour relish is one of my favorites for everything from chicken burgers to braised meats. The sunny yellow color really brightens winter meals.

Yield:	Prep time:	Process time:	Headspace:
7 pints	2 to 3 hours	15 minutes	½ inch

4 cups diced red bell peppers, stemmed and seeded (5 to 8 medium)

2 cups diced celery (6 medium ribs)

1 cup diced onion (1 to 2 medium)

1 qt. white vinegar (5%)

1⅓ cups granulated sugar

2 TB. canning or pickling salt

2 tsp. mustard seeds

2 TB. dry mustard

1 tsp. ground turmeric

8 cups fresh corn kernels (10 to 16 medium-size ears), or 5 (10-oz.) pkg. frozen corn

1. Review the section "General Procedure for Canning Savory Sauces, Relishes, and Chutneys" at the beginning of the chapter.

2. In a large stockpot, combine red bell peppers, celery, onion, white vinegar, sugar, canning salt, mustard seeds, dry mustard, and turmeric; bring to a boil over high heat. Reduce heat to medium-low and simmer 5 minutes, stirring occasionally. Add corn and simmer an additional 5 minutes. Keep mixture hot while filling jars.

PREPARING FRESH CORN

Remove husks and silk from ears of fresh corn; scrub gently with a vegetable brush to remove all fibers. Steam-blanch ears for 7 to 9 minutes. Cut whole kernels from the cob. Hint: Stand an ear on end in the center of a Bundt or other tubed cake pan and slice down the side with a chef's knife. The kernels will fall neatly into the pan. In recipes for soup or salad, you may cut raw kernels from the cob without blanching. However, for canning, blanch the corn to deactivate enzymes as quickly as possible.

Pickled Three-Bean Salad

This mild vegetable salad has a great balance. The sweet pickling solution offsets the earthy bean flavors. When green beans burst onto the scene in summer, the first thing I think is, "Oh boy, time for three-bean salad!"

Yield:	Prep time:	Process time:	Headspace:
7 pints	14 to 18 hours	15 minutes	½ inch

4 cups cut, blanched green beans

4 cups cut, blanched yellow wax beans

2 (15-oz.) cans pinto or black beans, drained and rinsed (about 3 cups)

1 cup peeled and thinly sliced onion (about 1 medium onion)

1 cup trimmed and thinly sliced celery (1½ medium ribs)

1 cup sliced red bell pepper (about 2 medium)

3 cups water

1⅓ cups white vinegar (5%)

⅔ cup bottled lemon juice

1½ cups granulated sugar

⅔ cup olive oil

1¼ tsp. salt

1. Review the section "General Procedure for Canning Savory Sauces, Relishes, and Chutneys" at the beginning of the chapter.

2. In a large bowl, gently toss together green beans, yellow wax beans, pinto beans, onion, celery, and red bell pepper.

3. In a large (8- to 10-quart) stockpot, combine water, white vinegar, lemon juice, and sugar; bring to a boil over high heat. Remove from heat, and stir in olive oil and salt until well blended. Add vegetables and bring to a boil over high heat. Remove from heat, and transfer to a large bowl. Cool, cover, and refrigerate for 12 to 14 hours.

4. Return bean salad to a stockpot over high heat and bring to a boil. Keep salad hot while filling jars.

Chutneys

Chutneys are a broad class of meal accompaniments that are a component of Indian cuisine. Think of chutney as a relish or condiment. There are generally three types of chutney: fresh vegetable, fresh herb, and preserved. Fresh chutneys are just that: chopped vegetables or herbs, perhaps mixed with salt, vinegar, or lemon juice, and accented with chopped ginger or mustard seeds. Fresh chutney is made and served within 2 hours.

Preserved chutneys are cooked. The acidity (low pH) of fruits used to make chutney—plus some added vinegar—prevents the growth of spoilage organisms when canned. Cooking chutney kills most microorganisms that may be present and lowers the moisture content that bacteria, yeasts, and molds need to be active. Canning pasteurizes the chutney and creates a vacuum seal, making it safe for storage at room temperature.

In this section, I offer two examples of preserved fruit chutneys. Underripe, acidic fruits must be used for safe canning.

Apple Chutney

Make this fruity, sweet, and sour chutney from tart apples or pears. Although these fruits are sour, the resulting relish is definitely sweet. Try it with beef or lamb stews or simple *hors d'oeuvres* of cheeses and almonds.

Yield:	Prep time:	Process time:	Headspace:
7 pints	2 to 3 hours	10 minutes	½ inch

2½ qt. chopped tart apples, peeled and cored (about 3½ lb. or 10 medium)

3 cups dried apricots (about 1 lb.)

3 cups seedless raisins (about 1 lb.)

2 TB. peeled and chopped fresh ginger

7 cloves garlic, crushed

4 cups brown sugar

2 TB. canning salt

½ tsp. cayenne, or to taste

1 qt. cider vinegar (5%)

1. Review the section "General Procedure for Canning Savory Sauces, Relishes, and Chutneys" at the beginning of the chapter.

2. In a large (8- to 10-quart) stockpot, stir together apples, dried apricots, raisins, fresh ginger, garlic, brown sugar, canning salt, cayenne, and cider vinegar; bring to a boil over medium heat. Reduce heat to medium-low and simmer 1 hour 15 minutes, or until thick. Stir occasionally during cooking. Keep mixture hot while filling jars.

Variation: For **Pear Chutney,** substitute pitted and chopped unripe (hard) pears for apples.

Mango Chutney

This tangy, hot, and sour chutney packs quite a bit of heat, which you can adjust to suit your taste. Serve it with ham, pork chops, grilled lamb, firm fish, as well as curry dishes.

Yield:	Prep time:	Process time:	Headspace:
7 pints	2 to 3 hours	10 minutes	½ inch

2½ cups brown sugar

5 cups white distilled vinegar (5%)

4 qt. coarsely chopped, unripe (hard) mangos (about 12 lb. or 12 medium)

1 cup finely chopped onion (about 2 medium)

2 TB. ground ginger

1 cup raisins

2 TB. ground coriander

2 tsp. canning salt

2 tsp. cayenne or chili powder

2 tsp. ground cumin

1 tsp. ground cloves

1 tsp. ground nutmeg

1. Review the section "General Procedure for Canning Savory Sauces, Relishes, and Chutneys" at the beginning of the chapter.

2. In a large (8- to 10-quart) stockpot, stir together brown sugar and white distilled vinegar, and bring to a boil over high heat. Reduce heat to medium-low and simmer 5 minutes, or until sugar is dissolved. Add mangos, ginger, raisins, coriander, canning salt, cayenne, cumin, cloves, and nutmeg, and return to a boil. Reduce heat to medium-low and simmer 25 minutes, stirring occasionally. Keep mixture hot while filling jars.

HANDLING GREEN MANGO

Green mango is irritating to the skin of some people. To avoid a reaction, be sure to wear latex or rubber gloves while handling or cutting unripe mango. If you do not wear gloves, wash hands thoroughly with soap and water and do not touch your face or eyes for at least 3 days to avoid irritation.

Canned Jam and Other Sweet Sauces

19

When you cook crushed fruit or fruit juice with sugar, the naturally present pectin will thicken to make jam (if using crushed fruit) or jelly (if using fruit juice). However, this can only happen when there is the right balance of fruit, pectin, acid, and sugar. (For more about fruit pectins, see Chapter 7.) You can guarantee that this thickening happens by adding commercial pectin. Jam with added pectin has a reliable flavor and texture, fresh fruit flavor, and tends to be sweeter than old-fashioned jam made without commercial pectin.

If you are new to jam making, you may want to begin with a recipe that adds commercial pectin. Or just dive in and make jam the old-fashioned way, with no added pectin. Oh, you can make your own pectin, too, from apples or oranges. See the recipe for homemade apple pectin later in this chapter.

General Procedure for Canning Jam and Other Sweet Sauces

For more details on the steps to prepare, process, and store canned foods, see Chapter 7. Use the following general procedure for all of the recipes in this chapter:

1. Prepare boiling water–bath canner, jars, and lids. Before proceeding, review your recipe; preparing the canner and jars is usually the first step, unless the recipe preparation is very lengthy.

2. Prepare jam or other sweet sauce as directed in each recipe.

3. Fill hot jars by the hot pack method as allowed in the recipe. Use the following general packing instructions, unless recipe directs otherwise.

   - Hot pack: Ladle hot product into hot jars, adjusting headspace as directed in recipe.

- Do not use raw pack for jams or jellies. All jam is filled into jars using hot pack only.

4. Clean the rim and secure the lid. Use process time as directed in recipe. Properly cool and store the jars up to 1 year for best flavor.

You should use only the packing methods, jar sizes, headspace, and processing times specified in the recipe. These requirements are not interchangeable from one recipe to another.

Guidelines for Adjusting Canned Jam Recipes

Jams using commercially made pectin need to be made one batch at a time using the package instructions for the type of pectin you are using. Doubling or adjusting these recipes usually results in a jam that fails to gel, overly stiff gel, or other problems such as weeping.

Old-fashioned jams with or without homemade pectin offer more flexibility. However, large quantities (more than 7 pints) can take a long time to cook and run the risk of burning before the jellying stage is reached. Practice with smaller quantities until you become an expert with the jam-making process before attempting larger batch sizes.

Old-Fashioned Cooked Spreads

The nice thing about cooked jam is you can use any type of fruit and cook it to your preferred consistency—runny, thin, or thick. You can combine low-pectin fruit with high-pectin fruit to get thicker jam. You can add acid to low-acid fruit to help it gel. Or you can make your own pectin and add some of that. Don't be afraid to experiment. The worst-case scenario is you end up with sauce instead of jam—which would do very nicely on a stack of pancakes.

The thickness of a jam or jelly is ultimately a matter of personal preference. Longer cooking tends to increase the caramel (some may say burnt) flavor that you may or may not prefer.

There are three methods for testing cooked jams and jellies to find out if they have cooked to the desired thickness. Use these tests for any jam or jelly made from the recipes in this chapter:

- **Temperature test:** A candy or instant thermometer reads 218°F to 222°F (above 1,000 feet elevation, subtract 2°F for every 1,000-foot increase). Lower temperatures create soft and runny jams and jellies; higher temperatures create firm and stiff ones.

- **Spoon or sheet test:** Dip a cold metal spoon into boiling jam or jelly mixture. Hold the spoon horizontally, so mixture runs off side of the bowl. In the early stages of cooking, liquid will easily drip from the spoon. As mixture continues to boil, liquid will thicken and fall off a couple drips at a time. When mixture falls off the spoon in a sheet instead of drips, it has reached the jellying stage.

- **Freezer test:** Chill a plate in the freezer for at least 15 minutes. Spoon a small amount of boiling jam or jelly onto the plate and put it back in the freezer for at least 1 to 2 minutes. Check consistency of cold jam or jelly for desired thickness.

Be sure to remove jam or jelly mixture from the heat during testing, so it doesn't overcook while you test the thickness.

Jam and Preserves

The following recipes represent the most popular jams made in homes today. Be sure to use a mix of mature and fully ripe fruit. Riper fruits contain less pectin that will prevent a strong gel from forming, resulting in a thin jam or fruit sauce. It is a good general practice to always use ¼ underripe fruit when making jam.

You can also combine high- and low-pectin fruits to make thicker jams. Some combinations to consider are rhubarb and currant, raspberry and blackberry, blueberry and cranberry, and tart apples with any other fruit.

Strawberry Jam

Sweetly simple and lush, strawberry jam is everyone's favorite. This succulent spread is great on toast, as a filling for cookies, and in a peanut butter and jelly sandwich.

Yield:	Prep time:	Process time:	Headspace:
1 half-pint to 7 pints	60 minutes	10 minutes	¼ inch

Strawberry Jam

1 Half-Pint	7 Half-Pints	7 Pints	Ingredient
1 cup (1 dry pt. whole strawberries)	7 cups (3½ qt. whole strawberries)	3½ qt. (7 qt. whole strawberries)	Crushed strawberries
¾ cup	5 cups	2½ qt.	Granulated sugar

1. Review the section "General Procedure for Canning Jam and Other Sweet Sauces" at the beginning of the chapter.

2. In a large (4- to 6-quart), heavy stainless-steel or enamel saucepan, stir strawberries and sugar until well blended. Bring to a boil over medium heat, stirring constantly until sugar dissolves.

3. Continue to boil, adjusting heat as needed to prevent boiling over, and stirring frequently to prevent sticking. Cook until thickened to desired consistency. Keep jam hot while filling jars.

Variation: For **Strawberry-Rhubarb Jam,** substitute diced rhubarb for half of strawberries. Sprinkle with half of sugar, cover, and let stand overnight in a cool location. (You can skip this step, but it tends to give better rhubarb texture.) Combine sugared rhubarb with remaining sugar and strawberries and proceed with step 1.

Raspberry Jam

Slightly tart, the bright, fresh flavor of this berry delight is a vibrant topping for buttery biscuits and creamy cheesecake.

Yield:	Prep time:	Process time:	Headspace:
1 half-pint to 7 pints	60 minutes	10 minutes	¼ inch

Raspberry Jam

1 Half-Pint	7 Half-Pints	7 Pints	Ingredient
1½ cups (3 cups whole raspberries)	10 cups (5 qt. whole raspberries)	5 qt. (10 qt. whole raspberries)	Crushed raspberries
1 cup	7 cups	3½ qt.	Granulated sugar

1. Review the section "General Procedure for Canning Jam and Other Sweet Sauces" at the beginning of the chapter.

2. In a large (4- to 6-quart), heavy stainless-steel or enamel saucepan, stir raspberries and sugar until well blended. Bring to a boil over medium heat, stirring constantly until sugar dissolves. Continue to boil, adjusting heat as needed to prevent boiling over, and stir frequently to prevent sticking. Cook until thickened to desired consistency. Keep jam hot while filling jars.

Variation: For **Seedless Berry Jam,** remove seeds from over 10 cups soft berries to make 10 cups (see the following sidebar). Proceed with recipe. Soft berries include blackberries, chokecherries, loganberries, marionberries, mulberries, raspberries, salmonberries, tayberries, and thimbleberries.

REMOVING SEEDS FROM BERRIES

To remove seeds from raspberries, blackberries, and other berries before making jams, place berries in a saucepan and crush lightly using a potato masher or the back of a large spoon. Place the pan over medium heat until berries soften. If needed, add a small amount of water (2 tablespoons) to prevent sticking. Press hot berries through a sieve or food mill. Some cooks like to add a small amount of seeds back into the strained purée for a little textural interest in their jam.

Plum Jam

Depending on the variety of plum used, this jam can range from deep, winelike, and perfumed to fresh, light, and gingery. Less cloying than berry jams, this jam works as a condiment for chicken and pork, as well as a sweet spread for breads.

Yield:	Prep time:	Process time:	Headspace:
1 half-pint to 7 pints	90 minutes	10 minutes	¼ inch

Plum Jam

1 Half-Pint	7 Half-Pints	7 Pints	Ingredient
1 scant cup (3 medium)	6 cups (18 medium)	3 qt. (36 medium)	Coarsely chopped, pitted plums
½ cup	3½ cups	7 cups	Granulated sugar
2 TB.	¾ cup	1¾ cups	Water

1. Review the section "General Procedure for Canning Jam and Other Sweet Sauces" at the beginning of the chapter.

2. In a large (4- to 6-quart), heavy stainless-steel or enamel saucepan, stir plums, sugar, and water until well blended. Bring to a boil over medium heat, stirring constantly until sugar dissolves.

3. Continue to boil, adjusting heat as needed to prevent boiling over, and stirring frequently to prevent sticking. Cook until thickened to desired consistency. Keep jam hot while filling jars.

Apricot Preserves

Candied, thick, and satisfying, how sugary you want this spread depends on the variety of apricot selected—which can be as sweet as honey or slightly sharp. I like deep, rich-flavored apricots for a spread that pairs well with cream cheese.

Yield:	Prep time:	Process time:	Headspace:
1 half-pint to 7 pints	90 minutes	10 minutes	¼ inch

Apricot Preserves

1 Half-Pint	7 Half-Pints	7 Pints	Ingredient
1 scant cup (4 to 6 medium)	6 cups (3 lb.)	3 qt. (6 lb.)	Blanched, peeled, pitted, and crushed apricots
1¼ tsp.	3 TB.	6 TB.	Bottled lemon juice
⅔ cup	4¾ cups	9½ cups	Granulated sugar

1. Review the section "General Procedure for Canning Jam and Other Sweet Sauces" at the beginning of the chapter.

2. In a large (4- to 6-quart), heavy stainless-steel or enamel saucepan, stir apricots, lemon juice, and sugar until well blended. Bring to a boil over medium heat, stirring constantly until sugar dissolves.

3. Continue to boil, adjusting heat as needed to prevent boiling over, and stirring frequently to prevent sticking. Cook until thickened to desired consistency. Keep jam hot while filling jars.

Variation: For **Peach or Nectarine Jam,** substitute chopped peaches or nectarines for apricots.

Fig Jam

Like plums, figs also create a spread that works with sweet as well as savory foods, from cookies or pastries to cheeses, ham, or roast pork crusted with rosemary and garlic.

Yield:	Prep time:	Process time:	Headspace:
1 half-pint to 7 pints	90 minutes	10 minutes	¼ inch

Fig Jam

1 Half-Pint	7 Half-Pints	7 Pints	Ingredient
1 scant cup (4 medium)	5½ cups (22 medium, 2½ lb.)	11 cups (4½ lb.)	Chopped, fresh figs
1 TB.	½ cup	1⅛ cups	Water

1 Half-Pint	7 Half-Pints	7 Pints	Ingredient
⅔ cup	4¼ cups	8½ cups	Granulated sugar
1¼ tsp.	3 TB.	6 TB.	Bottled lemon juice

1. Review the section "General Procedure for Canning Jam and Other Sweet Sauces" at the beginning of the chapter.

2. In a large (4- to 6-quart), heavy stainless-steel or enamel saucepan, stir figs, water, and sugar until well blended. Bring to a boil over medium heat, stirring constantly until sugar dissolves.

3. Continue to boil, adjusting heat as needed to prevent boiling over, and stirring frequently to prevent sticking. Cook until thickened to desired consistency. Add lemon juice and cook 1 minute longer. Keep jam hot while filling jars.

Low-Sugar Pineapple Jam

Like sunshine in a jar, this refreshing and chunky jam is packed with undeniable pineapple flavor. Use this bold and tasteful treat to brighten your breakfast bread or afternoon tea.

Yield:	Prep time:	Process time:	Headspace:
1 half-pint to 7 pints	90 minutes	10 minutes	¼ inch

Pineapple Jam

1 Half-Pint	7 Half-Pints	7 Pints	Ingredient
1⅓ cups (½ medium)	9 cups (2 medium)	4½ qt. (4 medium)	Peeled, cored, puréed fresh pineapple
3½ TB.	1½ cups	3 cups	Granulated sugar
2 tsp.	¼ cup	¼ cup	Water, or as needed
1½ tsp.	3½ TB.	7 TB.	Fresh lime juice
1 tsp.	2 TB.	¼ cup	Bottled lemon juice
¼ tsp.	1¾ tsp.	3½ TB.	Grated fresh lime peel

1. Review the section "General Procedure for Canning Jam and Other Sweet Sauces" at the beginning of the chapter.

2. In a heavy stainless-steel or enamel saucepan, stir pineapple purée, sugar, water, lime juice, lemon juice, and lime peel until well blended. Bring to a boil over medium heat, stirring constantly until sugar dissolves. If mixture sticks to pans, add more water as needed.

3. Continue to boil, adjusting heat as needed to prevent boiling over, and stirring frequently to prevent sticking. Cook until thickened to desired consistency. Keep jam hot while filling jars.

Tomato Jam

Essentially a sweetened, spiced tomato paste flavored with ginger for a slightly Asian flair, this unique jam adds richness to savory pancakes, burgers, and salad dressings.

Yield:	Prep time:	Process time:	Headspace:
1 to 7 half-pints	90 minutes	45 minutes	¼ inch

Tomato Jam

1 Half-Pint	7 Half-Pints	Ingredient
1½ cups (3 medium, 1 lb. fresh tomatoes)	2½ qt. (6 to 7 lb.)	Fresh tomato purée
1½ tsp.	3½ TB.	Peeled, grated, fresh ginger
¼ tsp.	1¾ tsp.	Ground cinnamon
⅛ tsp.	1 scant tsp.	Ground cloves
1½ TB.	⅔ cup	Bottled lemon juice
1 TB.	7 TB.	Cider vinegar
½ cup	3½ cups	Lightly packed brown sugar

1. Review the section "General Procedure for Canning Jam and Other Sweet Sauces" at the beginning of the chapter.

2. In a large (4- to 6-quart), heavy stainless-steel or enamel saucepan, stir tomato purée, fresh ginger, cinnamon, cloves, lemon juice, cider vinegar, and brown sugar until well blended. Bring to a boil over medium heat, stirring constantly until sugar dissolves.

3. Reduce heat to medium-low and continue to cook, stirring occasionally, for about 1 hour, or until thickened to desired consistency. Keep jam hot while filling jars.

Jellies

Jelly is the jewel of canned fruits. You start with fresh fruit, extract clear juice, and turn the juice into a softly gelled spread. The first step in making jelly is to make fruit juice. When you want to make a juice that will gel easily, be sure to use ¼ underripe fruit. The rest of the fruit needs to be fully ripe and full of flavor. (See Chapter 15 for more about making fruit juices.)

Grape Jelly

Plummy, fresh, and sweet, this is the classic PB&J spread.

Yield:	Prep time:	Process time:	Headspace:
1 or 4 half-pints	90 minutes	10 minutes	¼ inch

Grape Jelly

1 Half-Pint	4 Half-Pints	Ingredient
1 cup	4 cups	Homemade, filtered grape juice, or commercially bottled grape juice
¾ cup	3 cups	Granulated sugar
½ tsp.	2 tsp.	Strained fresh lemon juice (optional)

1. Review the section "General Procedure for Canning Jam and Other Sweet Sauces" at the beginning of the chapter.

2. In a large stainless-steel or enamel pot, stir grape juice, sugar, and lemon juice (if using) until well blended. Bring to a boil over high heat, stirring constantly, until sugar dissolves.

3. Continue to boil, adjusting heat as needed to prevent boiling over, and stirring frequently to prevent sticking. Cook until juice reaches the desired consistency. Remove from heat and skim off foam. Keep jelly hot while filling jars.

Variations: For **Apple Jelly,** substitute filtered apple juice for grape juice and be sure to include lemon juice. For **Blackberry Jelly,** substitute filtered blackberry juice for grape juice; lemon juice is optional.

OLD-FASHIONED JELLY FLAVORS

Apple, sour cherry, crabapple, cranberry, gooseberry, and some grape and plum varieties are the traditional juices used for old-fashioned jelly, made without pectin. For other fruits, you may want to add pectin for easy, foolproof jelly. Each type of juice lends its fruity goodness to the spread. The clearest juice makes the most impressive jelly. When perfectly made, it is a shimmering jewel and a burst of pure, sweet ambrosia.

Fruit Butters

Fruit butters contain less sugar than traditional jams and have most of the moisture cooked out, making them very thick and naturally sweet.

Low-Sugar Apple Butter

When cooked until thick, apples reveal earthy, plumlike flavors that are heightened with warm spices to make apple butter. Tart apple varieties tend to produce lighter, fresh-tasting butter, while sweet apples create a more cloying spread.

Yield:	Prep time:	Process time:	Headspace:
1 half-pint to 7 pints	120 minutes	10 minutes	¼ inch

Apple Butter

1 Half-Pint	7 Half-Pints	7 Pints	Ingredient
¾ lb. (2 medium)	5¼ lb. (16 medium)	10½ lb. (32 medium)	Apples, peeled, quartered, and cored
¼ cup	1¾ cups	3½ cups	Apple cider
⅓ cup	2½ cups	5 cups	Granulated sugar
⅛ tsp.	1¼ tsp.	2½ tsp.	Ground cinnamon
Pinch	½ tsp.	1 tsp.	Ground cloves

1. Review the section "General Procedure for Canning Jam and Other Sweet Sauces" at the beginning of the chapter.

2. In a large (6- to 8-quart), heavy stainless-steel or enamel pot, add apples and apple cider. Bring to a boil over medium heat. Continue to cook until fruit is soft. Press fruit through a food mill or strainer, or purée in a food processor. Rinse the pot and return fruit pulp to it. Add sugar, cinnamon, and cloves to fruit pulp and stir until blended. Bring to a boil over medium-high heat, stirring frequently. Reduce heat to medium and continue to boil gently, adjusting heat as needed. Cook until thick, stirring frequently to prevent sticking. Apple butter is done when it mounds on a spoon, or a spoonful on a plate does not weep clear liquid around the edge. Keep butter hot while filling jars.

Variation: For **Low-Sugar Pear Butter,** substitute pears for apples.

Plum-Ginger Butter

Plum butter has similar flavors to apple butter, earthy and comforting. Peach butters and pear butters (see Variations) tend to produce fruity, less complex, honeylike flavors.

Yield:	Prep time:	Process time:	Headspace:
1 half-pint to 7 pints	120 minutes	10 minutes	¼ inch

Plum-Ginger Butter

1 Half-Pint	7 Half-Pints	7 Pints	Ingredient
¾ lb. (4 or 5 medium)	5 lb. (30 medium)	10 lb. (60 medium)	Plums, pitted and quartered
¼ cup	2 cups	4 cups	Apple cider
¾ tsp.	2 TB.	¼ cup	Peeled, grated fresh ginger
⅓ cup	2½ cups	5 cups	Lightly packed brown sugar
⅛ tsp.	1 tsp.	1¾ tsp.	Ground cinnamon

1. Review the section "General Procedure for Canning Jam and Other Sweet Sauces" at the beginning of the chapter.

2. In a large (6- to 8-quart), heavy stainless-steel or enamel pot, add plums, apple cider, and fresh ginger. Bring to a boil over medium heat, stirring constantly. Continue to cook until fruit is soft. Press fruit through a food mill or strainer. Rinse the pot and return fruit pulp to it. Add brown sugar and cinnamon to fruit pulp and stir until blended. Bring to a boil over medium-high heat, stirring frequently. Continue to boil gently, adjusting heat as needed. Cook until thick, stirring frequently to prevent sticking. Butter is done when it mounds on a spoon, or a spoonful on a plate does not weep clear liquid around the edge. Keep butter hot while filling jars.

Variations: For **Peach-Spice Butter,** substitute blanched, peeled, pitted, and chopped peaches for plums. Omit apple cider, ginger, and cinnamon and add ¼ cup fresh orange juice and ⅛ teaspoon pumpkin pie spice. For **Pear-Wine Butter,**

substitute peeled, cored, and chopped pears for plums. Treat for browning. Omit apple cider, ginger, brown sugar, and cinnamon and add ¼ cup white wine, ½ cup granulated sugar, and ⅛ teaspoon ground cardamom.

Citrus Marmalades

Marmalade—a suspension of fruit in clear jelly—is something of a lost art. Today, marmalades are essentially citrus peel preserves. Citrus pith—the spongy white material between the peel and the fruit—contains high amounts of pectin. When cooked in sugar syrup, the peels become translucent. The pectin gels the liquid, and suspends the peels in glittering jelly.

Originally, marmalades were thick jams made from quince. Quince is in the same botanical family as apples and pears. In fact, they look like small, yellow-green, slightly misshapen pears. You can't eat them raw; the flesh is hard, gritty, and sour. However, when cooked, the flesh turns pink and sweet. (Actually, quince grown in tropical climates become soft and juicy when ripe, suitable for eating out of hand.)

The word marmalade comes from the Portuguese word for quince, *marmelo*. Greeks, Romans, Arabs, and especially the Portuguese made *marmelada* (a thick, sweet paste, similar to fruit leather today). The paste was poured into special molds and sent on Portuguese merchant ships. Find a recipe for quince paste in Chapter 10.

Mixed Citrus Marmalade

With clean, fresh flavor and beautiful color, citrus marmalade pairs nicely with roasted meats, as well as spread on toast.

Yield:	Prep time:	Process time:	Headspace:
3 or 7 half-pints	1 day	10 minutes	¼ inch

Mixed Citrus Marmalade

3 Half-Pints	7 Half-Pints	Ingredient
1 large	4 or 5 medium	Oranges or tangerines, cut in paper-thin slices and seeds discarded

3 Half-Pints	7 Half-Pints	Ingredient
1 small	1 medium	Lemon, cut in paper-thin slices and seeds discarded
1 small	1 medium	Lime, cut in paper-thin slices and seeds discarded
3 cups	2 qt.	Water
3 cups	7 cups	Granulated sugar, or as needed in step 3
1½ tsp.	3 TB.	Orange liqueur (optional)

1. Review the section "General Procedure for Canning Jam and Other Sweet Sauces" at the beginning of the chapter.

2. In a large (8- to 10-quart), heavy stainless-steel or enamel pot, add orange slices, lemon slices, lime slices, and water, and bring to a boil over high heat. Reduce heat, and boil gently about 1 hour, or until peels are tender and liquid is reduced by half. (Alternatively, boil mixture for 5 minutes, remove from heat, cover, and let stand in a cool location for 12 to 18 hours.)

3. Measure cooked fruit. Measure 1 cup sugar for each cup cooked fruit. Return cooked fruit to a boil over high heat. Add sugar slowly, maintaining a boil while stirring constantly. Raise heat to high and boil mixture rapidly until it reaches the jelly stage. Add orange liqueur (if using) and boil 2 more minutes. Remove from heat and skim foam. Keep marmalade hot while filling jars.

PERFECT PRESERVING

To achieve the best results with marmalade, make small batches. Cook fruit until tender before adding sugar. Boil the mixture rapidly to bring as quickly as possible to the jelly stage.

Rhubarb Marmalade

An uncommon marmalade, this rich-and-spicy spread tames mouth-puckering rhubarb with sugar. Red wine or grape juice further softens the flavor.

Yield:	Prep time:	Process time:	Headspace:
3 or 7 half-pints	1 day	10 minutes	¼ inch

Rhubarb Marmalade

3 Half-Pints	7 Half-Pints	Ingredient
1¾ lb. (10 or 11 medium stalks)	4 lb. (24 medium stalks)	Chopped rhubarb
1 small	1 medium	Orange, thinly sliced, seeds discarded
1 small	1 each	Lemon, thinly sliced, seeds discarded
3 cups	7 cups	Granulated sugar, or as needed
1½ tsp.	3 TB.	Red wine or grape juice

1. Review the section "General Procedure for Canning Jam and Other Sweet Sauces" at the beginning of the chapter.

2. In a large (8- to 10-quart), heavy stainless-steel or enamel pot, combine rhubarb, orange slices, lemon slices, and sugar; let stand for 30 minutes.

3. Add red wine and bring to a boil over medium heat. Adjust heat to maintain a gentle boil, and cook, stirring occasionally, about 1 hour, or until marmalade is thick. Keep marmalade hot while filling jars.

Conserves with Nuts

Traditionally, conserves always contained more than one kind of fruit, some citrus, and often nuts or raisins. Here are two delicious examples that are relevant today.

Cranberry-Orange Walnut Conserve

This tart, thick conserve has a traditional holiday flavor accented by nuts. Make it for Thanksgiving, to accompany any roast meat, or to top a slice of pound cake with whipped cream.

Yield:	Prep time:	Process time:	Headspace:
1 half-pint to 7 pints	60 minutes	15 minutes	¼ inch

Cranberry-Orange Walnut Conserve

1 Half-Pint	7 Half-Pints	7 Pints	Ingredient
¼ small	2 small	3 large	Unpeeled, finely chopped oranges; seeds discarded
¼ cup	1¾ cup	3½ cups	Water
1 cup	7 cups	14 cups	Cranberries, washed
2 TB.	1 scant cup	1¾ cups	Seedless raisins
¾ cup	5 cups	10 cups	Granulated sugar
2 TB.	1 scant cup	1¾ cups	Chopped, roasted walnuts

1. Review the section "General Procedure for Canning Jam and Other Sweet Sauces" at the beginning of the chapter.

2. In a large (6- to 8-quart), heavy stainless-steel or enamel pot, combine oranges and water, and bring to a boil over high heat. Reduce heat to maintain a gentle boil, and cook 5 minutes, or until orange peels are tender.

3. Raise heat to high. Stir in cranberries, raisins, and sugar, and bring to a boil, stirring frequently. Maintain a full rolling boil, stirring frequently, for 10 to 15 minutes, or until mixture thickens. Reduce heat to medium-low and stir in walnuts; cook gently for 5 minutes. Skim foam, if needed. Keep conserve hot while filling jars.

Plum-Almond Conserve

Toasted nuts superbly accent the rich flavors in this silky fruit jam. Use it as you would fig jam, in pastries and cookies, or served with cheeses and richly flavored meats such as ham, herb-roasted chicken, and game.

Yield:	Prep time:	Process time:	Headspace:
1 half-pint to 7 pints	60 minutes	10 minutes	¼ inch

Plum-Almond Conserve

1 Half-Pint	7 Half-Pints	7 Pints	Ingredient
1¼ cups (3 medium)	2¼ qt. (25 medium, 4¼ lb.)	4½ qt. (50 medium, 8½ lb.)	Pitted, chopped plums
¾ cup	5 cups	10 cups	Granulated sugar
¼ cup	1¾ cups	3½ cups	Seedless raisins
¼ teaspoon (about ⅛ medium lemon)	1 tablespoon (about 1 medium lemon)	2 tablespoons (about 2 medium lemons)	Lemon zest
2 tsp.	¼ cup	½ cup	Bottled lemon juice
¼ cup	1¾ cups	3½ cups	Toasted, slivered almonds

1. Review the section "General Procedure for Canning Jam and Other Sweet Sauces" at the beginning of the chapter.

2. In a large (6- to 8-quart), heavy stainless-steel or enamel pot, combine plums, sugar, raisins, lemon zest, and lemon juice; bring to a boil over medium heat. Reduce heat to maintain a gentle boil, and cook 30 minutes, or until mixture thickens. Add almonds during last 5 minutes of cooking. Keep conserve hot while filling jars.

Homemade Pectin

The easy, modern method for making jam and jelly simply adds commercially manufactured pectin. Commercial pectin reliably produces thick jams and jellies without any guesswork and captures the fresh flavor of ripe fruits. However, commercial pectin requires rather high levels of sugar. Using commercial pectin is detailed in the next section.

Another solution is to make homemade pectin and add it to any fruit when you want to make jam. Making and using homemade pectin takes practice, but can be fun and very rewarding. For more information about the pectin content of fruit, see Chapter 7.

Homemade Apple Pectin

This simple process produces homemade pectin. Add it to any low-pectin fruit or juice to achieve a thicker jam or jelly.

Yield:	Prep time:	Process time:	Headspace:
3 to 6 half-pints	90 minutes	10 minutes	¼ inch

Homemade Apple Pectin

3 Half-Pints	6 Half-Pints	Ingredient
2 lb. (6 to 8 medium)	4 lb. (12 to 16 medium)	Underripe apples, washed and cut into 1-in. pieces (do not peel or core)
2 cup	4 cups	Water
2 TB.	¼ cup	Fresh lemon juice

1. Review the section "General Procedure for Canning Jam and Other Sweet Sauces" at the beginning of the chapter.

2. In a large saucepan, add apples, water, and lemon juice. Cover and let stand 1 hour. Bring to a boil over high heat. Reduce heat to medium-low and simmer the mixture for 20 minutes, or until apples are tender. Pour into a jelly bag or a strainer lined with cheesecloth. (A jelly bag is composed of mesh material and is sold with a stand that holds the bag over a bowl while the fruit mixture drains.)

Allow to drain overnight. For best results, do not press on solids to extract more juice. Return juice to the saucepan and boil over medium-high heat until reduced by ½, or until liquid tests for adequate pectin content.

3. Use hot pack method to can homemade pectin, or refrigerate or freeze the pectin:

   • To refrigerate, transfer pectin to a covered container. Refrigerate and use within 3 days.

   • To freeze, pour cooled pectin into freezer-safe containers, leaving ½ inch headspace. Freeze up to 6 months.

4. Taste homemade pectin before using to make jam or jelly. Homemade apple pectin should taste like fresh apples.

Variation: For **Homemade Citrus Pectin,** substitute orange peels (especially the white pith), chopped fine, as well as pits, for apples. Bitter citrus may produce pectin with bitter flavors.

PERFECT PRESERVING

There are no hard-and-fast rules for making jam with homemade pectin. Start with a formula of 1 cup chopped low-pectin fruit, 4 to 6 tablespoons pectin, 1½ teaspoons fresh lemon juice, and 1¼ to 2 cups sugar. For example: 2 cups crushed strawberries, ½ cup pectin, 1 tablespoon lemon juice, and 2½ cups sugar. Bring the fruit, pectin, and lemon juice to a boil before adding sugar. Boil hard to the desired consistency. If it won't gel, add pectin, sugar, or acid. If you didn't test your homemade pectin, you may need to use as much as 1:1 with the fruit. Note that high-pectin fruits (such as blackberries) may not need any pectin at all; they have enough already.

Sweet Spreads with Commercial Pectin

Newer techniques for freezer, microwave, and low-sugar jams add easy-to-use commercially made pectin. Adding pectin allows you to make thick jam quickly and consistently.

When you use pectin, there is no need to learn jelling techniques or stir fruit over a hot stove. The flavor of added-pectin jams tends to be more like fresh fruit, without any caramel-like flavors sometimes present in long-cooked, traditional jams. However, these jams contain more sugar than traditional versions made without added pectin.

The recipes in this section cover the methods for using different varieties of pectin.

PERFECT PRESERVING

Manufacturers of pectin now offer packages of pectin in various sizes. Some are suitable for making small batches of jam. Others are packaged in bulk to make any size recipe, small or large. Look for these products where canning supplies are sold. Small-batch jam is great for trying new fruit combinations, experimenting with low-sugar jam, or making small amounts of jam that you don't plan to process for canning.

Cooked Jam and Jelly with Pectin

Commercial fruit pectin comes in two forms: powdered or liquid. Each form also has several types. For example, there is pectin for making low-sugar and sugar-free jams. Be sure to purchase the type you want, and follow the instructions that come with that pectin.

Either type of pectin—powdered or liquid—makes great jam easily. Liquid pectin is easier to combine, although powdered pectin dissolves readily. It may simply depend on which type is available where you buy canning supplies. If you are used to one type of pectin over the other, be aware that the steps for using each one is slightly different. Powdered pectin is heated to dissolve it completely before adding sugar; liquid pectin is added after the sugar. Butter or margarine, if you are using it in cooked jam, is always added with the first step (with powdered pectin, or with sugar for liquid pectin). This little bit of fat helps to reduce foaming when cooking fruits and sugar.

SPOILER ALERT

You cannot substitute one form of pectin for the other. Failure to follow the directions or measure fruit and sugar exactly usually results in runny sauce, instead of thick and luscious spread.

Pectin helps you make jam quickly and easily. However, there are important steps not to overlook to ensure a successful process and perfectly gelled jam. Be sure to measure crushed fruit and sugar accurately, use a large pot as volume increases greatly while boiling, stir in pectin and sugar quickly, and begin timing only when the mixture is at a full boil (one that continues to bubble rapidly even while you stir constantly). A small amount of butter or margarine helps to reduce foaming; this addition is optional. Also, you cannot double the recipe or the product will likely not gel. If you want to make more product, make the recipe multiple times.

Mixed-Berry Jam (with Powdered Pectin)

Mixed-berry jam is packed with fruity, plummy flavor. It's one of the easiest and quickest jams you can make.

Yield:	Prep time:	Process time:	Headspace:
8 half-pints	60 minutes	10 minutes	¼ inch

7 cups granulated sugar

5 cups washed and crushed berries (about 6 pt. any combination of strawberries, raspberries, blackberries, blueberries, or other berries)

1 (1.75-oz.) box powdered pectin

½ tsp. butter or margarine (optional)

1. Review the section "General Procedure for Canning Jam and Other Sweet Sauces" at the beginning of the chapter.

2. Measure sugar and have it ready before beginning to make jam. Remove seeds, if desired, before measuring berries (see the earlier sidebar "Removing Seeds from Berries"). In a large (6- to 8-quart), heavy stainless-steel or enamel saucepan, add berries, sprinkle evenly with powdered pectin, add butter (if using), and stir until well blended. Place over high heat and stir constantly while it comes to a full, rolling boil and pectin dissolves completely.

3. While mixture is boiling, pour in sugar. Continue to stir constantly, and return mixture to a full, rolling boil. Boil hard for 1 minute, adjusting heat as needed to prevent boiling over, and stirring constantly to prevent sticking. Remove from heat and skim off any foam. Keep jam hot while filling jars.

Variation: For **Strawberry Jam (with Powdered Pectin),** use 5 cups crushed strawberries.

Apricot-Pineapple Jam (with Powdered Pectin)

This jam looks and tastes like sunshine and has perfect spreading consistency. Beautifully golden, it has a harmonious blend of sweetness and tang.

Yield:	Prep time:	Process time:	Headspace:
8 to 10 half-pints	90 minutes	10 minutes	¼ inch

8 cups granulated sugar

3 cups unpeeled, pitted, and ground or chopped apricots (about 2½ lb.)

2½ cups peeled, cored, and finely chopped pineapple (about 1 medium)

½ cup fresh lemon juice

1 (1.75-oz.) box powdered pectin

½ tsp. butter or margarine (optional)

1. Review the section "General Procedure for Canning Jam and Other Sweet Sauces" at the beginning of the chapter.

2. Measure sugar and have it ready before beginning to make jam.

3. In a large (6- to 8-quart), heavy stainless-steel or enamel saucepan, stir apricots, pineapple, and lemon juice. Sprinkle evenly with powdered pectin, add butter (if using), and stir until well blended. Place over high heat and stir constantly while it comes to a full, rolling boil and pectin dissolves completely.

4. While mixture is boiling, pour in sugar. Continue to stir constantly, and return mixture to a full, rolling boil. Boil hard for 4 minutes, adjusting heat as needed to prevent boiling over, and stirring constantly to prevent sticking. Remove from heat and skim off any foam. Keep jam hot while filling jars.

PERFECT PRESERVING

Most pectin recipes make 8 to 10 half-pints, which can be stacked in a 7-jar canner in order to process all the jars at once. Just be sure there is 1 to 2 inches of boiling water above the stacked jars. Half-pint jars come in tall/narrow and wide/short versions. You may want to buy short versions in order to use the stacking method most effectively.

Blackberry Jam (with Liquid Pectin)

Prized for rich, full, old-fashioned berry flavor like Grandma used to make, wild blackberry jam is a favorite of many families. Seed the berries for a smooth texture.

Yield:	Prep time:	Process time:	Headspace:
8 half-pints	60 minutes	10 minutes	¼ inch

4 cups washed and crushed blackberries (about 6 pt., if seeded)

7 cups granulated sugar

½ tsp. butter or margarine (optional)

1 (3-oz.) pouch liquid pectin

1. Review the section "General Procedure for Canning Jam and Other Sweet Sauces" at the beginning of the chapter.

2. Remove seeds, if desired, before measuring blackberries (see the earlier sidebar "Removing Seeds from Berries").

3. In a large (6- to 8-quart), heavy stainless-steel or enamel saucepan, add blackberries, sprinkle evenly with sugar, add butter (if using), and stir until well blended. Place over high heat and stir constantly while it comes to a full, rolling boil and sugar dissolves completely.

4. Stir in liquid pectin and return mixture to a full, rolling boil. Boil hard for 1 minute, adjusting heat as needed to prevent boiling over, and stirring constantly to prevent sticking. Remove from heat and skim off any foam. Keep jam hot while filling jars.

Variation: For **Strawberry Jam (with Liquid Pectin),** use 4 cups crushed strawberries (about 4 pints).

Tomato Jam (with Liquid Pectin)

Homemade tomato jam is a sweet and mildly spiced sauce that you can use as a condiment like ketchup, add to salad dressings, or to brush on for flavorful roasted or grilled meats. Tweak your creation with a customized blend of seasonings.

Yield:	Prep time:	Process time:	Headspace:
7 half-pints	60 minutes	10 minutes	¼ inch

> 3 cups fresh tomato purée (about 4 lb. or 12 medium)
>
> 1½ tsp. freshly grated lemon peel
>
> ¼ cup fresh lemon juice
>
> 6½ cups granulated sugar
>
> ½ tsp. butter or margarine (optional)
>
> 2 (3-oz.) pouches liquid pectin

1. Review the section "General Procedure for Canning Jam and Other Sweet Sauces" at the beginning of the chapter.

2. In a large (6- to 8-quart), heavy stainless-steel or enamel saucepan, stir together tomato purée, lemon peel, and lemon juice. Add sugar and butter (if using) and stir until well blended. Place over high heat and stir constantly while it comes to a full, rolling boil and sugar dissolves completely.

3. Stir in liquid pectin and return mixture to a full, rolling boil. Boil hard for 1 minute, adjusting heat as needed to prevent boiling over, and stirring constantly to prevent sticking. Remove from heat and skim off any foam. Keep jam hot while filling jars.

Variation: Add with fresh lemon peel and lemon juice any of the following: 1 tablespoon Worcestershire sauce and 1½ teaspoons grated fresh ginger (for more savory flavor); or ½ teaspoon ground cinnamon, ¼ teaspoon ground cloves, and ¼ teaspoon ground allspice (for sweet-spicy jam). For heat, add ¼ teaspoon cayenne. You may also substitute cider vinegar for some or all of lemon juice, which tends to produce a tangier jam.

Herbed Garlic Jelly (with Liquid Pectin)

This interesting and versatile savory jelly adds aromatic flavor to many foods. Brush liquefied jelly on grilled steaks, chicken, or lamb; serve as a table condiment with roast chicken or pork; mix with vinegar and oil for a quick salad dressing; or blend with mayo for a tasty sandwich spread.

Yield:	Prep time:	Process time:	Headspace:
7 half-pints	60 minutes	10 minutes	¼ inch

1¾ cups dry white wine

¼ cup white wine vinegar

¼ cup minced garlic

2 TB. finely chopped fresh rosemary

3½ cups granulated sugar

½ tsp. butter or margarine (optional)

2 (3-oz.) pouches liquid pectin

1. Review the section "General Procedure for Canning Jam and Other Sweet Sauces" at the beginning of the chapter.

2. In a large (6- to 8-quart), heavy stainless-steel or enamel saucepan, stir dry white wine, white wine vinegar, garlic, and rosemary. Add sugar and butter (if using) and stir until well blended. Place over high heat and stir constantly while it comes to a full, rolling boil and the sugar dissolves completely.

3. Stir in liquid pectin and return mixture to a full, rolling boil. Boil hard for 1 minute, adjusting heat as needed to prevent boiling over, and stirring constantly to prevent sticking. Remove from heat and skim off any foam. Keep jam hot while filling jars.

Low- and No-Sugar Jam and Jelly

Low- and no-sugar jams are a boon to diabetics or anyone who wants to reduce their sugar intake. Modern pectin allows you to make satisfying sugar-free jams with ease. However, these recipes present some challenges over sugared jams and jellies. Jelling can be more difficult; for this reason, many cooks buy an extra package of pectin in case they need to increase the amount of pectin (some increase the pectin by just 20 percent and others simply double the amount of pectin). Low- and no-sugar jams have a shorter shelf life than those made with sugar. The color and flavor may fade after a few months for either canned or frozen jams; plan to store jams 6 to 12 months at most. Once opened, store them in the refrigerator and consume in 2 to 4 weeks.

PERFECT PRESERVING

When you want to make low- or no-sugar jam, be sure to locate and buy the pectin before you buy the fruit. Once you buy the pectin, check the instructions in the package to confirm the amount and kind of fruit that the pectin recommends. Pectin itself has a limited shelf life, so don't buy more than you plan to use within 1 year.

Mixed-Berry Jam (Low- or No-Sugar)

This fresh-tasting jam lets the full flavor of berries shine through without being too sweet.

Yield:	Prep time:	Process time:	Headspace:
6 half-pints	60 minutes	10 minutes	¼ inch

2 cups fruit juice concentrate or 4 cups of one of the following sweeteners:

(No sugar) 4 cups Splenda or stevia

(No sugar) 3 cups of fruit juice mixed with 1 cup of Splenda

(Low sugar) 2 cups of granulated sugar mixed with 2 cups of Splenda

(Low sugar) 2 cups of honey mixed with 2 cups of fruit juice

1 or 2 (1.75-oz.) boxes no-sugar powdered pectin

6 cups crushed berries of any variety (about 6 pt.), seeds removed before measuring, if desired

1 cup water or unsweetened apple juice

1. Review the section "General Procedure for Canning Jam and Other Sweet Sauces" at the beginning of the chapter.

2. In a small bowl, mix ¼ cup fruit juice concentrate or sweetener with 1 box powdered pectin. In a large (6- to 8-quart) saucepan, combine berries, water, and pectin mixture. Stir constantly over medium-high heat, until mixture comes to a full, rolling boil. Add remaining 1¾ cups fruit juice concentrate or sweetener. Continue to stir and boil for 1 minute.

3. Test jam for desired consistency. If the jam turns out runnier than you like, add more pectin from the second box; add ¼ (1.75-ounce) box pectin to the jam, boil

1 minute, and test again. Repeat as needed. Remove jam from heat. Let stand 5 minutes, and then stir any floating berries to mix evenly with liquid. Return pan to low heat and keep jam hot while filling jars.

LOW- OR NO-SUGAR JAM WITHOUT PECTIN

There are recipes available for low- or no-sugar jam using gelatin or artificial sweeteners such as Splenda instead of pectin. Many of these recipes make great jam; however, they have not been tested in the laboratory, so are not safe for canning. Make them in small batches, refrigerate, and use within 1 month. Freeze fresh fruit in summer and use to make low-sugar jams throughout the year, with or without pectin.

Strawberry Rhubarb Jam (No Sugar)

This jam is a perfect marriage of sugary and tart flavors. Rhubarb tames the sweetness of strawberries, leaving only fruity goodness.

Yield:	Prep time:	Process time:	Headspace:
6 half-pints	90 minutes	10 minutes	¼ inch

2 cups sliced (8 medium stalks) fresh rhubarb

¾ cup water

2 cups crushed strawberries (2 dry pt. whole berries)

1 (1.75-oz.) box low-sugar powdered pectin

1 cup granulated Splenda

1. Review the section "General Procedure for Canning Jam and Other Sweet Sauces" at the beginning of the chapter.

2. Place rhubarb and water in a large (6- to 8-quart) saucepan, and bring to a boil. Reduce heat to medium-low, cover, and simmer 5 to 8 minutes, or until rhubarb is soft. Cool to room temperature. Add crushed strawberries. In a small bowl, stir together pectin and Splenda. Gradually stir pectin mixture into fruit mixture, stirring until well blended. Place over high heat and bring mixture to a full, rolling boil. Boil 1 minute, stirring constantly. Reduce heat to low and skim off any foam. Keep jam hot while filling jars.

Canned Low-Acid Foods 20

Besides vegetables, other low-acid products include meats, poultry, seafood, and combinations of these ingredients. Canning these foods is not difficult, and produces tasty results.

For best quality and flexibility in meal preparation, can meats and vegetables in separate jars. However, you may prepare thin, unthickened soups that are safe for canning, if you limit the amount of meat and vegetables you put in the jar.

Before and after working with meat, poultry, or fish, be sure to clean and sanitize the work area (see Chapter 1 for guidelines).

If you haven't yet read Chapter 7, please be sure to read the section on botulism poisoning. Most of the food botulism cases reported to the Centers for Disease Control and Prevention (CDC) are due to home-canned meats, fish, and vegetables. Canning is safe if you use tested recipes, keep equipment clean, follow all procedures accurately, and never take shortcuts.

High-acid foods are inherently safer than low-acid foods. If you are new to canning, you may want to start with fruits, jams, relishes, or pickles. Each of these products will help you gain a solid understanding of the canning process. Once you have practiced on high-acid foods, you can tackle low-acid foods with confidence.

I recommend your first pressure-canning project be acidified tomatoes or one of the fruits in Chapter 15. You may process some tomato and fruit products by either method, boiling water–bath or pressure canning, as directed in a tested recipe.

General Procedure for Canning Low-Acid Foods

For more details on the steps to prepare, process, and store canned foods, see Chapter 7. Use the following general procedure for all of the recipes in this chapter:

1. Prepare the pressure canner, jars, and lids. Before proceeding, review your recipe; preparing the canner and jars is usually the first step, unless the recipe preparation is very lengthy.

2. Prepare low-acid foods (meat, poultry, seafood, and vegetables, and soups and sauces containing these foods) as directed in each recipe.

3. Fill hot jars by the hot-pack or raw-pack method as allowed in the recipe. Use the following general packing instructions, unless recipe directs otherwise. Add salt to the jar (if using) before or after filling with product: for quart jars, add 1 teaspoon salt; for pint jars, add 1½ teaspoons; and for half-pint jars, add 1¼ teaspoons.

   - Hot pack: *Method 1 (solid product such as meat or vegetables):* Fill hot jars loosely with hot, solid food. Add hot canning liquid, adjusting headspace as directed in recipe. *Method 2 (uniform product such as stock, soup, or sauce):* Ladle hot product into hot jars, adjusting headspace as directed in recipe.

   - Raw pack: *Method 1 (meats):* Do not add canning liquid to raw-packed meats; they make their own liquid during pressure canning. Fill hot jars loosely with raw meat. *Method 2 (vegetables):* Bring canning liquid to a boil, and then reduce heat and keep hot while filling jars. Ladle a small amount of hot liquid into the hot jar. Add raw vegetables; pack tightly without crushing, and add hot liquid to cover, adjusting headspace as directed in recipe.

4. Clean the rim and secure the lid. Use process time as directed in recipe. Properly cool and store the jars up to 1 year for best flavor.

You should use only the packing methods, jar sizes, headspace, and processing times specified in the recipe. These requirements are not interchangeable from one recipe to another.

Canning Meat, Poultry, and Seafood

Canning meat, poultry, or seafood is useful if you like to save money by buying these items in bulk or if you hunt or fish. It's a great way to preserve a bountiful catch—whether from the store or nature—for later use.

Meat or Poultry Stock or Broth

Prepare stock from beef bones to use as liquid in recipes or as a hot canning liquid for meats.

Yield:	Prep time:	Process time:	Headspace:
1 to 14 quarts	1 day	20 to 25 minutes	1 inch

Meat Stock or Broth, Hot Pack Only

1 Quart	7 Quarts	14 Quarts	Ingredient
1 lb.	7 lb.	14 lb.	Beef, chicken, or turkey bones
1 qt.	7 qt.	7 qt.	Water, or as needed

1. Review the section "General Procedure for Canning Low-Acid Foods" at the beginning of the chapter.

2. If desired for fuller flavor, roast bones in a single layer on rimmed baking sheets in a 400°F oven for 20 minutes, or until browned.

3. Place bones in a large stockpot, cover with water by 2 inches, and bring to a boil over high heat. Reduce heat to medium-low, partially cover, and slowly simmer 3 to 4 hours. Strain stock in a colander and discard bones. Chill stock overnight in the refrigerator.

4. Lift off solidified fat (discard fat or reserve for another use). Strain stock through a fine mesh strainer into a large stockpot and bring to a boil. (Small bits of meat may be canned with the broth; however, any meat should be ¼ inch or less in size and limited to a small area at the bottom of the jar. More or larger bits require that broth be processed longer, as cubed meat.) Keep broth hot while filling jars.

Process time for meat stock or broth (at 0 to 1,000 feet), in minutes:

- **Dial gauge at 11 pounds, hot pack:** pints, 20; quarts, 25

- **Weighted gauge at 10 pounds, hot pack:** pints, 20; quarts, 25

Boneless Meat Cubes or Strips

Cubed, chunked, or sliced meat in jars is ready to go for quick, nutritious, and hearty meals featuring meat stew, chili, or hot sandwiches.

Yield:	Prep time:	Process time:	Headspace:
1 to 14 quarts	3 to 4 hours	75 to 90 minutes	1 inch

Boneless Meat Cubes or Strips, Hot or Raw Pack

1 Quart*	7 Quarts*	14 Quarts*	Ingredient
2 lb.	14 lb.	28 lb.	Boneless meat
1 tsp.	2⅓ TB.	4⅔ TB.	Salt (optional)
1½ cups	2½ qt.	5 qt.	Canning liquid (water, broth, or tomato juice)

Estimated at an average of 2 pounds per quart.

1. Review the section "General Procedure for Canning Low-Acid Foods" at the beginning of the chapter.

2. Cut meat into uniform cubes or chunks for stews and braised dishes. Cut into thin strips for sandwiches. If desired to reduce strong flavors, soak wild game (venison, elk, bear, moose, caribou) for 1 hour in brine of 1 tablespoon salt per 1 quart water; rinse in cold water.

3. Prepare meat by one of the following methods.

   - Hot pack: Precook meat until rare by roasting, stewing, or browning in a small amount of fat; do not add flour when browning. Include meat juices with meat when packing. Bring canning liquid to a boil (water, broth, or tomato juice, especially with wild game) and keep hot while filling jars.

   - Raw pack: Keep meat well chilled until ready to pack into jars.

Process time for boneless meat cubes or strips (at 0 to 1,000 feet), in minutes:

   - **Dial gauge at 11 pounds, hot or raw pack:** pints, 75; quarts, 90

   - **Weighted gauge at 10 pounds, hot or raw pack:** pints, 75; quarts, 90

> **PERFECT PRESERVING**
>
> The best meat for canning is lean, and without fat, tendons, or silver skin. Raw-packed meat is less tender than hot-packed meat.

Ground Meat

Ground meat, meatballs, and seasoned sausage patties or links easily make delicious spaghetti sauce, enchiladas, sloppy joes, and other quick meals.

Yield:	Prep time:	Process time:	Headspace:
1 to 14 quarts	1 to 2 hours	75 to 90 minutes	1 inch

Ground Meat, Hot Pack Only

1 Quart*	7 Quarts*	14 Quarts*	Ingredient
1¾ lb.	12¼ lb.	24½ lb.	Ground meat or sausage patties or links
1½ cups	2½ qt.	5 qt.	Canning liquid (water, broth, or tomato juice)
1 tsp.	2⅓ TB.	4⅔ TB.	Salt (optional)

Estimated at an average of 1¾ pounds per quart.

1. Review the section "General Procedure for Canning Low-Acid Foods" at the beginning of the chapter.

2. For all ground meats, if desired, shape into patties or meatballs. Ground meat may also be left loose, without shaping. For ground venison, add 1 part high-quality pork or beef fat to 3 or 4 parts venison and grind them together. For link sausage, cut into 3- to 4-inch pieces. Prepare meat as follows.

   - Hot pack: Sauté meat in a skillet over high heat 3 to 5 minutes or until lightly browned. Do not add flour when browning. For large quantities, preheat the oven to 450°F and spread meat in a single layer in a roasting pan. Bake for 5 to 10 minutes or until lightly browned. Every 5 minutes, turn over patties and meatballs, or stir ground meat. Remove excess fat before packing. Bring canning liquid to a boil (water, broth, or tomato juice, especially with wild game) and keep hot while filling jars.

- Raw pack: Not safe. Use hot pack only for ground meats.

Process time for ground meat (at 0 to 1,000 feet), in minutes:

- **Dial gauge at 11 pounds, hot pack only:** pints, 75; quarts, 90

- **Weighted gauge at 10 pounds, hot pack only:** pints, 75; quarts, 90

SPOILER ALERT

Feel free to adapt your favorite sausage or meatball recipe for canning. However, use herbs and seasonings sparingly, because their flavors intensify when canned. Use salt, pepper, thyme, oregano, and basil in limited amounts. Although sage is a common seasoning in fresh sausage, it may cause a bitter off-flavor when the sausage is canned.

Canned Poultry

Canned chicken and other poultry such as turkey, duck, goose, or game birds have myriad uses, from vegetable soup to enchiladas.

Yield:	Prep time:	Process time:	Headspace:
1 to 14 quarts	2 to 4 hours	65 to 90 minutes	1 inch

Canned Poultry

1 Quart*	7 Quarts*	14 Quarts*	Ingredient
2 lb.	14 lb.	28 lb.	Bone-in poultry
1 tsp.	2⅓ TB.	4⅔ TB.	Salt (optional)
1½ cups	2½ qt.	5 qt.	Canning liquid (water or broth)

Estimated at an average of 2 pounds per quart for bone-in poultry.

1. Review the section "General Procedure for Canning Low-Acid Foods" at the beginning of the chapter.

2. For best flavor, do not pack liver or gizzards with poultry. If desired to reduce strong flavors, soak wild poultry for 1 hour in brine of 1 tablespoon salt per 1 quart water; rinse in cold water. Freshly killed and dressed poultry should be chilled for 6 to 12 hours before canning. Cut poultry at joints.

3. Prepare poultry by one of the following methods.

    • Hot pack: Place poultry on a baking sheet, and oven bake at 350°F. Alternatively, place pieces in a large stockpot, cover with cold water, and bring to a boil over high heat. Reduce heat to medium-low and simmer 30 to 40 minutes or until done (internal temperature at 165°F). Debone poultry (if desired), and can (with or without skin); use bones for broth. Bring canning liquid to a boil and keep hot while filling jars.

    • Raw pack: Raw poultry gives low yields per jar and tends to be chewy. For raw pack, cut poultry into pieces that will fit inside the jar.

Process time for canned poultry (at 0 to 1,000 feet), in minutes:

    • **Dial gauge at 11 pounds, bone-in, hot or raw pack:** pints, 65; quarts, 75

    • **Dial gauge at 11 pounds, boneless, hot or raw pack:** pints, 75; quarts, 90

    • **Weighted gauge at 10 pounds, bone-in, hot or raw pack:** pints, 65; quarts, 75

    • **Weighted gauge at 10 pounds, boneless, hot or raw pack:** pints, 75; quarts, 90

Variation: For **Canned Rabbit or Squirrel,** soak dressed animals for 1 hour in brine of 1 tablespoon salt per 1 quart water; rinse in cold water. Precook by poaching or steaming until skin can be removed easily. Discard skin and fat. Prepare and process like poultry, using hot pack or raw pack.

Canned Salmon, Steelhead, and Trout

Canning turns seafood into full-flavored, firm, steaklike products that you can use in many ways, including soups and sandwiches, salads, and seasoned patties for dinner entrées.

Yield:	Prep time:	Process time:	Headspace:
1 to 14 pints	3 to 4 hours	100 minutes	1 inch

Canned Salmon, Steelhead, and Trout

1 Pint*	7 Pints*	14 Pints*	Ingredient
1 lb.	7 lb.	14 lb.	Salmon, steelhead, or trout
1 tsp.	2⅓ TB.	4⅔ TB.	Salt (optional)

Estimated at an average of 1 pound per quart.

1. Review the section "General Procedure for Canning Low-Acid Foods" at the beginning of the chapter.

2. Clean fish within 2 hours after it is caught. Keep fish on ice until ready to can. Remove head, tail, fins, and scales. Wash and remove all blood. Keep well chilled until ready to pack.

3. Prepare fish as follows.

   - Hot pack: Not safe. Use raw pack only for fish.

   - Raw pack: Split fish lengthwise, if desired. Cut cleaned fish away from bones into 3½-inch lengths. Place skin side next to glass for nicer appearance.

Process time for canned salmon, steelhead, and trout (at 0 to 1,000 feet), in minutes:

- **Dial gauge at 11 pounds, raw pack:** half-pints or pints, 100
- **Weighted gauge at 10 pounds, raw pack:** half-pints or pints, 100

Variations: For **Canned Mackerel, Bluefish, or Other Fatty Fish** (except tuna), prepare and process as for salmon. For **Canned Cooked Tuna,** precook fish by baking at 350°F for 1 hour, or steam for 2 to 4 hours, or to an internal temperature of 165°F. Refrigerate cooked tuna overnight to firm meat. Peel off skin with a knife; remove blood vessels and any discolored flesh. Cut meat away from bones; discard bones, fin bases, and dark flesh. Cut fish in quarters, and then cut crosswise into lengths suitable for half-pint or pint jars. Pack into jars, pressing down gently to make a solid pack. Cooked tuna may be packed in water or oil, as preferred. Add tap water or oil to jars, leaving 1 inch headspace. Use only fresh oil and take extra care to carefully clean the rim to guarantee a good seal. Oil tends to soften the natural rubber-based lining and may result in loosening of the seal over time.

CRYSTALS IN CANNED SALMON AND TUNA

Glasslike crystals of magnesium ammonium phosphate sometimes form in canned salmon. The home canner has no way to prevent this from happening. They are safe to eat and usually dissolve when heated.

Canned Clams

Canned clams are chewy and briny, with the flavor of the sea. Use them in New England or Manhattan clam chowder as well as fritters and seafood stews.

Yield:	Prep time:	Process time:	Headspace:
1 to 14 pints	3 to 4 hours	60 to 70 minutes	1 inch

Canned Clams

1 Pint*	7 Pints*	14 Pints*	Ingredient
1 lb.	7 lb.	14 lb.	Clams in the shell
1 qt.	1 gal.	2 gal.	Water
1 tsp.	2⅓ TB.	4⅔ TB.	Salt
1 qt.	1 gal.	2 gal.	Boiling water
1½ tsp.	2 TB.	¼ cup	Lemon juice **OR**
⅛ tsp.	½ tsp.	1 tsp.	citric acid

1 Pint*	7 Pints*	14 Pints*	Ingredient
¾ cup	5¼ cups	2½ qt.	Canning liquid (water or clam broth)

Estimated at an average of 1 pound per pint or 3 cups per quart.

1. Review the section "General Procedure for Canning Low-Acid Foods" at the beginning of the chapter.

2. Keep clams live on ice until ready to can. Scrub shells thoroughly and rinse. Discard any shells that are not closed tight. In a steamer or wok fitted with a steaming rack, bring water to a boil, add clams, and steam 5 minutes or until opened. Discard any clams that don't open after several minutes of steaming.

3. Remove clam meat from shells. Strain and reserve clam juice for canning liquid. Rinse clam meat in water containing 1 teaspoon salt per quart. Drain.

4. In a large pot, add clam meat, boiling water, and lemon juice. Bring to a boil; boil 2 minutes and drain. For minced clams, grind clams with a meat grinder or food processor.

5. Prepare clams as follows.

   - Hot pack: Bring canning liquid to a boil, add clams, and keep mixture hot while filling jars.

   - Raw pack: Not safe. Use hot pack only for clams.

Process time for canned clams (at 0 to 1,000 feet), in minutes:

   - **Dial gauge at 11 pounds, hot pack:** half-pints, 60; pints, 70
   - **Weighted gauge at 10 pounds, hot pack:** half-pints, 60; pints, 70

Soups and Sauces

The general rule in canning is to can simple foods and add extra ingredients after you open a jar and heat the food for serving. Therefore, it is safest to can chicken cubes in broth, and separately can mixed vegetables. At serving time, combine these products to make chicken and vegetable soup.

Despite this recommendation, it is possible to create some simple meat and vegetable combinations to make meal preparation more convenient. However, to make safe canned soups, fill jars no more than half-full with solids, and add boiling broth to the correct headspace. Choose lean meats and fish, simmered until well cooked, with added beans or vegetables. When making spaghetti sauce or other recipes, be sure to use a tested recipe safe for canning. For other recipes, plan to freeze them.

Here are the guidelines for making safe canned sauces and soups:

- Do not add flour, cornstarch, or other starches to canned soups. Using thickeners can result in underprocessed and unsafe foods.

- Do not add barley, rice, noodles, or other grain or pasta to canned soups. These products reduce heat penetration and make canned products unsafe.

- Do not add butter, cream, or other dairy products. Dairy products reduce heat penetration and make canned products unsafe.

Of course, you can add any of these ingredients after you open a jar.

The following sauce and soup recipes include meat, poultry, seafood, and vegetarian combinations in several seasoning styles.

Spaghetti Sauce with Meat

This is a good basic sauce for pasta or lasagna. Do not increase onions or celery, but you can adjust seasonings to taste. If you have a family sauce recipe, you must freeze it; but don't try to can it, it's not a safe thing to do.

Yield:	Prep time:	Process time:	Headspace:
7 pints	3 to 4 hours	60 to 70 minutes	1 inch

23 lb. tomatoes

2 lb. ground beef or sausage

4 cloves garlic, minced

¾ cup chopped onions

¾ cup chopped celery, carrot, or green bell pepper

¾ lb. fresh mushrooms, sliced (optional)

3 TB. minced fresh parsley

3 TB. brown sugar, or to taste

1 TB. dried oregano, or to taste

1 TB. table salt, or to taste

2 tsp. ground black pepper

1. Review the section "General Procedure for Canning Low-Acid Foods" at the beginning of the chapter.

2. Wash tomatoes and dip in boiling water for 30 to 60 seconds or until skins split. Dip in cold water and slip off skins. Remove cores and quarter tomatoes. Boil, uncovered, in a large stockpot for 20 minutes. Put through a food mill or sieve. Return to the saucepan.

3. In a large skillet, sauté beef until brown. Drain fat. Add garlic, onions, celery, and mushrooms (if using). Cook 10 to 15 minutes or until vegetables are tender. Add mixture to tomato pulp in large saucepan.

4. Add parsley, brown sugar, oregano, salt, and pepper. Bring to a boil. Simmer slowly, uncovered, for 40 to 50 minutes or until thickened. At this time, initial volume will have been reduced by nearly $\frac{1}{2}$. Stir frequently to avoid burning. Taste and adjust seasonings, if desired. Keep sauce hot while filling jars. Stir sauce frequently while you fill jars to divide solids as evenly as possible across all jars.

Process time for spaghetti sauce with meat (at 0 to 1,000 feet), in minutes:

- **Dial gauge at 11 pounds, hot pack:** pints, 60; quarts, 70

- **Weighted gauge at 10 pounds, hot pack:** pints, 60; quarts, 70

SPOILER ALERT

For safe canning of combined meat and vegetable products like spaghetti and chili con carne, it is not safe when you allow some jars to contain a lot of solids, while others contain mostly sauce. These tested recipes have been carefully formulated to fill each jar no more than halfway with solids when evenly distributed across all of the jars. This allows for adequate heat penetration during canning and safe foods.

Chili Con Carne

Make this meat-and-bean chili as hot and spicy as you like.

Yield:	Prep time:	Process time:	Headspace:
9 pints	15 to 22 hours	75 minutes	1 inch

> 3 cups dried pinto or red kidney beans
> 5½ cups water
> 5 tsp. salt
> 3 lb. ground beef
> 1½ cups chopped onion
> 1 cup chopped fresh chiles or peppers of your choice (optional)
> 1 tsp. ground black pepper
> 3 to 6 TB. chili powder
> 2 qt. crushed or whole tomatoes

1. Review the section "General Procedure for Canning Low-Acid Foods" at the beginning of the chapter.

2. Wash pinto beans thoroughly and place in a 2-quart saucepan. Add cold water to a level of 2 inches above beans, and soak 12 to 18 hours. Drain and discard soaking water.

3. Cover beans with fresh water, and bring to a boil over high heat. Reduce heat to medium-low and simmer 30 minutes, until beans are just beginning to become tender. Add 2 teaspoons salt and cook until beans are tender. Drain beans and discard water.

4. In a medium (10-inch) skillet, brown ground beef. Add onion and fresh chiles (if using), and cook 5 to 8 minutes or until soft. Drain fat. Add remaining 3 teaspoons salt, pepper, chili powder, tomatoes, and drained cooked beans. Simmer 5 minutes, or until heated through. Keep chili con carne hot while filling jars. Stir chili frequently while you fill jars to divide solids as evenly as possible across all jars.

Process time for chili con carne (at 0 to 1,000 feet), in minutes:

- **Dial gauge at 11 pounds, hot pack:** pints, 75

- **Weighted gauge at 10 pounds, hot pack:** pints, 75

BEURRE MANIÉ

It's not advisable to add starches and thickeners inside the canning jar. But there are some easy ways to thicken your soups and sauces after opening. Simmer until thick before serving or add *beurre manié* (equal parts soft butter and flour). To make beurre manié: in a small bowl, using a fork, mix 4 tablespoons flour into 4 tablespoons soft butter or margarine until well blended. Stir 1 tablespoon beurre manié into simmering sauce or chili, and cook 2 minutes. Add additional beurre manié, stirring after each addition until you achieve the consistency you like. Cover and refrigerate leftover beurre manié up to 1 month.

Chicken and Vegetable Soup

Use this chicken and vegetable soup as a base to add other options at serving time, such as pasta, beans, or rice for a quick and hearty soup.

Yield:	Prep time:	Process time:	Headspace:
7 pints	2 to 3 hours	60 to 75 minutes	1 inch

8 lb. (2 medium) whole chickens, cut in pieces

1 TB. salt

½ tsp. ground black or white pepper

1 TB. chopped fresh parsley

Water to cover

1 cup chopped onion (about 1 medium)

2 cups chopped celery (4 to 6 medium stalks)

2 cups peeled and thinly sliced carrots (4 to 6 medium)

1. Review the section "General Procedure for Canning Low-Acid Foods" at the beginning of the chapter.

2. In a large heavy pot, add chicken pieces, salt, pepper, parsley, and water, and bring to a boil over high heat. Reduce heat and simmer 60 to 90 minutes, or until meat falls easily from the bone. Transfer chicken to a dish to cool for 30 minutes, or until it can be handled comfortably. Debone and shred chicken. Discard skin, fat, and bones.

3. Add onion, celery, and carrots to broth and bring to a boil. Return chicken to broth and heat through. Keep hot while filling jars. Stir soup frequently while you fill jars to divide solids as evenly as possible across all jars.

Process time for chicken and vegetable soup (at 0 to 1,000 feet), in minutes:

- **Dial gauge at 11 pounds, hot pack:** pints, 60; quarts, 75
- **Weighted gauge at 10 pounds, hot pack:** pints, 60; quarts, 75

Variations: For **Asian-Style Chicken and Vegetable Soup,** omit salt, pepper, and parsley. Add to simmering chicken 12 slices fresh ginger, 8 cloves garlic, 3 tablespoons soy sauce, and 2 teaspoons crushed red pepper. After chicken is cooked, strain from broth and discard ginger, garlic, and red pepper. Substitute for celery 2 cups sliced bamboo shoots, rinsed well.

Brazilian-Style Seafood Soup

This seafood and vegetable soup adds a kick with lime juice and crushed red pepper. Enjoy it served over rice.

Yield:	Prep time:	Process time:	Headspace:
7 pints	2 to 3 hours	100 minutes	1 inch

2½ lb. lean white fish, such as halibut

1 TB. salt

¼ cup fresh lime juice

1½ cups canned, rinsed, and drained black beans

1 cup diced canned tomatoes or fresh peeled tomato (1 medium)

½ cup chopped green bell pepper (about 1 medium)

½ cup chopped onion (about 1 medium)

1 TB. minced garlic

½ tsp. crushed red pepper

2 qt. water, or to cover

1. Review the section "General Procedure for Canning Low-Acid Foods" at the beginning of the chapter.

2. In a shallow dish, sprinkle white fish with salt and lime juice on both sides. Cover and refrigerate 30 minutes. Cut fish into ½-inch cubes.

3. In a large heavy pot, add fish, black beans, tomatoes, green bell pepper, onion, garlic, crushed red pepper, and water. Bring to a boil over medium heat. Reduce heat and cook gently 10 minutes, or until fish is cooked through. Keep hot while filling jars. Stir soup frequently while you fill jars to divide solids as evenly as possible across all jars.

Process time for Brazilian-style seafood soup (at 0 to 1,000 feet), in minutes:

- **Dial gauge at 11 pounds, hot pack:** half-pint or pints, 100
- **Weighted gauge at 10 pounds, hot pack:** half-pint or pints, 100

Mixed Bean Soup

Use as many different types of dried legumes as you like in this recipe, such as pinto, chickpea, red, black, navy, or white, as well as split peas, lentils, or black-eyed peas. When serving, add vegetables, greens, ham or sausage, canned tomatoes, and seasonings to customize soup to your taste.

Yield:	Prep time:	Process time:	Headspace:
7 pints	2 to 3 hours	75 to 90 minutes	1 inch

2 cups dried beans

Water to cover

2 tsp. minced garlic

2 tsp. salt, or to taste

½ tsp. ground black pepper, or to taste

1. Review the section "General Procedure for Canning Low-Acid Foods" at the beginning of the chapter.

2. Wash dried beans thoroughly and place in a large saucepan with water to cover by 2 inches. Bring to a boil, and boil 2 minutes. Remove from heat, cover, and soak 1 hour.

3. Drain and discard water. Add fresh water to cover soaked beans by 2 inches. Stir in garlic. Bring to a boil over high heat, cover, and boil 30 minutes. Add salt and

pepper. Keep soup hot while filling jars. Stir soup frequently while you fill jars to divide solids as evenly as possible across all jars.

Process time for mixed bean soup (at 0 to 1,000 feet), in minutes:

- **Dial gauge at 11 pounds, hot pack:** pints, 75; quarts, 90
- **Weighted gauge at 10 pounds, hot pack:** pints, 75; quarts, 90

Tex-Mex Vegetable Soup

This zesty vegetable soup is brimming with New World vegetables, including corn, tomatoes, and peppers. Control the heat by adding as much hot pepper sauce as you like.

Yield:	Prep time:	Process time:	Headspace:
7 pints	2 to 3 hours	55 to 85 minutes	1 inch

3 cups (4 medium ears) fresh corn kernels

3 cups (3 medium) peeled, cored, and chopped fresh tomatoes

1½ cups (3 medium) chopped onion

1 cup (3 to 4 medium) chopped tomatillos

1 cup (2 medium) stemmed, seeded, and chopped green bell pepper

1 cup (2 medium) stemmed, seeded, and chopped red bell pepper

4 cloves garlic, minced

3 TB. chopped fresh cilantro

2 tsp. chili powder, or to taste

1 tsp. cayenne, or to taste

¾ tsp. salt, or to taste

4½ cups tomato juice

1 cup water

1 TB. hot pepper sauce, or to taste

1. Review the section "General Procedure for Canning Low-Acid Foods" at the beginning of the chapter.

2. In a large pot, stir together corn kernels, tomatoes, onion, tomatillos, green bell pepper, red bell pepper, garlic, cilantro, chili powder, cayenne, salt, tomato juice,

water, and hot pepper sauce, and bring to a boil over high heat. Reduce heat and simmer 15 minutes. Keep soup hot while filling jars. Stir soup frequently while you fill jars to divide solids as evenly as possible across all jars.

Process time for Tex-Mex vegetable soup (at 0 to 1,000 feet), in minutes:

- **Dial gauge at 11 pounds, hot pack:** pints, 55; quarts, 85
- **Weighted gauge at 10 pounds, hot pack:** pints, 55; quarts, 85

Vegetables

Plain canned vegetables are easy to process. Pack them in water, with or without salt. They have myriad uses: add to soups and stews, drain and dress as a salad, or serve as a side dish.

Asparagus

Canned asparagus takes on an earthy flavor that many people enjoy as a side dish, in salads, or as a garnish for steak or seafood.

Yield:	Prep time:	Process time:	Headspace:
1 to 14 quarts	90 minutes	30 to 40 minutes	1 inch

Asparagus

1 Quart*	7 Quarts*	14 Quarts*	Ingredient
3½ lb.	24½ lb.	50 lb.	Asparagus
1½ cups	2½ qt.	5 qt.	Water
1 tsp.	2⅓ TB.	4⅔ TB.	Salt (optional)

Estimated at an average of 3½ pounds per quart.

1. Review the section "General Procedure for Canning Low-Acid Foods" at the beginning of the chapter.

2. Use tender, tight-tipped asparagus spears that are 4 to 6 inches long. Trim scales, cut or break off tough stems, and wash.

3. Bring a large stockpot of unsalted water to a boil. Prepare asparagus by one of the following methods.

- Hot pack: Cut spears into 1-inch lengths. Add asparagus to boiling water and cook 3 minutes. Keep hot while filling jars.

- Raw pack: Trim whole spears to fit jars or cut into 1-inch lengths.

Process time for asparagus (at 0 to 1,000 feet), in minutes:

- **Dial gauge at 11 pounds, hot or raw pack:** pints, 30; quarts, 40

- **Weighted gauge at 10 pounds, hot or raw pack:** pints, 30; quarts, 40

PERFECT PRESERVING

Use raw pack for some foods that are easier to pack when raw and firm, including asparagus spears, whole green beans, and carrot sticks. Other foods that can benefit from raw pack include citrus fruits, tomatoes, sliced meats, and brined fish. See Chapter 7 for more about using raw pack.

String or Snap Beans (Whole or Pieces)

Use these instructions for any type of green bean, including French beans, runner beans, Italian flat beans, or yellow wax beans. Use canned beans in soups and stews as well as salads.

Yield:	Prep time:	Process time:	Headspace:
1 to 14 quarts	60 minutes	20 to 25 minutes	1 inch

String or Snap Beans

1 Quart*	7 Quarts*	14 Quarts*	Ingredient
2 lb.	14 lb.	28 lb.	Green, wax, or broad beans
1½ cups	2½ qt.	5 qt.	Water
1 tsp.	2⅓ TB.	4⅔ TB.	Salt (optional)

Estimated at an average of 2 pounds per quart.

1. Review the section "General Procedure for Canning Low-Acid Foods" at the beginning of the chapter.

2. Use tender, young beans. Wash green beans and trim stem ends. Bring a large stockpot of unsalted water to a boil. Prepare beans by one of the following methods.

   - Hot pack: Cut spears into 1-inch lengths. Add beans to boiling water and cook 5 minutes. Keep hot while filling jars.

   - Raw pack: Leave beans whole, snap in half, or cut into 1-inch lengths.

Process time for snap beans (at 0 to 1,000 feet), in minutes:

   - **Dial gauge at 11 pounds, hot or raw pack:** pints, 20; quarts, 25

   - **Weighted gauge at 10 pounds, hot or raw pack:** pints, 20; quarts, 25

Dried Beans

Dried beans canned at home are great to have on hand to make dip, add healthy fiber to soup, combine with grain for a hearty pilaf, or make into earthy bean burgers.

Yield:	Prep time:	Process time:	Headspace:
1 to 14 quarts	90 minutes	74 to 90 minutes	1 inch

Dried Beans

1 Quart*	7 Quarts*	14 Quarts*	Ingredient
¾ lb.	5¼ lb.	10½ lb.	Dried beans
1½ cups	2½ qt.	5 qt.	Water
1 tsp.	2⅓ TB.	4⅔ TB.	Salt (optional)

Estimated at an average of ¾ pound per quart.

1. Review the section "General Procedure for Canning Low-Acid Foods" at the beginning of the chapter.

2. Select mature, dry beans. Pick over and discard discolored beans or debris. Soak beans by one of the following methods.

   - To cold-soak beans, place dried beans in a large pot and cover with water. Soak 6 to 8 hours in a cool place. Drain. (Cold soaking retains more nutrients.)

   - To quick-soak beans, place dried beans or in a large pot, cover with water, and bring to a boil. Boil 2 minutes. Remove from heat, cover, and soak 1 hour. Drain.

3. Cover beans soaked by either method with fresh tap water, bring to a boil over high heat, and boil 30 minutes. Reduce heat to medium and keep beans hot while filling jars.

Process time for dried beans (at 0 to 1,000 feet), in minutes:

- **Dial gauge at 11 pounds, hot pack:** pints, 75; quarts, 90

- **Weighted gauge at 10 pounds, hot pack:** pints, 75; quarts, 90

PERFECT PRESERVING

Shelling beans are available in the fall at farmers' markets. They can be enjoyed fresh, or dried for use throughout winter. If you grow beans or peas, simply dry them on the vine at the end of the season. They may need additional drying after harvest.

Beets

One vegetable that tastes as good canned as fresh is beets. Use smaller sizes to minimize cooking time. This avoids excessive bleeding of the color into the water, turning the beet white.

Yield:	Prep time:	Process time:	Headspace:
1 to 14 quarts	90 minutes	30 to 35 minutes	1 inch

Beets

1 Quart*	7 Quarts*	14 Quarts*	Ingredient
3 lb.	21 lb.	42 lb.	Beets
1½ cups	2½ qt.	5 qt.	Water
1 tsp.	2⅓ TB.	4⅔ TB.	Salt (optional)

Estimated at an average of 3 pounds per quart.

1. Review the section "General Procedure for Canning Low-Acid Foods" at the beginning of the chapter.

2. Use small beets with a diameter of 1 to 2 inches for whole packs. Use beets with a diameter of 2 to 3 inches for slices or cubes. Beets larger than 3 inches are often tough and don't take well to canning. Trim beets, leaving an inch of stem and taproot to reduce bleeding of color. Scrub well using a vegetable brush.

3. Place beets in a saucepan, cover with water generously, and bring to a boil over high heat. Boil 10 to 15 minutes or until skins slip off easily. Discard cooking water. Cool, trim stems and roots, and remove skins. Leave small beets whole. Cut larger beets into wedges, slices, or ½-inch cubes. Cut large slices in half.

4. Boil water for canning liquid. Prepare beets as follows.

   • Hot pack: Bring a large stockpot of unsalted water to a boil, add prepared beets. Keep hot while filling jars.

   • Raw pack: Not safe. Use hot pack only for beets.

Process time for beets (at 0 to 1,000 feet), in minutes:

   • **Dial gauge at 11 pounds, hot pack:** pints, 30; quarts, 35

   • **Weighted gauge at 10 pounds, hot pack:** pints, 30; quarts, 35

Carrots

Carrots are another vegetable that take well to canning. Their texture and flavor remains close to fresh after the canning process. Use them in soup, stew, salads, and side dishes.

Yield:	Prep time:	Process time:	Headspace:
1 to 14 quarts	90 minutes	25 to 30 minutes	1 inch

Carrots, Sticks or Slices

1 Quart*	7 Quarts*	14 Quarts*	Ingredient
2½ lb.	17½ lb.	35 lb.	Carrots
1½ cups	2½ qt.	5 qt.	Water
1 tsp.	2⅓ TB.	4⅔ TB.	Salt (optional)

Estimated at an average of 2½ pounds per quart.

1. Review the section "General Procedure for Canning Low-Acid Foods" at the beginning of the chapter.

2. Use small carrots, preferably 1 to 1¼ inches in diameter. Larger carrots are often too fibrous. Wash and peel carrots. Give them a second rinse before cutting.

3. Bring a large stockpot of unsalted water to a boil. Prepare carrots by one of the following methods.

   • Hot pack: Cut in slices or dice. Add carrots to boiling water and cook 5 minutes. Keep hot while filling jars.

   • Raw pack: Cut in sticks, slices, or dice.

Process time for carrots (at 0 to 1,000 feet), in minutes:

   • **Dial gauge at 11 pounds, hot or raw pack:** pints, 25; quarts, 30

   • **Weighted gauge at 10 pounds, hot or raw pack:** pints, 25; quarts, 30

> **PERFECT PRESERVING**
>
> Strong-tasting root vegetables, such as parsnips, turnips, rutabagas, and their aboveground cousin, kohlrabi, are delicious when pickled—as many cultures that use them do. They can also be frozen. However, they do not take well to canning, although it is safe to do.

Whole Kernel Corn

Along with beets and carrots, corn takes well to the canning process and tastes almost like fresh. Use it for soup, salads, salsa, and sides.

Yield:	Prep time:	Process time:	Headspace:
1 to 14 quarts	6 hours	55 to 85 minutes	1 inch

Whole Kernel Corn

1 Quart*	7 Quarts*	14 Quarts*	Ingredient
4½ lb.	31½ lb.	63 lb.	Corn
1½ cups	2½ qt.	5 qt.	Water
1 tsp.	2⅓ TB.	4⅔ TB.	Salt (optional)

Estimated at an average of 4½ pounds per quart.

1. Review the section "General Procedure for Canning Low-Acid Foods" at the beginning of the chapter.

2. Select ears with fully mature kernels. Sweeter varieties or immature kernels may turn brown after canning or during storage. Process one jar and check the color and flavor before canning a large quantity.

3. Remove husks and silk from corn; scrub gently with a vegetable brush to remove fibers. Cut whole kernels from cob, about ¾ the depth of kernel. Do not scrape cob; it adds starch to the jar and can make vegetables unsafe.

4. Bring a large stockpot of unsalted water to a boil. Prepare corn by one of the following methods.

- Hot pack: Add corn kernels to boiling water and cook 5 minutes. Keep hot while filling jars.

- Raw pack: Use raw kernels cut from cob.

Process time for whole kernel corn (at 0 to 1,000 feet), in minutes:

- **Dial gauge at 11 pounds, hot or raw pack:** pints, 55; quarts, 85

- **Weighted gauge at 10 pounds, hot or raw pack:** pints, 55; quarts, 85

PERFECT PRESERVING

To cut corn from the cob neatly and easily, stand an ear on end in the center of a Bundt pan and slice down the side with a chef's knife. The kernels will fall neatly into the pan.

Leafy Greens

This recipe can be used for cooking greens, including beet, chard, collard, kale, mustard, spinach, and turnip. Make a simple soup with diced meat, and season to taste with soy sauce. Use them as a side with roasted pork or ham.

Yield:	Prep time:	Process time:	Headspace:
1 to 14 quarts	2 hours	70 to 90 minutes	1 inch

Leafy Greens

1 Quart*	7 Quarts*	14 Quarts*	Ingredient
4 lb.	28 lb.	56 lb.	Greens
1½ cups	2½ qt.	5 qt.	Water
1 tsp.	2⅓ TB.	4⅔ TB.	Salt (optional)

Estimated at an average of 4 pounds per quart.

1. Review the section "General Procedure for Canning Low-Acid Foods" at the beginning of the chapter.

2. Select freshly harvested greens. Discard wilted or insect-damaged leaves. Wash greens one batch at a time in several changes of water, or until water is clear and free of grit. Cut out tough stems. Bring a large stockpot of unsalted water to a boil.

3. Prepare greens as follows.

   - Hot pack: Steam blanch one batch of greens at a time for 3 to 5 minutes, or until wilted. Keep hot while filling jars.

   - Raw pack: Not safe. Use hot pack only for greens.

Process time for leafy greens (at 0 to 1,000 feet), in minutes:

   - **Dial gauge at 11 pounds, hot pack:** pints, 70; quarts, 90

   - **Weighted gauge at 10 pounds, hot pack:** pints, 70; quarts, 90

Cultivated Mushrooms

Canned mushrooms are a handy kitchen staple and add a woodsy flavor to soups and stews.

Yield:	Prep time:	Process time:	Headspace:
1 to 14 pints	60 minutes	45 minutes	1 inch

Cultivated Mushrooms

1 Pint*	7 Pints*	14 Pints*	Ingredient
4 lb.	14 lb.	28 lb.	Cultivated mushrooms
1½ cups	2½ qt.	5 qt.	Water
1 tsp.	2⅓ TB.	4⅔ TB.	Salt (optional)
200 mg	1,500 mg	3,000 mg	Ascorbic acid, vitamin C, **OR** fresh or bottled lemon juice
¾ tsp.	2 TB.	¼ cup	

Estimated at an average of 2 pounds per pint.

1. Review the section "General Procedure for Canning Low-Acid Foods" at the beginning of the chapter.

2. Select only firm, very fresh, unblemished, small- to medium-size cultivated mushrooms with short stems and tight veils (unopened caps). Trim stems. Wash in several changes of clean water to remove dirt. Leave small mushrooms whole; quarter larger ones. Bring a large stockpot of unsalted water to a boil. For better color with white mushrooms, add ascorbic acid, vitamin C, or lemon juice.

3. Prepare mushrooms as follows.

   - Hot pack: Add mushrooms to boiling water and cook 5 minutes. Keep hot while filling jars.

   - Raw pack: Not safe. Use hot pack only for mushrooms.

Process time for cultivated mushrooms (at 0 to 1,000 feet), in minutes:

- **Dial gauge at 11 pounds, hot pack:** half-pints or pints, 45

- **Weighted gauge at 10 pounds, hot pack:** half-pints or pints, 45

SPOILER ALERT

Do not can wild mushrooms. There are no laboratory-tested processing times for wild mushrooms. Wild mushrooms have different textures from commercially grown mushrooms. Therefore, the processing time for cultivated mushrooms does not apply to wild mushrooms.

Peppers

Use these instructions for any variety fresh pepper, including sweet peppers, bell peppers, and hot chiles.

Yield:	Prep time:	Process time:	Headspace:
1 to 14 quarts	6 hours	35 minutes	1 inch

Peppers

1 Quart*	7 Quarts*	14 Quarts*	Ingredient
1 lb.	7 lb.	14 lb.	Peppers or chiles (hot, sweet, bell)
1½ cups	2½ qt.	5 qt.	Water
1 tsp.	2⅓ TB.	4⅔ TB.	Salt (optional)

Estimated at an average of 4½ pounds per quart.

1. Review the section "General Procedure for Canning Low-Acid Foods" at the beginning of the chapter.

2. Select peppers that are heavy for their size, smooth and symmetrical, bright in color, fresh, mature, and crisp. Wash peppers. Be sure to wear plastic or rubber gloves while handling or cutting hot chile. Blanch in boiling water or blister using one of the following methods.

   • Grill whole peppers on a barbecue over medium-high heat, using tongs to turn peppers every few minutes, until skins char on all sides.

   • On a gas stove or outdoor gas grill, cover burners with heavy wire mesh or griddle. Roast peppers, using tongs to turn peppers every few minutes, until skins char on all sides, between 30 to 90 minutes depending on how many peppers you have and how many you can tend to at one time.

   • Preheat the oven to 450°F. Place peppers on a baking sheet (line with aluminum foil for easy clean-up!), and put in the oven. Check and turn ¼ every 10 to 15 minutes, until charred on all sides. It will take up to 1 hour for one batch.

3. Wrap charred peppers in foil or a brown paper bag for 20 to 30 minutes, or until cool enough to handle. Peel skins.

4. Small peppers may be left whole; pierce two or three times with a small knife, and flatten. Large peppers may be quartered; remove stems and seeds. Bring a large stockpot of unsalted water to a boil.

5. Prepare peppers as follows.

   • Hot pack: Add peppers to boiling water. Keep hot while filling jars.

   • Raw pack: Not safe. Use hot pack only for peppers.

Process time for peppers (at 0 to 1,000 feet), in minutes:

- **Dial gauge at 11 pounds, hot pack:** half-pints or pints, 35

- **Weighted gauge at 10 pounds, hot pack:** half-pints or pints, 35

Potatoes

Use versatile canned potatoes to make potato soup, potato salad, mashed potato pancakes, or potato bread. Canned potatoes are delicious added to soups and stews, baked with a roast, sautéed with oil and rosemary, or mashed with cream and butter.

Yield:	Prep time:	Process time:	Headspace:
1 to 14 quarts	90 minutes	35 to 40 minutes	1 inch

Potatoes

1 Quart*	7 Quarts*	14 Quarts*	Ingredient
2¾ lb.	19¼ lb.	38½ lb.	Potatoes
1½ cups	2½ qt.	5 qt.	Water
1 tsp.	2⅓ TB.	4⅔ TB.	Salt (optional)
200 mg	1,500 mg	3,000 mg	Ascorbic acid or vitamin C

Estimated at an average of 2¾ pounds per quart.

1. Review the section "General Procedure for Canning Low-Acid Foods" at the beginning of the chapter.

2. Choose waxy, boiling, or all-purpose variety potatoes that have been stored at least 30 days after harvest at 45°F to 50°F. Select small- to medium-size mature, firm potatoes free from blemishes and any green color. If they are to be packed whole, choose potatoes 1 to 2 inches in diameter. Wash potatoes.

3. Peel potatoes. Leave potatoes up to 2 inches in diameter whole. Cut larger potatoes into uniform ½-inch cubes. Cover in water with ascorbic acid or vitamin C added to prevent darkening. Drain potatoes before adding to boiling water. Bring a large stockpot of unsalted water to a boil. Prepare potatoes as follows.

- Hot pack: Add potatoes to boiling water and cook potato cubes for 2 minutes and whole potatoes for 10 minutes. Keep potatoes hot while filling jars.

- Raw pack: Not safe. Use hot pack only for potatoes.

Process time for potatoes (at 0 to 1,000 feet), in minutes:

- **Dial gauge at 11 pounds, hot pack:** pints, 35; quarts, 40

- **Weighted gauge at 10 pounds, hot pack:** pints, 35; quarts, 40

Sweet Potatoes

Use canned sweet potato cubes in the same ways you would fresh: in biscuits, pancakes, breads, pies, custard, and cheesecake, as well as savory curries, black bean soup, stuffed ravioli, or as a side dish.

Yield:	Prep time:	Process time:	Headspace:
1 to 14 quarts	90 minutes	65 to 90 minutes	1 inch

Sweet Potatoes

1 Quart*	7 Quarts*	14 Quarts*	Ingredient
2½ lb.	17½ lb.	35 lb.	Sweet potatoes
1½ cups	2½ qt.	5 qt.	Water or light syrup (see Chapter 7)
1 tsp.	2⅓ TB.	4⅔ TB.	Salt (optional)

Estimated at an average of 2½ pounds per quart.

1. Review the section "General Procedure for Canning Low-Acid Foods" at the beginning of the chapter.

2. Select small- to medium-size mature, firm sweet potatoes, free from blemishes. Can within 1 to 2 months after harvest. Wash sweet potatoes.

3. Prepare boiling water or light syrup for canning liquid. Prepare sweet potatoes as follows.

    -   Hot pack: Boil or steam sweet potatoes for 15 to 20 minutes, or until partially soft. Peel skins. Cut sweet potatoes into uniform ½-inch cubes and add to boiling canning liquid. Do not mash or purée pieces. Keep mixture hot while filling jars.

    -   Raw pack: Not safe. Use hot pack only for potatoes.

Process time for sweet potatoes (at 0 to 1,000 feet), in minutes:

-   **Dial gauge at 11 pounds, hot pack:** pints, 65; quarts, 90
-   **Weighted gauge at 10 pounds, hot pack:** pints, 65; quarts, 90

Pumpkin or Winter Squash

Use sweet and succulent pumpkin or winter squash cubes in recipes from soup to pie.

Yield:	Prep time:	Process time:	Headspace:
1 to 14 quarts	90 minutes	55 to 90 minutes	1 inch

Pumpkin or Winter Squash

1 Quart*	7 Quarts*	14 Quarts*	Ingredient
2¼ lb.	15¾ lb.	31½ lb.	Pumpkin or winter squash
1½ cups	2½ qt.	5 qt.	Water or light syrup (see Chapter 7)
1 tsp.	2⅓ TB.	4⅔ TB.	Salt (optional)

Estimated at an average of 2¼ pounds per quart.

1. Review the section "General Procedure for Canning Low-Acid Foods" at the beginning of the chapter.

2. Select hard rind, mature squash of ideal quality for cooking fresh, such as acorn, butternut, carnival, or *kabocha*. Sugar pie pumpkins are ideal for canning. Wash squash.

3. Halve squash, remove seeds, cut into 1-inch-wide slices, and peel. Cut flesh into 1-inch cubes.

4. Prepare boiling water or light syrup for canning liquid. Prepare squash as follows.

   • Hot pack: Add squash cubes to boiling canning liquid and cook 5 minutes, or until barely tender. Do not mash or purée. Keep squash hot while filling jars.

   • Raw pack: Not safe. Use hot pack only for squash.

Process time for pumpkin or winter squash (at 0 to 1,000 feet), in minutes:

   • **Dial gauge at 11 pounds, hot pack:** pints, 55; quarts, 90

   • **Weighted gauge at 10 pounds, hot pack:** pints, 55; quarts, 90

CAN YOU CAN MASHED PUMPKIN?

The short answer is no. Canning is not a safe method for preserving mashed or puréed pumpkin or pumpkin butter. Mashed pumpkin products are thick and low acid. Despite several attempts, laboratory testing has not been able to establish safe processing times for any of these types of products. Thankfully, mashed pumpkin products are great for the freezer. So if you like to "put by" some pumpkin, plan to freeze it.

Glossary

 **A**

Acetobacter   A genus of acetic acid bacteria that oxidizes alcohol or sugar to form acetic acid, a primary component of vinegar.

alum   Short for potassium aluminum sulfate, this white powder is listed in old recipes for fermented pickles and was used to maintain a crisp texture.

anaerobic   Means "without air." Fermentation and canning processes are anaerobic; that is, they occur or result in containers without air.

ascorbic acid   Also known as vitamin C, used to prevent browning in fruits such as apples and vegetables such as eggplant.

Aspergillus oryzae   A fungus used in the production of miso, sake, rice vinegar, and soy sauce.

beurre manié   French for "kneaded butter," a mixture of equal parts butter and flour that is used as a thickener for soups and stews.

Bifidobacterium   *See* lactic acid bacteria.

blanch   To boil or steam food for a short period.

boiling-water bath (BWB)   A canning method that heats sealed jars in boiling water.

bresaola   An Italian-style cured and air-dried beef.

brine   A solution of salt dissolved in water.

brining   To soak in a brine or salt solution.

bushel   A dry volume measurement of 32 quarts (or 4 pecks) used to measure produce.

BWB   *See* boiling-water bath.

calcium citrate   A salt of citric acid that is used as a preservative, but adds salty as well as sour flavors, which may not be desirable. *See also* citric acid.

Campylobacter   A pathogenic family of bacteria that cause food-borne illness, usually from eating raw or undercooked poultry meat, or from cross contamination of other foods with these items.

canning   A method of food preservation that uses specially designed glass jars and lids. The jars are filled with food and heated. Heating methods are boiling-water bath and steam pressure.

canning salt   A pure salt without additives such as iodine, minerals, or anticaking agents. Used in brine and pickling solutions to prevent cloudiness or darkening of pickled foods.

case-harden   A condition that occurs in cured or dried foods when the surface dries prematurely and traps moisture inside. Foods with case-hardening will not be safely preserved and may spoil quickly.

check   A pretreatment used for fruits with tough, waxy skins to ensure even drying. There are two methods for checking: water blanching and physically piercing or slitting the peels. Fruits to consider for checking include blueberries, cranberries, cherries, figs, grapes, and small plums or fresh prunes.

chinois (pronounced *shin-wah*)   A large, funnel-shaped, fine-meshed strainer. Some models come with a stand—which holds the chinois steady over a bowl—and a pestle—which helps push food through the mesh. With these additions, the chinois can be used to purée and strain soft foods such as berries and cooked vegetables.

chow chow   A type of vegetable relish or pickle, often in a mustard-flavored sauce, and sometimes synonymous with *piccalilli*.

citric acid   A naturally occurring acid found in almost all foods; tart or sour fruits such as lemons and limes contain high levels of citric acid. The best use of citric acid in food preservation is when canning or curing to increase acidity that helps prevent microbial growth.

Clostridium botulinum (C. botulinum)   A pathogenic, anaerobic, gram-positive, spore-forming, rod-shaped bacterium that is widely found in nature and can release deadly toxins under certain conditions and cause botulism poisoning.

Clostridium perfringens   A pathogenic, anaerobic, gram-positive, spore-forming, rod-shaped bacterium that is widely distributed in the environment and the most common cause of food-borne illness in the United States.

cold pack   *See* raw pack.

cold smoke A preservation method that uses wood smoke and low temperatures between 50°F to 90°F to slowly dry out raw food such as meat or fish, and thoroughly penetrates the tissue with smoke.

curing salt #1 A pink-tinted mixture of 93.75 percent salt and 6.25 percent sodium nitrite. It is used as a fast cure on products that are cured up to a few weeks and will subsequently be smoked, canned, or cooked before eating.

curing salt #2 A salt mixture that contains sodium nitrite and sodium nitrate. It is used as a slow cure on products that are cured several weeks or longer and will subsequently be dry-aged, rather than smoked, canned, or cooked.

decomposition The breakdown of organic matter by the action of other living organisms (including bacteria, molds, and yeasts).

desiccant Any substance used as a drying agent to absorb moisture, oxygen, or both. In food preservation, desiccant controls excess moisture in dried foods.

dextrose A refined corn sugar that may be used instead of sugar when curing meats. It is only 70 percent as sweet as granulated sugar, blends easily, and helps to promote the formation of lactic acid in dry-cured meats.

Enterococcus *See* lactic acid bacteria.

enzymes Proteins that participate in important food preservation reactions. For example, enzymatic reactions produce lactic acid during fermentation.

Escherichia coli (*E. coli*) A large and diverse group of bacteria. Most E. coli serve a useful function in the digestive tract by suppressing the growth of harmful bacteria and synthesizing vitamins. However, some relatively rare strains produce verotoxin that can cause very serious food poisoning, leading to kidney failure and death, especially in very young children and the elderly.

fermentation An anaerobic decomposition process in which bacteria and/or yeasts consume sugars in food and create enzymes that break down the carbohydrates into alcohol and carbon dioxide.

food mill A handheld kitchen tool that purées and strains soft foods such as soups and sauces in one step. *See also* chinois.

food-borne illness Diseases caused by drinking water or eating food that is contaminated with pathogenic microorganisms.

fresh-pack pickles Unfermented pickles that are packed with vinegar solution and processed in a boiling-water canner. Fresh-pack pickles may or may not be cured or fermented in brine prior to packing and processing.

full boil (rolling boil)   Boiling water that breaks the surface and cannot be stirred down.

ghee   Rendered butterfat.

GRAS (Generally Recognized As Safe)   An acronym used by the U.S. Food and Drug Administration (USDA) for a food additive that is recognized among qualified experts as having been adequately shown as safe under the conditions of its intended use.

hot pack   A method for packing canning jars with food that puts hot food into hot jars with hot liquid before processing.

hot smoke   A complementary preservation method that uses wood smoke and temperatures between 180°F and 220°F to cook meats to a safe internal temperature and add flavor.

hull   A preparation method used for strawberries. The hull is the enlarged calyx of a fruit, such as a strawberry. It is usually green and easily detached. To hull a strawberry means to remove the hull or calyx.

hygrometer   An instrument that measures relative humidity.

lactic acid bacteria (LAB)   A group of gram-positive, non-spore-forming, round or rod-shaped bacteria that are important in the fermentation of many products such as wine, bread, yogurt, and sauerkraut. LAB increase the acidity (lower the pH), which inhibits the growth of pathogenic organisms and increases the storage life of foods.

lacto-fermentation   Fermentation caused by lactic acid bacteria.

Lactobacillus   *See* lactic acid bacteria.

lard   Rendered pork fat; made from leaf lard or fatback.

Leuconostoc   *See* lactic acid bacteria.

Listeria monocytogenes   A pathogenic, gram-positive bacterium widely found in soil, plants, and animals that can cause illness (listeriosis), especially in people at high risk for food-borne pathogens. It resists chilling, freezing, drying, and heating and is associated with raw milk, soft-ripened cheeses, raw vegetables, fermented raw-meat sausages, raw meats, and smoked fish.

lug   A container, usually a shallow box, used for produce that can hold a varying volume or count of fruit or vegetables. A lug can range from 10 to 30 pounds.

mortar and pestle   A grinding tool consisting of a bowl (mortar) and grinding tool (pestle) that is usually made of ceramic, marble, or stone.

mother   A component of unpasteurized, organic vinegar, which is composed mostly of cellulose, a type of soluble fiber, and the bacterium *Acetobacter*.

must   The unfermented crushed grape (or other fruit) mixture used to make wine. It includes juice and solids (called the *cap*), which may be composed of skins, pulp, stems, and seeds.

nitrates (NO_3)   Naturally occurring chemicals that are part of the "nitrogen cycle" and the process of decomposition. Common forms include sodium nitrate ($NaNO_3$) and potassium nitrate (NO_3), also known as saltpeter. Nitrates are used when curing meat to prohibit the growth of *C. botulinum*. However, to become effective, it must be broken down into nitrites by lactic acid bacteria.

nitrites (NO_2)   Naturally occurring and chemically manufactured chemicals. Nitrite is the active ingredient in meat curing and contributes the desirable reddish color and pleasing flavor, and controls the growth of *C. botulinum*.

pasteurization   Named for French chemist Louis Pasteur, this method of partial sterilization heats food at a specific temperature and time to kill microorganisms, without adversely affecting the physical qualities of the product.

pectin   A carbohydrate (polysaccharide) that thickens fruit jams and jellies. Pectin may be extracted naturally from tart or underripe fruits, or purchased in several powdered and liquid forms.

Pediococcus   *See* lactic acid bacteria.

piccalilli   A highly seasoned, often colorful pickle relish made from chopped vegetables. Many regional variations exist, but green tomato, peppers, and cabbage are common ingredients.

pickling lime (calcium hydroxide)   Used to firm pickled cucumbers and other vegetables, usually by immersing them in a solution for one or more days, and then rinsing well before pickling.

pickling salt   *See* canning salt.

pickling spice   A combination of whole spices used to flavor pickled vegetables. Many different blends are manufactured and may contain allspice, bay leaves, cardamom, cinnamon, cloves, coriander, ginger, mustard seeds, and peppercorns.

potassium nitrate   *See* saltpeter.

pressure canner   A canning method that uses pressure to heat-seal jars above the boiling point (212°F) of water to 240°F; it is used to process low-acid foods (such as meats and vegetables) safely and some high-acid foods for better quality.

pressure cooker   An energy-efficient cooking vessel that uses superheated steam to cook food up to 10 times faster. USDA does not have recommended processes for canning in a small pressure cooker. The recommendation for using USDA pressure processes for low-acid foods is to use a canner that holds at least four quart-size jars.

PSI (Pounds per Square Inch)   A measure of atmospheric pressure. At sea level, water boils at 212°F. By increasing the PSI in a pressure canner, water boils at higher temperatures.

purée   A method of mixing or blending food to give it a smooth texture.

rancid   Refers to the result of the chemical decomposition of fats and oils, often by overexposure to air. Rancid fats smell or taste unpleasant.

raw pack   A method for packing canning jars that puts raw food into hot jars with hot liquid before processing.

relative humidity (RH)   The amount of moisture in the surrounding air given as a percentage of water vapor.

rendering   A process used to extend the shelf life of solid fats like lard and ghee. The source fat (suet or butter) is melted over low heat and strained to remove solid particles.

rennin or rennet   An enzyme used in cheese making to coagulate or thicken milk into a solid ball.

ring   The metal screw band that holds a canning lid in place during processing.

Salmonella   Pathogenic, gram-negative, non-spore-forming, rod-shaped bacteria. They can cause food-borne illness in a wide variety of foods—including meats, poultry, seafood, dairy products, and produce—when products are improperly handled or incompletely cooked.

saltpeter (sodium or potassium nitrate)   A naturally occurring mineral form of nitrate that has been replaced by the use of nitrites in most modern curing processes. *See also* nitrates.

sea salt   Salt made from dried seawater that naturally contains minerals.

shelf-stable products   Foods that can be stored at room temperature and are safe to eat without additional preparation.

sodium chloride (NaCl)   Common salt. It is available for food use in many forms, including canning salt, sea salt, kosher salt, and table salt.

sodium erythorbate   A salt of ascorbic acid (vitamin C) used in commercial manufacturing to speed up the curing process, to prevent fats from going rancid, and to hold the color.

sodium nitrate   *See* saltpeter.

sodium nitrite   *See* nitrites.

Staphylococcus   Pathogenic, gram-positive, non-spore-forming bacteria that form clusters and are very common in the air, water, milk, and food and on surfaces. They are controlled by good sanitation practices.

starter culture   A known quantity of microorganisms used to introduce specific bacteria, yeasts, or mold into a fermentation process. Example starters include vinegar "mother" (*Acetobacter* bacteria); yogurt (LAB bacteria); *Saccharomyces* yeast for making beer, wine, or bread; and *Rhizophus oligosporus* mold for tempeh.

steam canner   A relatively new type of boiling-water canner that uses steam rather than boiling water to process jars. The use of steam canners is not currently recommended by the USDA because processing times have not been tested.

Streptococcus   Gram-positive, non-spore-forming bacteria. Pathogenic forms (e.g., *S. pyogenes*) cause mild illness, usually a sore throat. Beneficial strains (e.g., *S. lactis*) help preserve foods by producing lactic acid. *See* lactic acid bacteria.

suet   The solid fat from lamb or beef.

sulfiting   A process to help control microbial growth and preserve color in food preservation methods.

table salt   Salt with added anticaking additives to keep it free flowing. It may also be fortified with iodine.

tallow   Rendered fat from suet.

water activity (a_w)   A scientific term that describes the availability of water for microorganisms to live.

wort (pronounced *wert*)   Equivalent to must in wine making, wort is the raw beer liquid made by cooking malted grain before the hops are added and the mixture is fermented.

Produce Guides  B

These handy charts provide information about types of fruit and vegetables, yields, measurements, and recommended preservation methods.

Fruits

The following sections list types of fruit and their average yields. Keep in mind your results can sometimes vary from these averages, depending on the particular variety of fruit you want to preserve. Some fruits are juicier or have more seeds, and these issues can increase or decrease the amount of usable fruit. Finally, there is a chart suggesting the best preservation methods for different types of fruit.

Types of Fruit

Soft berries include blackberries, chokecherries, loganberries, marionberries, mulberries, raspberries, salmonberries, strawberries, tayberries, and thimbleberries.

Firm berries include blueberries, cranberries, currants, elderberries, gooseberries, grapes, huckleberries, lingonberries, Oregon grapes, rose hips, rowan fruit, and saskatoon berries.

Stone fruits include apricots, cherries, nectarines, peaches, and plums. Hybrids of these fruits include apriums, nectaplums, and pluots.

Pome fruits include apples, Asian pears, crabapples, loquats (Japanese plums) or medlar apples, mayhaws, pears, and quince.

Citrus fruits include blood oranges, citron (Buddha's hand), grapefruits, kumquats, lemons, limes, mandarins (clementines), oranges, pomelos, tangelos, and tangerines.

Melons include cantaloupes, casabas, charantais, Crenshaws, French breakfast, honeydews, and watermelons.

Tropical fruits include guavas, mangos, papayas, and pineapples.

Other fruits include those with distinct characteristics, which require unique handling:

- Bananas (tropical fruit)

- Figs (subtropical fruit)

- Rhubarb (a vegetable stalk that is often prepared as a fruit)

Fruit Yields

Average Yields for One Pound of Fruit as Purchased

Type of Fruit	One Pound as Purchased	Prepared	Purée or Juice
Soft berries	2 dry pints	4 cups whole or 3 cups sliced (strawberries)	$2\frac{1}{2}$ cups purée or $1\frac{1}{4}$ cups juice
Firm berries	2 dry pints	4 cups whole	$2\frac{1}{2}$ cups purée or $1\frac{1}{4}$ cups juice
Stone fruits	Apricots: 8 to 12 medium Cherries: 1 dry pint Nectarines: 3 medium Peaches: 3 medium Plums: 6 medium	2 cups halved or sliced (without stones or pits)	$1\frac{1}{2}$ to $1\frac{3}{4}$ cups purée
Pome fruits	3 medium	2 to 3 cups cored and sliced or chopped	$1\frac{1}{2}$ to 2 cups purée or 1 cup juice
Citrus fruits	Grapefruits: 1 medium Lemons: 4 medium Limes: 6 medium Oranges: 3 medium	$1\frac{1}{2}$ cups sections (without membrane), 3 to 4 tablespoons zest	1 cup juice

Type of Fruit	One Pound as Purchased	Prepared	Purée or Juice
Melons	1/3 medium	1 to 1½ cups cubed	¾ to 1¼ cups purée or ½ to ¾ cup juice
Tropical fruits	Guava: 3 medium Mango: 1 large Papaya: 1 medium Pineapple: ½ medium	2 cups cubed	1½ cups purée or 1 cup juice
Bananas	3 medium	1½ cups sliced	1 cup purée
Figs	8 medium	2½ cups chopped	n/a
Rhubarb	8 medium stalks	2 cups sliced or chopped	1 cup cooked purée

Fruit Preservation Methods

Summary of Fruit Preservation Methods

	Dry	Wine	Fresh Pickle	BWB Can	BWB Pickle Sauce	BWB Savory	BWB Jam	Cellar	Freeze
Soft berries	+	+	o	-	o	-	+	o	+
Firm berries	+	+	-	+	-	+	+	-	+
Stone fruits	-	-	+	+	+	+	+	-	+
Pome fruits	+	+	+	+	+	+	+	+	+
Citrus fruits	-	+	+	-	o		+	-	-
Melons	+	-	+	x	+	o	o	+	-
Tropical fruits	+	+	+	+	+	+	+	-	+
Bananas	+	-	o	x	x	x	x	o	+
Figs	+	+	+	+	+	+	+	-	-
Rhubarb	+	+	+	+	+	-	+	+	-

+ = Best method

- = Inferior method

o = Not recommended

x = Not safe

Vegetables

The following sections list types of vegetables and their average yields. Since these are average yields, your results may vary. Some varieties of the same type of vegetable may have more rind, seeds, or water, which can increase or decrease the yield. The last chart suggests preservation methods for different types of vegetables.

Types of Vegetables

Root vegetables include beets, carrots, kohlrabis, parsnips, rutabagas, and turnips.

Cruciferous vegetables include artichoke hearts, broccoli, brussels sprouts, cabbages, and cauliflower.

Greens/herbs include fresh herbs, leafy greens, and spinach. Leafy greens include cooking or braising greens such as rape or raab, collards, dandelion, kale, mustards, and Swiss chard. Lettuces and salad greens are not suitable for most preserving methods.

Bulbs include garlic and onions.

Tubers include potatoes, sunchokes, and sweet potatoes.

Radishes include daikon and globe or icicle radishes.

Squashes include pickling cucumbers, salad cucumbers, summer squashes, and winter squashes.

Beans and peas include pea pods, shell beans, shell peas, and snap beans.

Other vegetables that don't fit in any of these categories include asparagus, celery, chile peppers, corn, cultivated and wild mushrooms, eggplant, and tomatoes.

Vegetable Yields

Average Yields for One Pound of Vegetables as Purchased

Type of Vegetables	One Pound as Purchased	Prepared	Purée
Root vegetables:			
Beets	3 medium	3 cups sliced or 2 cups shredded	1½ cups purée
Carrots	6 medium	3 cups sliced or 2 cups shredded	1½ cups purée
Turnips, kohlrabi, rutabagas	3 medium	3 cups sliced or 2 cups shredded	1½ cups purée
Cruciferous vegetables:			
Artichokes	2 medium globe or 12 baby	n/a	½ cup artichoke heart purée
Broccoli and cauliflower	½ medium bunch or head	3 cups florets or 2 cups chopped	1½ cups mashed
Brussels sprouts	1½ dry pints	3 cups quartered or sliced	n/a
Cabbage (any variety)	½ medium head	4 cups sliced or shredded	n/a
Greens/herbs:			
Leafy greens	1 medium head or bunch	6 cups torn leaves; 1 to 1½ cups steamed	n/a
Spinach	1 medium bunch	6 cups torn leaves; 1 to 1½ cups steamed	n/a
Bulbs:			
Dry onions and garlic	Onions: 3 medium Garlic: 6 to 8 heads	4 to 6 cups sliced or 2 to 3 cups chopped	1½ cups grated onion or mashed garlic
Tubers:			
Sunchokes	1½ dry pints	2 to 3 cups shredded or sliced	1½ to 2 cups mashed
Potatoes or sweet potatoes	2 to 3 medium	2 to 3 cups shredded or sliced	1½ to 2 cups mashed

continues

continued

Type of Vegetables	One Pound as Purchased	Prepared	Purée
Radishes:			
Radishes and daikon	Globe: 50 1-inch radishes without tops Daikon or icicle: 1 long root, 6×2 inches	2 to 3 cups shredded or sliced	n/a
Squashes:			
Cucumbers	2 medium	2 to 3 cups sliced or 1½ to 2 cups peeled, seeded, and chopped	1½ to 2 cups peeled, seeded, and puréed
Squash, summer	3 medium	2 to 3 cups sliced or chopped	1½ to 2 cups peeled, seeded, and puréed
Squash, winter	⅓ medium	2 cups cubed	1½ cups cooked and mashed
Beans and peas:			
Beans, dried	1 to 1½ dry pints	2 to 3 cups dry or 2½ to 3½ cups soaked	2 to 3 cups cooked and mashed
Bean pods (snap beans)	1½ to 2 dry pints	2 to 3 cups trimmed and cut	n/a
Bean pods (snow peas, sugar peas)	2 to 3 dry pints	4 to 6 cups trimmed	n/a
Pea pods	1 to 1½ dry pints	1 to 1½ cups shelled	1 to 1½ cups cooked and mashed
Other vegetables:			
Asparagus	16 medium spears	3 cups trimmed and cut	1½ cups purée
Celery and celeriac	1 medium bunch, 10 medium stalks, or 1 medium root	3 cups trimmed and sliced	1½ cups purée, celery root

Type of Vegetables	One Pound as Purchased	Prepared	Purée
Corn	4 medium ears	2 cups whole kernels or 1 to 1½ cups dried corn	1 cup ground dried corn meal or flour
Mushrooms	24 medium or 2½ dry pints	4 cups sliced or 3½ ounces dried	⅓ cup dried mushroom powder
Eggplant	1 medium	3 to 4 cups cubed	1½ to 2 cups cooked and mashed
Peppers (sweet or hot)	3 to 4 medium sweet or bell peppers; 10 medium banana or 30 small hot peppers	2½ cups stemmed, seeded, and chopped	1 cup purée
Tomatoes	3 medium salad or 5 medium plum tomatoes; 1½ dry pints cherry tomatoes	2½ cups coarsely chopped; 1½ cups cored, peeled, seeded, and crushed	1½ cups purée, 1 cup thin sauce, ½ cup paste

Vegetable Preservation Methods

Summary of Vegetable Preservation Methods

	Dry	Wine	Salt/ Ferment	Fresh Pickle	BWB Pickle	BWB Relish	Pressure Can	Cellar	Freeze
Root vegetables:									
Beets	+	+	-	+	+	+	+	+	+
Carrots	+	+	-	+	+	+	+	+	+
Turnips, parsnips, kohlrabi, rutabagas	+	-	+	-	x	x	x	+	o

continues

continued

	Dry	Wine	Salt/ Ferment	Fresh Pickle	BWB Pickle	BWB Relish	Pressure Can	Cellar	Freeze
Cruciferous vegetables:									
Artichoke hearts	-	-	-	+	+	x	x	-	-
Broccoli	-	o	-	o	x	x	x	-	+
Brussels sprouts	-	-	-	-	x	x	x	+	+
Cabbages	o	o	+	+	-	+	+	-	-
Cauliflower	-	o	+	+	+	+	+	+	+
Greens/herbs:									
Leafy greens	-	-	+	+	x	x	+	-	+
Fresh herbs	+	+	-	-	o	o	o	-	+
Spinach	-	-	-	o	x	x	+	-	+
Bulbs:									
Spring onions	o	-	o	+	o	o	o	o	o
Dry onions	+	-	-	+	-	-	-	+	+
Garlic	o	-	-	+	-	-	-	-	o
Tubers:									
Sunchokes	+	+	o	+	x	x	x	+	-
Potatoes	+	+	o	x	x	x	+	+	+
Sweet potatoes	+	+	o	x	x	x	+	+	+
Radishes:									
Daikon	o	-	-	+	x	x	x	-	o
Globe	o	-	-	+	x	x	x	-	o
Squashes:									
Salad cucumbers	-	+	-	+	o	-	o	-	o
Pickling cucumbers	-	-	+	-	+	+	o	-	o

	Dry	Wine	Salt/Ferment	Fresh Pickle	BWB Pickle	BWB Relish	Pressure Can	Cellar	Freeze
Summer squash	+	+	-	-	-	+	o	o	-
Winter squash	o	+	o	-	+	o	-	+	+
Beans and peas:									
Snap beans	+	-	+	+	+	+	+	-	+
Shell beans	+	o	+	+	+	+	+	+	+
Pea pods	-	-	+	-	-	-	-	-	+
Shell peas	+	-	+	-	-	-	+	-	+
Other vegetables:									
Asparagus	-	-	-	+	+	-	+	+	+
Celery	+	+	-	-	-	+	+	+	-
Corn	+	+	+	+	+	+	+	+	+
Cultivated mushrooms	+	-	+	+	x	x	+	-	+
Eggplant	+	-	+	+	x	x	x	+	+
Peppers/chiles	+	-	+	+	+	+	+	+	-
Tomatoes	+	+	+	+	+	+	+	+	-
Wild mushrooms	+	-	+	+	x	x	x	-	+

+ = *Best method*

- = *Inferior method*

o = *Not recommended*

x = *Not safe*

Dry Measure (Agricultural Products)

1 dry pint = ½ dry quart

1 dry quart = 2 dry pints

1 peck = 8 dry quarts = 16 dry pints

1 bushel = 4 pecks = 32 dry quarts = 64 dry pints

Basket = varying sizes from $\frac{1}{4}$ or $\frac{1}{2}$ of a peck, to $\frac{1}{2}$ or 1 bushel

Box or lug (about $\frac{1}{3}$ bushel) = (approx.) 16 to 28 pounds

Carton or crate may be a lug or bushel or some portion of a bushel

Carton or box may come with one or more layers

Flats may contain 12 or 24 dry half-pints, dry pints, or dry quarts

Resources  C

If you're interested in learning more about some methods of preserving foods or where to buy supplies and equipment, the following resources provide plenty of helpful information.

Books and Journals

The following books and journals provide information on drying and cellaring foods, curing meat and fish, and preserving in general.

Drying Foods

Fodor, Eben V. *The Solar Food Dryer*. Gabriola Island: New Society Publishers, 2006.

Step-by-step plans for building a low-cost solar food dryer from readily available materials.

Kesselheim, Alan. *Trail Food: Drying and Cooking Food for Backpacking and Paddling*. Camden: Ragged Mountain Press, 1998.

Easy ideas and flexible recipes for making lightweight, portable foods for outdoor activities.

Curing Meat and Fish

Hull, Raymond, and Jack Sleight. *Home Book of Smoke Cooking Meat, Fish & Game*. Mechanicsburg: Stackpole Books, 1997.

Describes smokers you can build or purchase, different types of fuel, and tips on how to operate a smoker.

Marianski, Stanley, and Adam Marianski. *The Art of Making Fermented Sausages.* Seminole: Bookmagic LLC, 2009.

Information and recipes for making, drying, and fermenting sausages at home.

Cellaring Foods

MacKenzie, Jennifer, and Steve Maxwell. *The Complete Root Cellar Book.* Toronto: Robert Rose, Inc., 2010.

Detailed, illustrated construction guides for making four different kinds of root cellars.

General Reference

Belanger, J. D. *The Complete Idiot's Guide to Self-Sufficient Living.* Indianapolis: Alpha Books, 2009.

Provides information on gardening, raising livestock, keeping chickens, hunting, fishing, and other practical ideas for sustainable food.

Websites

The following websites provide information on drying, fermenting, cellaring, freezing, canning, or pickling foods; curing meat and fish; food safety practices; and additional preserving recipes.

Drying Foods

Build It Solar: builditsolar.com. Online articles on solar food drying, including plans for building solar dryers.

Fermenting Foods

Midwest Supplies: midwestsupplies.com. Online retailer for supplies for beer, cider, mead, wine, and sake making at home, including equipment, ingredients, and kits.

New England Cheesemaking Supply: cheesemaking.com. Online retailer for supplies for cheese making at home, including ingredients, equipment, and kits.

Ohio State University Extension: ohioline.osu.edu. Online food publications include *Making Cider Vinegar at Home.*

Sausage Maker Inc: sausagemaker.com. Online retailer for fermenting pots for pickles and sauerkraut.

Pickling Foods

Ohio Stoneware: ohiostoneware.com. Online retailer for American-made pickling crocks; also suitable for sealing foods.

Curing Meat and Fish

Butcher & Packer Supply Company: butcher-packer.com. Online retailer for making sausage at home, including equipment and ingredients.

Great American Spice Company: americanspice.com. Online source for buying spices, herbs, and seasonings.

IngredientStore.com: theingredientstore.com. Instructions for building your own smoker, including a cold smoker that repurposes a refrigerator.

Morton Salt, Inc.: mortonsalt.com. Makes and sells canning, kosher, and pickling salts; salt substitutes; and meat curing mixes.

SmokerCooking.Com: smoker-cooking.com. Instructions and video for building your own cold smoker using a soldering iron.

Canning Foods

National Center for Home Food Preservation: nchfp.uga.edu. Your source for current research-based recommendations for most methods of home food preservation and access to publications and tested recipes from extension agencies and university research throughout the country, including the *USDA Complete Guide to Home Canning.*

Cellaring Foods

Mother Earth News: motherearthnews.com. Online magazine features sustainable living information, including "Build a Basement Root Cellar."

University of Missouri Extension: extension.missouri.edu. Online articles, including "Building and Using Hotbeds and Coldframes."

Freezing Foods

Oklahoma Cooperative Extension Service: pods.dasnr.okstate.edu. Online publications, including "Buying Beef for Home Freezers."

Food Safety

Centers for Disease Control and Prevention: cdc.gov. Reliable information about healthy living, including food-borne illness prevention and education.

FoodSafety.gov: foodsafety.gov. Gateway to food safety information provided by several U.S. government agencies. Includes information about recalls, keeping food safe, and food poisoning.

U.S. Food and Drug Administration (FDA): fda.gov. Government-sponsored website that includes information about food safety, food-borne pathogens, and the online *Bad Bug Book—pH Values of Various Foods*.

Help and More Recipes for Preserving Foods

Carole Cancler: carolecancler.com. Ask questions, find more preserving recipes and techniques, or subscribe to get updates.

Index

P

pancetta, 62
pantry, 135
Papaya Salsa, 334
paprika, 224
paraffin sealing, 86
pasta, freezing, 151
pasteurization, 11, 14, 188, 316
pastry sealing, 87
Peach or Nectarine Jam, 351
Peach Pie Filling, 275
Peach Salsa, 334
Peach-Spice Butter, 357
Pear Chutney, 343
Pear Wine, 191
Pear-Wine Butter, 358
pectin, 31, 157, 345, 363
Pediococcus, 32
pemmican, 82
penicillin, 77
pepper relish, 211
Pepper-Herb Bacon, 239
Peppers, 399
Persian Eggplant Relish, 226
phosphates, 67
Pickle Crisp, 55
Pickle Spears, Chunks, or Slices, 318
Pickled Asparagus, 320
Pickled Berries, 256
Pickled Carrots, 322
Pickled Corn Salad, 340
Pickled Daikon and Carrots, 208
Pickled Fish, 225
pickled foods, 211. *See also* vegetables, pickled (canned)
fruit juice-pickled foods, 226
macerated foods, 231
pepper relish, 211

recipes
Brined Raw Eggs, 215
Citrus-Pickled Onions, 228
Cucumbers in Mustard Soy Sauce, 230
Easy Pickled Carrots, 218
Good Fortune Pickles, 229
Haitian *Pikliz*, 222
Indian-Style Hot Lime Pickles, 214
Indian-Style Pickled Vegetables, 220
Limoncello, 232
Macerated Cherries, 233
Miso-Pickled Vegetables, 231
Moroccan Preserved Lemons, 213
Original Bread-and-Butter Pickles, 217
Persian Eggplant Relish, 226
Pickled Fish, 225
Pickled Game Birds, 223
Quick Japanese Pickles, 221
Roasted Pepper Relish, 219
Salted Green Beans, 212
salted foods, 211
soy-pickled foods, 228
verjuice, 227
vinegared foods, 216
Pickled Game Birds, 223
Pickled Jalapeño Slices, 326
Pickled Marinated Mushrooms, 325

Pickled Melon with Ginger, 329
Pickled Pears, 258
Pickled Quince or Crabapple, 260
Pickled Red-Beet *Pkhali*, 323
Pickled Rhubarb, 264
Pickled Three-Bean Salad, 341
Pickled Yellow Beets with Fennel and Thyme, 324
pickling foods, 10, 49-51
brining vegetables, 58
dry salting of vegetables, 56
fermenting, 55
firming techniques, 54-55
food quality, 55
ingredients, 50-53
macerating fruits, 59
salt substitutes, 52
sanitary practices, 49
troubleshooting, 59
whey, 51
pickling salt, 39
pickling solutions, canning, 110
pie fillings, 273
piercing, fruit, 20
Pineapple-Chile Salsa, 333
pink salt, 63
Piper nigrum, 44
pit-fermented foods, 45
pit-oven drying, 16
Plum Jam, 350
Plum-Almond Conserve, 362
Plum-Ginger Butter, 357
polyphenol oxidase (PPO), 18
pome fruits, 107